# The Epic of the Islands

The history of the Caribbean includes such figures as Christopher Columbus, Sir Francis Drake, Blackbeard, Toussaint L'Ouverture, Fidel Castro, the Duvaliers, Maurice Bishop, Father Aristide.

It is set on islands ranging in size from Cuba, Dominica, and Puerto Rico to the tiniest specks of land in the Antilles.

Its peoples speak English, French, Dutch, Spanish, and Creole, reflecting their dramatic diversity of origins and cultures.

It encompasses vast economic booms and disastrous busts, hurricanes, epidemics, wars on land and sea, revolutions, and foreign interventions.

It all can be found in the finest single-volume history to cover all the islands through all their changes, including the ones going on today –

# A BRIEF HISTORY
## OF THE
# CARIBBEAN

JAN ROGOZIŃSKI received a Ph.D. in social and cultural history from Princeton University. He is the author of *Smokeless Tobacco in the Western World* and *Caste, Power, and Law,* a history of France. Dr. Rogoziński lives in Fort Lauderdale, Florida.

# A BRIEF HISTORY
# OF THE
# CARIBBEAN

## FROM THE ARAWAK AND THE CARIB TO THE PRESENT

■

### JAN ROGOZIŃSKI

A MERIDIAN BOOK

*For Paul Francis Hauch*

∎

MERIDIAN
Published by the Penguin Group
Penguin Books USA Inc., 375 Hudson Street, New York, New York 10014, U.S.A.
Penguin Books Ltd, 27 Wrights Lane, London W8 5TZ, England
Penguin Books Australia Ltd, Ringwood, Victoria, Australia
Penguin Books Canada Ltd, 10 Alcorn Avenue, Toronto, Ontario, Canada M4V 3B2
Penguin Books (N.Z.) Ltd, 182-190 Wairau Road, Auckland 10, New Zealand

Penguin Books Ltd, Registered Offices:
Harmondsworth, Middlesex, England

Published by Meridian, an imprint of Dutton Signet, a division of Penguin Books USA Inc.
This is an authorized reprint of a hardcover edition published by Facts on File.
For information address Facts on File, Inc., 460 Park Avenue South, New York, NY 10016.

First Meridian Printing, September, 1994
1  3  5  7  9  10  8  6  4  2

Ⓜ  REGISTERED TRADEMARK – MARCA REGISTRADA

LIBRARY OF CONGRESS CATALOGING-IN-PUBLICATION DATA
Rogoziński, Jan.
   A brief history of the Caribbean : from the Arawak and the Carib
to the present / Jan Rogoziński.
      p.    cm.
   Originally published: New York : Facts on File, c1992.
   Includes bibliographical references and index.
   ISBN 0-452-01134-5
   1. West Indies — History.  I. Title.
F1621.R72    1994
972.91 — dc20                                        94–15039
                                                        CIP

Printed in the United States of America
Designed by Donna Sinisgalli

BOOKS ARE AVAILABLE AT QUANTITY DISCOUNTS WHEN USED TO PROMOTE PRODUCTS OR SERVICES.
FOR INFORMATION PLEASE WRITE TO PREMIUM MARKETING DIVISION, PENGUIN BOOKS USA INC.,
375 HUDSON STREET, NEW YORK, NY 10014.

# CONTENTS

■

# LIST OF TABLES

■

# PREFACE

■

The following pages provide a descriptive and analytical history of the Caribbean islands. From the Bahamas in the north to Curaçao in the south, more than thirty million people share a common history and similar patterns of development. In recent years, the Caribbean sometimes has been more widely defined to include the mainland of Central America from Mexico down as far as French Guiana. However, the islands and the mainland really form two separate regions. These two geographic zones are endowed with very different natural environments, and they have followed divergent paths since the Spanish conquest.[1]

In recounting the history of the islands, this book focuses on the interrelated evolution of the economy, political institutions, and social forms. The Caribbean enjoys a rich intellectual, cultural, and religious life. A full appreciation of these aspects of its history would have required a much longer work.

The region's long and complex story is best understood from the inside looking out—from a point of view that begins with the islands rather than seeing them as an extension of the United States, Europe, or Africa. At the same time, the reader deserves a self-explanatory narrative, so that events are comprehensible without the use of reference books. When these must be mentioned, I have defined technical terms and identified non-Caribbean institutions and events. For example, in mentioning a treaty transferring sovereignty over an island, the text cites the signatory powers and date of signing. For many centuries, the islands formed part of large empires ruling over several continents. I describe these imperial institutions with special attention to the ways in which they evolved in the special circumstances of the Caribbean.

## MANY TRADITIONS, A SHARED HISTORY

Islands are different. The seas serve both as a barrier and as a highway. Island peoples are intensely attached and loyal to their birthplace. Yet, as economic needs dictate, they easily move to other islands or to the mainland—but always intending to return to their homeland. A strong sense of local particularism or even nationalism is especially characteristic of the Caribbean. The islands are scattered across a very large sea. Until the invention of the steamship and the airplane, the strong easterly trade winds and currents made it easier to sail from Europe to Barbados than from Cuba to Barbados. Moreover, the islands also enjoy a variety of landforms and climates, which make each different from its neighbors.

Rule by four major (and several minor) European empires increased the region's natural diversity. Island cultures were therefore more varied than in either North America (primarily northern European and Protestant) or South America (mainly Hispanic and Roman Catholic). Each empire imposed its own language, religion, habits, and prejudices on the governed. Their very different political systems also have left a lasting imprint. The Spanish tried to govern their empire from Europe. The British (at least before 1810) allowed the whites on each island to make their own laws. These distinctions were less sharp in practice than in theory. Simply because Spain was far away, it often left island élites alone to govern themselves. But the colonial centuries did leave different traditions—of one-man rule in one case, of parliamentary politics in the other.

Each of the islands has its own cultures and traditions. But they also share certain experiences that are different from those of the mainland. Since they supplied the same agricultural commodities to a world market, all have been affected by the same world-wide economic trends. With rare exceptions, all were once slave societies, to an extent never seen before or since. Their peoples thus practice similar social forms and habits, although sometimes with different names. While the island peoples have had the same experiences, they sometimes have had them at different times. Jamaica and Cuba both became major producers of sugarcane, grown by black slaves. However, Jamaica developed into a plantation society in the 18th century, Cuba during the 19th.

## FROM COLONIES TO SOVEREIGN NATIONS

Given their intense insular patriotism, all islanders consider political independence a decisive event—perhaps the most decisive—in their history. About half of the islands, with perhaps 90 percent of the population, now are independent. Like the abolition of slavery, self-rule came to the islands at different times. Haiti and the Dominican Republic have governed themselves since the 19th century. Cuba became independent when American troops withdrew in 1902. Guadeloupe and Martinique (with their dependencies) gained more local autonomy in 1946 when each became a province or *département* within the French Republic. Puerto Rico became an Associated Free State or Commonwealth in 1952, and the U.S. Virgin Islands also gained control over local affairs in 1968. In 1954, the six Dutch islands became self-governing territories associated with the Netherlands, although discussions about their eventual independence continue.

Most of the former British colonies also have become sovereign states since 1962. The drive for independence began with the formation of labor unions and trade associations, supported by the British Labour party and often led by men who had served abroad during the First World War. Since most islands depended on one or two major export crops, the great depression of the 1930s was severe. Demonstrations, strikes, and riots were frequent throughout the British Caribbean between 1935 and 1938. Other islands also suffered violence and political oppression. Rafael Trujillo imposed a police state on the Dominican Republic, while a civil war ended Gerardo Machado's attempt to establish one-man rule in Cuba. Nevertheless, a British commission chaired by Lord Moyne found much to blame in the Crown colony form of government. It called for stronger labor unions, increased self-government, and universal adult suffrage.

After the Second World War, the British authorities encouraged the formation of a West Indies Federation that included ten of their colonies. But the Federation enjoyed little popular support, and Jamaica and Trinidad withdrew and received independence in 1962. An attempt to create a smaller federation among the colonies in the Lesser Antilles also failed, and Barbados gained self-rule in 1962. Most of the remaining British colonies also became independent in the 1970s and 1980s. Anguilla, Montserrat, the British Virgin Islands, the Cayman Islands, and the Turks and the Caicos remain Crown colonies, enjoying a measure of internal self-government.

Some states remained under European rule until recently. But the United States long has been the main economic influence in the region. From the 1880s, American capital had a major role in developing the sugar industry in Cuba, Puerto Rico, and the Dominican Republic. The United States remains the region's largest trading partner—except for Cuba, which trades mainly with the Soviet Union.

The United States also intervened politically in several Caribbean states earlier in the century. For humanitarian reasons and to prevent interference by one of the warring European states, President Woodrow Wilson purchased the Danish Virgin Islands in 1917. He also sent American troops to occupy the Dominican Republic (1916–1924) and Haiti (1915–1934). In addition, the United States also intervened in Cuba on several occasions between 1906 and 1934. These American efforts failed in their avowed purpose: to establish honest, stable, and democratic governments. Thus the United States generally has taken a hands-off approach since the 1930s. However, it did send troops to intervene during civil wars in the Dominican Republic (1965) and Grenada (1983).

As they face their sixth century since Columbus irrevocably joined them to the world, the Caribbean nations may be judged a political success. Except in Haiti and Cuba, every island regularly holds elections, the winner takes office, and the loser retires—tests of democracy not met in most of the world.

The Caribbean islands continue to seek a secure economic base. Cane sugar made them the wealthiest colonies in the world during the 18th century. But the industry disappeared before the First World War from several of the islands in the Lesser Antilles. Since 1945, it also has declined in importance on the larger islands, except for Cuba. At the same time, the population has continued to soar as health care has improved, and unemployment has been high.

Efforts to find a substitute for sugar have enjoyed only mixed success. Several islands, especially Puerto Rico, that introduced manufacturing and processing industries before the mid-'70s have suffered from economic stagnation. A few governments have tried to manage the economy on the eastern European model—

Cuba since 1959, Jamaica during the 1970s, and Grenada under the Bishop regime. Their efforts failed to increase and probably hindered economic growth. Without local industry, most nations continue to pay for imported oil and industrial products with lower value agricultural products. Thus they suffer from chronic trade deficits and must depend on tourism to earn foreign currencies.

The island peoples face economic and social challenges directly linked to their history. In the Caribbean, Europeans created a plantation society unlike almost any other in human history. They settled the islands, invested large amounts of capital, and introduced sophisticated technologies for one purpose only. They replaced the extinct native peoples with hundreds of thousands of African slaves and drove them to grow sugar.

Although planters also developed other crops (notably coffee), all of the major islands were true monocultures by the middle of the 17th century. Sugar provided 80 percent or more of their exports, and many had to import food and other necessities. The sugar industry remained profitable into the 19th century. But almost all the profits were taken and remained in Europe. The islands were peopled to support one industry. That industry is no longer significant, and islanders must find alternative ways of making a living. The task for island leaders is difficult—but not impossible. A nation's history does not determine later events, and the future remains open.

For several centuries, a few white masters and many black slaves made up the societies of the sugar islands. Issues involving race thus are unavoidable in any study of Caribbean history. Over time, racial relations have taken many complex forms. In place of the stark division into two races found in some other parts of the world, island societies developed an elaborate network of shades and hierarchies. Because white laborers were few, slaves were everywhere and did every kind of work. Racial and ethnic blending began at an early period, and some members of racially mixed groups became wealthy and—especially on the French islands—owned slaves.

Precisely because they have played a crucial role throughout the history of the islands, it is essential to use meaningful and consistent language to describe racial relations. Throughout this book, I use the terms *black*, *white*, and *colored* with the meanings traditionally ascribed to them by the peoples of the islands. *Black* (French *noir*; Spanish *negro*) refers to persons perceived as being of African origin. *White* describes persons accepted by their neighbors as of European origin. *Colored* (*gens de couleur*, *gente de color*) refers to those perceived to be of mixed race, usually of mixed African-European descent. (Because the native Indians largely died out during the 16th century, alliances between Indians and other races were relatively rare.)

I have avoided the term *mulatto* because, over time, it had different meanings on various islands. Eighteenth-century authors—particularly those writing about Jamaica and Saint-Domingue—often present elaborate and complex systems of color coding with as many as eight, ten, or even sixteen categories. However, ordinary folk probably did not make these distinctions between small variations in whiteness.

Following most recent literature about the Caribbean, I use the term *freedman* to designate any male or female person of black or mixed ancestry who attained the legal status of non-slave. By the end of the 18th century, some sources distinguish between "free coloreds" and "free blacks." But these latter terms were not used consistently on the various islands.

During recent years, some in the United States have adopted the term *African-American* and prefer it to *black* and *colored*. However, a historian of the islands cannot use the analogous term "African-Caribbean." This new word would obscure a basic and important distinction. As used in the islands, African referred only to African-born slaves. The term *creole* indicated those—both black and white—born and raised in the region.[2] To make the same distinction, a writer using the term *African-Caribbean* would have to call black immigrants "African-born African-Caribbeans." Those traditionally called coloreds presumably would become "native-born African-Caribbeans of African-European ancestry." The islanders already have given us useful terms with positive connotations. Thus there seemed to be no reason to follow this new American coinage, which would have greatly lengthened the book.

\* \* \*

For their unfailing assistance, I am grateful to Marjorie Moorfield, at the Main Branch of the Broward County Library, as well as to Mimi Gewanter, head of the Interlibrary Loan Department, and her efficient staff.

# PART ONE:

## THE CARIBBEAN UNDER SPANISH RULE

■

# CHAPTER ONE:
## THE ENDURING ENVIRONMENT AND THE FIRST ISLANDERS

■

Taken together, the Caribbean islands create a kind of long narrow chain, almost 2,500 miles long but never more than 160 miles wide.[1] Running roughly north of and parallel to Central and South America, they enclose a body of water we call the Caribbean Ocean or Sea. The Caribbean can be distinguished from and is somewhat more salty than the Atlantic. But it is not a closed sea, and strong currents provide a constant interchange with the larger oceans.

On a map this long group of islands seems to form a bridge between North and South America. The historical reality has been more complicated. Merchants, planters, and job-seekers always have moved from one island to another or to the mainland. Until the end of the 19th century, however, the islands were colonies of four major European empires that sought to monopolize their resources. Thus the rivalries and the frequent wars of their foreign rulers sometimes hindered this natural flow of trade and migration.

Altogether thousands of islands rise from the Caribbean. They range in size from uninhabitable rocks and tiny cays to Cuba, which is among the world's largest islands, comparable in size to Sicily and slightly larger than Ohio. During the five centuries since their discovery by Columbus, their rulers have assigned the islands to various political and administrative divisions, and several have changed hands many times. Geographically, however, all of the islands fall into four major groupings—the Greater Antilles, the Bahamas archipelago, the lesser Antilles and the southern islands along the South American coast. These groups have different physical characteristics, and each island's natural resources have strongly influenced its economic and political fortunes.

## THE GREATER AND LESSER ANTILLES, THE BAHAMAS

The four larger islands of Cuba, Jamaica, Hispaniola, and Puerto Rico are known as the Greater Antilles. All are long and relatively narrow and generally lie more or less from west to east. Just above the Greater Antilles, more than 700 small islands and cays form the Bahamas group (which geographically includes the

## TABLE 1. THE CARIBBEAN ISLANDS
### (Reading from Northwest to Southeast)

| | SIZE (square miles) | HIGHEST POINT (feet) | ESTIMATED POPULATION mid-1991 (1,000s) |
|---|---|---|---|
| **GREATER ANTILLES** | | | |
| Cuba | 42,827 | 6,142 | 10,732 |
| Jamaica | 4,411 | 7,405 | 2,489 |
| **Hispaniola** | 29,530 | 10,417 | 13,671 |
| Haiti | 10,714 | | 6,286 |
| Dominican Republic | 18,816 | | 7,385 |
| Puerto Rico | 3,435 | 3,494 | 3,295 |
| Cayman Islands | 96 | 49 | 28 |
| **BAHAMAS GROUP** | | | |
| The Bahamas | 4,566 | 320 | 252 |
| Turks and Caicos | 169 | | 10 |
| **LESSER ANTILLES** | | | |
| **U.S. Virgin Islands** | | | 104 |
| St. Croix | 84 | 1,526 | 55 |
| St. Thomas | 28 | 1,300 | 50 |
| St. John | 20 | | 3 |
| **British Virgin Islands** | 67 | 1,700 | 12 |
| Tortola | 24 | | 9.2 |
| Anegada | 13 | | |
| Virgin Gorda | 9 | | 1.4 |
| Anguilla | 35 | 180 | 7 |
| Saint-Martin/St. Maarten | 13 | 1,391 | 37 |
| Saint-Barthélemy | 10 | | 3.5 |
| Sint Eustatius | 8 | 1,801 | 1.8 |
| Saba | 5 | 2,900 | 1.1 |
| Saint Kitts | 68 | 3,793 | 32 |
| Nevis | 50 | 3,232 | 8.8 |
| Antigua | 108 | 1,322 | 64 |
| Barbuda | 62 | 72 | 1.2 |
| Montserrat | 32.5 | 2,435 | 12.5 |
| Guadeloupe | 657 | 4,813 | 345 |
| Martinique | 421 | 4,584 | 345 |
| Dominica | 305 | 4,666 | 86 |
| Saint Lucia | 233 | 3,120 | 153 |
| Barbados | 166 | 1,109 | 255 |
| Saint Vincent | 133 | 3,868 | 113 |
| Grenadines | 17 | | 7 |
| Grenada | 120 | 2,756 | 84 |
| Trinidad | 1,864 | 3,087 | 1,245 |
| Tobago | 116 | 1,874 | 47 |
| **CURAÇAO GROUP** | | | |
| Aruba | 73 | 548 | 64 |
| Bonaire | 111 | 791 | 11.5 |
| Curaçao | 171 | 644 | 170 |

SOURCE: For population estimates, see U.S. Government, Central Intelligence Agency, *The World Factbook 1991*, Washington, D.C., 1991.

Turks and Caicos). To the east of Puerto Rico, the Lesser Antilles seem to trace a semicircle or arc that runs from the Virgin Islands in the north to Grenada in the south. Geographically and climatically, the Lesser Antilles actually fall into two groups. The larger inner arc is composed of mountainous volcanic islands. The smaller outer arc—Anguilla, Barbuda, Antigua, and the eastern half of Guadeloupe—are much lower in height. These are primarily formed of limestone, and have a dryer climate, characteristics which also are shared by Barbados to the south.

Trinidad, Tobago, and the three arid islands of Aruba, Bonaire, and Curaçao form a fourth grouping. The weather patterns of the Curaçao islands, located just off the coast of South America, are very different from those affecting other Caribbean islands. Although they sometimes were politically affiliated with the Lesser Antilles, Trinidad and Tobago are an extension of the South American mainland and share its climate.

## MOUNTAINOUS ISLANDS AND FLAT ISLANDS

Except for the Bahamas, almost all of the Caribbean islands represent the peaks of mountains that rise from the floor of the ocean, thrust up by enormous pressures under the earth's surface during two separate eras in the distant past. According to geological theories, these pressures deep below the surface of the planet cause the continents to move very slowly over long periods of time. The earth's crust is composed of large rigid sections, known as *plates*, that move alongside one another. One of these plates more or less coincides with the Caribbean Sea, with its outer edge being marked by the arc of the Lesser Antilles. It moves very slowly eastward relative to the North American plate, which in turn is tending toward the west. The boundary where these two plates meet in the Caribbean islands suffers from recurring volcanic activity as well as serious earthquakes.

In geological terms, the oldest islands are the Greater Antilles and the eastern or outer arc of the Lesser Antilles. Volcanic activity created both of these groups some 70 to 50 million years ago.[2] The Greater Antilles thus represent the peaks of three chains of volcanic mountains that were thrust up and extended east from the mainland. The first of these mountain ranges ran east along what is now the northern coast of Cuba and Haiti. A middle and much longer chain of volcanoes created the Cayman Islands. It then continued east along the southern coast of Cuba (the Sierra Maestre) and through the central regions of Haiti (the Cordillera Central) and Puerto Rico (El Yunque), finally coming to an end at what today is known as the Virgin Islands. A third and southernmost chain created the Blue Mountains of Jamaica and then extended along the southern coast of Haiti.

While Central America and the Greater Antilles were rising from the sea, similar volcanic forces created the Andes Mountains. Branches of this great South American chain continue north and east to make up the Caribbean Coast range. The highest peaks of one branch of this coastal mountain range form the islands of Aruba, Bonaire, and Curaçao just north of the mainland. Another

Volcanic islands: Vapor vents, Saint Lucia. Volcanic vents and hot sulfurous springs cover an extensive area near the coastal town of Soufrière. During the 18th century, the island exported sulfur dug from the springs, which also were used for medicinal baths.

branch stretches north from Colombia and Venezuela to Trinidad and Tobago, and perhaps to Barbados.

This age of great earth movements was followed by a quieter era—dated by geologists between the Middle Eocene and the Middle Miocene epochs. Volcanic activity died down. The sea again covered parts or all of the islands. Great deposits of sediment, such as sandstone and limestone, were laid down as the bodies of marine animals decayed. And some of the older islands—especially those along the outer rim of the Lesser Antilles—were flattened out and never again became active volcanoes. After several million years had passed, a second great period of mountain building took place during the late Miocene and Pliocene epochs. The four islands of the Greater Antilles again arose above the sea. And new volcanoes—several are still active today—created the inner arc of mountainous islands in the Lesser Antilles.[3]

The Bahamas group (including the Turks and Caicos) includes more than 700 small islands, innumerable rocks and cays, and hundreds of reefs lying only a few feet below the surface. Strictly speaking these islands and reefs are not found within the Caribbean Sea. And, unlike the Caribbean islands proper, they were not formed by volcanic eruptions. Instead they represent the highest points of the Bahamas Banks, two shallow blocks of rocks covered by limestone and sand that at various points in the ancient past probably rose above the water to form one landmass. Many of the Bahamas stand only a few feet above the water, with the highest hills—on Cat Island—reaching some 300 feet. Although their land surface taken together is close to that of Jamaica, only 22 are inhabited.

## THE TRADE WINDS BRING ENDLESS SUMMER

The Caribbean islands are uniformly warm, and all—including those that receive little rain—also are humid. Except for the most northern of the Bahamas, the islands lie south of the Tropic of Cancer. Moreover, they are surrounded by waters that are warm throughout the year. Because they are located within this warm sea, temperatures on the islands do not vary greatly with the seasons. Throughout the year, the average temperature ranges from around 78° Fahrenheit in the northern Bahamas to 80° in the south near Curaçao. Rarely is the difference between the warmest and coldest months greater than 8 degrees.

Indeed, daily variations in temperature usually are much greater than any seasonal change. Differences of 15° between day and night temperatures are common, and changes of 20° or more have been recorded. Throughout the year, the air temperature is at its coolest immediately before sunrise. It rises quickly to reach its highest point about noon, and then begins to fall off during the late afternoon. Relative humidity always is high, although this also varies during the day. Generally, humidity reaches a peak of more than 90 percent at dawn and falls as temperatures increase during the day. But the humidity never falls below 50 percent and rarely below 70 percent.

The pleasant climate of most islands is mainly due to the constant trade winds. During periods of lull, the constant heat and humidity can become unbearable. Some relief also can be gained by moving to the higher elevations. On average, the temperature falls by about one degree for every 300 feet in height. Some of the higher plateaus in the Greater Antilles thus enjoy a climate more suitable for temperate than tropical crops.

The northeast trade winds, originating in the Bermuda-Azores high pressure cell, are the prime "weather machine" of the Caribbean and the Gulf of Mexico. Month in and month out, the northeasterly trades (that is, coming *from* the northeast) blow at a steady 15 to 25 knots, varying no more than a compass point in any direction. Beginning at the latitude of Bermuda, the winds shift toward the north and east in a clockwise rotation. They then form the southwesterly trades that prevail at that latitude back across the Atlantic to England, France, and northern Spain. Because of the easterly trades, the Caribbean islands and parts of the Central American coast enjoy generally pleasant weather. However, summers are hot and rainy, with the end of summer (July through October) forming the dangerous hurricane season.

The ocean currents join the winds in carrying a ship west through the Caribbean and then north up the coast of North America. Sometimes reaching a velocity of 5 knots, Atlantic waters move westward through the channel between Cuba and the Yucatan peninsula until they turn northward in the Gulf of Mexico. Powered by the tropical sun, they sweep along the Cuban coast and squeeze through the 90-mile strait between Cuba and Florida, powering the great Gulf Stream along the American coast and back toward Europe.

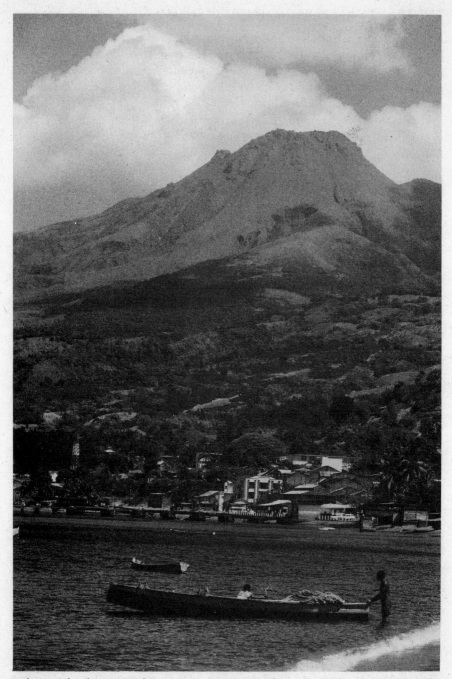

Volcanic islands: Mont Pelée, Martinique. At 4,700 feet, Mont Pelée towers above the small village of Saint-Pierre. An eruption in 1902 destroyed the original Saint-Pierre, the island's largest city. The areas bare of vegetation mark the course of the 1902 lava flows.

## TROPICAL ISLANDS AND DESERT ISLANDS

As they travel across the warm waters of the South Atlantic and the Caribbean, the trade winds become extremely humid and can produce very heavy rains when they are cooled. Generally speaking, this cooling can occur in two different ways, either through orographic effects—which are determined by the height of an island—or though convection—which is influenced by its size.

Orographic effects occur when the moisture-rich trade winds rise to pass over a high point on an island. As the trades rise, they become cooler, their moisture content condenses, and rain is produced. Even a relatively small island can cause this effect, but it increases with the height of the land. On average, low-lying islands thus receive less than half as much rain each year compared to mountainous ones. Moreover, especially on the larger islands of the Greater Antilles, the rain is heaviest at the top and on the windward (north and east) side of high mountains. As the winds descend on the leeward side, they have already lost most of their moisture. For this reason little rain falls on the southwestern coasts of many islands.

On the larger islands, such as the Greater Antilles, rain also is caused by convectional air currents. These are created because the land heats up and cools down more rapidly than water. When the air over the island becomes hotter during the morning and early afternoon, it rises and creates a powerful updraft or "convection." As the air rises, it also becomes cooler, and its moisture content condenses to form clouds. These clouds in turn cool the land, ending the upward flow of hot air. Toward mid-afternoon, the clouds may cool off enough to bring sudden and usually very heavy rains.

Since the temperature is essentially the same, the natural vegetation and the types of crops that can be grown on each island depend on the amount of rain it receives. For the reasons described, average precipitation can vary considerably in different regions of one island, depending on the location of mountain ranges. In general, however, mountainous islands receive more rain than flat islands, and smaller islands receive less than larger islands. For example, because of their size, the Greater Antilles generally are moist, although low-lying Cuba gets less rain than mountainous Jamaica. In contrast, the small, flat islands and cays of the southern Bahamas normally receive less than 25 feet of rain per year.

In the Lesser Antilles, similarly, the islands in the outer arc generally are arid compared to those in the inner arc with their volcanic mountains. Extremely dry conditions are found in the three islands (Aruba, Bonaire, and Curaçao) off the Venezuelan coast. In this region, the trade winds are least effective during the summer, when they produce rain on the other islands. On these islands, the brief "rainy season" actually occurs during the winter rather than during the summer.

The amount of rain received by each island is thus affected by its height above the sea and by its size. Except for the northern Bahamas and the Curaçao group off the Venezuelan coast, most islands tend to experience two distinct seasons each year—a dry season (usually from February to April) and a "rainy season" (from May or June to October or November). During the summer, troughs of low pressure, accompanying shifts in the global wind patterns, arise in the eastern Caribbean and move west. These unsettled periods, known as easterly waves (or "waves in the easterlies"), can bring overcast weather and occasionally very heavy rains.

## THE DEADLY POWER OF HURRICANES

Sometimes, especially during the late summer, one of these easterly waves develops into a hurricane. For reasons that to this day we do not completely understand, a powerful upward current of air arises. This air current sets up a circular area of extremely low pressure that spirals inward (counterclockwise in this hemisphere) around the storm's calm center or "eye." Although the heaviest damage is near the center of the storm, adverse weather may extend over an area 600 miles in diameter. Generally hurricanes bring very heavy rains; as much as 18 inches in one 24-hour period have been recorded. Except at the eye, wind speeds are severe. Velocities of 75 miles or more are common, and gusts near the center of the storm can exceed 200 miles an hour.

Hurricanes affecting this region arise in the eastern Caribbean or in the eastern Atlantic off the coast of Africa. Their course is totally unpredictable, but most tend to travel slowly westward, at about 10 miles an hour, across the Lesser Antilles and Greater Antilles. Next they may curve to the northeast or north, either striking the southeastern coast of the United States or dying out in mid-ocean. Only Trinidad and the three islands off Venezuela—far to the south of a hurricane's normal path—are safe from their destruction.

On average, eight hurricanes occur each year, but many do not touch land. Overall, 174 hurricanes were severe enough to be mentioned in local records between 1492 and 1800. Although they happen in every month (except May), more than 80 percent hit during August, September, and October. Since they occur haphazardly, hurricanes may pass by an individual island for decades. But when they do hit, they can cause extraordinary damage.

In October 1780, for example, a hurricane—probably the greatest storm known to us—ravaged Barbados, Saint Lucia, Martinique, Dominica, Sint Eustatius, Saint Vincent, and Puerto Rico. During its savage passage, it killed well over 22,000 people and totally destroyed large British and French naval fleets as well as hundreds of merchant vessels. No instruments existing at the time could measure the force of its winds. But maximum gusts must have been well in excess of 200 miles per hour, since raindrops stripped the trees of their bark.

## THE CARIBBEAN ENVIRONMENT: RAIN FORESTS AND CACTUS

Until the 20th century, all of the island peoples made their living from agriculture. Thus the resources of the islands—soil, water, and climate—both provided the potential for and also placed limits on growth. In fact, the history of individual islands often is the story of how successfully its settlers came to terms with the natural potential available to them.

Tropical islands: El Yunque rain forest, Puerto Rico. As the trade winds rise to pass over high mountains such as El Yunque, they produce heavy rains on the windward (north and east) sides. This is a true rain forest with three levels of evergreen leaves, the highest or canopy layer reaching 120 feet.

Beginning with Columbus, visitors to the islands have remarked on their lush, dense vegetation, which at first often hindered settlement. But appearances are deceiving. The environment of the islands is quite fragile. Because of the moist, warm climate, chemical weathering occurs rapidly, and soil erodes easily and massively. In hilly areas, even natural forests are subject to severe erosion during the heavy rains of the summer wet season. And erosion can dramatically increase when the forests are removed for cultivation. In the upland regions of Puerto Rico, Jamaica, and especially of Haiti, centuries of erosion have totally destroyed some areas, which are no longer able to support life.

Even before they were cultivated, the soil in most of the islands was not very fertile. In the rain forests, most of the nutrients are contained in the vegetation itself, and the soil is relatively sterile. In upland areas, the heavy showers tend to leach minerals and organic matter deep into the ground where they can be reached only by the roots of trees and shrubs. Once the trees are cut, the soil is exhausted quickly and requires heavy use of fertilizers to produce crops.

It is precisely because their soils are relatively poor that most of the islands originally were covered by forests rather than by grasslands. Even today, a great variety of vegetation can be found on each island. Overall, there are six main types of natural environment—tropical rain forests, seasonal rain forests, dry forests, savannah, thorny woodlands and cactus scrub, and mangrove swamps—with the prevalence of each type depending on the amount and frequency of rain an island receives.

*Tropical Rain Forests*   The rarest and most lush environment, tropical rain forests occur only in regions that receive 80 or more inches of rain and are wet at least ten months of the year. Throughout the islands, these areas are found primarily in lowland areas on the windward side of high mountains. Two or three levels of constantly green vegetation block the sun, with the highest leaf canopy rising as much as 120 feet about the ground. As the temperature falls at higher levels (above approximately 3,000 feet), the tall rain forest merges into the mountain (or montane) forest, even more thickly covered with ferns and mosses.

*Seasonal Rain Forests*[4]   These receive 50 to 80 inches of rain during seven to nine humid months. Originally they covered most of the lowland districts and are still found on the leeward sides of the Greater Antilles. During the early centuries, several species had significant commercial value, including cedar and some trees used to make dyes, such as logwood. Only two layers of leaf canopy are found, and many trees lose their leaves during the dry season. At higher elevations in Cuba and Hispaniola, these seasonal rain forests merge into grasslands containing extensive forests of pine trees.

*Dry (or Tropical Deciduous) Forests*   These grow in regions with between 30 and 50 inches of rain and five to seven humid months. While frequently merging into the seasonal rain forest, the dry forest can be recognized by its more open nature. Trees rarely are more than 30 feet high, do not form a continuous canopy, and lose their leaves during the dry season. Since the ground is not shaded, it often is filled by a dense thorny brush, which is extremely difficult to pass through.

Desert islands: Small cabins (said to be former slave huts) on Curaçao. Low-lying islands do not break the flow of the northeast trade winds, and they thus receive little rain. The three flat islands of Aruba, Bonaire and Curaçao are especially arid.

*Savannah*   Flat dry grasslands containing scattered scrub trees originally occurred only in areas of seasonal drought and hard, coarse soils in Cuba,
Hispaniola, and the northern Bahamas. Man-made savannahs are found now on
most islands, where they have been created by burning the dry forest or seasonal
rain forest.

*Thorny Woodlands and Cactus Scrub*   These are found in areas with less than
30 inches of rain and only three to four humid months. Occurring on the dry
leeward coasts of many islands, they cover much of the Bahamas and the three
arid islands off Venezuela. Although only 6 or 7 feet high, often they are almost
impenetrable.

*Mangrove Swamps*   Originally encircling the more humid windward coasts of
most islands, some species of mangrove swamps can tolerate salt water. Above
the waterline, coastal areas were covered by low dense thickets of salt-tolerant
plants such as sea-grape and sometimes by palm trees.

## ISLAND ANIMAL LIFE

Until the invention of modern steamships, the history of the islands was
continuously influenced by the strong flow of the trade winds and currents more
or less from east to west. Because of these winds and currents, it is much easier
to move through the Caribbean from Venezuela than from Florida. And, as far
as we know, virtually all plant, animal, and human life did migrate from east to
west—from the northern coast of Venezuela to Trinidad, up through the lesser
Antilles and Virgins, and then across the Greater Antilles to Puerto Rico,
Hispaniola, Jamaica, and Cuba.

When Europeans reached the islands in 1492, they found relatively little
animal life. Apparently, few of the larger species had been able to cross the water
from South America. Among wild animals, a variety of small mammals was
found only on Trinidad, which is closest to the mainland. These included the
sloth, anteater, tiger cat, racoon, and a small deer. On the other islands, the only
mammals, other than bats, were various rodents, including the large and tasty
hutia, which reminded the Spanish of a rabbit. One kind of frog and a wide
variety of reptiles also thrived, including the caiman, crocodiles (found only in
Cuba), several snakes, and many lizards, such as the giant iguana.

The native peoples added very few domesticated animals over the years. The
Caribs kept Muscovy ducks, and the Arawak may have raised guinea pigs as well
as small dogs (called *alco*), which did not bark. The Spanish themselves
introduced many European plants and animals, some of which thrived and
became major export crops. The most important of these are cane sugar, cattle,
pigs, chickens, goats, donkeys, and horses.

## THE ARAWAK AND THE CARIB

When the Spanish reached the islands in 1492, they found three major groups
of people. All had come to the islands from South America in the relatively recent
past. Small groups commonly referred to as the Ciboney (or Siboney) lived on

the northwestern tips of Cuba and Hispaniola. The Island Arawak dominated the Bahamas, the Greater Antilles, and Trinidad. The Carib were found on the Virgin Islands, many of the Lesser Antilles, and the northwestern tip of Trinidad. The Arawak, the first native group they encountered, told the Spanish that they had come after the Ciboney and were being chased by the Carib—and most archaeologists believe this story to be true.

The history of these native peoples is inherently fascinating, they play an important role during the first decades of European settlement, and they have left us much of their material technology and a few descendants of mixed blood. But their story cannot be summarized easily and is largely conjectural. Since none of these peoples had a written language, we must rely on Spanish accounts and archaeological evidence.

The three major groupings of Indians are linguistic, with each group speaking similar and mutually comprehensible languages. Various scholars have distinguished a number of separate cultures, and they have given various names to these subgroups. However, none of these systems is generally accepted—except possibly for the use of Lucayan for the Arawak inhabiting the Bahamas.

Because of the importance of marine protein in their diet, all of the native peoples tended to live near or along the coasts. The most primitive and probably the oldest group were the Ciboney. By 1500, they primarily lived in rock shelters and caves along the northwest coasts of Cuba and Hispaniola. Small family groups apparently survived by collecting shellfish, wild fruits, and herbs as well as by hunting or culling fish, turtles, and reptiles (such as the iguana). Like all of the native peoples, they wore few clothes and painted their bodies, and their only implements were chipped and ground stone tools. Thus their sites reveal no evidence of cultivated plants, pottery, domestic utensils, or weapons.

## CONUCO AGRICULTURE AND ITS SURVIVAL TODAY

In contrast to the Ciboney, the Arawak and Carib carried more advanced ways of life with them from their original homeland in the Amazon basin. The Arawak and Carib were in frequent contact, and both peoples used essentially the same material technologies. They farmed, hunted, and fished in comparable ways; and they used similar methods to make canoes, build huts, weave cloth, and make pottery. There do seem to have been significant differences in their social and political organization and in their religious beliefs, although these differences may have been exaggerated by some of the first Spanish observers.

Both peoples brought from South America a system of raising root plants known as *conuco*. This method produces large amounts of starch and sugar with relatively little effort, and it also is well suited to the fragile soil of the Caribbean islands. Toward the end of the dry season, the Indians first burned off the forest or brush. This released nutrients into the soil, which was then heaped up into mounds, more or less knee-high and some 3 to 6 feet across. Using pointed sticks, the women placed in these mounds cuttings from several types of root plants. The most important of these was the bitter yuca (called *manioc* in Brazil). Since its roots are poisonous, they are shredded or grated and drained of their juices before being baked into a kind of flat, unleavened bread known as *cassava*. A sweet form of yuca and yams or sweet potatoes also were grown and eaten boiled or baked.

The bitter yuca provided the Arawak and Carib with an abundant and constant supply of starch and sugar. The yuca is ideally suited to the islands. Because the *conuco* mounds provide drainage and prevent erosion, it can be grown on both in lowlands and on slopes. The plant grows in almost any soil, resists winter droughts and summer hurricanes, and can be stored (in the form of cassava bread) for months. Moreover, since the mounds require only modest weeding and can be harvested continuously, there is little urgency about work in the fields. While the crops become less abundant with time, the same mounds can be used for up to ten or fifteen years. For all of these reasons, yuca later became one of the main foods of the African slaves, and it continues to be very widely grown throughout the Caribbean by peasant farmers.

Yuca and yams were the main crops. In addition, the mounds also produced several other types of root plants, including arrowroot, peanuts, peppers, and gourds. And the Indians also grew smaller amounts of seed plants such as tobacco, corn (maize), beans, and squash. For variety these could be supplemented by local fruits, including the pineapple, the guava, and possibly the cashew.

Fishing and hunting provided additional protein. The native peoples mainly hunted the hutia, the iguana, and several kinds of birds (pigeons, doves, and parrots), and they sometimes ate snakes, worms, spiders, and insects. The seas were much richer than the land, providing many varieties of shellfish, crabs, and fish as well as large marine mammals such as the manatee, or sea cow. The Arawak and Carib also caught many types of waterfowl, and they especially relished the eggs and flesh of the giant green turtle, which can weigh as much as 1,500 pounds. By contrast, freshwater fish were of comparatively less importance. Whether meat or fish, most of what they caught was placed with vegetables such as the sweet yuca into a pepper pot, a bowl left on the fire to simmer continuously.

## THE GENTLE ARAWAK

The Spanish described the Arawak as peaceful, gentle, hospitable, friendly, and ceremonious. No doubt individual Arawaks suffered pain and unhappiness, but the islands of the Greater Antilles and the Bahamas probably did form a kind of tropical paradise. As Carl Sauer has noted, the *conuco* method "would have been a competent agricultural system without yuca. With this great staple it was productive as were few parts of the world."[5]

Because of the climate, there was little need for elaborate housing or artificial heat. With their food needs so easily met, the Arawaks had the leisure to design and make pottery (by the coil method), baskets, woven cotton clothing, simple stone tools, and elaborate stone sculptures. Both men and women painted their bodies and ornamented them with jewelry made of gold, stone, bone, and shell. Gold was especially prized. Although the island Arawak did not mine gold, they

Arawak ceremonial ballpark, Puerto Rico. The Arawak played a ball game (something like soccer) on these rectangular courts found in almost every village. This park, which includes paved walks and plazas outlined with colored stones, may also have been used for religious ceremonies.

recognized its natural form and collected usable amounts from riverbeds. These nuggets were pounded into smooth plates and then shaped into ear and nose rings, necklaces, and masks. Gold ornaments later proved their undoing by attracting the attention of the Spanish, who enslaved the Arawak to obtain more of the precious metal.

When they were not hunting or fishing, the Arawak spent much of their leisure time in games. These included a kind of ball game (something like European soccer) that was played on rectangular courts found in almost every village. Informal feasts and dances also were frequent, sometimes in connection with games. And the village chiefs organized more solemn festivals on religious and ceremonial occasions. If anything, dances were even more common among the Carib, who accompanied them by drinking alcoholic beverages made from fermented corn, sweet potatoes, cassava, and pineapple juice. In later years, many Arawak also drank routinely, but some authorities believe that they did not use alcohol before the Spanish conquest. Both peoples also enjoyed tobacco, which they rolled into a kind of primitive cigar and also took as a nasal snuff.

The Arawak had organized systems of religion and government. They believed that good and evil spirits inhabited both human bodies and also many natural objects. They sought to control these spirits through their priests or shaman as well as by capturing them in icons or statues called *zemis*, sometimes made of gold.

To the first Spanish explorers, the Arawak political system seemed very similar to their own. Each island was divided into provinces ruled by paramount chiefs known as *caciques* (five or six in Hispaniola, perhaps as many as eighteen in Puerto Rico). The provinces were in turn allocated into districts ruled by sub-chiefs and villages governed by headmen. While the village headmen are said to have exercised despotic powers over their own villagers, the caciques' rule seems to have been looser or even merely ceremonial. In either case, chiefs and headmen owed their authority, at least in part, to their possession of superior zemis that contained the most powerful spirits.

## THE WARLIKE CARIB

Government was more decentralized among the Carib, perhaps because they did not possess zemis. Each village was independent, and one or more war chiefs were elected for each island. Carib men spent their time hunting, fishing, and practicing their military skills, while women did the other work. Both the Arawak and the Carib divided up tasks among the genders, but the division was far more rigid among the Carib.

In both cases, women maintained the *conucos*, prepared food, wove cloth, and made household baskets and pottery. But Arawak women were relatively equal in many areas, and they were not segregated before marriage. Virginity was not considered desirable; indeed, Arawak men preferred sexually experienced wives. By contrast, Carib men lived together in communal houses and kept their wives in separate huts. They treated their wives as servants, who had to dress and feed their husbands, clean their houses, and carry all burdens in addition to working in the fields.

Carib men were experts in building and managing boats. They also were fearless warriors, who almost always defeated the Arawak and even had some success against Europeans. Although their skills were excellent and they considered war the highest art or game, battles actually took up only a small percentage of their time.

Because the Carib fought attempts to enslave them, the Spanish described them as bloodthirsty savages. Indeed, the English term *cannibal* is derived from their Spanish name (*caribal*). But human meat had no place in their regular diet. Cannibalism was practiced as part of a religious rite in which their captors tortured, killed, and ate the bravest warriors taken in a battle. The Carib's reputation for violence and cruelty almost certainly is exaggerated. When the French and British settled the Lesser Antilles in the 1630s, the Carib initially were friendly and provided food to the starving adventurers. They turned hostile only after they were attacked by the Europeans.

## THE CARIBBEAN DISEASE ENVIRONMENT

Millions of tourists come to the Caribbean islands each year to rest and relax from their everyday cares. They are convinced, correctly, that their trip will improve their physical and spiritual health. Until this century, however, most

Europeans believed, again correctly—that the islands were one of the least healthy places on earth, that they were the proverbial "whiteman's graveyard." For four centuries, the Caribbean's semitropical climate provided an ideal environment for microbes and a deadly environment for humans.

The earth's winds and currents make the Caribbean a natural highway both for men and for parasites traveling from Europe and Africa to the Americas. The port cities of the islands provided a meeting place for the diseases endemic to three continents. Here Europeans and their African slaves gave each other diseases against which the other race had no immunity. As many as a third of both races died during their first two years on the islands—often of different diseases.

Humans and microbes coexist, and they adapt to one another over time. As a disease becomes broadly endemic within a society, changes or adjustments in the human immune system may result in genetic immunity. Total immunity usually is acquired only through actual contact with a disease. However, when a disease is endemic, a group develops a partial or relative immunity so that the disease affects it in a less virulent form. Most individuals suffer though a mild case in childhood and thus acquire the antibodies needed to protect them from further infection as adults.

Prior to the 15th century, the peoples of Europe and Africa rarely mingled, and the indigenous peoples of the Americas existed in total isolation. A distinctive disease environment developed on each of these continents. The people developed relative immunities to some—but not all—of the diseases endemic among them, which thus became relatively mild or "childhood" illnesses.

Until Europeans and Africans arrived, a host of illnesses—including smallpox, measles, typhus, yellow fever, malaria, tuberculous, and pus infections— were totally unknown in the Americas. The native peoples were not immune to these diseases. Thus they died in staggering numbers when Europeans and African slaves introduced them. The Spanish enslaved the natives and wanted to use them as laborers. Within a decade, they accidently exterminated them. When Columbus touched land in 1492, the Caribbean islands were home to at least a quarter-million Arawak and Carib Indians—perhaps as many as six million, according to some archaeologists. Within twenty years, almost all were dead.

Europeans and Africans have roughly the same tolerance for diseases endemic on both continents—smallpox, diphtheria, whooping cough, measles, mumps, and influenza. Although these diseases originated in Africa, Africans are more likely than whites to suffer from yaws, leprosy, and intestinal worms. They also are more susceptible than Europeans to bacterial pneumonia, tuberculosis, and tetanus. By contrast, most West Africans are at least partially immune to two diseases—yellow fever and falciparum malaria—found only in Africa.

Africans coming to the Caribbean fared better than European colonists. Most islands were decidedly unhealthy for whites, who today form only a small minority—5 percent or less—of their population. Europeans coming to the islands brought their own diseases with them. They also were exposed to yellow fever and falciparum malaria, two deadly African fevers to which they did not have natural immunity. Only in this century have physicians begun to understand the complex ways in which these two diseases are transmitted. Until about 1900, the causes of both diseases remained a mystery, thus increasing the fear and horror they incited.

Yellow fever and malaria are among the diseases carried by mosquitoes. Both travel from one victim to another through the insect, and neither passes directly from human to human. The pattern of transmission is from man to mosquito to man—and back to mosquito. However, the mosquitoes carrying malaria and yellow fever belong to separate species with distinct habits. Thus they spread the two diseases in somewhat different ways.

Falciparum malaria was endemic on some islands but not on others. Primarily a rural disease, it quietly winnowed children and immigrants. Over the centuries, it killed as many or more victims than yellow fever, but its ravages often passed unnoticed. Yellow fever, the other great killer, is dramatic in its onset and terrible in its ferocity. Yellow fever was not endemic to the islands, but it sporadically visited all of them with devastating effects. Primarily an urban disease, yellow fever suddenly descended upon a crowded port city or the packed tents of an invading army. Over the course of a few weeks or months, many—half or even more—of the citizens or soldiers died horrible deaths. Then the plague disappeared, sometimes returning in a few years, sometimes not for decades.

*Falciparum Malaria*   One of the oldest and most widespread of diseases, malaria is an infection by one of four species of the *Plasmodium* parasite (protozoa). It is normally transmitted to humans by the bite of the female Anopheles mosquito, widespread throughout both Africa and the Americas. As the tiny mosquito feeds on human blood with a lancet smaller than the head of a pin, the malaria parasites rapidly enter the liver and multiply. They then break out into the bloodstream and feed on the victim's red blood cells.

Two types of malaria afflicted the Caribbean islands, making its peoples shake with fever and ache with pain. Europeans brought *Plasmodium vivax*. This milder form rarely is deadly. But it leaves its victims weak and anemic and thus can contribute to death from other causes. *Plasmodium falciparum*, a much more severe form, is a tropical disease endemic in West Africa but not in Europe. African slaves brought it to the islands during the 16th century, and it later reached the American mainland.

Before the 1840s, when quinine became available in a purified form, falciparum malaria was a major killer among newly arrived adult Europeans. At least 25 percent—sometimes as many as 75 percent—of whites died following their first encounter with the disease. Malaria also killed Africans, but whites died more rapidly and in greater number. West Africans, who lack certain hemoglobin determinants, are almost totally resistant to malaria vivax and they enjoy a relative immunity to falciparum malaria. Victims (black or white) surviving falciparum malaria acquire partial immunity. But they remain infested with the parasite for life, and they thus pass it on when bitten by a anopheline mosquito.

Anopheline mosquitos breed in profusion in standing water, with some species preferring dank, stagnant swamps. Since mosquitoes cannot survive, this disease did not exist on the relatively dry islands of Barbados, Saint Kitts, and Anguilla; and it was rare in the Bahamas, Antigua, and Saint Vincent. But malaria was endemic in the more humid islands of the Greater Antilles (Cuba, Jamaica, and Hispaniola), as well as on Guadeloupe, Martinique, Dominica, Saint Lucia, Grenada, Trinidad, and Tobago.

*Yellow Fever*   A mosquito also carries yellow fever from man to man. The *Aëdes aegypti* mosquito (formerly called *Stegomyia fascinata*) has an eccentric life-style that makes yellow fever primarily an urban disease. This mosquito is a domestic pest that flourishes in the company of humans. It breeds only in standing water, and it favors water kept in open containers with solid sides and flat bottoms, such as cisterns or water casks. It cannot fly very far, only a few hundred yards at most. *Aëdes aegypti* and the virus need a closely packed population to supply the blood that is their food. Thus those threatened by the disease could escape it both by rigidly quarantining the sick and also by immediately leaving the infected area.

The yellow fever virus affects some victims lightly—especially children— and they may show few visible symptoms. Nonimmune European adults suffer a terrible death, but fortunately one that comes swiftly. After a brief period of remission, the disease reappears and involves the kidneys. Fever increases, causing extreme prostration, frequent vomiting, and jaundice (the yellow skin giving the disease its English name). As the disease progresses, its victims suffer internal hemorrhage and vomit blood (hence the Spanish name *vomito negro*, black vomit), delirium, coma, and death. There is no cure for yellow fever. Even with care in a modern hospital, the death rate in severe cases approaches 50 percent. In earlier centuries, 75 percent or more died among those encountering the disease for the first time.

The death rate from yellow fever was much higher among whites than among blacks. Since the disease is endemic in West Africa, many West African peoples have developed a relative immunity. They can become infected with yellow fever, but their power to resist and survive the virus' effects is much greater than that of whites or Indians. In contrast, Europeans almost never acquired immunity to Yellow Fever before coming to the islands.[6]

Whether the illness is mild or severe, it leaves its victims with total lifelong immunity, and survivors are safe from further symptoms. Indeed, their blood will not support the disease, and they cannot act as a carrier. In the Caribbean, once an epidemic finished its course, the virus ran out of nonimmune hosts. It died out—often for many years—until an infected individual reintroduced it into a population.

Yellow fever thus was never endemic to the islands. But it visited and revisited them all with devastating effects. Africans brought both the yellow fever virus and *Aëdes aegypti* to the New World. The mosquito remained, but the virus died and was periodically reintroduced to a nonimmune population. Invariably epidemics were associated with slave ships newly arrived from Africa. Port cities crowded with European sailors, businessmen, and immigrants supplied nonimmune hosts. The packed tents of soldiers provided the mosquitoes and the virus with an ideal environment. Thus invasions during wartime set off several of the worst epidemics.

For more than 300 years—from about 1600 to the end of the 19th century—malaria and yellow fever had a major influence on the life of the islands. Over and over again during these centuries, they struck down thousands of white settlers. On several occasions, these diseases literally determined who would control the region by destroying an invading fleet or army. Indeed, these diseases often were—as the following chapters document—the creole population's best defense against invading armies of nonimmune Europeans.

Because both the malaria parasites and the yellow fever virus require masses of nonimmune hosts, they probably spared the sparsely settled Spanish islands during the 16th century. These fatal microbes were present by 1598, when yellow fever and other diseases killed most of an British army that had taken and planned to occupy San Juan, Puerto Rico. After 1625 they continued to ravish northern Europeans trying to settle the Lesser Antilles and Jamaica. In 1655, the French landed 1,500 men at Saint Lucia. A few months later, only 89 remained alive. During some years after the British captured Jamaica in 1655, the death rate among new settlers was almost as staggering.

At all times the islands were fatal for new arrivals. The creoles, who caught relatively mild cases in childhood, thus acquired immunity to yellow fever and malaria. But the death rate was extraordinary among healthy young Europeans. One-third to one-half of the indentured servants arriving during the 17th century did not live to complete their five-to-seven-year term of bondage.

The toll was as great two hundred years later. From 1817 through 1836, 12 percent of white troops in Jamaica died of disease each year on average, compared to a death rate of only 3 percent among black troops. The entire regiment had to be replaced every eight years. If individuals quickly succumbed, the death rate was even higher among the compact ranks of troops fresh from Europe. During their invasion of Saint-Domingue (1793–1797), the British sent some 20,500 soldiers to occupy that island. About 12,500 died, mostly of malaria and yellow fever.

Perhaps because there often is a significant interval between the mosquito bite and the onset of illness, physicians were extraordinarily slow to identify the causes of malaria and yellow fever. Carol Finlay of Havana correctly identified *Aëdes aegypti* as the species carrying yellow fever in 1881, and Ronald Ross described the complex life cycle of the plasmodia parasite in 1898. During the early 1900s, public health authorities accepted their findings. Killing the mosquitoes stopped the spread of the two diseases, which became rare by World War One.

*Aëdes aegypti* was easily exterminated because it needs to live close to humans. The American army occupying Havana eradicated the pest in 1901 by treating standing water with oil and requiring that all home supplies be kept in mosquito-proof containers. Within a year yellow fever no longer originated in that city. Other Caribbean countries also adopted anti-mosquito measures with marked success, and the last case of yellow fever among European troops at Port Royal, Jamaica, occurred in 1904.

Humans could not as easily get rid of the indigenous anopheles mosquito. But malaria killed fewer victims from the 1840s, when a purified form of quinine became widely available both as a prophylactic and as a treatment. Improved sanitation and public health measures also indirectly reduced the urban mosquito population. Public authorities provided Kingston, Jamaica, with water flowing through filtered pipes in 1871, and they built a street sewage system by 1895.

Improved shipping also helped to eradicate malaria and yellow fever. Wooden ships take in water from leaks on the keel, providing many damp refuges for insects. Pests are less likely to infest steel ships, which are comparatively water-tight. And water condensed from steam replaced stagnant casks. By the 1890s the governors of Jamaica and several other islands began to tout their healthy climate, although tourism did not develop as a major industry until after the First World War.

# CHAPTER TWO:
# DISCOVERY OF THE ISLANDS

■

On October 12, 1492, Christopher Columbus (1451–1506) reached the Bahama Islands, landing—according to tradition—on San Salvador, today known as Watling's Island. Carried by the easterly trade winds into the unknown, the three small ships under his command had made a smooth voyage of 2,400 miles in only 36 days. Believing that some 2,500 miles (rather than 7,500) of ocean separated China and Japan from Europe, Columbus thus sought to sail to the Indies by a westward passage. When he reached the Bahamas, he was convinced that he had achieved his goal, and he continued to claim the islands as part of Asia until his death in 1506.

The history of the Caribbean islands is strongly affected by their geographical situation and by the environmental qualities discussed in Chapter One. And until recently their history also has been closely tied to events in Europe. Columbus is said to have "discovered" America, and that statement is largely accurate. Columbus probably was not the first man to cross from the Old World to the New. But, by returning to Spain, he became the first to make the Americas widely known to Europeans, who now entered the region in force.

## THE ISLANDS UNDER THE RULE OF CHRISTIAN KINGS

The Caribbean was the first part of the New World to be reached by Columbus. Moreover, Europeans remained in the islands longer than in most other parts of the Americas. Until the 1960s, many islands were directly attached to European states as political and economic dependencies. And their peoples, or at least the ruling groups, often considered themselves to be Europeans even though they had been born in the islands.

When Columbus discovered the Americas, Europe was only beginning to emerge from its medieval past. During the next few centuries, both technology and the ways in which Europeans viewed the world changed dramatically. Thus the history of the islands largely is the story of adaptation to developments in Europe or, in later centuries, in the United States. Europeans—to take one example—imposed slavery on the islands. Later, when European governments turned against slavery, they forced island planters to free their bondsmen.

"An Indian Cacique of the Island of Cuba, addressing Columbus concerning a future state." Columbus reached Cuba on his first voyage in December 1492.

Before leaving on his first voyage, Columbus negotiated with Queen Isabella of Castile the terms of a contract in the form of a royal grant (*capitulación*). In the event that he succeeded, the Crown would grant Columbus hereditary nobility and the title of admiral, make him viceroy of the mainlands and islands he reached, and give him one-tenth of the profits taken from them. The privileges granted to Columbus were unusually generous. But the *capitulación* itself was a traditional device through which the Crown delegated specific royal powers to the leader (*adelantado*) of an expedition. Most of the conquistadors who followed Columbus into the Americas solicited and operated under these contracts. Normally, the expedition's leader combined most of the administrative authority of a governor with the powers of a military captain-general.

Queen Isabella believed that she could delegate such great powers to her captains because the lands of pagan peoples were hers by right of conquest. A legitimate king did not invade the territory of another Christian king without just cause. But he was obligated to bring under his rule territories occupied by pagans (or Christian heretics). By right of conquest, the king owned everything in these territories. And he could in turn distribute this conquered property to various subjects in whatever ways seemed most likely to facilitate settlement by Christians or the conversion of the present inhabitants.

In theory, a Christian king was not a tyrant because he exercised his control in accordance with law and followed legal procedures. He was above all other men, but he could not act capriciously. His actions thus were limited by the laws and customs of his realm, by divine and natural law, and by his obligation to take counsel with experts (secular and spiritual) and with those affected by his decisions.

In actual practice, the king's powers also were limited by his financial resources and by the small number of officials available to carry out his decrees. Particularly in the case of Spanish America, royal authority was restricted by the technology of the day. Local officials had a great deal of latitude in applying royal decrees simply because it literally took months and even years for these to reach the Americas from Madrid.

## COLUMBUS RULES THE CARIBBEAN

Guided by the Lucayo Indians, Columbus sailed south from the Bahamas to Cuba, and spent six weeks exploring its northern coast. By December 6, 1492, he reached the northeastern tip of a second large island, which he named Isla Española (Anglicized as Hispaniola). On Christmas Day, his flagship, the Santa Maria, was grounded on a sandbank and destroyed. Leaving behind 39 men at the first European settlement of Navidad, Columbus sailed back to Spain. To impress the queen, his two remaining ships carried some gold nuggets and six Lucayos. His return elicited popular excitement as well the applause of his monarch, who granted him the rewards promised in his contract.

Judging by its small size, the queen and her counsellors had viewed Columbus's first voyage as a kind of tentative exploration that might open up trade with the East. They rapidly prepared a second and much larger expedition to establish a permanent foothold on the islands he had reached. In September 1493, Columbus—now an admiral of Spain—again sailed, this time in command of seventeen ships. In addition to perhaps 1,500 men, 1,200 of them armed soldiers, his fleet carried horses, sheep, cattle, and hogs as well as European plants such as wheat, barley, grapes, and sugarcane.

On this second voyage, the admiral steered further south and made landfall on Dominica. Turning west, he passed through and named the entire chain of the Lesser Antilles—Santa Maria de Guadalupe, Santa Maria de Montserrate, Santa Maria la Antigua, Santa Maria la Redonda, Santa Cruz, San Juan Bautista (Puerto Rico)—before arriving in Hispaniola in November 1494. Here he remained for almost seventeen months until March 1496.

Columbus again sought to stake out Spanish claims against those of Portugal or other nations. This time he also intended to establish permanent settlements under his control. Above all, he wanted gold. In these latter aims, he was largely unsuccessful. Finding Navidad deserted and its men killed, he founded the city of Isabella in an unhealthy and poorly located site on the northwest coast and put it under the command of his brother Bartholomé. He then sailed away for six months, discovering Jamaica and exploring along the southern coast of Cuba.

Neither Christopher nor Bartholomé Columbus could rule the new colony. Both alienated the Spanish by demanding that they work. And Columbus also disrupted the production of food on the native *conucos* by forcing each Indian to dig up a set amount of gold. Many Indians died, and those that rebelled were harshly punished. When Columbus sailed for home in March 1496, Hispaniola was in poor condition. Food was in short supply, and the natives were much diminished in numbers. Many settlers had returned to Spain with complaints about his rule.

## THE ENCOMIENDA: INDIAN SLAVERY

The admiral remained in Spain until May 1498 while the Crown sought to regulate the sorry affairs of the colonies and to encourage their development. Up to this point, the settlers theoretically were Columbus's salaried employees, although seldom paid. One royal decree authorized the distribution (*repartimiento*) of land, all legally owned by the Crown. Individual settlers were expected to work the land, build dwellings, and remain on it for four years. In return they received the use of their property in perpetuity and could sell it, give it away, or will it to their family. This decree was repeated by Emperor Charles V in 1513, and it later became one basis of land ownership in the Greater Antilles. However, when Columbus returned on a third voyage to the islands in 1498, it was distorted to justify the virtual enslavement of the Indians.

During his absence, Columbus again left his brother Bartholomé in charge as *adelantado*. In August 1496, Bartholomé transferred the capital from Isabella to the new city of Santo Domingo, located on the southeast coast in a productive region with a good harbor. The administrative capital of the Spanish empire until 1526, Santo Domingo was a natural destination for ships following the easterly trades from Europe and the Lesser Antilles. Thus it proved an excellent base from which to explore South America during the next fifty years, and it remained economically important until the 1560s, when a change in sailing routes made Havana the preferred port.

Bartholomé's efforts to rule the settlers were even less successful than those of his brother. Perhaps half of those remaining in Hispaniola joined a revolt led by Francisco Roldan, who set up an independent administration in the southwest. Instead of working, the Spanish squatted on the Indian communities and lived off their labor. In May 1498, Columbus returned on his third voyage with a modest fleet of six ships. Sailing through the passage between Trinidad and Venezuela, he landed in Santo Domingo in August to face Roldan's revolt. To placate the rebels he distributed to them not land but Indian communities.

Individual settlers could legally force "their" Indians to work without wages in a kind of semi-slavery or serfdom, known in Spanish both as *repartimiento* and as *encomienda*.

The institution of Indian *encomienda* dominated Spanish America for centuries. Strictly speaking, it was illegal. Moreover, it tended to create a dangerous group of overpowerful subjects, independent of the Crown. Despite its reservations, the royal government believed it had to allow the Indian *encomienda* to make the colonies profitable. The initial groups of settlers did not go to the Americas to work, and the economy could not survive without Indian labor. Thus Queen Isabella confirmed the practice in 1502–1503 with certain limits, and Charles V again regulated it by the laws of Burgos in 1512.

## THE FORMATION OF ROYAL GOVERNMENT FOR THE INDIES

While Christopher Columbus was a superb navigator, his direct rule of the Indies did not prove successful. Beginning in 1499, Queen Isabella acted in three ways to take back the powers she had delegated to the Admiral. She appointed Francisco de Bobadilla as "royal governor and judge of all the islands and mainland of the Indies." At the same time, the Crown now began to license other expeditions under new leaders. Finally, the queen also created the Casa de Contratación (Board of Trade), the first of two councils in Spain charged with commissioning and overseeing both these royal officials and adventurers in the Indies.

In approving Columbus's second voyage to the Indies in 1493, the queen assigned Juan Rodriguez de Fonseca (1451–1524), her chaplain and archdeacon of the Cathedral of Seville, to coordinate preparations. From then until his death in 1524, Fonseca effectively was in charge of government in the Indies, making or approving appointments and royal orders to the colonies. Seeking to increase overseas revenues, Fonseca set up a disciplined organization at Seville, which was formalized in 1503 as the Casa de Contratación. For more than two centuries, this powerful bureaucracy regulated emigration and trade, collected revenues due to the Crown, and supervised all expenditures authorized by the Crown or the Council of the Indies.

## THE SETTLEMENT OF HISPANIOLA

For the first royal governors of the Indies, the Queen choose two experienced administrators. Both were also officers in hybrid military/monastic orders that had developed to reconquer Spain from the Moors and that now managed large properties. When Francisco de Bobadilla (d. 1502), commander of the Order of Calatrava, arrived in Hispaniola in August 1500, he found a full-scale civil war in progress. Carrying out the queen's orders, he immediately arrested the Columbus brothers, sending them back to Spain in chains. During the next two years, Bobadilla restored order to the island and substantially increased the production of gold by offering incentives to individual entrepreneurs. All minerals were held to be royal property, and each mine was worked under royal license. Bobadilla initially may have set the Crown's share at 50 percent of output, but he apparently forgave payment of some of the first royalties.

Under this system of monopoly licenses, which became the standard in Spanish America, gold soon was produced in some quantity, perhaps as much as 600 pounds in 1501 alone. Only estimates are possible because a hurricane sank most of the fleet leaving for Spain in July 1502, taking with it Bobadilla, his records, and all of the gold he had collected. Hispaniola was now a going proposition, and his successor laid out the new city of Santo Domingo on a grander scale on the west bank of the river.

It was Brother Nicholas de Ovando, commander of the military order of Alcantara, who finally established royal control over Hispaniola. Arriving in April 1502 with a fleet of 30 ships and 2,500 settlers (including the first women and children), Ovando ruled the island until 1509. He imposed strict discipline upon the settlers, and treated the natives with great harshness. Spanish troops now conquered the rest of the island, treacherously murdering the chiefs (*caciques*) of the western regions at a banquet. Their communities were broken up, and the Arawak became serfs. Most were assigned to individual settlers as workers in the fields or gold mines. But the *encomienda* grants were made at Ovando's pleasure, and he reserved the right to transfer Indians to those settlers who got the most work out of them.

Under Ovando's severe rule, Spanish Hispaniola enjoyed a brief era of prosperity. The number of residents soared from perhaps 300 in 1502 to as many as 8,000 to 10,000 in 1509. To bring these settlers under his jurisdiction, Ovando founded fifteen towns. Food production rose, with the number of cattle increasing rapidly. And, by reducing the Crown's share from 50 to 20 percent, Ovando encouraged entrepreneurs to increase gold production, which reached its peak in 1509.

By that year, however, the very harshness of Ovando's regime had helped to kill off the native peoples, on whose labor Hispaniola's prosperity was based. An official Spanish census in 1509 counted only 60,000 adult Indians, and another in 1518 found as few as 11,000. With the approval of the royal government, the settlers raided the Bahamas islands and even the Lesser Antilles, bringing their inhabitants back to Hispaniola as slaves. And they also began to import black slaves, at first from Spain or from the Canary Islands and then from West Africa. Neither effort provided enough labor to maintain gold and food production. Moreover, the mines on Hispaniola now began to fail. Very little gold was produced after 1515, and all mining virtually ceased by 1519.

In 1509 Ovando retired, and King Ferdinand restored the governorship of the islands to Diego Colón (1509–1515, 1520–1523), Christopher Columbus's only legitimate son. To control Colón, the Crown also sent Miguel de Passamonte as royal treasurer reporting directly to Juan de Fonseca in Seville. Disputes soon arose over Colón's authority to distribute Indians to the settlers in *encomienda*, to approve town councils, and to appoint the governor of Puerto Rico. To resolve these, the king sent three judges, who arrived in 1512, to form an *audiencia* or royal appellate court, the symbol of royal justice since the Middle Ages.

## THE CONQUEST OF CUBA, JAMAICA, AND PUERTO RICO

By the end of Ovando's reign, the settlers were ready to undertake new conquests. Ruthless adventurers with money made in gold mining staked their new fortunes by outfitting expeditions. They found ample recruits among their less prosperous neighbors, who were eager to try their luck again in a new colony. The Crown also sought gold, and its agents licensed each expedition against a share of the spoils.

Overall, the occupation of other islands followed the pattern set in Hispaniola. The expeditionary forces marched quickly through the island, terrorizing the natives and crushing any rebels. A brief gold rush drew in thousands of Spaniards, who divided up the natives in *encomienda*. After only a few years, with the natives dead and the mines exhausted, the colonists moved on, leaving behind their cattle and pigs to take over an empty landscape.

In July 1508, Governor Ovando authorized Juan Ponce de León (c.1460–1521) to lead an expedition to Puerto Rico. Ponce founded towns near the richest pockets of gold at Camparia (now San Juan) and at San German, whose *vecinos* (male citizens) divided up the Indians. Some historians believe that Ponce treated the natives less harshly than most other Spanish conquistadores. Nevertheless, early in 1511, the Arawak rebelled with the help of more warlike Caribs, who had entered the island from San Croix. Ponce and his troops brutally crushed the rebellion. But the gold was quickly exhausted, and the Carib continued to raid the coasts. By 1518, most of the colonists drifted back to Hispaniola or moved on to Cuba or Panama. Replaced as governor by a protégé of Diego Colón at the end of 1511, Ponce moved on to discover Florida (Paschua Florida) on Easter Sunday 1513.

Because of his dispute with the Crown, Diego Colón rushed to appoint Juan de Esquivel as governor of Jamaica, with Panfilio de Narváez (c. 1470–1528) second in command. Earlier, both had played a leading part in brutally putting down Indian rebellions in Hispaniola. Their occupation of Jamaica began in 1509 near St Ann's Bay, where they founded Sevilla Nueva. Since they did not find gold, they gave out the Indians to settlers who intended to sell their crops to expeditions exploring the mainland. Horses, cattle, pigs, and goats were brought in and soon increased prodigiously in the absence of natural predators. Within ten years, nearly all the natives were dead. In 1519, most of the remaining colonists followed the royal governor, Francisco de Garay, on an expedition to Mexico. A few remained to raise and hunt cattle for sale to passing ships.

The Spanish Crown largely abandoned Puerto Rico and Jamaica. After Hispaniola, the most important settlement was Cuba, which was first colonized in 1511. In that year, the king approved a contract between Diego Colón and Diego Velázquez de Cuellar (c. 1460–1524?), one of the two captains in charge of Ovando's treacherous 1504 massacre of native chiefs. Velazquez landed in the northeast to capture a party of Arawak under the cacique Hatuey, who had earlier fled Hispaniola. (Hatuey has since become an adopted national hero in modern Cuba.) Western Cuba was conquered by Panfilio Narváez and other Spaniards from Jamaica, whose march through the island was marked by unprovoked massacres of Indians. Within a year the entire island was under Spanish control.

Events in Cuba followed the same course as in Hispaniola and Puerto Rico. In 1512, significant amounts of gold were found in the central mountains. Settlers rushed in from Hispaniola and the mainland, and Velázquez founded seven towns, disbursing the entire native population in *encomienda*. Once again, most Indians died within a decade, although small groups did survive in the Sierra Maestre mountains and on some of the offshore islands. As in Jamaica, the native population was supplanted by cattle and especially pigs, whose numbers increased at an extraordinary rate.

By 1519, the Cuban gold placers were exhausted and most of the towns deserted. Ignoring the superior harbor at Havana, Velázquez maintained the capital at Santiago on the southeast coast. Western Cuba was largely abandoned by the restless, gold-seeking Spanish. Its population dropped precipitously in November 1519, when Hernando Cortés (1485–1547)—after quarreling with Governor Velázquez—sailed for Mexico, taking with him 600 men, 16 horses, and many of the Cuban hogs to supply meat and breeding stock. Those settlers that stayed lived by herding semi-wild cattle and horses on open-range ranches.

## THE SPANISH IN PANAMA AND THE LESSER ANTILLES

Between 1502 and 1512, invasions from Hispaniola subdued Puerto Rico, Jamaica, and Cuba. Beginning in 1499, what today is known as Panama and the northern coast of Venezuela were visited by several expeditions that combined exploration, trade, looting, and slave hunting. Most were tentative until 1509 when the Crown authorized Alonso de Ojeda (*c.* 1466–1515?) to take the northern coast of Colombia and gave Central America to Diego de Nicusea. Both expeditions were routed by the Indians, but a few survivors grouped themselves at Darien, where Vasco Nuñez de Balboa (*c.* 1475–1519) seized power.

A comparatively humane leader, Balboa was the first to cross the Isthmus of Panama to the Pacific Ocean in 1513. He lost power in the same year, when the Crown sent out Pedro Arias de Ávila (called Pedrarias; *c.* 1440–1531) as royal governor. Under Pedrarias, who beheaded Balboa in 1519, the Spanish ferociously ransacked the peninsula for gold, killing virtually all the native population in the process. When Pedrarias stepped down as governor in 1529, the few settlers left in the city of Panama (founded in 1519) had to import Indian slaves from other regions.

Several of the excursions to the mainland apparently touched on various of the Lesser Antilles. An expedition under Alonso de Ojeda is know to have discovered Bonaire, Curaçao, and possibly Aruba in 1499. Columbus himself landed on Martinique during his fourth and last voyage in 1502. But the Spanish did not attempt to settle these islands.

King Ferdinand and leaders such as Cortés and Pedrarias were interested only in gold. Hispaniola, Puerto Rico, and Cuba all saw perhaps ten years of furious activity and were abandoned when their gold was exhausted. Since the Lesser Antilles had no gold at all, they were ignored. In the words of Diego

Colón, these were "useless islands" (islas inutiles). Their population was seen only as a source of slaves to replace the Indians who had died out on Hispaniola.

In 1511, King Ferdinand authorized slaving expeditions to the Lesser Antilles and the Curaçao group. Enslavement of the Carib was justified, the king said, because they were cannibals who refused to obey the Spanish. By 1520, the northern or Leeward islands from the Virgins to Barbuda were depopulated except for Saint Kitts and Nevis. To the south, the Spanish also removed to Hispaniola the inhabitants of the Curaçao group, Barbados, Saint Lucia, and Tobago. On the remaining islands, the Carib retreated to the mountainous interiors, where they resisted with some skill.

By the 1570s, the Spanish had virtually forgotten about the Lesser Antilles. Between 1525 and 1540, a few hundred Indians were transferred back to Curaçao to work on the land. Then the Curaçao group also was abandoned until the 1620s, except for occasional visitors from Venezuela. As Carl Sauer suggests, "The political geography of the West Indies is starkly simple: the French, English, and Dutch colonies of the seventeenth century occupied islands that had been emptied of their natives early in the sixteenth century in order to keep Española going. To a great extent the North European successors were able to live off the Spanish livestock that had replaced the Indians."[1]

## THE EXTERMINATION OF THE ARAWAK

The Spanish Crown abolished Indian slavery in 1542, and it outlawed the encomienda system of semi-slavery in 1550. In South America, where substantial numbers of Indians had survived, Spanish settlers resisted these laws and continued to demand forced labor for centuries. In the Greater Antilles, the royal decrees had almost no significance simply because most of the Arawak had died out decades earlier. The few survivors on each island grouped themselves into one or two villages. Here they often intermarried with runaway slaves and gradually lost their ethnic and cultural identity.[2]

There can be no question that the Spanish occupation totally destroyed Arawak society and led to the extinction—literally the genocide—of the Arawak race. Although the subject has been studied in depth for more than 70 years, what is less certain is how many Indians were killed or why they died. After analyzing all the competing theories, Lynn McAlister concluded that "No one knows how many Indians inhabited the Western Hemisphere in 1492 and, indeed, the problem has generated one of the liveliest controversies in American ethnohistoriography."[3]

The problem of an accurate count began with the first settlers. Almost as soon as the islands were taken, some Spanish observers harshly criticized the way in which their contemporaries were treating the Indians. Among the most consistently outspoken of these critics were members of the Dominican religious order. As early as 1511, for example, Antonio de Montesinos, a Dominican preaching before the governor, officials, and citizens of Santo Domingo, told his distinguished congregation that they would burn in hell because of their mortal sins against the Indians.

The Dominicans found their greatest spokesman in Bartholomé de Las Casas (1474–1566), the famous "Apostle to the Indies," who joined their religious order in 1522. Las Casas had arrived in Santo Domingo in 1502 with Governor Ovando. He participated in the conquest of Cuba in 1511 and acquired a large *encomienda* of Indian serfs, which he gave up in 1515. For the next fifty years he dedicated his life to the defense of the Indians, preaching, writing tracts, and lobbying the royal government.

He was a first-hand observer almost from the beginning. The unanswerable question is whether he exaggerated his charges. While other early Spanish observers reported that about one million Indians lived on Hispaniola, Las Casas wrote that between three and four million were present in 1492. Early anthropologists thought his estimates were incredible; more recent scholars tend to accept them. Since it was the most heavily populated island, most studies assume that the total Indian population was roughly twice that of Hispaniola. Assessments of the number of Indians throughout the Caribbean thus range from a low of 225,000 to as high as six million. All are simply educated guesses based on conflicting assumptions about how many people the Indian system of *conuco* agriculture could support.

How and why the Arawak died is even less certain than their original numbers. Traditionally, the "Black Legend" of Spanish settlement (especially favored by Protestants) asserted that the colonists wantonly tortured the Indians and literally worked them to death. Las Casas and other contemporary critics, who stress the brutality of individual masters, provide evidence that can be used to support the Black Legend. Taken as a group, however, the Spanish did not want to kill off the Indians. They wanted to make them work. But even relatively benign masters may inadvertently have hastened their death by herding the Indians together, especially at gold mines in the center of the islands. Here the Arawak were both exposed to new diseases and also cut off from the sea, which supplied their main source of protein.

It is said that the Europeans and especially their animals destroyed the native *conucos*. This was not generally true, since there is no evidence that cassava was ever in short supply. But cassava and yams supply only starch and sugar. They do not provide protein, animal fat, and salt—all of which are absolutely necessary to sustain life. Thus, even though they were well fed, the captive Arawak were malnourished and susceptible to sickness.

Isolated for thousands of years, the Arawak did not have natural immunity to the diseases carried by Europeans or Africans, including influenza, small pox, measles, malaria, and the common cold. These diseases, which elsewhere were endemic childhood illnesses, spread rapidly and killed men and women of every age. Since the women of child-bearing age died, demographic losses could not be made up by an increased birthrate after the plague was gone.

Another mystery is why the Arawak did not fight against the Spanish, even though they vastly outnumbered their captors. The mountains and dense scrub of the Greater Antilles are a natural environment for guerrilla warfare. And the weapons carried by the Spanish—especially their single-shot, smooth-bore muskets—were clumsy, slow, and inaccurate. During the 18th century, runaway black slaves (known as *maroons*) easily defeated professional solders with far better guns. While isolated rebellions did occur, most of the Arawak apparently let themselves be enslaved without resisting.

Many contemporary observers protested the fate of the Arawak, and the settlers may have doomed the Indians through their ignorance of disease and diet rather than through deliberate sadism. Nevertheless, the extermination of the Arawak was a crime. And, as Brother Antonio de Montesinos told Diego Colón in 1511, it also was a sin. Indeed, according to the teachings of Christianity espoused by the Spanish, their sin was equally as damning whether they killed 225,000 or six million.

# PIRATES FIGHT FOR SPANISH GOLD

■

From the 1530s, the Caribbean formed only a minor part of a vast Spanish empire, whose heart was in upland Mexico and Peru. On the mainland, Spanish adventurers finally found the untold riches—in gold and especially in silver—that the islands could never provide. Henceforth, the islands were important only because Spanish treasure fleets had to pass by them on their way to Seville. For more than two centuries, the Caribbean played a crucial role in commerce, but solely as the highway that carried treasure from the mainland to Spain.

The rulers of other European states envied the wealth of Spain's king and allowed their subjects to plunder it. Piracy became an accepted business in many French and British ports, with the Dutch joining in after 1599. Thousands of pirate ships attacked Spanish shipping and ports in the Caribbean and along the coast of Central America. The greatest booty was taken by Sir Francis Drake (1540?–1596), who captured an entire year's yield of Peruvian silver in 1573.

To protect its treasure fleets from pirates, Madrid imposed a system of economic regulation that endured until the 1750s. Spain closed its American empire to outside trade, and it limited trade with Europe to two yearly convoys. Under this restrictive system (the famous Laws of the Indies), Spain paid little attention to its island possessions. It fortified the ports used by the treasure fleets but did little to defend the other cities in the Caribbean.

## THE COCKPIT OF EUROPE

For more than two centuries, Spanish kings claimed that all of the Americas were their property because Columbus had sailed under the authority of Queen Isabella. By virtue of conquest, the Crown was said to possess all political, judicial, and religious authority, own all property, and retain all powers of taxation throughout the Indies. Anyone of any nationality entering the Americas must obey the royal laws. In theory, only Spaniards could move to or trade with the colonies, and all goods had to be brought over from Spain in the annual fleets of licensed Spanish ships.

Rulers of other states soon resented Spain's claim to a monopoly over the Indies. Francis I of France (1515–1547) reportedly asked where in Adam's will did the first man leave the Indies exclusively to the Spanish king. But the Dutch, British, and French did not begin to plant colonies in Spain's island world until about 1625. Seizing territory involved expensive problems of governance and defense. Spain's enemies preferred to weaken the Spanish economy and kingdom by licensing (or ignoring) pirates and "privateers" who seized Spanish ships on the high seas. Until the 1620s, piracy was the most common—and probably the most effective—form of warfare in the Americas. Since the Caribbean formed the narrow choke point through which passed all of Spain's trade with the Indies—including the great silver fleets—it inevitably bore the brunt of foreign attacks.

In seeking to maintain a total monopoly over all the Americas, the Spanish government ironically permitted, or even invited, its enemies to invade its American empire. The Spanish Crown focused its attention on Europe, and it depended on the Americas primarily as a source of treasure to support its European wars. The Spanish government showed little interest in Cuba, Jamaica, and Hispaniola after the discovery of gold and silver in Mexico and Peru. The Spanish Crown built great forts to defend the route of its treasure fleets. It left the other settlements to fend for themselves, even to the point of deliberately depopulating them. Spanish settlers on the islands were poor and ill-defended by the cumbersome colonial government—both overcentralized and over-complicated. They fell easy prey to the buccaneer raids that brought death and devastation for the next two centuries.

## THE SPANIARDS DISCOVER A MOUNTAIN OF SILVER

During these centuries, Spanish rulers had a number of goals—not always articulated and sometimes contradictory—for their American kingdoms. Above all else, they wanted to maintain ownership by preventing others either from occupying their overseas territories or from dominating them economically. The Spanish government also wanted and desperately needed revenue for the royal treasury in Spain.

Most of the first settlers had one aim only: to make quick fortunes by finding gold and other precious substances. If gold could not be found, they would attempt to become lords over Indian serfs. Between 1520 and 1550, some Spanish adventurers did achieve these goals. Driven by their dreams of personal glory, great military captains conquered the native empires of the Aztecs and Incas, carving out a great empire for Spain that stretched from Arizona to Argentina.

In the conquest of Central and South America, the Greater Antilles played a major role as a staging area and source of supplies and fresh meat. In 1519, Hernando Cortés sailed from Cuba with an expedition that captured the Aztec capital of Tenochititlán in 1521. From this city, renamed Mexico by its conquerors, his lieutenants quickly took over the remainder of the Aztec empire. During the same years, Spanish forces operating from a forward base in Panama followed the Pacific coast of South America to Peru. By 1533, the forces led by Francisco Pizarro (c.1476–1541) had occupied Cuzco, the capital of the Inca empire. Following the Inca road system, Spanish expeditions soon occupied Colombia, Chile, and Upper Peru (now Bolivia).

In Mexico and Peru, Spanish adventurers and their king finally found the wealth they had been seeking, although it largely took the form of silver rather than gold. Given the available technology, Spanish miners could profitably take gold ore only from high grade surface ores. The gold ore available through existing methods usually was fully exploited within ten to twenty years. Thus the mines in Santo Domingo, Cuba, and Puerto Rico largely were played out by the end of the 1520s. Similarly, the output from mines in Central America dropped off sharply in the 1550s.

But the diminishing gold quickly was replaced by immense amounts of silver from enormously rich veins in Peru and Mexico. In 1545, explorers discovered what was literally a mountain of silver at San Luis de Potosí in Upper Peru. Other major strikes were made in the 1530s in central Mexico (at Taxco) and in the 1540s and 1550s in northern Mexico (at Zacatecas, Guanajuato, and Pachuca). For about a hundred years, from the 1530s to the 1620s, silver production continuously rose. Altogether, the Casa de Contratación in Seville registered 16,887 tons of silver and 1,813 tons of gold as legally imported from the Americas between 1501 and 1650. Almost as much may have been smuggled out as illegal contraband.

Given the changes in the purchasing power of money, the value of this immense hoard cannot be precisely stated. However, the king's share—perhaps 40 percent of the total registered amount—became absolutely essential to the Spanish monarchy. American silver provided as much as 20 percent of all royal revenues at the end of Philip II's reign (1556–1598). Although royal receipts dropped dramatically after 1620, this reduced amount of treasure still provided Philip IV (1621–1665) with perhaps one-tenth of his funds.

Moreover, unlike many other taxes, the American treasure took the form of ready cash on hand. Thus the government of Philip II could pledge the treasure as security in borrowing from German and Genoese bankers. During the last third of the 16th century, these loans allowed the Spanish Crown to assemble the Great Armada that invaded England in 1588, send mercenary soldiers to crush the rebellion in the Netherlands, and subsidize the Catholic forces in France. The government borrowed lavishly against the arrival of the next treasure fleet. Seeing to it that the fleet arrived safely became its overriding concern.

## FRENCH AND BRITISH PIRATES INVADE THE CARIBBEAN

Almost from the beginning, the sailors of other nations began to attack Spain's treasure fleets and American colonies. Operating out of a series of different bases, pirates remained a threat for many generations. At first they sailed from Europe itself, easily following the trade winds to and from the Caribbean. For more than

GALLI CHIORERAM URBEM OCCUPANT, PRÆDANTUR, 7
& tandem, ob incolarum perfidiam, igne abfumunt.

Ho RE RA, quæ in Infula Cuba eft, à Gallis occupatur, in qua exiguam prædam inve-
niunt, quia Hifpani, aliquoties ante à Gallis fpoliati, omnem fere fuppellectilem in
fuis prædiis repofitam adfervabant.  Occupatis tamen in conquirenda præda Gallis, bini Hifpani mittuntur, qui obfervarent, quantus effet Gallorum numerus: eo tamen præ-
textu, ut cum illis agerent de captivorum lytro, & oppido ab incendio redimendo, Gallorum

French pirates capture, plunder, and burn Havana in 1555. ("Galli chioreram urbem occupant, praedantur, et tandem, ob incolarum perfidiam, igne absumunt.") Pirate bands continued to loot Caribbean ports during the next three centuries.

150 years, until the final collapse of Spanish power in the 1670s and 1680s, Spanish ships and ports provided the main prey in the Caribbean. The Spanish, with the only settlements in the region, remained the traditional victims—although by 1600 their towns had been raided so often, later pirates sometimes found slim pickings.

During the 16th century, pirates sailed almost continuously from ports in western England and northern France, where entire cites became dependent upon their infamous trade. The number of voyages to the West Indies rose and fell. But French and British captains (often with crews from several nations) left virtually every year, during times of truce as well as during hostilities. All sought booty. But many also were strong, even fanatical Protestants (many followers of Jean Calvin, called Huguenots in France), who added hatred of the Catholic Spanish to their greed for loot.

## NORMAN FRENCH CORSAIRS

The French, who were almost continuously at war with Spain until 1559, were the first to attack Spain's Caribbean ports. As early as 1522 and 1523, naval squadrons belonging to Jean d'Ango of Dieppe in Normandy managed to seize four ships carrying back to Spain Montezuma's fabled treasures and other riches seized by Cortés in conquering Mexico. In 1537, another of d'Ango's fleets captured nine ships carrying silver from Peru.

These hauls were taken near the Azores. But their extraordinary richness encouraged French captains to invade the Caribbean itself during the 1530s. By the mid-1550s, as many as 30 French ships raided the Indies each year, virtually controlling the seas and repeatedly pillaging costal towns on Hispaniola, Puerto Rico, and Cuba. The climax of their campaign came in 1555, when the French corsair Jacques de Sores captured Havana itself and burned it to the ground.

The 1559 peace treaty ending hostilities in Europe brought little respite to the Spanish colonies in the West Indies. As France was torn by religious civil wars during the next half-century, the government was too preoccupied and too weak to make the effort needed to stop pirate ships operating out of Normandy. Individual French ships and small squadrons continued to ply the Caribbean into the 1620s, operating as both privateers and smugglers. Indeed, Norman French pirates may well have outnumbered those from other nations even during the Anglo-Spanish war that broke out in 1585.

## THE CARRERA DE INDIAS

In response to these pirate attacks, the Spanish government created a system of annual convoys, with warships protecting merchant vessels sailing to and from Seville. In 1503, the Crown had required most ships to use the one port of Seville. From an early stage, many ships sailed in groups as security against increasing pirate attacks, and the convoy system reached its final form in the 1560s. In 1564, the Spanish Crown ordered that all ships must sail in two armed fleets for New Spain (Mexico) and Tierra Firme (mainland Central America). The Mexican fleet (called the *flota*), which included any ships bound for the Greater Antilles, was supposed to leave in April. The Terra Firme fleet (the *galeones*) was to sail in August. Both were assigned a naval escort. Usually two galleons accompanied the *flota*, and eight were assigned to the Terre Firme fleet—the famous *armada de la guardia de la carrera de las Indias*.

Each year the two fleets left Seville (although rarely on schedule), caught the northeasterly trades just south of Spain near the Azores, and followed them to Dominica or another island in the Lesser Antilles. Here their routes divided. Ships from the Terre Firme fleet proceeded either to Cartagena or to Nombre de Dios or (after 1598) to Portobelo in Panama. To the waiting galleons in these ports, the great treasures from Peru arrived after an overland journey from the Pacific across the narrow neck of Panama.

The other fleet proceeded north to Vera Cruz or to the nearby port of San Juan de Ulúa to pick up the cargoes brought along the treasure trail leading down from the Mexican highlands. To beat the hurricane season, both fleets reassembled in Havana in the late spring or early summer. In one great convoy, the heavily laden ships made their way through the narrow channel between Florida and the Bahamas until they reached the Carolinas and could catch the westerly trades across the Atlantic back to Seville.

The convoy system succeeded in its main goal, that of protecting the silver fleets. For more than two centuries, when Spain was so frequently at war with the northern maritime powers, the corsairs—both licensed and free-lance—sought to capture the source of its power. Year after year, they prowled the broad channel between Cuba and the Yucatan as well as the narrower Florida strait, ready to seize any unfortunate ship that might be separated from its fellows by a storm or accident. Almost never, however, were their arduous efforts rewarded. Occasionally, a pirate or privateer might cut off one or two merchant ships. But a royal galleon, heavily armed and carefully guarded, was taken on fewer than a dozen occasions. On only three occasions (in 1628, 1656, and 1657) was the entire treasure fleet taken, each time by a large squadron of enemy warships.

## THE MILITARY WEAKNESS OF THE SPANISH CARIBBEAN

While the Spanish government succeeded in protecting its treasure ships, it did little to protect the cities on the islands. And, given the fragmented and ineffective nature of Spanish local government, the islands could do little to defend themselves. Spanish officials did not form a chain of command in the military sense. Because of the juridical and legalistic nature of Spanish government, every group of officials in practice became an independent agent. There was no central command post for the entire Caribbean, and the various local authorities often did not even cooperate with each other.

In response to dozens of French raids, colonial governors began to fortify important ports and to organize militia companies to defend them. But the poor and sparsely inhabited Antilles colonies could afford little, and only Santo Domingo had a reasonably complete set of permanent works by 1560. In the following decades, the Crown gradually began to use taxes from the mainland (called the *situado*) to defend the Caribbean, which was so vital to the entire Americas.

Pedro Menéndez de Avilés (1519–1574) deserves credit as the Spanish leader who began the royal fortresses at major Caribbean ports. Menéndez, first appointed captain-general of the *armada de la carrera* in 1554, took out the Indies fleets in 1555, 1560, and 1562, bringing each safely back to Spain. His experience convinced him of the crucial importance of the lands along the Bahama Channel. In 1565, as *adelantado*, he led an expedition to Florida, wiping out a French colony and establishing a Spanish base at Saint Augustine. In the following year, he toured the islands and left soldiers and guns at Santo Domingo, San Juan, and Santiago de Cuba. As governor of Cuba (1568–1572) he ordered new defenses for Havana. However, these were not constructed until the 1580s, after a series of devastating raids by Britain's greatest sea raider.

## SIR FRANCIS DRAKE

While the French alternatively traded with and pillaged isolated towns and merchant vessels, the richest hauls now went to the British. The glory of taking the king's treasure at Panama fell to the famous English captain Sir Francis Drake. During a period of thirty years, Drake and his teacher, John Hawkins (1532–1595), made no fewer than seven voyages to the Spanish Main. Scholars dispute the purpose of Hawkins's voyages in the 1560s. But Drake's goal in the early 1570s was clear: to seize the Peruvian silver, which each year was brought by mule train across the isthmus from Panama to Nombre de Dios.

During his first two voyages in 1570 and 1571, Drake spied out the coast of the Spanish Main and made friends with the *Cimarrones*, African slaves who had run away from their Spanish masters. In January 1573, following several failed attempts, Drake finally succeeded in taking the Peruvian silver, after joining forces with the Norman Huguenot Guillaume Le Testu. Le Testu was killed during the struggle, but the Anglo-French pirates captured the mule train just north of Nombre De Dios. Although they had to leave behind 15 tons of silver, the pirates made off with gold worth the enormous sum of 100,000 pesos.

In 1577 Drake led a small fleet through the Straits of Magellan (at the tip of South America), probably intending to attack Panama from the east. Off the coast near Valparaiso, the British seized the Spanish ship *Cacafuega* carrying another rich treasure. Drake then sailed east around the world, returning to England in 1580. This was his last great haul in the New World. In 1585–1586, this time carrying royal orders, Drake returned and ransacked Santo Domingo and Cartagena. But he did not capture any treasure, and the ransom paid by the two cities did not cover his costs. In 1595, a fleet of 27 ships captained by both Hawkins and Drake tried to repeat the earlier successes. This time, Drake's good fortune totally failed him. San Juan was guarded by the new fort of El Moro, both Hawkins and Drake died during the siege, and the fleet returned without booty.

## ENGLISH PIRACY BECOMES BIG BUSINESS

Drake's fantastic hauls in 1573 and 1578 aroused feverish enthusiasm in England and are still remembered today. Over the years, however, the economy of the islands suffered greater damage from the dozens of other English privateers who flocked to the Caribbean during the Anglo-Spanish War. Especially during the 1590s, certain ports in the west of England, such as Weymouth and Southampton, gave themselves over to the business of fitting out privateer ships and disposing of their cargoes. No less than a hundred private warships sailed from these ports each year. Not all went to the Caribbean, but at least ten to twenty did each year.

No one was able to repeat Drake's seizure of royal treasure. At all times, few pirates actually gained great heaps of gold and jewels. Most seized merchant cargoes. Captured slaves were taken into small ports along the coast of Hispaniola or Cuba. Since the pirates sold these slaves at a price well below the official tariffs, they found eager buyers on the Spanish islands. The pirates then brought back other booty to their base ports in England and France and sold it for cash. Although less fabulous than the treasure of the Andes, their hauls were impressive. By a conservative estimate, the owner of a privateer ship could expect a 60 percent return on the capital invested, even after deducting the shares of the crew and captain.

Although convinced of the need to fortify the major ports, the Spanish Crown did little until 1585, when Francis Drake attacked and easily captured Santo Domingo and Cartagena. Finally, stung to action, Philip II in 1586 sent out the Italian engineer, Juan Bautista Antoneli, who devoted the next twenty years of his life to the defenses of the Caribbean. At Havana and San Juan, Antoneli sketched the works for the immense forts—both popularly known as El Moro— that ultimately came to dominate the entrance to the two harbors. Fortifications also were designed for San Juan de Ulúa, Portobelo, and Cartagena.

Many years and large sums of money were needed to complete these defenses. The great forts at San Juan and Havana, as we see them today, were not completed until the 18th century. Moreover, the Crown sought primarily to protect the ports essential to the defense of the silver fleets. Two galleys unsuccessfully were stationed for a time at Santo Domingo, Cartagena, and

El Moro Fortress, San Juan, Puerto Rico. To protect its treasure fleets from pirate attacks, Spain built large fortresses guarding the ports of Havana, San Juan, Portobello, Cartagena, and Vera Cruz. Begun in the 1580s, this massive fort was completed nearly two centuries later.

Havana. Otherwise, the smaller cities and rural areas in the Caribbean effectively were left to their own, totally inadequate, devices. Constant pirate attacks on shipping and coastal cities increased the poverty of the islands, as the insecurity of life along the coasts forced their inhabitants to move inland to isolated farms.

## THE FIRST DUTCH ATTACK, 1599–1609

The Dutch were remarkably slow to enter the Caribbean. From 1568 to 1609, the seven northern provinces forming the United Netherlands fought a long and often savage war against the king of Spain, their hereditary overlord. During these years, Dutch corsairs attacked enemy (and neutral) shipping in European waters. But only rarely did a Dutch ship venture to the Spanish Main. The majority of marauders during these years were British and French, and regular Dutch traffic began only in the years 1593–1594.

Dutch attacks on the islands suddenly and dramatically increased when the Spanish government in August 1598 imposed a general embargo on Dutch traders in the Iberian Peninsula. Two products in particular drew them to the Caribbean. The first of these was high-grade salt, previously taken from the east coast of Portugal and absolutely necessary to their enormous trade in herring. The second was tobacco, which was beginning to become popular throughout western Europe. A substitute for Portuguese salt was found near the tip of the Araya Peninsula on the coast of Venezuela. About one-third of a mile inland from Araya Bay lies an inexhaustible natural salt pan, 4 to 5 miles long and 1 to 2 miles wide. From March 1599 to December 1605, a minimum of 768 Dutch vessels sailed to Araya to load up with salt.

While the large salt hulks lay at anchor in Araya Bay, some of their crews ranged throughout the Caribbean in armed pinnaces and sloops brought over on the mother ships. Together with other Dutch pirates and smugglers, they robbed and sank Spanish coastal shipping, literally sweeping it from the seas by 1606. They also traded widely with the Spanish colonies throughout the area for hides, ginger, tobacco, and sugar. To a lesser extent, French smugglers also used the protection provided by the Dutch salt hulks, and British merchants reentered the West Indian trade in 1602 for the first time in more than 30 years.

In response to this invasion, the Spanish government, which literally was bankrupt, decided it could not afford to send ships to police the Caribbean. Instead it took the drastic measure of destroying the crops the aliens wanted or even depopulating the regions most likely to trade with the enemy. At the end of 1605, a Spanish fleet from Lisbon swept through the region, seizing the salt ships at Araya and other smugglers and killing their crews. Steps were taken to stop the inhabitants of Cuba from trading with the enemy. In Venezuela tobacco growing was prohibited for ten years. Most drastically, armed force was used to depopulate northwestern Hispaniola. These measures forced the tobacco trade to shift eastward to Trinidad and the Orinoco River, until this trade also was suppressed in 1612.

## THE GUYANA CONNECTION

The years from 1606 to about 1620 saw a brief lull in foreign incursions into the Spanish Caribbean. British privateering became illegal piracy when the Peace of London with Spain was signed in December 1604. Whatever his other faults, King James I was the first British king totally to shun privateering, issuing no commissions of his own and outlawing British captains who took commissions from other princes. Dutch efforts in the region also fell off after a twelve-year truce was concluded in 1609, reopening access to Portuguese salt.

A few Dutch smugglers continued to visit the Greater Antilles, as did a small number of British and French pirates. In 1598, the Treaty of Vervins ended seventy years of almost continuous war between France and Spain. However, by a secret restrictive article added to the treaty, the two governments agreed that the peace applied only in Europe and did not extend south of the Tropic of Cancer and west of the meridian of the Azores. "Beyond the lines," French and Spanish ships might attack each other and take fair prize as in open war. Despite this clause, French piracy probably did decline after 1605. Most of the cities in Cuba and Santo Domingo or along the Spanish Main had been raided so frequently that they now offered pirates little to plunder.

The Spanish respite in the Caribbean was brief. During the first two decades of the 17th century, several British and Dutch treasure-hunting and tobacco-planting expeditions headed for the Wild Coast, the region stretching south from Trinidad and the Orinoco delta to the Amazon. Spanish colonists believed that a rich Incan kingdom existed inland from the Wild Coast. Its fabled capital was ruled by El Dorado, called the "gilded one" because he covered his body with gold dust before bathing. Several major expeditions attempted to discover this city of gold. Antonio de Berrio established the first Spanish colony in Trinidad in 1592 as a base for his explorations on the mainland. Similarly, Sir Walter Raleigh (1554?–1618), the English statesman and adventurer, led expeditions up the Orinoco in 1602 and again in 1616.

Particularly after 1612, when the Spanish banned the Trinidad tobacco trade, other Dutch and British adventurers tried to establish tobacco plantations along the Wild Coast. Because of the harsh environment, most failed within two or three years or were destroyed by Spanish and Portuguese forces. But tobacco prices remained high, and the failure of the Guyana expeditions indirectly contributed to the settlement of the Lesser Antilles by the British, French, and Dutch.

# SPAIN'S CARIBBEAN COLONIES

■

The kings of Spain claimed absolute authority in their American dominions. Here they considered themselves free of any constitutional constraints limiting their power in Europe. Obviously the kings could not rule the Americas in person. (Indeed, they never went there.) Over the years, they thus delegated various of their powers to different officials and administrative bodies. Despite the absolutist claims of the Crown, the great distance between Seville and the Americas ensured that these officials enjoyed a great deal of latitude or even autonomy in interpreting royal laws.

Spain's laws closing its empire to foreign trade hindered economic growth. As Table 2 indicates, the population of the islands stagnated. The Crown virtually abandoned the Antilles, and most Spaniards coming to the Americas preferred the mainland. Havana became a major port for the Spanish fleet. Otherwise the few isolated settlers remaining on the islands had to become self-sufficient cattle ranchers and smugglers.

## FORMS OF GOVERNMENT IN THE SPANISH EMPIRE

During the first 25 years of settlement, significant steps were taken to enforce royal powers. The Crown established the Casa de Contratación to supervise and control all movement of men and goods. It sent out royal governors and treasurers to each of the territories as they were conquered. In 1511, it established in Santo Domingo an appellate court—the *audiencia*—to resolve conflicts between local officials. Between 1520 and about 1560, these institutions were modified to handle the vast new territories conquered in Mexico and Peru. The laws and institutions thus established remained in effect for more than two centuries, until reforms were introduced by the Bourbon kings in the 1760s. Under the protection of these laws, a system of society and ways of life developed in Spanish America which differed significantly from those of the British or French colonies.

The Spanish concept of governance was juridical rather than political. Spanish officials primarily thought of government as a system of laws. In this view, the king's duty was to embody in regulations appropriate to a specific province the ideal and universal laws of God and of nature. For this reason, the

| TABLE 2. POPULATION ESTIMATES FOR THE SPANISH ISLANDS, 1570–1673 | | | | |
|---|---|---|---|---|
| | TOTAL | WHITES | SLAVES | FREE NON-WHITES |
| **Cuba** | | | | |
| 1570* | 17,550 | 1,200 | 15,000 | |
| 1610 | 20,000 | — | — | — |
| 1662* | 30,000 | — | — | — |
| **Hispaniola** | | | | |
| 1570* | 35,500 | 5,000 | 30,000 | — |
| **Puerto Rico** | | | | |
| 1530* | 3,039 | 368 | 1,523 | — |
| 1570* | 11,300 | 1,000 | 10,000 | |
| 1673 | 1,523 | 820 | 667 | 304 |
| **Jamaica** | | | | |
| 1570* | 1,300 | 300 | 1,000 | — |

* The estimated "Total" includes Native Americans for the years indicated: Cuba—1570 (1,350) and 1662 (3,500); Hispaniola—1570 (500); Puerto Rico—1530 (1,148) and 1570 (300). (In 1570, Spanish sources mention a small but unspecified population of Native Americans on Jamaica.) For 1673, the data for Puerto Rico include the township of San Juan only.

SOURCES: Salvador Brau, *Historia de Puerto Rico* (San Juan: Editorial Coqui, 1966), 70–71 (1530); Lyle McAlister, *Spain & Portugal in the New World*, 131 (1570); Angel Rosenblat, *La población indigena y el mestizaje en América*, 2 volumes (Buenos Aires: Editorial Nova, 1954), I:218–19 (1610, 1662, 1673).

government of the Spanish colonies differed from current practices in major ways. Councils or groups of officials made important decisions, and there was no "separation of powers." These bodies made regulations, administered them, and acted as a court to consider disputes about their application. Every colonial council had a delegated rather than an independent authority. Thus it always was possible to appeal from its decisions to the Crown. Moreover, there was no real distinction between local and central government. Every town council—like every governor—acted under powers delegated by the king.

## THE COUNCIL OF THE INDIES AND THE CASA DE CONTRATACIÓN

Under the Crown, the chief body for ruling the colonies was the Royal and Supreme Council of the Indies, set aside as a permanent committee of the Council of Castile in 1511 and transformed into a sovereign court in 1524. Until it was abolished in 1834, the council theoretically enjoyed absolute authority, and every aspect of colonial life fell within its jurisdiction. It appointed the highest judicial, military, and administrative officials (including bishops), prepared most of the laws governing the Americas, saw to it that officials enforced these laws, and sat as a supreme court to judge appeals from the highest courts in the colonies.

Although the Casa de Contratación, created in 1502, legally was subordinate to the Council of the Indies, it was largely autonomous in economic matters. For more than two centuries, the Casa controlled all trade with Spanish America. This immensely powerful bureaucracy registered, licensed, and supervised all immigration to the Indies as well as all ships and merchandise to and from the New World. It suggested and supervised the laws relative to navigation and commerce, served as a court for all cases involving trade with the Americas, and collected duties on exports and imports. In return for a monopoly granted in 1543, the merchant's guild (*consulado*) of Seville worked closely with the Casa in organizing and unloading the fleets. Henceforth, virtually all trade with the colonies had to be funneled through the congested and inadequate port facilities at Seville. In many matters, a local governor was responsible first to the Casa and then to the Council of the Indies.

## THE AUDIENCIA OF SANTO DOMINGO

In the American colonies, the Casa de Contratación and the Council of the Indies primarily dealt with governors, the highest courts (*audiencias*), and town councils. Colonial government was complicated because the Crown kept adding new levels of officials. Originally each island or region was ruled by a royal governor, with the first governor being the leader (*adelantado*) of the expedition that conquered the territory. Over the centuries, the Crown tended to limit the autonomy of local governors. In 1511, the king thus created the *audiencia* of Santo Domingo (which became permanent in 1524).

An *audiencia* was a kind of permanent committee. The governor—in Santo Domingo given the title and powers of a military captain-general—presided over its meetings. He was joined by a varying number of judges (*oidores*), three in the case of Santo Domingo. Under the Council of the Indies, an *audiencia* exercised judicial, administrative, and legislative powers. As the highest provincial court, it handled civil and criminal cases for the town in which it was located, and it also heard cases on appeal from lower courts. As the regional council, it prepared laws on local matters and helped supervise subordinate officials. In the interim between two governorships, it wielded all royal authority in the colony. From 1535, the captain-general and *audiencia* of Santo Domingo nominally were subordinate to the viceroy of New Spain in matters of defense. Because Mexico City was so far away, however, they generally communicated directly with the Council of the Indies.

At first the *audiencia* of Santo Domingo governed all of the Americas. After the appointment of a second *audiencia* for Mexico City in 1528, Santo Domingo retained jurisdiction over the Caribbean islands, Florida, and the settlements on the northern coast of Venezuela. Its *audiencia* thus had jurisdiction over Puerto Rico, Cuba, Jamaica, and (until 1662) Trinidad. In theory, the *audiencia* was both the supreme court of appeal and the regional council responsible for supervising government throughout the islands. As such, it always had the right to send out special judges who could overrule the decisions of local authorities. Over time, however, the *audiencia* increasingly found it difficult to exercise these powers. Under the onslaught of French and British corsairs, the governors of Cuba and Puerto Rico also began to deal directly with the Council of the Indies. Symbolizing this change, the Council granted both governors the military powers of a captain-general.

## TOWN GOVERNMENT

For most people in Spain's American colonies, the most important instrument of royal power was always the town council or *cabildo*. In medieval and early modern Spain, men and women participated in politics not as individuals but as members of corporations. In Spanish America, the most important of these corporations was the municipality or town.[1] Neither the Spanish Crown nor the settlers could conceive of any other way of organizing society. Unlike those living on the British and French islands, most Spanish colonists lived in towns from the very beginning.

A town included more than just the urban center. The area under its authority included all of the surrounding countryside up to the boundaries of the next town. In Puerto Rico, for example, the entire island was legally divided into the two townships of San Juan and San Germán until 1752, when Ponce was founded. Even though some colonists might spend most of the year on a farm or ranch, the population of each town included registered male citizens (*vecinos*) who owned a certain amount of property, as well as their families, black slaves, and Indian dependents.

Under the supervision of the royal governor and *audiencia*, each town was administered by a city council (*cabildo*) made up of four to twelve councillors (*regidores*) and two municipal magistrates (*alcaldes ordinarios*) appointed by the *regidores*. The founder of the city named the first councillors, and these usually appointed their successors. In a few cases during the first years of settlement, some town councils were democratically elected by all *vecinos*. By the 1600s, however, the position of town councillor had become—as was also the case in Europe—a lifetime and hereditary position. In most cases, the council effectively was controlled by a few of the wealthiest creole families. However, the office of councillor was usually not sold by the king, as sometimes happened in the wealthier mainland colonies.

## THE ISLANDS SUFFER FROM THE CONVOY SYSTEM

While it protected the American silver fleets, the Spanish system of annual convoys created powerful monopolies that prevented economic growth on the islands. The system gave great powers to the merchant guilds (*consulados*) in Seville, Mexico City, and Lima. Their representatives controlled the annual fairs in Portobelo and Vera Cruz, where prices were set for European goods and arrangements were made for their distribution throughout the Americas. As the years passed, these merchants found less and less room for cargoes to or from the Antilles.

The annual fleets provided only a precarious life-line between the Caribbean islands and Europe. Even when they brought goods to the Antilles, the system tremendously increased prices of imported goods. Taxes were only a small part of the problem. More fundamental was the series of high markups inherent in the entire monopoly system. Moreover, the system began to falter altogether after 1623, and both the number and tonnage of ships fell at least 50 percent by 1650. The fleet system continued for the rest of the century, though not on an annual basis. But tonnage remained at a fraction of former levels, and legal trade virtually ceased during the War of the Spanish Succession (1701–1714). Although Spain's new Bourbon dynasty permitted a somewhat looser system of licensed ships, it did not decree free trade until 1765. From that year, with only slight restrictions, any Spanish captain of a Spanish ship might trade at any time between numerous ports in Spain and the Antilles.

The economic situation in the islands was bleak. Years might pass between the arrival of a ship from Spain, and trade between the islands almost ceased during the second half of the 17th century. After about 1620, the inhabitants of each of the islands had to become self-sufficient. Urban life declined, and most of the population, living on isolated cattle ranches, governed themselves with little interference from representatives of the Crown. Although conditions may have improved somewhat earlier in Cuba, the economy and the pulse of civilized life did not really revive until the 1760s.

## THE NATURAL RESOURCES OF THE ISLANDS

To purchase manufactured goods and foods not grown on the islands, their inhabitants had to produce products they could export profitably. In the days of sail, the Caribbean was very far away from Europe in time as well as in distance. On average, the passage from Seville to Havana or Panama lasted 75 days or a little more. The return voyage to Spain took 65 days from Havana—the closest port to Europe—and as long as three months from Trinidad. To this direct distance must be added the months that ships might spend in Havana, while they waited for the yearly fleet to assemble. Thus, to be profitable, any product for export had to be something that grew easily in the Caribbean, that Europeans wanted but could not produce as cheaply themselves, and that was neither perishable nor so heavy or bulky that the long trip back to Seville ate up all the profits.

Since it is rare, imperishable, and highly valuable for its weight, Mexican and Peruvian silver clearly met all of these tests. Unfortunately for the islanders, their mines were played out by the 1530s. In choosing among possible export crops, the inhabitants of the Caribbean have found that while the tropical environment is kind to some plants and animals, it is also deadly for others.

## CATTLE RANCHES FLOURISH IN THE CARIBBEAN

Spanish colonists at first tried to introduce into the islands the plants and especially the animals with which they were familiar at home. Certain European animals immediately took to the region, which lacks any natural predators. The tough Spanish pig multiplied at an incredible rate. Cats, chickens, goats, and Spanish cattle also took readily to life in the Indies. Horses were more fragile and slower to multiply, but they also were widespread by the 1530s. Only sheep did not find the heat and humidity of the Antilles congenial.

For almost three centuries, until the end of the 18th century, most of the inhabitants of the Spanish Caribbean—both black and white—earned their living through subsistence farming and as open-range cattle ranchers. Cattle and hogs provided meat for the towns. Further, their hides and fat (tallow) found a ready market in Europe both through legal exports (when these were possible) and through sales to foreign smugglers.

Throughout the Greater Antilles, the land was divided up into great cattle estates—although local laws also provided for smaller land grants (called *estancias*), which could be located next to or even within cattle ranches. In the absence of royal laws, rights to land generally were distributed by the *cabildos* or town councils, usually for a small charge. Most of these grants were not approved by the king until much later (as late as 1778 in Puerto Rico). However, they were given de facto legal approval in 1574 by a magistrate of the Santo Domingo *audiencia*, who was reviewing the administration of an outgoing Cuban governor.

## SUGAR IS INTRODUCED TO THE ISLANDS

The conquest of the Antilles and South America brought about a transfer of plants and animals as well as of peoples. The Spanish and Portuguese sent samples of native plants back to Europe. Some now are widely grown in Europe, Asia, and Africa—including tobacco, corn (maize), potatoes, tomatoes, red peppers, and even cassava. Tobacco at first provided a valuable export, but the Americas soon lost their monopoly over its production. By the 1650s, tobacco had been carried from the Americas to Europe, Asia, and Africa. Henceforth, it was grown everywhere from Sweden and Siberia in the north to the Cape of Good Hope in the south. But due to Spanish regulations, tobacco provided a commercial crop only in Cuba prior to the 19th century.

Although they ultimately came to enjoy corn, yams, and even manioc (cassava), Spanish colonists tried out many types of European plants in their efforts to find a valuable export crop. Most did not flourish. Seed crops, such as wheat and barley, are not successful in the tropics, where they tend to mildew and run to stalk instead of head. Grapes and olive trees later were carried to parts of South America and Mexico, but they can not be grown successfully in the Caribbean. Other crops did adapt well on the islands as well as on the mainland. These included bananas and all forms of citrus trees (oranges, lemons, and limes) as well as various garden vegetables from cabbages to garlic.

Ultimately, the most successful European import was sugarcane, which found ideal environmental conditions in the Antilles. On some of the islands taken from the Spanish by the British and the French, sugar became virtually as good as gold during the late 1600s. However, sugar plantations largely disappeared from the Spanish Caribbean (except for Cuba) in the 1570s. They were destroyed by the trade monopoly enforced through the convoy system, and sugar did not again become an important crop until trade policies were changed at the end of the 18th century.

If the Spanish government had not subordinated the immediate interests of the Antilles to the trade regulations of a large empire, sugar certainly would have flourished there. The Greater Antilles and Trinidad provide an ideal environment for sugar and became major producers in later centuries. It is true that a sugar plantation requires considerable technical skills, substantial capital to build mills, and large amounts of labor. But European demand was growing during the 17th century, and capital was available. Sufficient labor could have been acquired by opening up the African slave trade. Moreover, Spanish planters long had grown sugar successfully in the Canary Islands, using techniques similar to those that later succeeded in Jamaica and Saint-Domingue.

Sugar was brought from Europe to the Caribbean with the very first Spanish expeditions. Columbus carried cane from the Canaries to Hispaniola in 1493, and sugar again was planted in 1503 under Governor Ovando. Although these initial attempts failed, a wealthy surgeon had built a mill using the best available technology by 1517, and Santo Domingo exported sugar to Europe in 1522. Progress was rapid at first, and King Charles V encouraged the industry with loans, tax exemptions, and experts from the Canaries. By the late 1530s, 34 mills already were in operation, most located along the coast just west of Santo Domingo. And efforts were made—again with royal loans—to expand the industry to Puerto Rico and Jamaica.

The sudden collapse of the Caribbean sugar industry in the mid-1570s almost certainly is tied to the development of the annual convoy system. Most of the newer and larger ships were now carrying silver bullion from Mexico and Peru, and only a diminishing number of the smaller (and thus more expensive) freighters continued to call on Santo Domingo. Moreover, sugar now could be produced more cheaply on the mainland, especially in Brazil, which was ruled by the Spanish Habsburgs from 1580 to 1640. Brazilian sugar production boomed after 1570, flooding the Iberian market.

## THE SLAVE TRADE BEGINS

Until the 19th century, sugar and black slavery were linked together. Almost all sugar plantations were worked by slaves, and the brief sugar boom from 1530 to 1570 thus saw the origins of the slave trade. Spain's Mediterranean cities and the Canary Islands imported African slaves, and blacks—both slave and free—took part in the first Spanish expeditions. In 1513, the government began to grant licenses to bring slaves directly from Africa. It legalized the trade partly to forestall Portuguese smuggling and partly because of requests by Dominican friars on Hispaniola, including Bartholomé de Las Casas. The Dominicans suggested that white and black slaves be imported to prevent the extermination of the Arawak.

Until the 1590s, the slave trade was carried out through individual licenses, although sometimes a monopoly was granted for a number of years. The Casa de Contratación granted or sold licenses to import a specific number of sales at a set fee per slave. From 1595 to 1640 (with brief interruptions), a series of Portuguese merchants purchased a monopoly over the slave trade, known as the *asiento*. In return for annual payments, the king granted these merchants the exclusive right to bring slaves into the Americas, and the latter in turn sold licenses to shippers. Until the 1560s, Santo Domingo was the main slave market for the islands. Under the *asiento*, all slaves first had to be taken to Cartagena.

Under the license system, the Crown collected a large fee for each slave, and it also limited the total number of slaves brought over each year. As a result, slaves became very expensive, and planters on the islands could not compete for legal imports with richer buyers on the mainland. We cannot measure the precise number of slaves imported under the *asiento* system, parcticularly since many other slaves were smuggled into the islands by foreign merchants and pirates. But it is known that slaves never outnumbered owners as dramatically as later became the case in the British and French colonies. As the economy stagnated during the 17th century, slavery also declined in importance. From the 1570s, free blacks and coloreds outnumbered whites on all the Spanish islands.

Given the sparsity of evidence, it is difficult to judge how well slaves were treated. However, slave revolts began early. Black slaves aided an Arawak revolt on Hispaniola in 1519. Three years later, some forty slaves owned by Diego Colón held out for some months before being caught and executed, and in 1527 another revolt occurred in Puerto Rico. In later years, when large parts of the islands were only sparsely settled, flight into the deserted countryside apparently became more common than revolt. Judging by the enactment of harsh local laws, substantial numbers of runaway slaves existed in Hispaniola, Cuba, and Jamaica. These runaways were called *cimarrones*—a word which was later corrupted to *Maroons* on the British islands.

## THE EMERGENCE OF HAVANA, CUBA

Santo Domingo remained the administrative capital of the Spanish Antilles. From the 1560s, however, Havana became the most important settlement in the Caribbean because of its vital importance in protecting the treasure fleets carrying American silver to Spain. In July 1519, Cortés, who was quarreling with the governor of Cuba, ordered a subordinate to reach Spain by sailing directly north from Vera Cruz through the Bahama Channel; in this way he avoided any contact with officials in Santiago or Santo Domingo. This route soon replaced the Windward Passage as the ordinary route for ships sailing from Mexico and Panama to Seville.

Havana effectively became the capital of Cuba under Hernando de Soto (*c.* 1500–1542), who used the island as a base to support his invasion of Florida in

1538. The permanent residence of the governors from 1550, Havana soon became the only major city on the island. For more than two centuries, Havana owed its importance to its domination of the Old Bahama or Florida Channel, through which passed all legal shipping from the New World to Spain. The Gulf Stream, the strongest ocean current in the world, carries ships through the Bahama Channel at up to 10 kilometers per hour. Thus only a little over two months was needed to complete the entire passage from Mexico to Seville. Moreover, the harbor at Havana is one of the finest in the world. Its spacious anchorage is deep enough for the largest vessels, and a promontory along the western shore of the harbor mouth provided an excellent location for defensive fortifications.

Since Vera Cruz does not have a natural harbor, ships left Mexico for Havana as soon as possible. There they refitted for the ocean voyage, and waited—often for months—for other vessels to join the one annual convoy or *flota* to Seville. From the 1560s, the Crown also designated Havana as the assembly point for all ships from Terre Firme (Central America). The fleets now totally bypassed Santo Domingo and Santiago de Cuba, and these lost their commercial importance.

Because the law made Havana the main port for convoys to Seville, Cuba was somewhat more prosperous than the other islands. The fortunes of Havana itself rose and fell with the annual convoys. Moreover, the city's role as an international port also opened the island to trade both with Europe and with other islands. Because land communications were very difficult, most industry was confined to regions near Havana or on the coasts. From the 1550s, immigrants from the Canary Islands established tobacco farms, which produced a very high quality tobacco much esteemed by the state monopoly in Seville. Cuban tobacco was a relatively sensitive plant, and the need to ensure a high-quality product gave the industry a relatively democratic nature. Most farmers worked the fields besides their families, although the more prosperous might own a slave or two.

As early as the 1590s, some holders of *estancias* (small farms) received state loans to build sugar mills near Havana. But only small amounts of sugar were produced for more than a century. Cargo space was limited, freight charges were very high, and tobacco received preference as cargo on the annual trade convoy to Spain. Moreover, because of the inefficient *asiento* system, slaves were expensive and in short supply. Sugar harvests increased after 1700, but they did not really take off until the British conquered the island in 1762.

## HISPANIOLA, PUERTO RICO, AND JAMAICA

For two centuries, Hispaniola suffered from many buccaneer attacks. As on other Spanish islands, economic life reached its lowest ebb during the second half of the 17th century, when inter-island trade almost disappeared. An energetic governor, Alonso de Feunmayor, completed the building of the cathedral and erected walls and forts around Santo Domingo between 1533 and 1556. Hunkered down behind its walls, the capital survived as a "city of lawyers" dealing with the legal work of its *audiencia*.

Almost all of the other fifteen cities established under Governor Ovando were totally forgotten by 1605. That year, to curb smuggling by Dutch ships, the captain-general was ordered to burn the remaining towns in the western part of the island. The inhabitants were removed by military force to the Santo Domingo region, and their cattle ran wild. The deserted region was left wide open to invasion first by buccaneers and then by the French, who in 1697 gained formal control of the western third of the island, henceforth called Saint-Domingue.

With the extinction of the sugar industry after 1600, plantations and slaves also disappeared from Puerto Rico. Through intermarriage and more casual contacts, the population became predominantly colored. Away from the fortress at San Juan, Puerto Rico's few thousand inhabitants raised cattle on open-range ranches and grew crops for their own subsistence. From 1651 to 1662, not a single ship arrived at the island.

Jamaica largely escaped royal control because of the special position of the Columbus family. In 1536, the family gave up its rights under the 1492 contract granted by Queen Isabella. In return, the Crown gave Christopher Columbus's grandson the titles of duke of Veragua and marquis de la Vega and possession of Jamaica. According to the royal grant, the Columbus family received all royal revenues and powers, "supreme jurisdiction [only] remaining to us and nothing else."[2] Until 1640, the family continued to collect taxes, but it otherwise took no interest in the island, which fell under the corrupt misrule of a series of petty local tyrants.

Under the absentee rule of the Columbus family, Jamaica was isolated from the rest of the Spanish America, and all contact between the island and Spain ended in 1634. When the pirate William Jackson plundered Spanish Town (the only urban settlement) in 1642, he found four or five hundred houses, five or six churches, and one Franciscan monastery. His description of the island's fertility indirectly encouraged the British invasion and conquest in 1655.

## TRINIDAD GOES ITS SOLITARY WAY

During the 16th century, Trinidad served the Spanish as a source of Arawak slaves. The Carib had begun to raid the island even before the Spanish conquest and had established camps on the northern coast. In response to Spanish and Carib slaving attacks, the Arawak moved their villages inland, where fishing was difficult and the soil was less fertile. Overall, as in the Greater Antilles, the Spanish invasion led to a severe drop in the Arawak population.

The Arawak and the Carib now began to resist further Spanish encroachment, and their attacks probably contributed to the failure of Spanish attempts at colonization in 1532–1534 and in 1569. It was not until 1592 that a permanent settlement was established at San José de Oruña (Saint Joseph). The city's founder, Antonio de Berrio, planned to use it as a forward base for expeditions searching the neighboring mainland for El Dorado, the mythical city of gold. Since it had not authorized De Berrio's act of possession, the Spanish Crown ordered him to leave the island. He refused, and the government was powerless to evict his followers. This initial act of rebellion symbolizes Trinidad's isolation from the main centers of Spanish settlement during the next two centuries.

A second town soon was established near the present capital of Port of Spain (Puerto de España). But the Governor continued to reside in Saint Joseph until 1754 and shared his powers with the town's council (*cabildo*). Both supposedly were answerable to higher authorities at Santo Domingo or (after 1662) on the mainland, but they had virtually no contacts with these distant courts.

Since Trinidad was not situated on a shipping route useful to the empire, there was no Spanish market for its products. No Spanish ship arrived in Trinidad for twenty years after its settlement in 1592. In 1613, because of the growing presence of foreign ships in the area, the Crown ordered that one ship a year should go to the island with the convoy for New Spain (Mexico). However, trading contacts continued to be rare and intermittent, especially after the entire convoy system began to break down in the late 1600s. Spanish ships again failed to visit Trinidad from 1702 to 1716.

Few Spaniards lived on Trinidad until reform governments in Spain began to encourage settlement in the 1770s. During the 17th century, the number of male householders (vecinos) rarely exceeded 100, largely consisting of free blacks and coloreds. These normally lived on their farms, and Saint Joseph consisted of a few mud huts roofed with thatch. At the beginning of the century, the settlers were able to sell small amounts of tobacco to Dutch, British, and French merchants. But this industry could not compete with the British colonies in North America, and it also was harmed by Spanish efforts to end the contraband trade.

Throughout the colonial period, the settlers at Saint Joseph relied on food produced by the Indian villages. Four *encomienda* villages existed during the 17th century. But most Indians continued to live in independent communities outside direct Spanish control. In 1687, the Spanish government introduced Capuchin missionaries, who gathered several thousand Indians into a number of settlements. Complaints by landowners, who wanted labor for their cocoa plantations, led the Crown to abolish both the missions in 1713 and the *encomienda* in 1716. Henceforth, *corregidors*, responsible to the governor, acted as magistrates in the native villages and organized the distribution of Indian workers to Spanish landowners.

For three centuries, Spain treated the Caribbean islands as mere way-stations along the route of their treasure fleets. The Spanish government did not develop the economies of the islands, and it repressed all attempts by their minuscule creole populations to trade with foreign nations. These Spanish policies were intended to keep other nations out of the Caribbean, but they actually facilitated French, British, and Dutch settlement. During the 17th century, Spain permanently lost the Lesser Antilles, Jamaica, and the western third of Hispaniola (which became the French colony of Saint-Domingue). A British fleet easily took Trinidad in 1799, and Santo Domingo fell in 1802. Spain retained Cuba and Puerto Rico. But these islands could not prosper until after the 1760s, when Spanish reformers finally abolished the restrictive "Laws of the Indies" imposed under Queen Isabella almost three centuries earlier.

# PART TWO:

## NORTHERN EUROPEANS COME TO STAY

■

# CHAPTER FIVE:

# THE DUTCH EMPIRE

■

After pillaging Spain's empire for 150 years, northern Europeans finally planted permanent colonies in the 1620s. They concentrated first on the smaller, still unoccupied islands of the eastern Caribbean. After 1650, they moved west into the Greater Antilles. The success of these expeditions often depended on events in Europe. In particular, islands often changed hands during wars in Europe, as local forces or naval expeditions seized control. Until the 1700s, European events directly affected the islands, but the latter did not in themselves cause wars between European states. The Caribbean was only one of many areas in which Europeans were interested, and some Dutch merchants initially considered them valuable mainly as the gateway to Spanish America.

Since wars between European rulers decided who controlled the islands, historians often treat each nation's expeditions separately. But the settlement of the islands was an international movement.[1] During the first half of the 17th century, all of the new colonies depended on Dutch traders, and the merchants that funded the settlements had interests in many regions. Men from all the northern European states (who usually were Protestant) worked together against the Catholic Spanish until at least the 1650s. Pirate ships sailing from any of the Atlantic ports were manned by crews of mixed nationality—Norman French, British, Dutch, and even Scandinavian. In the same way, the first settlers cooperated in order to survive, and sometimes divided up small islands amicably.

Governments played only a limited role in the initial settlement and economic development of the islands. The first colonies were established by individual adventurers, often acting for groups of merchants. Governments were not directly involved in settling the islands for two important reasons. Their rulers were more interested in European adventures, and they literally had no money to spend on foreign colonies. European rulers during the 17th and 18th centuries were chronically short of the revenues needed to obtain their goals, and were content to leave exploration and settlement to private enterprise.

Just as Queen Isabella drew up a contract with Columbus, so did other European governments give adventurers exclusive licenses to exploit specific parts of the world in return for a share of their profits. In France and the Netherlands, the state usually granted a monopoly to a joint-stock company, such as the Dutch West India Company. In England, the Crown often granted monopoly rights to looser merchant groups or to noblemen acting as agents for individual merchants. But in no country did the Crown put up its own cash or (usually) provide ships and settlers for expeditions.

## NORTHERN EUROPEANS CREATE SEVERAL TYPES OF COLONIES

During the first half of the 17th century, merchant groups in France, Britain, and Holland continued to sponsor pirate attacks on Spanish shipping. But they also began to plant their own colonies, which were intended to accomplish a variety of goals. Some expeditions had as their aim the creation of trading posts where goods could be stored for sale or for later transport to Europe. Their owners did not make any attempt to bring over European settlers to these colonies—the major examples being the Dutch colonies of Curaçao and Sint Eustatius. Other colonies were established as plantations where precious metals might be mined or tropical products grown for sale in Europe. Only a few colonies deliberately were founded as settlements for European immigrants. Often these were planted by dissident groups, such as the Pilgrims and Puritans of New England, who wanted to create alternative societies.

In the Caribbean, most of the British and French colonies—Saint Christopher, Barbados, Martinique, and Guadeloupe—were settled as tobacco plantations. Jamaica and the Dutch islands initially were meant to be trading posts, bases from which to carry on privateering and to trade with Spanish America. Some of the trading posts later developed into plantations; the Dutch islands provided salt while Jamaica produced sugar. But none of the islands taken over by northern Europeans became a place of settlement that attracted thousands or even millions of European immigrants—as did the British North American colonies.

## THE DUTCH OPEN UP THE CARIBBEAN TO NORTHERN EUROPEANS

The Dutch entered the Caribbean in force in the 1620s, and British and French colonists depended on their help in the settlement of the Lesser Antilles. A massive influx of Dutch raiders swept Spanish shipping from the seas in 1618, and Dutch attempts to conquer Brazil in the 1620s and 1630s tied down Portuguese and Spanish resources. This Dutch invasion thus provided a shield behind which the French and the British were able to plant settlements in the region.

The Dutch also helped the British and French to create the plantation society based on sugarcane that dominated the islands during the following centuries. The Dutch remained the main carriers of products in the Caribbean until the end of the century. During the first years of the new settlements, when their inhabitants often came close to starvation, Dutch traders took their crops in return for food and tools. Finally, Dutch merchants transformed the entire society of the British islands by helping to introduce the cultivation of sugar, by providing the African slaves needed to produce it, and by marketing and popularizing the crop in Europe.

Viewed from Amsterdam, however, the islands were only one area in which Dutch commerce was expanding. During the 17th century, the Netherlands led all other European nations combined in manufacturing, commerce, and finance capitalism. Citizens of this tiny state owned at least half of the world's total stock of shipping, and Amsterdam was the world center of international trade through which passed goods and products from every part of the globe. Building on their domination of European commerce, the Dutch now sought to expand into the "rich trades" in luxury goods. During the first decades of the 17th century, they entered and soon dominated trade with the Far East, Africa, and the Caribbean as well as (during some periods) the Mediterranean and the Levant.

In all these regions, Dutch merchants came both to trade and raid. Their efforts succeeded in part because of the close collaboration between the Dutch government and the nation's merchant elite. The Dutch state set up, promoted, and protected—through war if necessary—a variety of cartels, organizations, and joint-stock companies, including the powerful Dutch East India and West India Companies. Backed by the power of their government, Dutch traders followed two contradictory policies, in neither case allowing conventional morality to interfere with business. When a variety of competitors existed, they called for "freedom of the seas" and opposed any restrictions other governments might place on trade. Carefully avoiding political entanglements, they succeeded by undercutting competitors. By contrast, in areas far from Europe or major European colonies—most successfully in Ceylon and Indonesia—they sought a total monopoly over luxury goods such as spices, tobacco, or sugar. In these areas, they set up forts from which they controlled the native populations and ruthlessly drove off or sank ships from other nations.

In the Caribbean, Dutch traders initially followed both of these policies. As the Spanish were their enemies in Europe, they sank Spanish ships without mercy and pursued illegal or contraband trade with the Spanish colonies. Yet they took a more friendly attitude toward the fledgling (and much weaker) French and British colonies, providing them with essential supplies and at times financing their industries. At first the Dutch were often the only available carriers. After 1650, despite the complaints of their home governments, many French and British planters continued to prefer Dutch traders simply because these gave them better terms.

The relative sophistication of Dutch finance and insurance meant that they could offer planters loans with lower interest charges and for longer terms. Because Dutch ships were smaller and better designed, their freight rates were cheaper, and they could sell European goods at lower prices. Since tariffs and freight charges were lower, French and British planters often made a larger profit on sales to Holland. Some also believed that Dutch captains took better care of their cargoes. In the 1650s, however, England and France turned on the Dutch and drove them from the region during several wars. The Dutch were allowed to retain only six small conquests—three tiny Leeward Islands (Sint Maarten, Sint Eustatius, and Saba), and a larger but semi-desert group (Aruba, Bonaire, and Curaçao) off the coast of Venezuela.

## THE DUTCH WEST INDIA COMPANY

In the 1620s and 1630s, large fleets employed by the Dutch West India Company (WIC) dominated the Caribbean. During these decades, the company was an instrument of war, although one that also sought to conduct war profitably. With the ending of the twelve-year truce in 1621, Spain and Portugal (united under the Habsburg Crown between 1580 and 1640) again were at war with the Republic of the Netherlands. Until 1648, while the armies of the two states fought in Europe, their navies battled throughout the world. The Republic set up the West India Company in 1621 primarily to carry this war into the Caribbean through piracy and conquest. Although permitted to engage in trade and to set up colonies, the company at first subordinated these activities to its naval and military ambitions.

As chartered in 1621, the WIC largely resembled the East India Company (founded in 1602), although its management was less centralized. The state assigned the WIC a twenty-five year monopoly in every territory not already given to its older sister—the Atlantic, the west coast of Africa, and the Americas. In its structure, the company combined public and private powers. Like a private corporation, it sold stock listed on the Amsterdam exchange. At the same time, it was set up, supervised, and guaranteed by the States-General, which provided continuing subsidies. In cooperation with the state, overall management was administered by five chambers representing different regions, and these in turn elected the Heren XIX—a central governing board with nineteen members.

Until 1624 the company left the Caribbean to the small-scale raiding of independent corsairs, who often were allied with British and French captains. In that year, it launched large-scale attacks with three ambitious goals: to occupy the Portuguese sugar plantations in Brazil, to conquer the Portuguese slave stations in West Africa, and to seize the treasure fleets that carried Peruvian and Mexican gold from Havana to Seville. In all these efforts, the company ultimately failed after enjoying astounding initial victories.

In 1624 the company captured Bahia, the chief town in northeast Brazil, but lost it again the following year to a joint Spanish-Portuguese armada. In 1630 it took Pernambuco (Recife) and Olinda, and its forces controlled a large area of sugar plantations by 1637. To supply Brazil with West African slaves, an expedition from Pernambuco in 1637 captured the Portuguese fortress at Elmina. Other company forces further overran Angola, Axim, and the island of São Tomé. The Dutch now controlled both the international sugar trade and the Atlantic slave trade. However, in 1645, the Portuguese Catholics rose up in a devastating revolt. They soon swept the Dutch out of most of their Brazilian territories, although the company retained the fortress of Recife until 1654.

Brazil represented the company's most important adventure. But its fleets also scoured the Caribbean, both plundering merchant shipping and seeking to capture the Spanish treasure fleets. Small Dutch fleets returning from Brazil were present throughout the 1620s and 1630s, and the company sent major expeditions to the region in 1625 and again between 1628 and 1635. On land, the great Spanish fortresses built since Drake's invasion in the 1580s held, and the company's forces failed to take El Moro in San Juan during a five-week siege in 1625. Although they devastated Spanish shipping, the company's fleets took too little plunder to pay for their enormous cost.

The company's greatest victory in the Caribbean came in 1628 and was never repeated. In September of that year, ships captained by Piet Heyn (1578–1629) managed to trap the entire Mexican treasure fleet in Matanzas Bay off Cuba. Heyn's men took an enormous treasure in gold, silver, and goods estimated at 11 million guilders—enough to pay the cost of the entire Dutch army for eight months. Because of this one haul, the company in 1629 paid its shareholders a cash dividend of 70 percent.

Until 1635, the company continued to mount large and costly expeditions to pillage Spanish settlements and shipping in the West Indies. Overall (and including its Brazilian campaigns), the company by 1637 had sent out over 800 ships manned by some 67,000 sailors. From its point of view, their take was meager, and its shares sank to record lows on the Amsterdam exchange. However, the company's attacks—together with those of smaller fleets of Dutch, British, and French pirates—did succeed in destroying Spanish commerce and communications. Between 1625 and 1635, Dutch maritime forces changed the balance of power in the Caribbean, making it possible for Dutch traders to control most of the region's commerce for decades.

## SINT MAARTEN, SINT EUSTATIUS, SABA

While it engaged in the struggle to control Brazil and the West African slave trade, the West India Company also continued to look for a secure source of salt, of particular interest to its Zeeland branch. During the 1630s, their need for salt led Dutch traders to occupy three tiny islands, closely grouped together at the northern tip of the Leeward chain.[2] All three are very small and relatively infertile. Saba and Sint Eustatius form part of the inner or volcanic arc of the Lesser Antilles. Indeed, Saba is simply the rocky remains of an extinct volcano rising abruptly from the sea to a peak almost 3,000 feet high. On Sint Eustatius, a large plain extends between volcanic hills to the northwest and Quill, another but more attractive extinct volcano, 1,800 feet high. Sint Maarten, part of the outer or limestone arc of islands, is comparatively flat. However, it also is arid and lacks an adequate water supply.

The desire to exploit the salt pans on the Araya Peninsula of Venezuela had led the Dutch to invade the region in 1599. After the renewal of war in 1621, construction of a new Spanish fort effectively closed off Araya. From the mid-1620s, the Dutch found alternative sources on Sint Maarten and on Tortuga Island, near Venezuela.[3] Spanish countermeasures made it difficult to keep Tortuga open. Thus the company in 1631 sent a fleet to occupy Sint Maarten, possibly unaware that some 14 French families already lived on the other side of the island. The salt flats on Sint Maarten proved to be of extremely high quality, and the island soon attracted hundreds of Dutch, French, and British ships. According to one source, Sint Maarten's salt paid most of the cost of the company's 6,000 man garrison in Pernambuco.

The Spanish Council of the Indies took the Dutch occupation of Sint Maarten seriously. In June 1633, the annual Panama fleet stopped at the island, landing 1,300 soldiers who easily overcame the company's 80-man garrison. The Spanish fleet left behind a force of 250 soldiers, who remained in place for the next 15 years. In 1644, this garrison bravely beat off a Dutch attack led by Peter Stuyvesant (c.1610–1672), during which the governor of Curaçao—and later of New Amsterdam—lost a leg.

With peace imminent in 1648, the Spanish withdrew from Sint Maarten. A few Dutch and French civilians stayed on the island, and the governors of Dutch Sint Eustatius and French Saint Kitts sent troops to defend their nation's claims. In March 1648, the leaders of the two groups negotiated a settlement dividing Sint Maarten along customary boundaries, with the Dutch retaining the valuable salt pans.[4] During the 18th century, residents of both parts of the island also developed cattle ranches and sugar plantations.

Unlike the other Dutch colonies, Sint Eustatius was settled as a tobacco plantation. In 1635, a company of merchants sent out two ships to Saint Croix. Finding that the island already was occupied by the British, 50 colonists chose to stay at Sint Eustatius. On the ruins of a former French fort (possibly built in 1627) overlooking the bay, they erected Fort Orange (Oranjestad). During the 18th century, Sint Eustatius flourished as a free port, from which the French and British islands illegally imported goods to avoid their government's tariffs.

In 1640, several Dutch planters from Sint Eustatius built a small fort on the southern coast of Saba. Agriculture never flourished, and Saba's few inhabitants survived by fishing, shipbuilding, and making shoes. Since its people owned few slaves, Saba remained, until the Second World War, one of the rare Caribbean islands with a predominantly white population.

## CURAÇAO

Aruba, Bonaire, and Curaçao form the southern end of the Lesser Antilles. Because of their location, they are all extremely arid. Although Curaçao produced some sugar during the 18th century, the island owes its importance to its site just off the coast of Venezuela and its excellent harbor (present-day Willemstad). The Spanish reconquest of Sint Maarten in 1633 left the West India Company without a secure source of salt. Since the late 1620s, Dutch ships returning from Brazil had stopped at Bonaire and Curaçao to take on salt, and the Heren XIX apparently were misled about the value of the pans on these islands. They also hoped that Curaçao would serve as a military base from which to monitor and plunder the Spanish treasure fleets.

With the help of a state subsidy, the West India Company sent six ships to seize and hold Curaçao—which it considered "a suitable place where we can procure salt, hard-wood and other items, and from where we can infest the

Mounds of salt sparkle in the sun, Bonaire. The Dutch initially settled Sint Maarten (1631), Curaçao (1634), and Bonaire (1636) to secure a safe supply of salt. Sea water was pumped into a series of ponds. The water evaporated, leaving rough salt crystals like those shown.

enemy in the West Indies." The Dutch forces easily overran Curaçao in July 1634 and occupied Bonaire and Aruba in 1636. The conquerors transferred the few Spanish colonists and their Indians to the mainland; and Spain, occupied during these years with the war in Brazil, could not launch an effective counterattack.

During the next twenty years, the island proved to be an expensive liability for the company, which seriously considered abandoning it. As long as the war lasted, trade with the Spanish mainland colonies was practically nonexistent. During the 1640s, Curaçao served as a base for company forces raiding coastal settlements in Puerto Rico, Cuba, and the mainland. Peter Stuyvesant, the island's only famous governor, similarly led an abortive attack against Sint Maarten in 1644. After the loss of Brazil, the Heren XIX made Stuyvesant governor of New Amsterdam in 1645, and he ruled both colonies from North America until New Amsterdam became British New York in 1664.

## THE DUTCH COLONIES AFTER 1648

As the West India Company's fortunes waned, it gradually gave up its commercial monopoly, at first for a fee. It allowed individual traders—Dutch, Jewish, and later Portuguese—to carry salt (1633) and to trade with Brazil (1638), Curaçao (in the 1640s), and later West Africa (1734). In 1646, the directors accepted the failure of the company's grandiose schemes. They reorganized it as a commercial organization that would supply slaves and goods to the colonies of other powers, relying for protection on the Dutch state. With these more modest goals, the company was rechartered in 1647. When it became bankrupt in 1674 during the Third Dutch War, the state reorganized it under the same name, and it survived until 1799 as the administrator of the Dutch colonies and as a slaving company of some importance. The Republic now focused its main efforts on the East India Company, which continued to provide a profitable outlet for Dutchmen with an ambitious and aggressive spirit.

Curaçao, created as a war base, began to make a profit for the company only after the conclusion of peace with Spain in 1648. The Treaty of Muenster recognized the Dutch colonies in the Americas but expressly prohibited trade with the Spanish islands or mainland. However, the Dutch were now the principal carriers in the Caribbean, and trade with the British and French colonies in the Lesser Antilles flourished from the 1640s. Some merchants operated directly from Amsterdam, bypassing Curaçao. But the company largely controlled the supply of West African slaves, and Curaçao now became an enormous slave depot.

From 1662, Spain allowed Dutch merchants to ship slaves through Curaçao into its American colonies, and they enjoyed a virtual monopoly until 1689. Although it remained illegal, the Spanish government also tolerated commerce in other goods from 1654. Dutch ships called on Cuba and Hispaniola, and Curaçao became the main depot for an extensive trade with Venezuela and Peru until 1713. Contacts with the mainland again declined during the 18th Century, but Curaçao (and Sint Eustatius) remained prosperous ports for trade with the islands. Dutch ships carried goods and slaves legally to the Danish Virgin Islands, and they also illegally smuggled them into the British and French colonies. Throughout these years, Aruba and Bonaire—where the salt pans proved unprofitable—served mainly to support commerce through Curaçao. The company maintained Aruba as a vast cattle ranch, and it grew corn on Bonaire to feed the slaves passing through its depots on Curaçao.

# CHAPTER SIX:

## SETTLEMENT OF THE LESSER ANTILLES

■

With the outbreak of the Thirty Years War (1618–1648), a brief truce in Europe's dynastic wars ended. Spain's enemies were glad to see their subjects menace the source of Spain's wealth, and new waves of Dutch, British and French marauders descended on the Caribbean. This time, they intended to stay.

Many influences came together during the 1620s to help the northern European settlements survive and succeed. In Britain and France, the first expeditions directly grew out of the privateering voyages of the preceding fifty years. Ships were available with crews that knew the islands well, and the profits from pirate voyages also provided merchants with the capital to fund settlements. Pirate raids had impoverished the Greater Antilles, and Spanish efforts to end smuggling had only made things worse. The way was open, and tropical products, such as tobacco and sugar, fetched high prices. Few investments at home were as profitable, and young men could be induced to leave Europe to find work.

The pursuit of economic gain was the paramount reason for the settlement of the Caribbean, which was facilitated by the naval weakness of Spain. As always, individual colonists had variable, complex, and obscure motives. A desire for fame and honor clearly drove many leaders, and economic and religious nationalism also were a significant influence with some. Old habits die hard, and the decline of the Spanish empire probably is more obvious now than it was at the time. All of the northern European colonists thus tended to join together in their hatred of Spain.

From the 1650s and 1660s, the French and British governments imposed greater controls on the various trading posts and plantations under their flag. Both governments needed to supply their colonies with men and money. They wanted their colonies to repay these expenses by producing products for sale in Europe. Both wanted to keep control over their colonies and ensure that they traded only with the homeland. Until the late 1800s, they enforced a system of economic regulations—sometimes called mercantilism—that kept out foreign imports through high tariffs. However, neither could totally enforce these rules.

Both British and French colonists happily smuggled in foreign goods through Dutch Sint Eustatius or Danish Saint Thomas.

## TOBACCO AND SUGAR

The first French and British settlements were established in the early 1620s to grow tobacco. During the 1590s, most of the tobacco entering England had been taken by pirates from captured Spanish merchant ships. Since quantities were small, prices rose dramatically, reaching 90 shillings a pound in 1598 and averaging 40 to 60 shillings from 1600 to 1613. Its high price made tobacco one of the most lucrative commodities, and many merchants wanted to secure their own exclusive source of supply. Thus the cultivation of tobacco provided the main incentive for the settlement of the Lesser Antilles. In fact, British merchants sponsored the settlement of Saint Kitts and Barbados for tobacco farming. And tobacco also encouraged the creation of French colonies on Saint Kitts, Martinique, and Guadeloupe.

Unfortunately, tobacco is a weed that will grow anywhere, and the tobacco boom in the Caribbean was short-lived. By 1629 exports from Virginia (founded in 1607) reached 1.5 million pounds, and the high prices even encouraged production in England itself. Supply quickly outstripped demand from the late 1620s. Prices fell drastically to a few pennies a pound, and they remained depressed until the end of the century. All the colonies suffered a severe setback, until tobacco was replaced by sugar as their main crop. Barbados became the richest colony in the 1640s because its planters were the first to introduce sugarcane.

## BRITISH COLONIES IN THE
## LESSER ANTILLES

By 1623, the Dutch West India Company had driven Spanish ships from the seas. As usual, the islands bore the full force of these attacks, to the extent that towns along the southern coast of Cuba could not deliver their products to Havana. The absence of Spanish forces removed the fear that they would slaughter the colonists during their first months on an island.

Many British captains already were familiar with the Caribbean islands. Since Columbus's second voyage, ships from Europe usually had followed the trade winds to the outer islands of the Lesser Antilles, halting there to make needed repairs and obtain fresh meat and water. By the 1620s, many captains had established regular bases on some of these islands, where they might stay for several months while they launched raids against the Greater Antilles. The southern or Windward Islands were occupied by hostile Carib, who annihilated at least three British attempts at settlement between 1605 and 1614. But pirates maintained camps throughout the Leewards, where fewer Carib lived—especially on Saint Kitts, Nevis, and on several of the Virgin Islands, including Virgin Gorda and Saint Croix.

## SAINT KITTS

On January 38, 1624, Thomas Warner (1575–1649), accompanied by fewer than 20 "gentlemen adventurers," landed on the small island of Saint Kitts and founded the first permanent British settlement in the Caribbean. A Suffolk gentleman of limited means and large ambitions, Warner in 1620 joined an ill-fated expedition to the Amazon. Leaving in 1622, before the colony failed, he sailed through the Lesser Antilles until he came to Saint Kitts, which he judged to be "a very convenient place for the planting of tobaccoes which ever was a rich commodetie." Back in England in 1623, Warner gained the financial support of a syndicate of British merchants led by Ralph Merrifield and Maurice Thomson, launching his adventure early in 1624.

Under Warner's control, the adventurers first killed or drove off a small group of Carib and then planted tobacco. A hurricane destroyed their first crop in September 1624, but another crop was ready by the next summer. In the spring of 1625, Warner's party was joined by the crew of a disabled Norman privateer under Urbain du Roissey and Pierre Belain d'Esnambuc (1585–1636). With their help, Warner defeated a force of Carib who sailed to the island to avenge the massacre of the preceding year. From the beginning, the two groups divided the island between them, with the British receiving the center and more mountainous sector, and the French inhabiting the two extremes. In 1625, Warner returned with the first tobacco crop to England, where he obtained a royal commission naming him governor of Saint Kitts, Nevis, Barbados, and Montserrat.

The tomb of Sir Thomas Warner, Saint Kitts. Thomas Warner founded the first permanent British settlement in January 1624 and governed Saint Kitts until his death in 1649. From Saint Kitts, parties of settlers established colonies on Nevis, Montserrat, and Antigua.

## BARBADOS: THE CARLISLE GRANT

Saint Kitts soon was surpassed by Barbados, which was permanently settled in 1627 and grew at a very rapid rate. Barbados is larger and was not occupied by the Carib. Moreover, it lies 100 miles to the east of the other islands so that any hostile force has to approach it by sailing against the strong trade winds. For these reasons, Barbados is the only island in the Lesser Antilles that was never taken by a hostile naval force.

As on Saint Kitts, a syndicate of merchants sponsored the settlement of Barbados. The dominant partner was Sir William Courteen (1572–1636), an Anglo-Dutch trader with many interests in Amsterdam and along the Wild Coast in South America. Between 1627 and 1629, Courteen's group poured money and men into the island—carrying over, according to one estimate, more than 1,500 people at a cost exceeding 10,000 pounds.

Two merchant syndicates now had set up tobacco plantations in the Lesser Antilles, but neither had a clear title. Following Spanish precedent, all lands the French or the British acquired in the West Indies were deemed possessions of the Crown. Both groups thus sought to purchase a member of the court nobility who could secure a proprietary grant from the king. The Merrifield (Saint Kitts) syndicate bought the support of the bankrupt James Hay, earl of Carlisle. The Courteen group (Barbados) purchased that of William Herbert, earl of Pembroke. After a sordid story of intrigue and backroom dealings, Carlisle's grant was upheld in February 1629, and the Merrifield group thus ended up in control of both Saint Kitts and Barbados. The Crown confirmed Sir Thomas Warner as governor of Saint Kitts and the other Leewards, an office he held until his death in 1649.

## BARBADOS: THE FIRST SUGAR BOOM

The royal privilege to Carlisle (as well as the abortive grant to Pembroke) was a revival of a kind of "feudal" grant no longer found in England itself. In return for a small yearly payment, the proprietor received both ownership of all land and all governmental powers. He appointed the governor and judges, and he could make laws with the assent of the freeholders. In 1641, the Civil War in England cut the island off from its proprietor (and his merchant backers). Until then, his governor apparently acted in a harsh and unpopular way, ruling through an appointed council and arbitrarily levying heavy taxes and fees.

Because of the Pembroke-Carlisle dispute, Barbados until 1641 was divided between two groups of settlers, who made the first "starving years" worse by burning each other's crops. As on other islands, many new settlers died in transit or during their first year. An unspecified "plague" also killed off perhaps 1,200 whites on Barbados between 1647 and 1650.

Despite these political and economic difficulties, the first colonies of Saint Kitts and Barbados initially attracted a rush of settlers. Barbados had 10,000 white settlers by 1640, and the governor had distributed virtually all of the island's land. The population doubled again by 1655, leaving Barbados more densely populated than most regions in England or Europe. For the first two decades these settlers experimented with various crops, looking for a product they could export at a profit. Most at first planted tobacco. When the price of that crop fell drastically, some switched to sea-island cotton, and others tried indigo and ginger. During the 1640s, the largest planters finally found in sugar a crop that not only paid their bills but that made them the richest men in British America by the 1680s.

Traditionally, the Dutch receive credit for introducing to the French and British islands both the sugar plant and the technical expertise needed to grow it. From 1630 to 1654, the Dutch West Indies Company occupied the Permanabuco region of Brazil. And Permanabuco planters introduced both the plantation system and the technology—three-roller mill and copper furnace pots—later used on Barbados. However, the Barbados planters were eager students, and several went to Brazil to see for themselves how the system worked. What the Dutch did provide was a ready market for the product and the large loans needed to create and maintain a sugar plantation. The success of the first sugar crops in the early 1640s set off a frenzied boom. By 1647 most of the large planters had switched to the new crop, and production, land prices, and the demand for labor soared. Until about 1710 Barbados was the main sugar producer in the Caribbean, and it soon caught up with and even overtook Brazil in the world market.

Successful sugar planting required large estates. For Barbados the optimum probably was about 200 acres. Although smaller estates continued to exist, many were now combined into large plantations. At first most of the workers on the sugar estates were white indentured servants. Some planters probably preferred African slaves, who were widely used in Brazil, but these were in relatively short supply during the 1640s. The number of both white and black servants probably continued to increase until the 1660s. But black slaves made up the overwhelming majority of the population by the 1680s. (See Table 3.)

As a result of the sugar boom, Barbados was the first Caribbean island to develop the plantation society later found on the smaller Leeward Islands, Jamaica, and Saint-Domingue. A few big planters owned the best sugar acreage, reaped most of the profits, and dominated island politics. Perhaps one-fourth of all white males could vote under a 10-acre property qualification. But the smaller planters deferentially elected their betters to the important offices on the island.

| TABLE 3.  BARBADOS POPULATION ESTIMATES, 1635–1684 | | | |
|---|---|---|---|
| | TOTAL | WHITES | SLAVES |
| 1635* | 1,227 | 1,227 | — |
| 1639* | 8,707 | 8,707 | — |
| 1655 | 43,000 | 23,000 | 20,000 |
| 1684 | 68,743 | 21,941 | 46,802 |

*For 1635 and 1639, figures include only adults age 14 years or older.

SOURCE:  Richard S. Dunn, *Sugar and Slaves* (New York: Norton, 1973), 55, 87.

Drax Hall, Barbados. James Drax, a planter of Anglo-Dutch lineage, helped to build the first sugar mill on Barbados during the 1640s. Constructed before 1700 as a copy of an English manor house, Drax Hall was totally unsuited to the Caribbean climate.

## COLONISTS IN BONDAGE

The colonists who created cane estates on Barbados during the 1640s and 1650s were at least moderately well-off in the home country. Below this élite, most of the settlers came over as indentured servants. The landowner paid for a servant's passage to the island and provided him (for most were very young men) with food, clothing, and shelter. In return he worked, usually in the fields, for three to five years. Only at the end of this term did he receive wages called "freedom dues." Initially in the form of land, later in a set amount of sugar, these provided him with the chance to become an independent farmer or laborer.

Contemporaries often compared indentured servants to slaves, and their status fell somewhere between freeman and slave. During the term of his contract, a servant was the property of his master and could freely be sold or given away. He could not run away, marry without his owner's permission, and was usually not allowed to engage in commerce. At the same time, he could (unlike an African slave) own personal property, sue, and testify in court. He further was protected by the terms of his indenture and the island's apprenticeship laws, and he might apply to a local magistrate if he was grossly mistreated.

While the indentured servant's condition may seem barbarous today, temporary servile status as an apprentice or servant was a normal part of growing up in 16th-century England. Indentures, of course, were not limited to the Caribbean islands. Most of those immigrating to the southern colonies in North America also came as servants.

At first most of the servants in the West Indies came over voluntarily, drawn by the hope of acquiring their own land. During the 1640s and 1650s, some were kidnapped, and "Barbadosed" took on the same meaning that "Shanghaied" has today. After the British Civil War ended, captives from Cromwell's expeditions to Ireland and Scotland were forcibly brought over between 1649 and 1655. But fewer criminals entered the islands as servants than were sent either to British America or later to Australia.

Fewer indentured servants came to Barbados or the Leewards after 1660, although some continued to go to Jamaica throughout the 18th century. On most islands, African slaves now did most of the hard field work and formed the majority of the population. Alarmed by this trend, the island legislatures from the 1670s unsuccessfully tried to encourage white immigration. They required planters to bring in indentured servants and sometimes subsidized their cost. Most also passed laws requiring better treatment of white servants. Masters had to give servants a minimum amount of food and clothing, and they needed a magistrate's permission to flog them.

In the early days, working conditions were brutal, and some owners cruelly punished shirkers. Antagonism was increased by religious differences between Irish Catholic servants and Anglican masters. Discontented servants regularly burned cane fields on Barbados and planned an armed uprising in 1649. In the Leewards, Irish Catholic servants similarly cooperated with invasions by the Spanish and the French, and an outright rebellion took place on Saint Kitts in 1689.

## THE ORIGINS OF AFRICAN SLAVERY

It was the combination of sugar and tropical diseases that made the Caribbean islands into colonies populated almost entirely by African slaves. The introduction of sugar to Barbados between 1640 and 1645 did not in itself make African slavery inevitable. European laborers can grow sugar, and white labor produced much of the sugar grown in Barbados into the 1650s. Indentured servants stopped coming during the 1660s, because the islands became deadly for whites. The African slaves sold by the Dutch in the 1640s introduced several diseases to which whites have no immunity. Whether colonists came from Europe or Africa, they faced a new disease environment in the islands, but blacks fared less badly than whites in adjusting to this new climate. As a general rule, about one out of three slaves died during the first two years in the islands. As many as three out of four white settlers perished soon after arrival.

Indentured servants began to avoid Barbados both because its planters gained a reputation as cruel masters and because emancipated servants often could not find satisfactory work. A servant's meager "freedom dues" were not enough to set up a sugar estate. As planters increasingly trained their slaves in most forms of skilled labor, white wage earners could not compete. During the mid-1600s, moreover, black slaves were becoming cheaper than white servants, since the price of Africans fell while British wages were rising. But the main obstacle to European immigration—now and for two centuries to come—was the Caribbean's reputation as a white graveyard. Why go to Jamaica or Marti-nique, where an indentured servant faced a high risk of a horrible death? By opting for North America instead, British laborers chose a region with a better disease environment than Europe.[1] Unlike those going to Jamaica or Barbados, they could at least expect to survive their years of voluntary slavery and become independent workers or farmers.

## BARBADOS GOES IT ALONE

The British Civil War that began in 1642 freed the Barbados planters from their proprietor and temporarily made them independent of the home government. Governor Philip Bell (1641–1649) consolidated and expanded the island's independent executive and judicial system. The legislative assembly (first called together in 1639) gained the power to make new laws, abolishing those of England. Under Governor Bell, it sought to remain neutral in the Civil War afflicting the home country. Above all, whatever their private beliefs, the planters wanted to maintain free trade with Amsterdam. They argued that the Dutch offered better prices, brought in superior goods, and offered longer credit.

The death of the king and the establishment of the Commonwealth govern-ment (1649–1660) of Oliver Cromwell (1599–1658) ended this truce between Barbados' Cavaliers and Roundheads—the names given to the Royalist and Parliamentary factions. With the fighting over in England, members of both factions came to the islands, some with money to purchase estates. A long series of plots and counterplots ended with the victory of the Cavaliers. In May 1650, the assembly declared its loyalty to the late king's exiled son and adopted a program of free trade with Holland and Hamburg.

## THE NAVIGATION ACTS

Barbados' free-trade policy ran head-long into the mercantilist goals of the Commonwealth government, which sought to destroy the Dutch commercial monopoly. Cromwell's government responded in October 1650 by prohibiting trade with four colonies—including Barbados and Antigua—that had recog-nized the exiled Charles Stuart as king. In October 1651, the Council of State extended these rules by the Navigation Act. This established the mercantilist and exclusionary policies that regulated trade with the North American and Caribbean colonies until after 1776. Primarily directed at the Dutch, the act proclaimed that all imports into England or its colonies must be brought in on ships that were built, owned, and captained by British subjects. European products could be imported into the colonies only on ships sailing from England, its colonies, or the country where the goods were produced.[2]

To enforce its rule over Barbados, the Commonwealth government sent a fleet under Sir George Ayscue (d. 1671). Led by Lord Francis Willougby (d. 1666)—who had leased Carlisle's rights and also acted as governor—the plant-ers reinforced the island defenses. By the time Ayscue arrived in October 1651, his fleet could blockade but not take the island. After three months, this stalemate was broken in January 1652 when both sides accepted articles of surrender generally favorable to the islanders. The Barbadians accepted a new governor appointed by the Commonwealth. In return, they gained liberty of conscience, local control of taxation and justice, and restoration of free trade with the Dutch. The home government latter reneged and tried to exclude Dutch traders, but Barbados retained political autonomy.

The restored monarchy was as determined as the Commonwealth to control colonial trade, and it passed additional and even stricter Navigation Acts in 1660 and 1663. These laws effectively required the islands to deal only with England. They provided that the trade of British colonies, both import and export, must be carried in British ships. The most important products (including sugar and tobacco) could be sent only to England or to other British colonies. Goods not of British origin first had to be brought into England and then reshipped to the colonies. Another law, enforced until 1678, required the planters to buy their slaves from the monopolistic Royal Africa Company.

Passage of these acts ended one era of British colonialism in the islands and, indeed, throughout British America. In economic matters, successive British governments now sought to bring the colonies under centralized control. By the outbreak of the Second Dutch war in 1665, the government had excluded most Dutch ships from the British islands. The resulting increase in transportation costs helped to bring an end to the first golden age for sugar planters. In September 1663, moreover, the government forced Barbados to accept a 4.5 percent tax on all goods exported from the island. In return, the Crown permitted the planters to retain significant control over local finance.

The economic effect of the Navigation Acts has been debated. Caribbean planters lost access to foreign buyers operating through Amsterdam. At the same time, they gained a protected market in England, with prohibitive tariffs set against foreign sugars. However, most historians agree that the islands were harmed by the 4.5 percent export tax, which in practice was paid by the individual planter. The island legislatures sought to end this hated tax until it was repealed in 1798.

## SAINT KITTS, NEVIS, ANTIGUA, AND MONTSERRAT

The first settlers on the other Leewards came from Saint Kitts. Thomas Warner, governor until 1649, successfully promoted immigration to Saint Kitts, and the best land soon was taken. Servants who had completed their term of indenture readily moved to neighboring islands and even to British America. In 1628, Anthony Hilton, a relatively wealthy planter, led a group of 150 settlers to Nevis, first obtaining the title of governor from the earl of Carlisle. According to tradition, the first immigrants from Saint Kitts arrived on Montserrat and Antigua in 1632.

All of the British Leewards legally were under the authority of the earl of Carlisle's lieutenant governor at Barbados. But the great distance separating them from the larger island made them virtually independent colonies. Each island had its own deputy governor and assembly, who were jealous of any outside authority. As on Barbados, conflicts during the British Civil War led to greater local control.

After the monarchy was restored in 1660, the British government tried but failed to impose a federated system of government. In 1664, the assemblies of the four islands made the same bargain with Charles II that the Barbadians earlier had agreed to. In return for self-government and confirmation of their land titles, they granted the Crown a 4.5 percent tax on all exports. To their disappointment, however, the king placed them under the governor of Barbados.

The Leeward colonists resisted their subordination to Barbados, their main economic rival. Moreover, federation soon proved ineffective during the Second Dutch War, when French naval forces seized and plundered Saint Kitts, Antigua, and Montserrat. These defeats convinced the London government that it needed to separate the northern islands from Barbados. In 1671, Charles II tried to create one unified government, with one governor-general and one General Assembly for the four Leeward islands. Despite the continuing French menace, however, the planters on each island remained intensely jealous of their own independence. Since they refused to grant revenues, the General Assembly seldom met, although it survived on paper until 1798.

While each of the four northern Leeward Islands has a distinctive personality, they are all much smaller than Barbados. Each also presented problems to settlers. Like Barbados, Antigua is generally flat with higher volcanic hills along the Leeward and southern coasts. The island is quite dry, but it possesses exceptionally fine harbors. English Harbor, now restored and renamed Nelson's Dockyard, became the British fleet's home port during the 18th century. Saint Kitts, Nevis, and Montserrat represent the upper slopes and cones of volcanoes. The hillside fields are difficult to clear and erode easily, and Nevis is generally arid. None of these three has a natural harbor.

Settlers on these four islands repeated the history of Barbados fifty to sixty years later. Throughout the 17th century, most settlers were small tobacco and cotton farmers, and society had a rough-hewn frontier quality. Except on Saint Kitts, larger sugar plantations were developed toward the end of the 17th century. But the industry really began to expand only with the end of the War of the Spanish Succession in 1713, when the French part of Saint Kitts passed to England.

War and a lack of money held back the introduction of sugar on the Leewards. Until the 1660s, most colonists were former servants who lacked the capital to purchase milling equipment or slaves. British investors tended to focus on wealthier Barbados. After the Restoration in 1660, efforts to create plantations were thwarted by the destructive wars with the French, Carib attacks, and the general slump in the sugar industry. Except for Saint Kitts, all were thinly settled for several decades, and planters tended to rely on white servants rather than black slaves. (See Table 4.) Many of the settlers were Irish—with Irish settlers forming 70 percent of the white population on Montserrat in 1678.

| TABLE 4.  BRITISH LEEWARD ISLANDS POPULATION ESTIMATES, 1678 | | |
|---|---|---|
| | TOTAL | WHITES | SLAVES |
| Antigua | 4,480 | 2,308 | 2,172 |
| Saint Kitts | 3,333 | 1,897 | 1,436 |
| Montserrat | 3,674 | 2,682 | 992 |
| Nevis | 7,370 | 3,521 | 3,849 |
| SOURCE:  Dunn, *Sugar and Slaves*, 127. | | | |

## THE BRITISH VIRGIN ISLANDS AND ANGUILLA

Under the law of 1671 separating the Leewards from Barbados, the British government gave the governor of the Leewards authority over Anguilla and the Virgin Islands. The small populations of these islands could not support a representative assembly, and a deputy or lieutenant-governor and six-man advisory council represented the Crown. Although their arid climates discouraged planters, the British government kept them for military reasons. An enemy with a base on these islands would have easy access to Barbados and the British Leewards.

British forces took the Dutch colony on Tortola—the most important of the Virgins—in 1665 and 1672. The governor of the Leewards again occupied it during the Nine Years War (1688–1697) and forcibly resisted Danish efforts to expand from Saint Thomas. Into the 18th century, Tortola and the other British Virgins mainly served as bases for pirates and smugglers, and visitors described their people as lawless, immoral, and riotous. Although planters grew some cotton for export, the government in 1710 and 1735 rejected requests for a separate government. With the sugar boom of the 1750s, the white and slave population grew as cane plantations were introduced on Tortola. In 1773, the Crown finally conceded a representative assembly to the freeholders of Tortola, Spanish Town (Virgin Gorda), and Josh Vandyke. In return, the islanders granted the 4.5 percent export tax levied in the other Leeward Islands.

Anguilla, north of Saint Martin (Sint Maarten), is flat and built of limestone. Like the Virgins, it receives little rainfall and is covered by spare dry woodlands. Because it is too arid for sugarcane, Anguilla's population lived from fishing and salt making. Already investigated by the Dutch in 1631, the salt ponds attracted British settlers after 1650. A few planters also grew tobacco and tried to make rum. As late as 1774, however, fewer than 400 planters with some 2,000 slaves inhabited the island.

## THE FRENCH IN THE LESSER ANTILLES

French pirates, who had long attacked Spanish shipping and cities, founded permanent camps from the early 1600s on Tortuga, Hispaniola, and several of the Lesser Antilles. In 1625, more peaceful colonists settled Saint Kitts, which until 1669 remained the political capital of the French Antilles. In 1635, colonists from Saint Kitts landed on Martinique, while another group from France settled Guadeloupe. From these first colonies, French settlers slowly spread south into the Windwards, and they also moved west to Hispaniola. Although both islands remained independent pirate kingdoms for a long period, French governors planted the flag on Tortuga in 1628 and on Hispaniola in the 1660s.

French and British colonization began at the same time, and both nations claimed many of the same islands. But the French colonies grew more slowly than the British. Until after 1713, the sugar industry on the French islands lagged behind that of the British partially because it lacked workers. As Table 5 indicates, the French simply did not move to the islands in large numbers. Fewer indentured servants (known in French as *engagés*) went to Martinique or Guadeloupe than to Barbados, and the French also imported fewer slaves. In 1665, when the French and the Dutch went to war against the British, the latter outnumbered them by more than three to one.[3]

Like the British, the French colonies developed out of the piracy of the preceding century, and they similarly sought to profit from high tobacco prices. However, the first French colonies were not settled by individual merchant groups. They were created under state guidance by two powerful prime ministers, Richelieu in the 1620s and 1630s and Colbert in the 1660s. Richelieu believed that individual settlements needed protection, and the French government created several companies with monopolies in this region. However, these official companies proved to be economic failures. Since the companies could not provide either needed provisions or slaves, the colonists ignored their representatives. Instead they sold their tobacco and other products to Dutch traders, who dominated Caribbean commerce during these years.

The first years were marked by economic hardship, political conflict, and even civil wars. The governors ruling each island for the company tended to act

## TABLE 5. POPULATION ESTIMATES FOR THE FRENCH ISLANDS, 1664–1699

|  | TOTAL | WHITES | SLAVES | FREE NON-WHITES |
|---|---|---|---|---|
| **Martinique** |  |  |  |  |
| 1664 | 15,401 | 2,681 | 12,704 | 16 |
| 1696 | 20,066 | 6,435 | 13,126 | 505 |
| **Guadeloupe** |  |  |  |  |
| 1670 | 8,696 | 1,227 | 5,267 | 47 |
| 1699 | 10,111 | 3,687 | 6,076 | 349 |
| **Saint-Dominique** |  |  |  |  |
| 1681 | 6,648 | 4,336 | 2,312 | — |

SOURCES: Orlando Patterson, *Slavery and Social Death: A Comparative Study* (Cambridge, Massachusetts: Harvard University Press, 1982), 480–81; Guy Lasserre, *La Guadeloupe: Etude géographique* (Bordeaux: Union Française d'Impression, 1961), 284.

as independent rulers. Often nobles of high rank with strong and dominating personalities, these governors frequently clashed with each other and with the less submissive colonists on their islands. During the 1650s, the French government simply gave up and sold the islands to their governors. In 1664, Colbert again imposed French control, and the islands for the first time became directly subject to the king.

## SAINT-CHRISTOPHE

The small northern island of Saint Christopher/Saint-Christophe was the mother colony for both the French and the British. When the British captain Thomas Warner arrived on Saint Kitts in January 1624, he may have found a small French party already there. Early in 1625, these pioneers were joined by a pirate crew led by two Norman nobles, Urbain du Roissey and Pierre Belain, sieur de Esnambuc. Finding that Saint-Christophe produced excellent tobacco, Esnambuc decided to settle down and proved to be an energetic and popular leader. He returned to France with a valuable cargo and approached (through Roissy's relatives) the powerful Cardinal de Richelieu. Impressed by Esnambuc, Richelieu created the Compagnie de Saint-Christophe, granting it a monopoly for 20 years over Saint Kitts, Barbados, and the neighboring islands.

Four ships carrying 500 passengers left Normandy in February 1627. On their arrival in May, Esnambuc and Thomas Warner—acting as representatives of their governments—divided Saint Kitts among the two parties. The first years proved difficult, and the Compagnie de Saint-Christophe soon ran out of funds. Most of the first colonists died, the French and British quarreled, and a Spanish fleet forced both groups to flee the island in October 1629.

This dismal beginning did not discourage Cardinal Richelieu, who decided to expand the French colony to other islands. In February 1635, the Compagnie de Saint-Christophe was folded into a new and more powerful Compagnie des Isles d'Amerique. The Crown gave the new company both possession and full lordship over virtually all the Lesser Antilles. (Its possessions thus overlapped those granted to the earl of Carlisle in 1627.) In June 1635, some 500 men landed on Guadeloupe under the leadership of Charles Liénard, sieur de l'Olive. Esnambuc believed that l'Olive had stole his plans. When he heard of the Guadeloupe expedition, he angrily led his own small group of 150 settlers to Martinique the following September.

## GUADELOUPE AND MARTINIQUE

French settlers worked for decades to settle Martinique and Guadeloupe. Much larger in size than Saint Kitts, both had significant Carib populations, and both contain difficult terrain. Along the northern coast of Martinique, Mont Pelée rises more than 5,000 feet from steep hills. Still an active volcano, Pelée erupted in 1902, killing the 30,000 inhabitants of Saint-Pierre. Since it lies to the leeward of these high mountains, the plain covering the southern part of the island is arid. Given Martinique's harsh landscape, plantations developed slowly. However, Fort-de-France, built over a large enclosed bay on the leeward side of the island, soon became a major port. The first stop for French ships following the trade winds from Europe, it was from 1669 the seat of the governor-general and the political capital of the French Antilles.

Two separate islands, separated by the narrow Rivière Salée, make up Guadeloupe. The dividing line between the inner volcanic and the outer limestone arcs of the Lesser Antilles runs between these two islands, which thus offer totally different environments. The western island, called Basse-Terre, is mountainous with fertile soil and ample water.[4] Running parallel to the west coast, a mountain ridge rises almost 5,000 feet. It is dominated by Mont Soufrière, a volcano that erupted in 1956 and is still unstable. By contrast, the eastern island, called Grande-Terre is flat and arid with brackish water. The French under l'Olive soon moved to Basse-Terre, and sugarcane was not planted in Grande-Terre until the 18th century.

## INTERNAL CONFLICTS AND CARIB WARS

Civil wars and wars with the Carib devastated Guadeloupe and Martinique until the 1660s. On Guadeloupe, the Carib initially aided the French, providing them with food during their first nine months on the island. However, in January 1636, the governor attacked the Carib in order to steal their provision grounds (*conucos*). The resulting war lasted until June 1640, when a new governor defeated the Carib during a thirty-hour battle. The colonists on Martinique also warred with the Carib, and the latter retired to their strongholds on Dominica and Saint Vincent. Reciprocal massacres continued until the French signed a peace treaty in 1660.

Political turmoil also disturbed the young colonies, with Guadeloupe especially torn by conflict. Under the charter of the Compagnie des Isles, the Crown named a governor-general over the governors of particular islands. A civil war now broke out between the two rivals for this office. In February 1638, the king appointed Philippe, sieur de Lonvilliers de Poincy (1587–1660), a captain in the royal navy and a high officer in the Knights of Malta.[5] During the next twenty-one years, de Poincy proved to be a strong military leader, but he often acted for his own benefit. In 1645, he refused to step down when the Crown sent out a new governor-general. De Poincy won out only after two years of civil war, during which the governors on each island took sides.

## THE FRENCH ATTACK THE CARIB IN THE WINDWARDS

This period of anarchy and Dutch control of shipping contributed to the failure of the Compagnie des Isles d'Amerique during the 1640s. To regain their capital, the directors sold each of the islands to its governor, who became its proprietor and hereditary lord. In September 1649, Charles Houël purchased Guadeloupe and the smaller islands around it. The following September, Esnambuc's nephew, Jacques Dyel Du Parquet (1606–1658), bought Martinique as well as the company's claims over to Saint Lucia, Grenada, and the Grenadines. Acting for the Knights of Malta, de Poincy in May 1651 acquired the French rights on Saint-Christophe and Saint Martin (Sint Maarten) as well as the company's claims over Saint Croix, Saint Barthélemy, and Tortuga.

The new proprietors aggressively extended the territories under the rule. De Poincy pushed north from Saint Kitts. At his direction, an expedition took Saint Barthélemy and another drove a small Spanish force from Saint Croix. Meanwhile, the lords of Martinique and Guadeloupe sought to drive the Carib out of the islands to the south. From Guadeloupe, Houël occupied the Saintes and Marie Galante and in 1653 dispatched an expedition to Grenada. His troops massacred all the Carib on the island, 40 of whom jumped to their deaths from a cliff often called the Morne des Sauteurs (Leapers' Bluff).

In 1654, Du Parquet similarly dispatched a punitive expedition to Saint Vincent. To save this island—one of their last refuges—the entire Carib community counted a concentrated attack. Those on Saint Lucia rose up and massacred the small French settlement, while some 2,000 warriors temporarily overran Martinique. Four years later, a new governor of Martinique organized a general slaughter of the Carib remaining on that island. In 1660, de Poincy and Houël finally signed a treaty—accepted by the British governors of Saint Kitts and Montserrat—reserving Dominica and Saint Vincent to the Carib. The small number of Carib left on these two islands generally remained at peace with the French, who sometimes instigated their raids on the British colonies.

## THE FRENCH ISLANDS COME UNDER ROYAL CONTROL

Independent rule by proprietors ended soon after 1661, when Louis XIV assumed power as king. Needing tax revenues to support his expensive European wars, Louis put the economy under the control of Jean-Baptiste Colbert, his finance minister. Colbert enacted laws—similar to the British Navigation Acts—that excluded foreign imports and encouraged French exports. For Coblert, the immediate threat was Dutch control of world trade, and he sought to increase his control over the French colonies. In his view, the colonies existed for, and were the exclusive property of, the home country. Their interests must be subordinated to those of France.

The situation in the West Indies was totally unsatisfactory to Cobert. Hundreds of Dutch ships visited the main port at Martinique each year, gathering up tobacco and sugar for sale in Amsterdam. Thus the colonies, which had been chartered and subsidized to make a profit for France, actually returned nothing to the home country. Colbert distrusted private enterprise and preferred large monopolistic companies under governmental regulation. In April 1664, the Crown chartered the Compagnie des Indes occidentales (West Indies Company)—based on the Dutch West India Company—and gave it a monopoly over all Atlantic shipping. The king also repurchased the rights of the existing proprietors and replaced them with royal governors.

The new company did succeed in taking over trade with the islands and in removing Dutch merchants through military action. However, it lost large sums of money during the Second Dutch War and through its own financial mismanagement. In 1670 Colbert opened West Indian commerce to all French nationals, while continuing to forbid entry to foreigners. In 1674, the Crown liquidated the over-ambitious company. The islands now became part of the royal domain, legally provinces of France itself.

France governed its colonies directly from Europe. French planters paid lower taxes than British colonists. But they also lacked the representative assemblies that made laws for many British islands. The French Ministry of the Marine appointed the military, administrative, and judicial officials for each colony. A governor supervised military affairs and the many courts, while an *intendant* controlled the civilian administration and finance. *Conseils supérieurs*—appointed by the governor—claimed the right to discuss and register laws. Saint-Domingue had two such *conseils*, reflecting the geographical divisions that effectively made it three colonies rather than one (page 114). Not until 1788 did the French Crown create representative assemblies with limited powers for Martinique and Guadeloupe—but not for Saint-Domingue.

Although the islands were under direct royal rule, the government did not subordinate their interests to those of the homeland. In political and economic matters, the French Crown was less absolute than it liked to claim. In practice, the Crown had to balance the interests of organized groups at home (for example, sugar refiners and shippers) against the competing aims of planters and merchants on the islands. It could not impose its will by force and gave up trying to enforce unpopular laws. Caribbean planters often got their own way in commercial matters, and they largely controlled government on the islands themselves.

## THE VIRGIN ISLANDS

Rising from the sea 40 miles east of Puerto Rico, a group of more than 100 small islands and cays represents the culmination of the mountain chains forming the Greater Antilles. All are relatively mountainous, and only Saint Croix has an extensive plain. Because of their small size, the Virgins are relatively dry or even semiarid, and droughts frequently cause serious water shortages.

In 1493 Columbus called the largest island Santa Cruz and named the northern group after Saint Ursula and the 11,000 virgins martyred at Cologne by the Huns. The Spanish left the Virgins uninhabited, and informal occupation by other Europeans began in about 1600. Pirates, privateers, and smugglers coming from Europe set up camps on several of the islands. Here they could obtain fresh water and food while planning expeditions to the major Spanish colonies in the Greater Antilles. The smaller islands remained pirate bases for a long time. But Saint Croix also attracted planters from the 1620s, and sugar plantations developed there and on Saint John during the 18th century. Saint Thomas is less fertile, but it has an excellent harbor and commands the Anegada Passage, a major channel between the Atlantic and the Caribbean. Thus it mainly served as a depot for Dutch and Danish traders carrying slaves from West Africa.

## SAINT CROIX UNDER THE DUTCH, BRITISH, AND FRENCH

In about 1625, separate parties of British and Dutch planters occupied Saint Croix. The Dutch, governored by the West India Company, occupied the harbor at Christiansted, while the British took the southwestern shore, near Frederiksted. By 1645, the British settlers had driven out the Dutch, who migrated to Sint Maarten and Sint Eustatius. The Spanish authorities did not welcome a large British colony so close to San Juan, Puerto Rico. In August 1650, Spanish troops attacked and expelled the British.

De Poincy, the French governor at Saint Kitts, took advantage of this opportunity to add to his empire. He sent soldiers to expel the Spanish garrison, and he brought Saint Croix (as well as Saint Kitts) for the knights of Malta in 1651. De Poincy spent large sums on the Saint Croix colony. However, the island proved unhealthy, and a drought burned up the cane fields. In 1696, Governor Bertrand d'Ogeron de la Rivière (1615–1676) evacuated the remaining inhabitants and resettled them in his colony at Saint-Domingue. The French abandoned their claim to the island in 1713, and its ownership reverted to the Knights of Malta. In 1733, the latter sold it to the Danish West India Company, which already occupied Saint Thomas.

## THE DANISH WEST INDIA COMPANY

Dutch planters unsuccessfully tried to settle Saint Thomas from the 1640s onward. Permanent occupation began under the Danish West India and Guinea Company, chartered by Christian V of Denmark-Norway in 1671. This venture was modeled after the Dutch West India Company and was given broad powers in Africa and the Americas. Its sponsors believed they could gain substantial profits by carrying slaves to Saint Thomas for resale throughout the West Indies.

Like the Dutch, the Danish company functioned as a commercial venture and attracted few European immigrants. Few Danes ever came to the Americas, and the Danish islands economically formed part of the Dutch empire. From 1685 to 1718, Denmark also allowed an Africa company chartered by the Duke of Brandenburg-Prussia to sell slaves on Saint Thomas.

Like its Dutch and French rivals, the Danish West India Company rarely made a profit, and it went out of business in 1754. Except for the slave trade, the company gave up its monopoly rights at Saint Thomas in 1724, permitting ships of all nations to trade there on payment of small export and import taxes. Since this era, Saint Thomas has been described as a "free port." (Saint Croix received the same privileges in 1831.) Ten years later, the company also opened the slave trade to all Danish subjects in the West Indies. Nevertheless, its losses continued, and the Danish king purchased all of the shares held by private investors in 1754. The three islands became Crown colonies, directly subject to royal governors.

Although the company itself failed, the islands developed as major sugar producers. Cane and cotton plantations developed from the 1680s on Saint Thomas. To encourage their expansion, the company settled Saint John in 1717

| TABLE 6. DANISH VIRGIN ISLANDS POPULATION ESTIMATES, 1686–1835 | | | |
|---|---|---|---|
| | TOTAL | WHITES | SLAVES | FREE NON-WHITES |
| Saint Thomas | | | | |
| 1686 | 633 | 300 | 333 | — |
| 1720 | 4,752 | 565 | 4,187 | — |
| 1775 | — | — | 3,979 | 500 |
| 1803 | — | — | 5,968 | — |
| 1835 | 14,022 | 3,520 | 5,298 | 5,204 |
| Saint Croix | | | | |
| 1742 | 2,080 | 174 | 1,906 | — |
| 1755 | 10,220 | 1,323 | 8,897 | — |
| 1792 | — | — | 22,420 | — |
| 1803 | — | — | 27,161 | — |
| 1835 | 26,681 | 1,892 | 19,876 | 4,913 |
| Saint John | | | | |
| 1728 | 800 | 123 | 677 | — |
| 1739 | 1,622 | 208 | 1,414 | — |
| 1787 | 2,383 | 167 | 2,200 | 16 |
| 1803 | — | — | 2,598 | — |
| 1835 | 2,475 | 344 | 1,929 | 202 |

SOURCES: Paterson, *Slavery and Social Death*, 482; William Boyers, *America's Virgin Islands: A History of Human Rights and Wrongs* (Durham, North Carolina: Carolina Academic Press, 1983), 40, 48, 53 (1835).

and Saint Croix in 1735, offering tax exemptions and subsidies to attract planters. The sugar industry rapidly developed on both islands and prospered throughout the 18th century. By the 1830s, a few hundred planters—most not Danish—controlled several thousand slaves.

From the beginning, merchants at Saint Thomas welcomed ships of all nations. Its excellent harbor soon served as a refuge both for merchant ships chased by pirates and for corsairs selling their loot. Collusion with pirates was most obvious during the 1680s. Buccaneers chased from Jamaica by a reforming governor sought new havens to the north. They received a warm welcome from Adolph Esmit, who seized the governorship from his brother in the autumn of 1682. Esmit's obvious collusion with buccaneers caused an international incident the following year. The governor refused to turn over a pirate ship to a British man-of-war and even fired a canon at the British ship. Subsequent Danish governors were less blatant in their support, but buccaneers continued to call on Saint Thomas for several decades.

## CHAPTER SEVEN:

# THE BUCCANEERS OF JAMAICA, SAINT-DOMINGUE, AND THE BAHAMAS

■

French, British, and Dutch companies planted commercial colonies on several of the Lesser Antilles during the 1620s and 1630s. From 1655, northern Europeans moved west into the Greater Antilles. Here the British conquered Jamaica, while the French occupied the western third of Hispaniola, which they renamed Saint-Domingue. In contrast to Barbados, Hispaniola and Jamaica prospered through piracy rather than by growing sugar. Initially settled by buccaneers, these islands remained pirate havens until almost 1700, attracting thousands of men who chose a life of adventure over drudgery on the sugar plantations of Barbados or Martinique.

Jamaica and Hispaniola were ideally located to be centers of piracy. Port Royal in Jamaica, with its strategic location in the center of the Caribbean Sea, provided a perfect base for strikes against Spanish shipping and raids on ports in Cuba and Central America that guarded the Spanish treasure fleets. The northwestern coast of Hispaniola and the island of Tortuga are situated between two straits—the Windward Passage and the Mona Passage—that carry merchant shipping from Europe or North America into the Caribbean.

Until the 1690s, pirates openly operated out of a series of havens, first out of Tortuga and Hispaniola and then, after 1655, from Port Royal in Jamaica. After they were chased from these bases, many carried on their trade from the Bahamas during the following century. All of these pirates traditionally are known as buccaneers. Strictly speaking this name is not accurate. It initially referred to groups of men who caught the wild cattle and hogs that were abundant on both islands. However, British settlers expanded the meaning of buccaneer during the 1660s, and it is now used to refer to any pirates based in the Caribbean rather than in Europe.[1]

## THE BUCCANEERS ON HISPANIOLA

The natural environment of Hispaniola and Jamaica also made these islands ideal pirate bases—while hampering governmental control and the development of plantations. Rugged mountains and hills cover both islands. These mountain chains run more or less from west to east, hindering transportation and communications across the islands from north to south. Although long stretches of their coasts are hazardous to shipping, landings are possible in many locations. Governments based on the coasts could not control the fertile central valleys, which provided a haven for pirates and for runaway slaves. Because of their mountainous terrain, both islands receive abundant water. Dense forests of tropical hardwood trees initially covered the fertile sections, and it took planters decades to cut down these woodlands and plant cash crops such as sugar.

The climate of the islands provides cattle and pigs with a favorable climate, plenty of food, and no natural predators. As early as the 1530s, escaped or freed animals had multiplied into vast herds covering Cuba, Jamaica, and Hispaniola. Around 1600, many Spanish colonists made their living from these wild cattle and hogs, selling their hides, meat, and fat to French or Dutch smugglers and pirates. To stop this illegal industry, the governor of Santo Domingo burned the homes of the settlers in northwestern Hispaniola and ordered them to move to Santo Domingo (page 42).

This evacuation program of 1605 backfired against the Spanish government. The illegal hide trade continued, and the now empty land soon began to draw outsiders. Presumably some of the Spanish cattle-hunters escaped the 1605 roundup, and they soon were joined by free spirits and beachcombers of many nations and races. Hunting bands and settlements maintained themselves through the hide trade on Hispaniola until well into the 1670s.

Sometime, perhaps long before 1600, the island of Tortuga—far removed from the main Spanish port of Santo Domingo—became a stopover for smugglers and pirates. A multinational settlement developed that was perhaps the earliest independent European community in the new world, owing allegiance to no king and trading with every nation. In the 1630s, it gained strength through a curious alliance with the leaders of the Puritan party opposing the royal government in England.

## PURITAN PIRATES ON PROVIDENCE ISLAND

While the first British colonists struggled to survive on Saint Kitts and Barbados, another and more daring group entered the western Caribbean, the heart of the Spanish empire. Chartered by the Crown in 1630 and sponsored by the principal Puritan politicians of England, the Providence Company planted settlements on three islands. Toward the end of May 1631, its men established bases on Providence (Santa Catalina) and Henrietta (San Andreas), less than 250 miles from the strategic town of Portobelo. In the same year, it extended its claims to include Tortuga Island and sent Anthony Hilton to act as its governor. Hilton, a persuasive rogue who founded the first colony on Nevis in 1628, had been chased away by the Spanish the following year, leaving behind large debts in Saint Kitts.

The company advertised its intention to create a godly commonwealth such as the one in Massachusetts. But both of its colonies—well placed to harass the Spanish but badly located to trade with other British settlements—devoted themselves to piracy. Some settlers on Providence and Tortuga did try farming. Since they sold their hides and tobacco to Dutch traders, the Providence Company did not receive a return on its investment. The company wholeheartedly endorsed piracy after suffering Spanish raids on Providence and Tortuga in 1635. The settlers on Providence drove off a Spanish fleet, and the colony survived for another six years. But Spanish forces quickly overran Tortuga, hanged the male residents, deported the women and children, and razed the settlement. Although the Spanish troops soon departed, the Providence Company abandoned Tortuga. But the pirates, once again without any ties to a European government, soon drifted back to the island.

In reprisal for these Spanish attacks, the king granted the Providence Company the power to commission privateers. Piracy, long secretly practiced from Providence, now became the company's main purpose. Goaded by increasing attacks on Spanish ships and cities, the governor of Cartagena launched a larger and more carefully planned attack that occupied Providence in May 1641 and carried its male residents to captivity in Spain.

The Providence Company went bust and abandoned both Providence and Tortuga, but it continued to issue privateering commissions for some years. In July 1642, Captain William Jackson, armed with letters of reprisal, sailed from England with three ships and recruited four more at Barbados. For the next three years, Jackson's fleet cruised the Caribbean, plundering several cities. In 1643, his forces easily seized Villa de la Vega (presently known as Spanish Town), the principal settlement on Jamaica. Jackson extracted from it a miserable ransom of only 7,000 pieces of eight. But the island was fruitful, and Jackson's men liked it so much that many of them deserted and remained with the Spaniards after the fleet sailed. Moreover, Jackson's account of his raids, which stressed Spanish weakness, helped to persuade Oliver Cromwell to launch the 1655 campaign that added Jamaica to the British empire in the West Indies.

## THE WESTERN DESIGN AND JAMAICA

The British conquest of Jamaica in 1655 was the one result of a failed campaign to capture the entire Caribbean from Spain. England itself was torn by a civil war from 1642 to 1649 between supporters of King Charles I and various factions associated with the Parliament. Ultimately the army seized power under the leadership of Oliver Cromwell, who executed the king in 1649 and ruled supreme until his death in 1658. Cromwell's government sought both to expand abroad and to bring the British dominions under one centralized rule. It conquered Ireland in 1649 and Scotland in 1650, sending captives to the islands as indentured servants. In 1651, it sent a fleet to bring the existing British colonies in Barbados and the Leewards under its control, and it passed the Navigation Act to prevent their trading with the Dutch. Until that time, the planting of colonies had been almost entirely a matter of private initiative. But from then on, trade and national finance became dominant considerations, and settlement concerned the Crown as well as individual merchants.

In 1654, Cromwell's government and his ministers conceived a grandiose scheme called the Western Design. Convinced of Spanish weakness, they sought to take over the entire Caribbean, even though the two nations were then at peace. The government hurriedly assembled a fleet and an army of 2,500 men, placing them under the command of Admiral William Penn (1621–1670)—father of the founder of Pennsylvania—and General Robert Venables (1612?–1687).

Late in January 1655, the expedition arrived in Barbados. There its commanders spent ten weeks recruiting additional soldiers, including perhaps 3,500 men from Barbados and at least 1,200 more from Saint Kitts, Nevis, and Montserrat. Having decided to make Hispaniola their first target, the commanders besieged Santo Domingo. Although the British forces outnumbered the city's defenders at least ten to one, they were hopelessly defeated. In all, the army made two attempts to reach Santo Domingo. But the landings had been made 40 miles from it, and the walls were never reached. The untrained and undisciplined soldiers taking part in this disastrous campaign lacked food, weapons, and medicine. Moreover, Penn and Venables—who were not on good terms—frequently quarreled, and the fleet took little part in the siege.

The British commanders feared Cromwell's wrath if they returned without a prize. They thus decided to turn against Jamaica, which they knew to be thinly populated and weakly garrisoned. On May 10, 1655, 38 vessels with some 6,000 men cast anchor at Passage Fort, at the western end of the present Kingston Harbor. Opposition was useless, and the invaders easily took the small Spanish forts. The British allowed the Spanish colonists to leave the island but confiscated their lands and all of their possessions. General Venables gave the governor a week to consider these terms of surrender. Led by Cristóbal Arnaldo de Ysassi, many Spaniards instead freed their own slaves and fled north to the mountains. There the Spanish colonists held out for five years while they waited for reinforcements from Cuba and Mexico.

In their fierce resistance, the Spanish formed an alliance with escaped slaves, who controlled the region, northeast of Spanish Town, still called Juan de Bolas after one of their chiefs. On June 27, 1658, a new British governor, Edward d'Oyley, finally defeated an invading Spanish army in a pitched battle near Rio Nuevo—east of Saint Ann's Bay on the northern coast. The former Spanish governor held out for two more years in the mountains until Juan de Bolas went over to the British side. In May 1660, the last Spaniards sailed away to Cuba, according to tradition from a pleasant beach at Runaway Bay. However, a small number of slaves (called Maroons) retained their independence, making their new headquarters at Nanny Town on the northern slopes of the Blue Mountains.

## THE BRITISH SETTLEMENT OF JAMAICA

During the 1700s, Jamaica became an immensely wealthy producer of sugar. During its first thirty years under the British flag, however, it was a second Tortuga, offering hospitality to generations of pirates drawn from Europe and throughout the Caribbean. Despite the government's efforts to promote agricultural development, few acres were cleared and put under cultivation during the 17th century. Establishing a sugar plantation required large amounts of capital and labor, and most of the first settlers had little money and few slaves. Thus there really were two Jamaicas from 1655 to 1689—an agricultural colony of small farms and cattle ranches and the wealthy buccaneer capital of Port Royal.

The proprietary system used to plant Barbados and the Leewards now was discredited. Cromwell's government ruled Jamaica under martial law, and Charles II (after the Restoration in 1660) retained the island as a Crown property. Both governments sought to develop the island as a source of tropical products. They encouraged white settlement by guaranteeing settlers British citizenship and by offering generous grants of land. Under Sir Thomas Modyford, governor from 1664–1673, most of the best farmland along the south-central coast was distributed, much of it in large allotments.

Despite the government's offers, the population of Jamaica grew very slowly during the 17th century. (See Table 7.) Due to the introduction of tropical diseases such as malaria, Jamaica was an unhealthy place during these years. In addition to soldiers and settlers from England, many white servants and poor planters from overcrowded Barbados and the Leewards moved to Jamaica, searching for better opportunities on a bigger island. Most died during their first year of residence. The mortality rate among the soldiers was very high, and immigrants from other islands fared little better.[2]

Altogether, perhaps 12,000 white settlers came to British Jamaica during its first six years, but the population in 1661 was only 3,470. It increased more rapidly under the Modyford administration but fell again toward the end of the century. The earthquake of 1692 damaged the entire island and wiped out Port Royal. A severe malaria epidemic took many lives, and a French invasion almost captured the island in 1694.

Jamaican planters had only begun to clear the thick tropical forests by 1713, when a general European peace finally allowed agriculture to take off. The first sixty years proved to be a harsh winnowing process. Only a few of the men arriving during the first decades survived. But those that did endure founded dynasties that became immensely wealthy during the 18th century. As on Barbados, as the number of white settlers shrank, the survivors took over their property and imported African slaves. Few white servants wanted to go to Jamaica, and black slaves outnumbered their masters almost seven to one by 1700. Most of the best land henceforth was held in very large estates. The gulf between large and small planters had grown very large, and the chief sugar planters dominated local offices. Most of their property still lay fallow, and sugar production remained low until the 1720s. However, the stage had been set for the rapid development of a classic plantation society during the 18th century.

| TABLE 7.   JAMAICA POPULATION ESTIMATES, 1661–1673 | | | |
|---|---|---|---|
| | TOTAL | WHITES | SLAVES |
| 1661 | 3,470 | 2,956 | 514 |
| 1673 | 17,272 | 7,768 | 9,504 |
| SOURCE:  Dunn, *Sugar and Slaves*, 155. | | | |

## JAMAICA'S PLANTERS GAIN CONTROL OVER LOCAL GOVERNMENT

During the Restoration period (1661–1689), the Jamaican planters succeeded in gaining control over local taxation as well as the power to initiate laws regulating property and slavery. As in Barbados and the Leewards (and later in British America), the planters took British government as their model. Thus they claimed for their assembly the same powers enjoyed by the British House of Commons. Since the West Indian colonies were regarded as Crown property, they were not immediately subject to the Parliament in England. The Crown delegated administrative and military authority to a royal governor. The king also appointed the judges and the governor's Council, generally on the governor's recommendation.

Planters in all the colonies opposed the Navigation Acts and the Royal Africa Company's monopoly over slave imports. But the major constitutional issues came down to control of taxation for local defense and the general purposes of administration. In Jamaica, several governors gained temporary control by manipulating conflicts between the planters and the buccaneers. Nevertheless, the planters ultimately won on the main point and did not grant a permanent revenue to the king.

The commission issued to the first royal governor in 1661 permitted him to convoke an assembly. The first elections were held two years later, beginning the assembly's often stormy career that lasted until its suppression in 1866. Under the royal instructions, it could initiate laws for the colony, but such laws had to be approved within two years by the Crown as well as by the governor and council. For the next 28 years, a series of governors struggled to control the assembly. The main issue was the grant of a permanent revenue to the Crown similar to the 4.5 percent export duty in Barbados and the Lesser Antilles. A compromise was reached in 1689, when the Glorious Revolution brought William II to the throne of England. The new government, which needed the Jamaica customs revenue, confirmed the constitution as it existed in 1661. For the next two centuries, the large planters controlled local taxation and largely governed the island according to their own views.

## THE BAHAMAS

The Bahamas group was uninhabited after the Arawak died out in the 1520s, victims of Spanish slaving expeditions and disease. Its many islands and cays first were settled by Bermudians, fleeing religious conflicts during the British Civil War. During the 1640s, Bermudians belonging to the Puritan faction planted the first permanent colony in the Bahamas, and the two groups of Atlantic islands remained closely associated until the Bahamas became a pirate haven in the 1680s.

British sailors stranded by a hurricane landed on Bermuda in 1609, and the Crown granted the island to the Somers Islands Company in 1615. The small island enjoyed a short period of prosperity based on tobacco and fishing, and its population grew to more than 2,000 by the 1620s. As in Barbados, conflicts between the proprietors and settlers marked Bermuda's early years. The Somers Company was controlled by the earl of Warwick and other men with Puritan views, who preferred colonists of their own persuasion. But the majority of the islanders, who apparently supported the Royalist and Anglican cause, sought independence from the company's rule. In 1632 the Somers Company appointed Captain Philip Bell, previously governor of Bermuda, as governor of their new colony on Providence Island. Bell led about a hundred Bermudians to the Bahamas. (After the Spanish closed down Providence in 1641, Bell became the governor of Barbados.)

Puritans continued to form a minority in Bermuda after the outbreak of the Civil War in 1642, and members of that sect made several attempts to settle in the Bahamas. In 1647, Captain William Sayle—a moderate Puritan—traveled to London, where he founded the Company of Eleutherian Adventurers. Although it never actually received a charter, the company enjoyed support at high levels and wrote an elaborate constitution. The following year, Sayle led some 80 adventurers from Bermuda and founded a settlement, probably at Spanish Wells.

Plantation crops do not flourish in the arid climate and thin soil of the Bahamas. Sayle's colony was not a success, and only a few settlers remained at Eleuthera, eking out a miserable livelihood from occasional shipwrecks. Tiny communities also may have existed at Exuma, Inagua, and in the Turks and Caicos, part of the Bahamas until 1848. As Bermuda continued to be overcrowded, other expeditions ventured into the Bahamas. About 1666, one of these groups colonized Sayle's Island, renaming it New Providence in memory of the Puritan colony destroyed in 1641. By 1671, New Providence had become home to 900 settlers, who established an assembly and asked Jamaica to confirm their choice as governor.

Agriculture never has prospered in the Bahamas. But the islands are strategically placed next to both the Windward Passage and the Florida Strait leading to the Gulf of Mexico. Thus New Providence soon became a major center for British pirates. In 1670, Charles II, ignoring previous grants, gave the Bahamas to six of his Lords Proprietors of Carolina. If the settlers looked to their new lords for aid, the latter sent them only a succession of incompetent, corrupt, and ineffectual governors. From the 1670s, when the government of Jamaica tried to curb the pirates of Port Royal, the proprietary governors of the Bahamas happily sold the buccaneers commissions as privateers.

In 1684, Spanish forces retaliated by attacking New Providence and sacking the main settlement (called Nassau from 1695). Some of its inhabitants returned in 1686, and the island once again became a pirate haven. Particularly after the outbreak of war with France in 1689, British pirates based at Tortuga reestablished themselves in the Bahamas. Its inhabitants welcomed the buccaneers' trade, and several of the proprietary governors openly helped them. Not until 1718 was a serious effort made to suppress their activities.

## PIRATE SOCIETY IN THE CARIBBEAN

For the next fifty years, hungry, adventurous, or criminal men from the established colonies in the Lesser Antilles constantly replenished the pirate bands. Failed planters, disgruntled former servants, runaway black slaves, petty criminals, and religious and political malcontents all drifted north and west to the thinly populated islands of Puerto Rico, Hispaniola, and Jamaica. A party of men merely had to find a boat and follow the prevailing winds and currents. When they arrived at the larger islands they found these inhabited mainly by enormous herds of wild cattle descended from the flocks abandoned by the Spanish in the 1530s and 1540s. Some joined the cow hunters who made their living by selling smoked meat and hides to passing ships. Others turned to piracy, using small boats against Spanish merchant and treasure ships sailing past their coast.

## THE PIRATE KINGDOM OF TORTUGA

Many hardened pirates gathered on the island of Tortuga, which remained virtually an independent pirate kingdom until the end of the 17th century. After the Spanish destroyed the Providence Company's Tortuga settlement in 1635, British and French buccaneers soon returned to the island, from which they attacked merchant ships of many nations. But the two groups quarreled, and the French on Tortuga asked de Poincy (the French governor-general at Saint Kitts) to send them a governor.

In response, de Poincy sent 50 Huguenots and other troublesome settlers under the command of Jean Le Vasseur in 1642.[3] A Norman nobleman and a professional military engineer, Le Vasseur forced his followers to construct an impregnable fortress or citadel on the summit of a steep crag. From this citadel armed with two dozen canon, Le Vasseur defied his French patron and beat off repeated Spanish attacks. Ruling as a cruel and greedy king over the buccaneers, Le Vasseur collected a share of their plunder and taxed the hides brought into Tortuga from Hispaniola. For a dozen years, he reigned in barbaric splendor. Finally, in 1653, he was killed by a treacherous lieutenant, whose mistress he had appropriated.

Le Vasseur's death did not end pirate control over Tortuga. A Spanish force in January 1654 defeated the new governor sent by de Poincy. However, with the approach of Cromwell's fleet in 1655, the Spanish deported the French and withdrew their own troops back to defend Santo Domingo. As soon as the coast was clear, the buccaneers poured back in greater strength than before.

## D'OGERON IN SAINT-DOMINGUE

For the next ten years, the French and the British, now occupying Jamaica, continued to dispute control of Tortuga. Beginning in 1665, Tortuga and the western third of Santo Domingo were brought under the French flag by Bertrand d'Ogeron de la Rivière. As governor for the new French West Indies Company, d'Ogeron's instructions ordered him to impose some order at Tortuga and settle farmers along the western coast of Hispaniola. During the next ten years, d'Ogeron skillfully accomplished both of these goals.

Since they formed the colony's only defense, d'Ogeron could not expel the buccaneers. Instead he transferred those on the mainland to Tortuga. Through his energetic efforts—and sometimes at his own expense—d'Ogeron replaced the pirates with more peaceful colonists from France. By 1681, perhaps four thousand settlers lived on the French section, centered around the town of Port-de-Paix, opposite Tortuga. (See Table 5, page 76.) The small Spanish colony still living in the eastern half of Hispaniola could hardly challenge their possession, especially as the mountainous central part of the island separated the two groups.

As on other islands, tobacco initially formed the main cash crop on Saint-Domingue. The government encouraged sugar planting after 1697, when the Treaty of Ryswick tacitly recognized French occupation. The industry took off after 1713, when slaves became available through Jamaica. Saint-Domingue then underwent a spectacular boom, as planters created hundreds of sugar estates on its virgin soil. By 1740, these estates produced more sugar than all the British islands taken together.

D'Ogeron and his successors were less successful in controlling the pirates of Tortuga. Henceforth, these were primarily French in nationality and generally did not seize French shipping bound for Saint-Domingue. But their raids against Spanish and British shipping actually increased during d'Ogeron's administration. The Tortuga buccaneers of the 1660s and 1670s—men such as François l'Ollonais and Michel le Basque—are still famed for their daring and their cruelty.

## THE BUCCANEERS COME TO PORT ROYAL

In 1657, Governor d'Oyley, seeking help against the Spanish, invited the British buccaneers at Tortuga to transfer their headquarters to Jamaica. Spanish settlers soon were thrown off the island. The buccaneers remained for decades. By 1665, more than two thousand buccaneers regularly sailed in a dozen large ships from Port Royal, a small spit of land at the south of Kingston Harbor. Most were desperate men, accustomed to living at sea and with no trade save burning and plundering. Electing their own captains, they followed men—such as Henry Morgan—whose missions promised enormous rewards. They obeyed royal laws only when these were backed by stronger and faster frigates.

On his restoration in 1660, Charles II officially ended the war against Spain begun by Cromwell in 1655. But violence continued to rage "beyond the line" in the Indies. In naming Sir Thomas Modyford (1620?–1679) governor of Jamaica in 1664, the king instructed him to control piracy and forbade him to commission privateers. Nevertheless, pirates openly flourished at Port Royal during the next two decades. Governor Modyford and other Jamaicans shared in their profits. Prominent merchants bought whatever the pirates brought in, and planters belonging to the island's assembly and governor's council sponsored their voyages.

Jamaica also depended on the pirates for protection against foreign enemies. In times of war, the buccaneers, licensed as privateers, were the only available defense against enemy attack. Neither the French in Tortuga nor the British in Port Royal could suppress their own pirates unless they could be sure that the other side would do so the same. During the Anglo-Dutch Wars (1652–1674), it would have been simple for the pirates to find a new base in Dutch Curaçao. Piracy could not be suppressed until all nations turned against it. But that did not happen until the end of the 1720s.

# CHAPTER EIGHT:
# WAR AND PIRACY, 1665–1720

■

The Second Dutch War (1665–1667) marked the end of one era in Caribbean history and the beginning of another. Until that point, northern Europeans generally had worked together to plunder the Spanish possessions in the Caribbean. From 1665 to 1815, England and France fought a long series of wars to gain colonies and to control world trade. The Spanish empire, now terminally weakened, often sat out most of these conflicts but still suffered from the pirate raids that accompanied them.

Both Britain and France placed a high value on the Caribbean islands, and they sent large naval fleets and soldiers from Europe to attack each other's colonies. During these almost constant wars, several of the islands were conquered and reconquered many times—only to be restored to their original owners at the final peace conference. These were true world wars, and the islands were only one chip in a massive poker game played for high stakes. They often were traded back for gains on other continents.

For islanders, the wars between 1665 and 1713 were almost wholly destructive. Both French and British colonists took advantage of them to destroy rival sugar producers. They were especially eager to steal slaves from the enemy, and these wars often resembled nothing more than enormous reciprocal slave raids. Moreover, this half-century of international war provided an environment in which piracy flourished. Neither Britain nor France could keep a navy permanently in the islands. Both used the pirates during times of war. When peace came they found it impossible to disband their now unwanted allies, who continued to pillage the sea-lanes. Until the 1720s, there were two parallel societies in the Caribbean. Planters, merchants, and slaves peacefully grew sugar and other tropical products for sale in Europe. The buccaneers attacked the ships connecting the islands to Europe and bringing slaves from Africa.

## THE SECOND DUTCH WAR, 1665–1667

In contrast to modern wars, the Second Dutch War was purely a commercial struggle, instigated by British merchants suffering from Dutch competition and monopoly. Hostilities began in West Africa, where British forces in 1663 captured most Dutch strongholds along the slave coast. In retaliation, the Dutch dispatched a fleet under one of their greatest admirals, Michiel de Ruyter (1607–1676). De Ruyter retook the forts and brought his fleet across the Atlantic early in 1665. There he attacked British merchant ships off Barbados, Nevis, and Montserrat, effectively destroying that season's export crops.

From Jamaica, Governor Thomas Modyford suggested that the government turn the Port Royal buccaneers against the Dutch naval bases in the region. The Crown agreed that Modyford should use the pirates "to dispossess the Dutch from Curaçao and their other plantations." This, the first inter-island war, began with a pirate raid against Sint Eustatius, Saba, and Curaçao. Modyford gave a privateer's commission to Edward Morgan, uncle of the more famous Henry Morgan, who gathered ten ships and five hundred pirates. Morgan promised them their pay in plunder, and the king provided only gunpowder and shells. In the event, however, the pirates were unreliable allies, who preferred not to fight regular troops.

Morgan's fleet easily defeated the small garrison guarding Dutch slave pens on Sint Eustatius and Saba. Meanwhile another group of Jamaican pirates looted the Dutch settlements on Tobago. However, the pirate crews refused to go on to Curaçao, which they knew to be more heavily armed. The British sent out a second privateer fleet in January 1666 under Edward Mansfield and Henry Morgan, both of whom later became notorious pirate chiefs. Again, the crew choose not to take on the Dutch forts at Curaçao. Instead they turned south against the weaker Spanish, looting Providence Island and the colonies along the coasts of Honduras and Mexico.

## FRENCH TROOPS PILLAGE THE LEEWARD ISLANDS

The war began with quick British victories, but the Dutch soon gained their revenge through their French allies. Dutch privateers attacked British shipping throughout the region, while French pirates raided the coast of Barbados. The French colonists also seized the British part of Saint Kitts, which the two nations had shared since 1627. The British governor of Saint Kitts had brought over militia from Nevis and also hired some of the buccaneers from Sint Eustatius. Fearing these preparations, the French in April 1666 decided to strike first and soon forced humiliating terms of surrender on the British. British plantations were devastated, more than 8,000 planters left with their slaves, and the rest took an oath of allegiance to the French Crown. In July 1666 a hurricane off Martinique sank most of the eight British ships carrying 1,000 men sent from Barbados to retake the island.

The French and British governments now sent men-of-war from Europe to aid their colonies. Local forces supported by regular French troops took Antigua and Montserrat in December 1666 and in February 1667. On both islands, many indentured servants—primarily Irish Catholics—aided the invaders. On Antigua, the French also were assisted by Carib from Guadeloupe, Dominica, and Saint Vincent. The war ravaged plantations on both islands, and the French seized hundreds of slaves. Only Nevis escaped, and it took in the white refugees from neighboring islands. The tide of battle turned in May 1667, when a fleet from England defeated a mixed Dutch-French armada off Nevis. The British soon recaptured Antigua and Montserrat, but they could not take the strongly fortified French positions in Saint Kitts.

The Treaty of Breda (1667) restored all colonies to their previous owners with one exception: Tobago passed from the Netherlands to France. Nevertheless, the war is significant because it set the boundaries between the French and British colonies until 1763. It also marked the end of Dutch ambitions in the region. The war proved a mortal blow to the Dutch West India Company, and the British and French now rigidly enforced restrictions against Dutch traders.

In the Caribbean, the Second Dutch War seriously disrupted economic growth, ended a century of Anglo-French cooperation, and fostered piracy. All the islands suffered from the disruption of trade and heavy taxation, and several British colonies had been ruined. The French did not hand back Saint Kitts until 1671, and they kept the captured slaves and other war booty. The British had to rebuild Saint Kitts from scratch, and Antigua had been devastated from end to end. The material damage could be repaired. However, the violence of the fighting in the Leewards left behind lasting bitterness, creating a tradition of antipathy between French and British colonists.

## HENRY MORGAN AND THE PORT ROYAL BUCCANEERS

During the 1660s and 1670s, thousands of pirates made their homes at Port Royal and Tortuga, with smaller groups operating out of other bases, such as Saint Croix, the Virgin Islands, and Curaçao.[1] The French and British governments had recognized the buccaneers by granting them commissions during the Second Dutch War. After the war ended, they went back to attacking Spanish shipping and ports. Of all the pirates, the most infamous was the Briton Henry Morgan (1635?–1688), who led three notorious raids between 1667 and 1671.

During the Second Dutch War, Morgan commanded a ship in the 1666 expedition that took Providence Island. When the Spanish captured and killed Mansfield shortly afterward, the buccaneers elected Morgan as their "admiral." The next year, fearing an invasion from Cuba, Governor Modyford commissioned Morgan to capture Spanish prisoners. Collecting ten ships with 500 to 700 men, he pillaged Puerto Principe in Cuba and then turned against the Spanish Main. There Morgan took by storm the fortified and well-garrisoned town of Portobelo and held it for thirty-one days against successive attacks. Seeing that his forces could not drive out Morgan's men, the governor of Panama agreed to an enormous ransom of more than 100,000 pounds.

The Portobelo raid obviously exceeded the terms of Morgan's commission. And the buccaneers under his command acted with horrible cruelty, torturing their prisoners to discover where they had hidden their treasures. Nevertheless, Modyford soon commissioned him to lead another expedition against Cuba. In January 1669, Morgan almost lost his life when the pirates on board accidentally blew up his flagship during a drunken party. Escaping with most of his officers,

Morgan nevertheless sacked the Cuban towns of Maracaibo and Gibraltar, destroyed three Spanish ships waiting to intercept him, recovered a considerable treasure, and again exacted a heavy ransom from the Spanish authorities.

## HENRY MORGAN SACKS PANAMA

For his third and final raid in 1670–71, Morgan assembled about 2,000 buccaneers in 36 ships and again turned them against Panama. Recapturing Providence Island, he then seized the castle at the mouth of the Chagres River, slaughtering its garrison of 300 men. With some 1,400 buccaneers, he ascended the Chagres over difficult terrain. Appearing before Panama in January 1671, Morgan again defeated a much larger force than his own and took the city.

However, Morgan's behavior after the battles somewhat tarnished the glory of this victory. Morgan's men sacked Panama, torturing and slaughtering its inhabitants. While the buccaneers enjoyed drunken orgies, the captain and crew of a Spanish galleon escaped and sailed away with much of the captured loot. Enough remained to enrich all the participants. But, on returning to Chagres, Morgan cheated the other members of the expedition out of their fair share. Morgan escaped with a few ships to Jamaica, leaving the rest to find their own way home.

In July 1670, England and Spain signed the Treaty of Madrid. For the first time Spain officially recognized British holdings in the Caribbean, and both nations agreed to prohibit piracy against the other. Since Morgan had raided Panama after the signing of this treaty, the British arrested him and Governor Modyford, taking them to London. There Morgan gained the favor of Charles II, who knighted him in 1674 and sent him back to Jamaica as lieutenant governor. Morgan was now thirty-nine, immensely rich, and the owner of a plantation of 6,000 acres. He spent the next fourteen years in drunken idleness. By his death in 1688—ousted from his offices for incoherence—he was so immensely fat that he no longer could move from his hammock.

Although their raids now were totally illegal, other pirate captains continued to sail throughout the 1670s, and their stolen cargoes remained welcome in Port Royal. Not until 1682 did a new governor, Sir Thomas Lynch, finally convince the Jamaican Assembly and Council to enforce the laws. Even then, other islands and other ports continued to welcome their trade, and the pirates simply moved on.

The earthquake of 1692, during which Port Royal sank under the sea, was a fitting punishment for the sins of that new Sodom. But it did not mark the end of the British buccaneers. From the 1680s, pirate ships found new havens with more friendly governors in the Danish and British West Indies and finally in the Bahamas. After again serving their king as commissioned privateers (during the War of the Spanish Succession, 1701–1714), thousands of buccaneers settled in the Bahamas, which became their last haven during the great era of pirate terror.

## THE THIRD DUTCH WAR, 1672–1678

Despite the hostility between their colonists in the Caribbean, England and France joined against the Netherlands in the Third Dutch War. This war marked another attempt by England and France to abort Dutch supremacy in world commerce and shipping. It was decided by land and sea battles in Europe, and the islands suffered comparatively little damage. Since the British withdrew from the war in 1672, Dutch and French forces fought the main battles in this region.

Both the Netherlands and France considered the islands extremely important. Their sugar was increasingly valuable, and they also provided a base for trade with the Spanish mainland. Seeking total conquest of their enemy's colonies, both nations sent large armadas carrying soldiers from Europe. However, European troops could not take fortified bases. Local pirates (and merchant vessels commissioned as privateers) again proved the most effective weapon.

When the war began in July 1672, the French and British seized the Dutch forts on Sint Maarten, Sint Eustatius, and Saba as well as the Dutch bases on Tortola and Virgin Gorda. However, the West India Company held on to the Curaçao islands, and two massive French expeditions against Curaçao in 1673 and 1678 failed disastrously. During the 1673 French attack on Curaçao, the French governor-general wanted to use Bertrand d'Ogeron and the Tortuga buccaneers. But d'Ogeron and his fleet disappeared in bad weather off the northern coast of Puerto Rico. Without their help, the Dutch at Curaçao repulsed the royal warships. The second French expedition in 1678 proved an even greater disaster. Seven large warships and three belonging to buccaneers ran aground on a hidden reef near Bonaire, drowning more than more than 500 sailors. Before this abortive attack on Curaçao, however, the French fleet did take Tobago.

Two large armadas sent from Holland also met with disaster. In July 1672, soldiers from a fleet commanded by Admiral de Ruyter were defeated with large losses at Cul de Sac in Martinique. In 1676 a second expedition temporarily regained Tobago and Sint Maarten but failed to take the buccaneer colony at Saint-Domingue.

After the war, the Dutch regained the small islands of Sint Maarten, Sint Eustatius, and Saba in the Leewards. The British retained Tortola and Virgin Gorda, and the French kept (but did not settle) Tobago. The Dutch state now permanently ended its involvement in West Indian commerce. The enormous expense of its failed campaign against Martinique in 1673 bankrupted the original West India Company, which was dissolved in 1674. However, individual Dutch merchants continued to trade successfully from Curaçao and, in later years, from Sint Eustatius.

## SAINT-DOMINGUE BECOMES THE PIRATE CAPITAL

For a decade after the Treaties of Nijmegen (1678–1679), the European states officially were at peace. But piracy on a large scale continued to plague the region. Since the British finally denied them Port Royal, pirates from many nations now gathered on Tortuga and Saint-Domingue. There Louis XIV of France followed a duplicitous policy. Although refusing royal commissions to freebooters, he permitted Governor de Pouançay to issue privateering licenses under his own name. As usual, Spanish ports provided the most lucrative targets, but the pirates also seized Dutch and British ships.

In 1683, buccaneer captains from Tortuga attacked Vera Cruz, the Spanish treasure port on the coast of Mexico. Plundering its houses, churches, and convents, they seized a fortune, which they later divided into more than 1,000 shares, each containing 800 golden pieces of eight. Enraged by this attack, the Spanish briefly went to war, until the French government agreed to the Truce of Ratisbon (August 1684) pledging peace in the West Indies as well as in Europe.

The following year, England and France similarly promised not to encourage buccaneering expeditions against each others' colonies. Despite these solemn treaties, pirates from Tortuga in 1685 looted Campeche, Nicaragua, gaining a large booty. The European nations were not yet ready to end their toleration of pirates. Without permanent naval garrisons in the islands, they still depended on privateers as their first line of defense in time of war.

## THE NINE YEARS WAR, 1688–1697

In yet another reversal of alliances, England, Holland, and Spain (and many other European states) now fought France. Louis XIV declared war on Holland in November 1688. England joined the anti-French alliance in May 1689, after William III replaced James II on the throne. (For this reason, some histories call this "King William's War.") Battles in Europe again decided the war, but it soon spilled over into the colonies. The Dutch no longer took an active role in the Caribbean, but both the British and the French launched expeditions that caused extensive damage.

As in the previous war, both sent warships from Europe, and the French also enlisted the Saint-Domingue and Tortola pirates. The 1695 attack on Cartagena was, after Morgan's rape of Panama, among the largest of pirate raids. Both regular forces and privateers again caused heavy damage in the Leewards. And they also carried the war west into the Greater Antilles. For the first time since the British conquest in 1655, Jamaica and Hispaniola suffered devastating raids.

Early in 1689, the French destroyed the Dutch settlements on Sint Eustatius, and they once again occupied the British part of Saint Kitts. Irish Catholics on Nevis, Antigua, and Montserrat rebelled in support of the deposed king, James II. Thus British prospects in the Leewards looked bleak. They were saved by the leadership of Christopher Codrington (d. 1697), governor-general of the Leeward Islands. Codrington managed to head off the Irish rebellion, and retook Saint Kitts and Anguilla in June 1690. Determined to put an end to the French presence on Saint Kitts, Codrington packed the French settlers off to Saint-Domingue and distributed their lands to British settlers.

In March 1691, Codrington, who wanted to force the French out of all the Leewards, then invaded Guadeloupe. There the British razed French sugar plantations and burnt the principal towns, but Codrington had to withdraw when his naval support suddenly pulled out. In 1693, an British invasion of Martinique came to a similar end. Codrington's troops quickly took most of the island and destroyed its plantations. But they again had to withdraw, devastated by disease while besieging the fort at Saint-Pierre.

For the first time in many years, the larger islands of the Greater Antilles also suffered major war damage. On Hispaniola, both the French and the Spanish tried to conquer or destroy each other's colonies. In 1690 French settlers and buccaneers burned the Spanish settlement of Saint Iago. The following year, in revenge, a strong Spanish force burned the port city of Cap Français, massacred whatever men they could find, and carried off the women, children, and slaves to Santo Domingo.

To replace the governor of Saint-Domingue—killed in this raid—the French Crown turned to Jean Du Casse (1640–1715), himself a leading buccaneer captain. Taking advantage of the 1692 earthquake, Du Casse sent French buccaneers to pillage and to steal slaves from plantations along the coast of Jamaica. In June 1694, Du Casse personally led a fleet of 22 ships that ravaged Jamaica's southern coasts at Port Morant, Cow Bay, and Carlisle Bay, burning 50 sugar plantations and capturing some 1,300 slaves.

While Du Casse pillaged Jamaica, the British planned to attack Saint-Domingue while a Spanish army marched across the island from Santo Domingo. In July 1605, this joint expedition took the northern coast, destroyed Cap Français for a second time, and thoroughly plundered the capital at Port-de-Paix. Once again, an outbreak of disease halted a successful invasion, and the British fleet withdrew.

*The Sack of Cartagena*   Du Casse prepared a counterattack on Santo Domingo. But the French king instead decided to take Cartagena, the main port for the Spanish treasure fleet carrying silver from Peru. Obedient to his orders, Du Casse assembled more than 700 buccaneers on seven ships. In March 1697, these joined thirteen royal warships brought over from France by their admiral, the arrogant and dishonest Jean-Bernard Desjean, baron de Pointis (1645–1707).

Before the combined fleet sailed, de Pointis gave his word that the men could divide any loot in equal shares, following pirate custom. Only after a savage battle was the French force able to take Cartagena, which the Spanish had heavily fortified since Drake's conquest in 1573. Its defenders finally surrendered, when the French admiral agreed to spare civilians and their homes. Working rapidly, de Pointis's regular soldiers collected gold and silver worth perhaps 20 million French *livres*. They then prepared to sail for France.

Du Casse, who had to live with the buccaneers in Saint-Domingue, demanded that de Pointis honor his word and give them their promised share of the loot. When de Pointis refused, Du Casse managed to restrain the pirates until the royal fleet could leave. He promised to present their claims and gain their share from the French courts.

At first the buccaneers also prepared to sail home. But four of the seven captains decided that gold in hand was better than Du Casse's promise. Heading back to the prostrate city, the buccaneers ruthlessly sacked Cartagena, until its inhabitants agreed to pay them another five million *livres*. Much more than the destruction of Port Royal, the pirates' final departure for Saint-Domingue marks the end of their reign. Henceforth, individual pirate ships might take individual merchant or treasure ships. But the sack of Cartagena in 1697 represents the last time that a joint force of buccaneers in many ships sailed home with immense booty from a looted port.

## THE WAR OF THE SPANISH SUCCESSION, 1702–1714

The Treaty of Ryswyck in September 1697 ended the Nine Years War. All sides again returned the colonies they had taken, and they formally recognized the French colony at Saint-Domingue governed by Du Casse. Only five years later, in May 1702, Austria, England, and the Netherlands declared war on France and Spain. The allies fought mainly to prevent the uniting of the French and Spanish empires. The French royal house of Bourbon now occupied both thrones because Charles II of Spain had willed his kingdoms to Philip V, Louis XIV's grandson. As one of their war aims, the British sought the right to trade with the Spanish mainland. They particularly coveted the *asiento*, the contract to import slaves into the Spanish colonies.

Only France and Britain sent troops to the Caribbean. In this region, privateering raids had continued even during the brief peace after 1697. The war simply continued the hostilities between the two empires that had begun in 1665. Initially, both sides hoped to take colonies from the other, and each sent a fleet to the region in 1701. However, tropical diseases soon killed so many of their crews that both navies accomplished little. Local forces again proved more effective than imported troops, and the war turned into a series of destructive raids in the Leewards. The British wanted to destroy their economic rivals and to steal their slaves. The French, outnumbered by British colonists, needed help from the Saint-Domingue pirates. The buccaneers only sought booty.

Under Christopher Codrington Junior (1668–1710), governor of the Leeward Islands from 1699 to 1704, the British won the first battles. In July 1702, Codrington seized the French portion of Saint Kitts. The next year, he invaded Guadeloupe with 3,600 troops and inflicted great damage during a two-month campaign. Although Codrington could not defeat the French troops on the island, his men totally ruined the enemy's sugar plantations.

Unable to send a navy from Europe, the French government sought revenge for these raids through an alliance with the Saint-Domingue pirates. In 1706, the king put the local forces under the command of Pierre Le Moyne, sieur d'Iberville (1661–1706), a famous French-Canadian solider and seaman of great ability. Iberville was ordered to seize Barbados and Jamaica with the aid of the buccaneers, and he planned the expedition as a classic pirate raid. Iberville and his associates outfitted the ships, and the king sent only 600 soldiers. The Crown expected the buccaneers and French colonists to do most of the fighting, and it offered them the majority of any booty that might be taken.

Iberville and his pirate allies harshly revenged the earlier British raid on Guadeloupe. In February 1706, they plundered Saint Kitts, systematically stripping and burning every plantation beyond the reach of the British canon. They then turned on Nevis. There the British planters quickly surrendered under humiliating terms. The French seized all of their property (except for their houses and clothes), including 3,187 slaves. The British also promised to catch and hand over another 1,400 slaves who had escaped to the hills. With both islands in ruins, the British government in 1711 gave out £28,000 to the planters on Saint Kitts and distributed another £75,000 among the sufferers on Nevis.

*Rebellion in Antigua*  Iberville died in Havana soon afterwards, but French buccaneers continued to raid the British islands. In July 1712, a privateer squadron (estimated at 3,500 men) threatened Antigua and then took Montserrat, carrying off 1,200 slaves. During these years of danger, the Leeward Islands certainly needed a strong governor. The royal army and navy could not protect them against French privateers, and the wealthy planters commanding the local militia had refused to fight at Nevis. However, Colonel Daniel Parke, appointed governor of the Leewards in 1706, was the wrong choice.

Governor Parke soon earned the hatred of the planters, especially on Antigua where he usually resided. He apparently made too many reforms too quickly, and he also was greedy and possibly demented. His assailants shot at the governor several times in 1708 and 1709, wounding him in the arm. In December 1710, after Parke took control of the local regiment, armed rebels surrounded his house and demanded that he leave for Nevis. In the ensuing tumult, the rebels murdered Parke and brutally killed or wounded most of the seventy soldiers guarding him. None of the participants was punished. When the Crown tried to investigate the rebellion, no Antiguan would testify, and the new governor could not punish the entire colony.

## THE BUCCANEER REPUBLIC IN THE BAHAMAS

The buccaneers again had proved the most effective force, and this war also strengthened pirate control of the Bahamas. In 1703 and 1704, a joint French-Spanish force raided New Providence and destroyed the small settlement there. The surviving inhabitants took refuge in the woods or fled to the smaller out islands. By 1714, only 200 families still lived in the entire Bahamas group, and the pirates totally dominated New Providence.

This Bahamian era of piracy was brief. In the 1680s, pirates began to move to Nassau. After 1713, they were joined by thousands of former privateers who had lost their livelihood with the peace of Utrecht. But these pirates went into the trade not to fight but to gain easy money by looting merchant ships. Their easy pickings ended in 1718 with the appointment of Captain Woodes Rogers (d. 1732) as first royal governor of the Bahamas.

A man of strong character and a skilled captain, Woodes Rogers was, like many of the pirates, from the west of England and had served as a privateer.

During the War of the Spanish Succession, he became famous by sailing around the world, taking as prizes the Manila treasure fleet of 1709 and more than twenty other galleons. Because Rogers lacked a strong fleet of his own, he cleverly turned the pirate captains of the Bahamas against one another. He granted an amnesty to pirates willing to surrender. And he paid prizes to former pirates who captured those still at large and brought them into Nassau to be hanged. By 1720, most of the remaining buccaneers sought less dangerous waters, usually in the South Seas.

During their brief reign of terror during the 1710s, several pirate captains gained lasting fame. As their double-crosses indicate, most were greedy robbers without scruples. Partly because they often did not work well together, none carried out large raids or gained the enormous wealth of earlier buccaneers such as Henry Morgan. Unlike some of their predecessors, few pirates now hesitated to attack ships flying the flag of their own country, as long as they appeared to be easy targets.

## BLACKBEARD—PIRATE CRUELTY REACHES NEW LOWS

Some of these last buccaneers were superb navigators who could sail out of sight of land for months. Although based in the Bahamas, they brought terror from one end of the globe to the other. They sought their prey throughout the Caribbean, along the Atlantic coast as far north as Maine, and even marauded across the Atlantic to West Africa and the South Seas. Their exploits became famous in their own day because they were eagerly covered by the new popular newspapers and novels, including Daniel Defoe's novel *Robinson Crusoe* and his *General History of the Pirates*.[2]

Nearly all of the pirates found in Defoe's colorful pages made their home in Bahamian waters. The most notorious undoubtedly was and is Edward Teach (originally Edward Drummond), alias Blackbeard (d. 1719). Blackbeard enjoyed torturing his victims and, sometimes, his crew. The legend of his cruelty may have been deliberately created by Blackbeard to frighten his opponents into immediate submission.

The Blackbeard of this legend is vile beyond belief. Ranting into battle, he wore twelve pistols and several cutlasses in a special belt. A physical giant with an enormous appetite, he was reputed to have had fourteen wives and to have drunk enormous amounts of rum long after his crew had passed into a stupor. When finally cornered, he reportedly went on fighting for several minutes after receiving five musket wounds and three sabre-thrusts.

# PART THREE:

## THE SUGAR EMPIRE

■

## CHAPTER NINE:

# SUGAR RULES THE ISLANDS

■

Following the Treaty of Utrecht (1713) that ended the War of the Spanish Succession, the Caribbean enjoyed almost 80 years of relative peace and prosperity. The economy—especially the sugar industry—grew rapidly. Today, the islands supply only a small fraction of Europe's sugar. During the 18th century, however, the islands—as shown in Table 8—produced 80 to 90 percent of the sugar consumed by western Europeans. The European homeland always wanted more sugar, and the British and French planters increasingly grew nothing else.

### TABLE 8. SUGAR PRODUCTION IN THE AMERICAS, 1741–1824
(Annual Averages in Tons)

|                         | 1741–1745 | 1766–1770 | 1820–1824 |
| ----------------------- | --------- | --------- | --------- |
| French West Indies      | 64,675    | 77,923    | 47,658    |
| British West Indies     | 41,043    | 74,452    | 147,733   |
| Brazil (Portuguese)     | 34,000    | 20,400    | —         |
| Virgin Islands (Danish) | —         | 8,230     | 23,000    |
| Surinam (Dutch)         | 9,210     | 6,800     | —         |
| Cuba (Spanish)          | 2,000     | 5,200     | 50,384    |

NOTE: For possessions other than British, data available only for some years during the period reported.

SOURCES: Richard Sheridan, *The Development of the Plantations to 1750* (Aylesbury, England: Ginn and Company, 1970), 22 (1741–1770); David Watts, *The West Indies: Pattern of Development, Culture and Environmental Change since 1492* (Cambridge: Cambridge University Press, 1987), 287–288 (1820–24); Franklin Knight, *The Caribbean: The Genesis of a Fragmented Nationalism* (New York: Oxford University Press, 1978), 241 (Haiti/Saint-Domingue, 1820).

## THE COLONIAL EMPIRES IN 1713

A century after northern Europeans established their first settlements, the decaying Spanish empire still retained Cuba, Puerto Rico, and the eastern part of Hispaniola (Santo Domingo). In 1713, the main centers of French and British occupation remained the Lesser Antilles. There the French controlled Martinique and Guadeloupe, and the British ruled Barbados, Saint Kitts, Antigua, Montserrat, Nevis, and the British Virgins. In the Greater Antilles, the British occupied Jamaica, and the French held the western third of Hispaniola (Saint-Domingue). During the 18th century, Britain and France rapidly developed these larger islands, which became their most important colonies by the 1750s.

Only the Windward Islands remained largely uninhabited by Europeans until after 1763. Dominica and Saint Vincent both retained large settlements of Carib, whose ownership had been guaranteed by a treaty in 1660. Expeditions from the French and British Leewards tried to settle Saint Lucia and Saint Vincent from time to time, but the other side usually drove them off. French settlers from Martinique did set up plantations on Grenada, which produced significant amounts of sugar by the 1760s as well as coffee and cocoa. Further south a few Spanish colonists clung to survival on Trinidad, while Tobago (nominally under French control) had only a small population.

## THE NON-SPANISH ISLANDS GIVE THEMSELVES WHOLLY TO SUGAR

All of the Caribbean islands became integrated into the tropical plantation system during the 18th century. On the British islands sugar became virtually the only crop, and a true monoculture developed. The French islands enjoyed a somewhat more diversified economy, but sugar was their main and most important product. The plantation system reached out to dominate the economies even of islands that grew no sugar. At the far north, the Bahamas remained unsettled because they were unsuited to sugar. To the far south, the Dutch retained the Curaçao islands as outposts of trade to Latin America through Venezuela. But everything between Curaçao and the Bahamas was dominated by the plantation system. The Danish Virgin Islands and the Dutch Leewards— Sint Eustatius, Saba, and half of Sint Maarten—served as free ports selling slaves to the British and French islands. As the sugar industry flourished, sugar plantations also came to dominate Danish Saint Croix.

The very success of the sugar islands retarded development of the Windwards. Sugar plantations require large amounts of capital. British Jamaica and French Saint-Domingue did not reach full development until the 1750s, and there was little money to spare for the smaller Windwards. Moreover, the shipping schedules were tied to the needs of the sugar islands, especially during times of war. Captains were loath to go to the remoter territories, such as Grenada or even Guadeloupe, which had to send their crops to Martinique for pick up.

## EUROPEANS CRAVE MORE AND MORE SUGAR

Overall, the four centuries from 1550 to 1950 saw a sharp increase in per capita sugar consumption, and prices generally rose until the 1820s. Particularly during the 18th century, Europeans of all classes increasingly drank tea, coffee, and cocoa, and ate processed foods, jams, and candy. Northern European consumers (except for the French)—especially the British and their colonies—always have eaten more sugar than others. Thus the sugar habit grew throughout northern Europe during the 1700s, but it increased most rapidly in England. In 1700, on average, Britons ate 4 pounds of sugar a year. By 1750, per capita consumption doubled, and then doubled again by 1800, reaching 18 pounds a year. Consumption doubled once more in the late 1840s after the British government removed import taxes on sugar. The British craving for sweets peaked in the early 1960s, when the average Briton ate more than 110 pounds of sugar each year.

Over the longer term, prices generally rose until the 19th century. Nevertheless, sugar went through a series of boom and bust periods with serious effects on the islands. Prices soared to new records after 1645, when the revolt against the Dutch devastated Brazilian plantations. Planters on Barbados enjoyed profits of 40 to 50 percent a year during the 1650s, and they rapidly expanded production. By 1661, a glut had developed on the European market, and prices fell by as much as 70 percent between 1646 and 1680. They remained depressed until about 1690 and then rose again until a minor slump in the 1730s.

With constantly rising demand, the market again rose from the mid-1740s. Planters on the British islands did especially well during times of war (1748, 1756–1763). Although they never again equaled those on Barbados in the 1650s, profits were generous. They soared again during the Napoleonic wars from 1791 to 1815, when the price of sugar on the London market reached its all time high. From the 1840s, both prices and profits began to fall dramatically. European governments subsidized the beet sugar industry, Cuban production soared, and the British Empire found new sources in Asia.

## THE MERCANTILIST SYSTEM DURING THE 18TH CENTURY

The French and British governments both sought to make their colonies—the most important sugar producers—benefit the mother country. Both forbade islanders from importing or exporting goods on ships not owned by their own subjects. At home, both placed prohibitive duties on any kind of sugar imported from a foreign nation or its colonies. To protect domestic sugar refiners, both also taxed imports of semi-refined (clayed) sugar at a much higher rate than the raw product (muscovado).

Despite their shared "mercantilist" philosophies, the French and British regulations also differed in important ways that significantly affected the economies of their islands. Neither government followed a totally consistent policy over the years, since both had to please many constituencies with divergent interests. In general, however, the British government followed a high tax policy to increase its own revenues. The French government collected lower taxes and mainly sought to increase its exports to other countries.

The British government always burdened consumers with high import duties on tropical products—especially sugar, tobacco, and tea—that had to be brought into the British isles. The import duties first imposed on sugar in 1650 continued to rise until 1705. Moreover, planters on Barbados and the Leewards (but not Jamaica) also paid a 4.5 percent duty on all their exports.[1] But the French government primarily wanted to increase France's exports rather than to raise revenues. It thus emphasized the sale of tropical products, especially sugar, to other European countries. From the 1660s, the government organized its empire to encourage commercial growth with the main benefits accruing to French merchants. From 1717 it did away with taxes—except for a three percent tax on all colonial exports—on sugar reexported from France.

In 1739 the British government also eliminated duties on sugar exported directly from the West Indies to Europe. Nevertheless, French West Indian sugar remained cheaper than British products, and French sugars dominated the Amsterdam and Hamburg markets during times of peace throughout the 18th century. Thus the British islands primarily shipped their sugar to the large protected market in England. Because of the tax laws, British planters were restricted to making raw sugar, but they were guaranteed high prices.

Because the French planters made more clayed sugar, they also had an abundance of molasses, a byproduct of the claying process. Throughout the 18th century, British North American merchants purchased inexpensive rum from the French islands, as well as molasses for their rum distilleries. As a result, British planters lost the American market. To placate planter interests, the Parliament in 1733 placed prohibitive duties on sugar, molasses, and rum imported from non-British islands. British customs officials did little to enforce this Molasses Act, and American merchants openly and brazenly violated it until the 1760s. When the British government did attempt to prohibit French rum and molasses through the 1764 Sugar Act, it infuriated American merchants and shippers. This act became a major grievance leading to the American Revolution of 1776.

## THE PROFITS AND POWER OF THE SUGAR LORDS

The Caribbean colonies justified mercantilist theories by supplying sugar and other staples in return for North American provisions and European manufactured goods. By the early 1770s, Jamaica, Barbados, and the Leewards thus supplied about 24 percent of all goods imported into Britain and took 13.4 percent of all British exports. The direct duties on sugar were only a small part of the revenues Britain and France took from the islands. Sugar and slaves were lucrative trades, and most of the profits went to the homeland. Payments to absentee landlords, commissions, freight, insurance, and other charges took the greater part of the income of the islands.[2]

European states invested nothing to finance, govern, and defend their Caribbean colonies. On the contrary, the plantations largely financed themselves after the first investments in the 1600s, and their profits found a permanent home in Europe. Moreover, the sugar colonies were at the heart of a complex "triangular trade" that indirectly returned revenues to the mother country considerably in excess of official customs taxes. By this system of trade from Europe to Africa to America (and then back to Europe), as Basil Davidson notes, three separate profits were made and taken, all high and all in Europe: the first profit was that of selling consumer goods to the slavers; the second derived from selling slaves to the planters and mine-owners of the Americas; while the third (and biggest) was realized on the sale of American and West Indian cargoes in Europe. It was largely on the steady and often stupendous profits of this circuitous enterprise that France and England would ground their commercial supremacy.[3]

But neither sugar nor slavery in itself tells the entire story. European consumers paid high prices that covered all taxes and all the costs of producing sugar (as well as any profit to the planters). Thus the sugar and slave trades supported many European interests—from wealthy merchants, refiners, and shipowners through prosperous insurers and lawyers down to humble grocers. Many, both then and now, have exaggerated the total profits from sugar and slavery, which formed only a fraction of Europe's gross national product.[4] The important point is that British and French statesmen considered sugar and slavery essential to the national economy. Capital put into these trades brought in much higher profits than alternative investments, and they thus increased national income and government revenues.

Even if they had wanted to, governments could not ignore sugar merchants and slavers, who were concentrated in several large cities. In France, the three great ports of Nantes, Bordeaux, and Marseilles dominated the French slave trade and supplied most of the sugar and coffee consumed in Europe during the 18th century. Given the steady rise both in sugar prices and the volume of consumption, the French sugar trade soared throughout the 18th century. Despite wartime interruptions, the total value of French sugar imports increased five-fold—from 15 million *livres* in 1730 to 75 million in 1790. Thus these ports became much richer than the rest of France. The French government felt it had to maintain its hegemony over one of Europe's largest trades. It protected its Caribbean colonies, even if this meant (as in 1763) abandoning North America and India.

A few large cities also captured the sugar and slave trades in England. London, with an estimated 180 refineries by the 1780s, dominated sugar refining, followed by Bristol, Liverpool, and Glasgow. Liverpool became the world's leading slave port, eclipsing Bristol and London in the 1740s. These British merchants joined with West Indian sugar planters to form one united "West India Interest." Shared profits and needs bound together wealthy absentee planters, merchants, manufacturers, bond-holders, agents of colonial governments, and military officers serving in the West Indies. In addition to creating formal associations, the West Indians formed a close social circle, bound together by family and marriage ties as well as lasting friendships.

In England, the "West India Interest" was able to express its concerns through a large and generally united voice in Parliament. Seventy West Indian merchants and absentee proprietors purchased seats in Parliament from 1730 to 1775. The leading planter families of Jamaica, Saint Kitts, and Antigua sat throughout the century. Taken all together, the 1766 Parliament held "forty members who are either West Indian planters themselves, descended from such, or have concerns there that entitle them to pre-eminence."[5] While the Parliament also represented competing interests and industries, the West Indian bloc had no difficulty making its concerns known to the government.

## THE VARYING FORTUNES OF THE ISLANDS

During the 18th century, as sugar dominated the islands, planters adopted one relatively uniform plantation system. Innovations often began on Barbados and then spread north to the Leewards and west to Jamaica and Saint-Domingue. Despite the wars between their two nations, French and British planters were willing to learn from each other. Although they used relatively uniform agricultural methods, the pace of economic development varied—because of each island's different resources, the policies of England and France, market fluctuations, wars, and natural disasters. At one extreme were the small, intensively cultivated estates of Barbados, at the other the vast holdings of Jamaica and Saint-Domingue.

Natural resources partially determined which regions formed part of the fabled sugar empire. Sugarcane grows best when heat and water are plentiful year-round. An ideal climate provides a predictable sixty to seventy inches of rain per year, with no prolonged droughts. These conditions are common along the coasts of the larger islands in the Leewards. By contrast, rainfall is highly localized on the Greater Antilles because of their high mountains. Here different parts of the same island can receive from 20 to 200 inches a year. In the dryer areas, cane could not be profitably produced without irrigation.

Cane grows well both in the volcanic soils found on Guadeloupe and Martinique and also on the limestone soils of geologically older islands like Barbados. However, the soil rapidly loses fertility after trees are removed, and cane itself further takes minerals out of the soil. The productivity of older plantations quickly falls unless the cane fields are heavily fertilized—during the 18th century through the application of animal dung. New plantations always enjoyed an advantage that was accentuated by improvements in technology over time.

Planters on the smaller islands of Barbados and the Leewards initially could produce more cheaply than Jamaicans because of their easterly location and because of the high ratio of coastline to landmass. Since the prevailing winds are from the east, ships carrying goods from Europe and slaves from Africa reached Barbados and Martinique several weeks before arriving at Jamaica or Saint-Domingue. Similarly, ships carrying sugar from Barbados to Europe could tack north against the easterlies. In contrast, ships leaving Port Royal in Jamaica had to sail downwind south of Cuba to catch the Gulf Stream through the Florida Passage and up the Carolina coast. Simply because the voyage took longer, Jamaica sugar cost more than Barbadian sugar by the time it reached Liverpool.

Until the 19th century, plantations along the sea also enjoyed a cost advantage. Even milled sugar is quite heavy. Most of the best sugar land was near the coast, so that barrels of sugar could be rolled to the beach and carried in small boats to seagoing vessels. Inland plantations on Jamaica and Saint-

Domingue either had to produce more efficiently or enjoy smaller profits. Ultimately, Cuba surpassed all the other islands when railroads opened up access to its interior provinces during the 19th century.

## BARBADOS AND THE BRITISH LEEWARD ISLANDS

Each island enjoyed its Golden Age at slightly different eras. Sugar planters on Barbados enjoyed the highest profits ever during the 1650s and 1660s. Planters in the Leewards naturally tried to follow Barbados's lead. However, a lack of capital and slaves held back the development of cane estates, and French invasions depopulated the islands during the War of the Spanish Succession. After 1713, Barbados maintained and even expanded production, but it soon was surpassed by the Leewards. By the 1750s, these small islands were producing three times as much sugar as Barbados, and Saint Kitts was the richest colony in the British Empire by 1776. Sugar prices then fell, but the islands enjoyed a final burst of prosperity during the first decades of the 19th century.

Sugar estates totally dominated Barbados and the British Leewards, which developed into extreme examples of monoculture. By 1770, sugar products counted for 93 percent of Barbados's exports and more than 97 percent of exports from the Leewards. Cane was planted on every possible piece of land, and the islanders depended upon outside sources for food, clothing, building materials, and draft animals.

Sugarcane exhausted the natural fertility of the soil, but planters managed to increase production by using better technology and more slaves. Although they used relatively primitive mills and distilleries, Barbados planters introduced many innovations that became standard throughout the islands. These included planting the cane in holes, the heavy use of animal manure or dung, and construction of windmills to power their mills. Intense human labor was needed to dig cane holes and to carry dung to each plant. The planters devoted more and more slaves to each acre, and the number of slaves constantly rose. Partially because they were hard driven and received inadequate amounts of imported food, slaves on Barbados and in the Leewards died at a rapid rate.

Only the wealthiest could afford to buy sugar estates with their heavy investment in machinery and slaves. A few families owned virtually all the land. By 1750, 74 families on Barbados owned 305 of the 536 cane estates. An even smaller number of families—often living in England—controlled the Leewards, where consolidation of estates and concentration of ownership increased throughout the 18th century. On Nevis, perhaps the most extreme case, planters consolidated the hundred sugar plantations existing in 1719 into less than three dozen a century later. Some families among this sugar aristocracy, especially on Barbados and Antigua, were descendants of the original settlers. Most were newcomers (many Scots) who bought estates as an investment or came to the islands as merchants or lawyers and bought up the estates of failed owners.

With their soil devoted entirely to cane production, Barbados and the Leewards could not support a white population. The planters trained their slaves as managers, slave drivers, bookkeepers, and domestic servants. There was no work for wage laborers, and white settlers preferred to emigrate to British North America. Thus the white population stagnated or (in the case of Montserrat and Nevis) fell while the number of black slaves soared. The Leewards had virtually no white population at all. (See Table 9.) Here slavery reached its most extreme state, with the slaves outnumbering the small number of estate employees fifteen or even twenty to one.

| | 1724 | | 1834 | |
|---|---|---|---|---|
| | WHITES | SLAVES | WHITES | SLAVES |
| Anguilla | 360 | 900 | 350 | 2,000 |
| Antigua | 5,200 | 19,800 | 1,980 | 23,350 |
| Saint Kitts | 4,000 | 11,500 | 1,612 | 15,667 |
| Montserrat | 1,000 | 4,400 | 330 | 5,026 |
| Nevis | 1,100 | 6,000 | 700 | 7,225 |
| Virgin Islands | 760 | 1,430 | 447 | 4,318 |

**TABLE 9. BRITISH LEEWARD ISLANDS POPULATION ESTIMATES, 1724–1834**

NOTES: For 1724, the Virgin Islands estimate includes Virgin Gorda and Tortola only. Under 1834, the estimates for Anguilla refer to 1790.

SOURCES: Alan Burns, *History of the British West Indies* Second edition, revised (London: Allen & Unwin, 1954), 461 (1724); Noel Deerr, *The History of Sugar*, 2 volumes (London: Chapman & Hall, 1949–50), II:279 (1834); Elsa Goveia, *Slave Society in the British Leeward Islands at the End of the Eighteenth Century* (New Haven: Yale University Press, 1965), 203 (Anguilla, 1790).

Barbados, the original British colony, retained a substantial white population—with one white for every four slaves. (See Table 10.) But only a small number of whites shared in the profits of the sugar industry. Many poorer planters had emigrated to Jamaica in the 1660s, and the more ambitious continued to leave. Those that remained lived in squalid poverty. By 1834, three-fourths of the whites remaining on Barbados belonged to the class known as "Redlegs" (because of their sunburned legs). Most earned a marginal living by fishing or by planting a few acres.

**TABLE 10. BARBADOS POPULATION ESTIMATES, 1712–1834**

| | TOTAL | WHITES | SLAVES | FREE NON-WHITES |
|---|---|---|---|---|
| 1712 | 54,498 | 12,528 | 41,970 | — |
| 1757 | 80.417 | 16,772 | 63,645 | — |
| 1786 | 79,115 | 16,167 | 62,115 | 833 |
| 1833–1834 | 100,242 | 12,797 | 80,861 | 6,584 |

SOURCES: Dunn, *Sugar and Slaves*, 87 (1712); Deerr, *History of Sugar*, II:278 (1757); Jerome S. Handler and Arnold A. Sio, "Barbados," *Neither Slave nor Free: The Freedmen of African Descent in the Slave Societies of the New World*, edited by David Cohen and Jack Greene (Baltimore: Johns Hopkins University Press, 1972), 218–219 (1786–1834).

## JAMAICA AND SAINT-DOMINGUE

Jamaica and Saint-Domingue—as Table 11 shows—became the world's main sugar producers during the 1740s. Both had an abundance of good land and ideal climates, but their greater size actually held back settlement until the 18th century. By 1750, Jamaica became the greatest sugar producer in the British Empire, a position it retained until the 1830s. Saint-Domingue ultimately the richest of all the sugar islands developed in two stages. Many cane estates were created in the 1720s and 1730s along the coastal region. By the 1740s, these produced more sugar than the British islands taken together. To increase production, French engineers then built an elaborate series of irrigation system in the central province that ensured Saint-Domingue's dominance of the sugar trade until 1791. Other tropical crops also flourished. Coffee, indigo, and cotton thus represented about one third (by value) of Saint-Domingue's exports in 1770.

| TABLE 11. SUGAR PRODUCTION OF SELECTED CARIBBEAN ISLANDS, 1741–1770 (Annual Averages in 1,000 U.S. tons) | | |
|---|---|---|
| | 1741–1745 | 1766–1770 |
| Saint-Domingue* | 42.4 | 61.3 |
| Jamaica | 15.6 | 36.0 |
| Antigua | 6.2 | 10.7 |
| Saint Kitts | 7.3 | 9.7 |
| Martinique | 14.2 | 8.8 |
| Saint Croix | — | 8.2 |
| Guadeloupe | 8.1 | 7.9 |
| Barbados | 6.6 | 7.8 |
| Grenada | — | 6.6 |
| Cuba | 2.0 | 5.2 |

NOTES:  Saint-Domingue became Haiti in 1804.

SOURCE:  Sheridan, *Development of the Plantations to 1750*, 23.

*Jamaica*   Wars, Maroon raids, and low sugar prices held back Jamaica's settlement until the 1720s. The French devastated the island in 1692, and Barbados continued to attract most of the available capital and slaves. Jamaicans could make their fortune more rapidly as buccaneers and smugglers or by raising cattle and cutting logwood. The government gave out large grants of land to potential sugar planters, but few developed their estates at this time. Only 70 sugar estates existed in 1675, most of them along the easily defensible southern coast near Kingston.

The Jamaican sugar industry began to flourish in the 1740s. Treaties with the Maroons in 1738 and 1739 ended their raids (page 155), British traders began to bring in many more slaves, and sugar prices remained high after 1748. Jamaica increasingly became a colony of large sugar estates. As in the Leewards, a very small population of white planters, estate managers, and other professionals controlled black slaves outnumbering them at least ten to one. In 1758, 18,000 whites supervised 180,000 slaves, and 455 sugar plantations produced 24,000 tons of sugar. (See Table 12.)

| TABLE 12.  JAMAICA POPULATION ESTIMATES, 1730–1834 | | | |
|---|---|---|---|
| | TOTAL | WHITES | SLAVES | FREE NON-WHITES |
| 1730 | 82,183 | 7,658 | 74,525 | — |
| 1758 | 198,300 | 17,900 | 176,900 | 3,500 |
| 1775 | 216,000 | 18,700 | 192,800 | 4,500 |
| 1800 | 340,000 | 30,000 | 300,000 | 10,000 |
| 1834 | 376,200 | 20,000 | 310,000 | 46,200 |
| SOURCE:  Patterson, *Slavery and Social Death*, 477. | | | |

This plantation economy, almost wholly devoted to sugar produced by black slaves, expanded rapidly during the next 25 years. By 1775 fewer than 19,000 whites ruled over 193,000 slaves. Both the size of the average plantation and output per slave had increased dramatically. Jamaican sugar exports, produced on 775 much larger plantations, had doubled to more than 40,000 tons.

Historians at one time believed that the British West Indies's economy suffered a severe decline after 1763. Supporting this interpretation was the natural inclination of the planters to exaggerate their difficulties and hide their profits from the British Parliament. Studies by present-day economic historians have now shown this interpretation to be false. The planters' private accounts indicate that Jamaica and the other British colonies remained prosperous until the 1820s. The planters were hurt by the American Revolution, but prosperity soon returned. Sugar consumption grew rapidly in Great Britain after the duty on tea was reduced in 1786, and a slave rebellion in 1791 eliminated exports from Saint-Domingue. The Napoleonic wars opened new markets on the continent, and Britain officially reopened the islands to United States shipping in 1793. Prices on the London market boomed, reaching the highest level ever recorded in March 1815.

Sugar planters significantly increased production by improving their mills, introducing superior varieties of cane and grasses, growing more food crops, and using more dung. By 1806, 859 estates—even larger and much more productive than in 1775—produced more than 80,000 tons of sugar. While the slave population had increased by 50 percent since 1775, sugar exports had doubled, and Jamaican coffee production also boomed.

*Saint-Domingue*  The natural environment divides Saint-Domingue (and present-day Haiti) into three distinct provinces, whose citizens communicate with each other as well as with France by sea. The western end of Hispaniola is shaped

Château Murat, Marie-Galante. French planters constructed island big houses in the baroque and rococo styles. A great slave rebellion (1791–1804) destroyed the French plantations on Saint-Domingue (today Haiti). This estate house survives on Marie-Galante, near Guadeloupe.

something like a capital U lying on its side. The two arms of the U (called the North and South provinces) are continuations of the great mountain chains that stretch from Central America through Cuba and on to Puerto Rico. The central sector (known as the West Province) also is mountainous, but it is cut by several major river valleys.

Sugar plantations rapidly developed in the 1720s and 1730s in the lowlands along the northern coast. The region south and east of Cap Français possessed rich soils and adequate rainfall. Moreover, planters could ship their harvest through the island's largest city and political capital.

The central or West Province, with its capital at Port-au-Prince, developed more slowly. To grow cane, planters first had to construct a sophisticated irrigation system using surface water. Parts of the province then enjoyed an abundance of fertile soil. But some of the best land received little rain because it lay within a rain-shadow to the leeward (west) of high mountain ranges. Beginning in the 1730s, French engineers constructed an elaborate system of reservoirs, diversion dams, levees, aqueducts, and canals. Altogether, more than 100,000 acres were brought under irrigation by 1791. Although the cost of these projects was huge, they quickly paid off. With irrigation, some plantations became the most productive in the Caribbean. From the 1740s to 1791, Saint-Domingue's planters produced almost as much cane (much of it in a semi-refined or clayed form) as the British West Indies put together.

The South Province, the bottom arm of the U, was the last to develop. Using irrigation, planters created substantial sugar estates on the coastal Les Cayes plain. Elsewhere in this region, coffee provided the main product from the 1730s. This crop was grown on many, comparatively smaller, estates in the hills, some owned by colored freedmen. Only a few small towns—Jérémie, Les Cayes, and Jacmel—served the area.

## GUADELOUPE AND MARTINIQUE

Tobacco remained important on Guadeloupe and Martinique until about 1660, when the French tobacco monopoly switched to Virginia leaf. These islands developed cane estates more slowly than Saint-Domingue. Thus they had fewer inhabitants, both white and slave, and planters were more likely to reside on the island. Fort Royal (today Fort-de-France) was the political capital of the French Antilles, while Saint-Pierre (destroyed by a volcanic explosion in 1902) was a major commercial center and the first stop for slave ships from Africa. Thus both islands served the French empire as trading posts more than as producers of tropical products. Both islands had a significant number of free coloreds (Table 18 page 163), but they were less affluent than on Saint-Domingue. More free coloreds worked as artisans or retailers in the towns, and fewer owned plantations and slaves.

## THE WINDWARD ISLANDS

By the Treaty of Paris in 1763, Great Britain gained control of Saint Vincent, Dominica, Grenada, and Tobago. Britain returned Saint Lucia to France, but British forces reoccupied the island in 1778 and 1794 (page 141).

La Pagerie, Martinique. This estate was the birthplace of Marie-Rose Tacher de la Pagerie, later Empress Josephine, first wife of Napoleon Bonaparte. Pictured is La Pagerie's massive stone kitchen, now a museum. A hurricane destroyed the plantation big house in 1766.

Thousands of British and Scotch adventurers descended on the islands, hoping to repeat the success of planters in Barbados, the Leewards, and Jamaica a century earlier. They quickly cleared the forests, built mills, and imported thousands of new Africans.

The newly established sugar plantations flourished for 20 years on Saint Vincent and Grenada. But they were devastated by rebellions in 1795 (page 168). The Black Carib held Saint Vincent for six months, while rebel slaves controlled Grenada for more than a year. By the time British military forces reoccupied the islands, the rebels had killed many white settlers and sacked their plantations.[6] It was even more difficult to subdue rebellious slaves on Dominica. The island's mountainous terrain allowed runaway slaves to establish Maroon communities, which the British could not eradicate until 1814. Because of these disturbances, some planters left Saint Vincent, Dominica, and Grenada. Most moved on to Saint Lucia and Trinidad, which were comparatively tranquil and contained large areas of unoccupied land.

| TABLE 13. WINDWARD ISLANDS POPULATION ESTIMATES, 1763–1832 | | | | |
|---|---|---|---|---|
| | TOTAL | WHITES | SLAVES | FREE NON-WHITES |
| **Dominica** | | | | |
| 1763 | 8,090 | 1,718 | 5,872 | 500 |
| 1788 | 16,648 | 1,236 | 14,967 | 445 |
| 1805 | 26,449 | 1,594 | 22,083 | 2,822 |
| 1832 | 19,225 | 791 | 14,387 | 4,077 |
| **Saint Lucia** | | | | |
| 1765 | 13,717 | 2,397 | 10,270 | 1,050 |
| 1789 | 21,778 | 2,198 | 17,992 | 1,588 |
| 1825 | 18,595 | 1,194 | 13,530 | 3,871 |
| **Saint Vincent** | | | | |
| 1763 | 5,263 | 695 | 3,430 | 1,138 |
| 1787 | 13,603 | 1,450 | 11,853 | 300 |
| 1825 | 22,239 | 1,301 | 18,114 | 2,842 |
| **Grenada** | | | | |
| 1753 | 13,426 | 1,262 | 11,991 | 173 |
| 1771 | 27,872 | 1,661 | 26,211 | — |
| 1829 | 28,732 | 801 | 24,145 | 3,786 |
| SOURCES: Watts, *West Indies*, 316, 318; Patterson, *Slavery and Social Death*, 479. | | | | |

## THE SPANISH ISLANDS

From 1713, the British and French islands followed Barbados in adopting sugar as their main or only crop. Yet the islands ruled by Spain long remained *hacienda*, or rancher, societies, not unlike those later found in the western United States.

Here vast herds of cattle roamed open ranges between isolated towns. Governmental regulation rather than a lack of natural resources hindered the development of sugar estates in the Spanish colonies. Under the Laws of the Indies, Spain limited trade to two convoys a year. Only Spanish ships could trade with her islands, but few Spanish ships called at their ports. Economic development thus became possible when the reforming Bourbon dynasty eased trade restrictions during the 1760s. Cuban planters now began to create cane estates, setting the stage for rapid growth during the 19th century. Change came more slowly to Puerto Rico and Santo Domingo, where large sugar estates were created only during the 20th century.

## CUBA COMES UNDER SPANISH CONTROL

During the 1600s, Havana had prospered as the main port of the yearly fleets that carried Mexican silver to Spain. Because of the port's strategic importance, its captain-general received political and military authority over the entire island. In fact, the captain-generals had little power in the countryside, especially in the central and eastern provinces. There local property owners governed through town councils (*cabildos*). The sharp contrast between prosperous western Cuba and the sparsely populated eastern provinces thus began early. Since the early 1600s, most Cubans have lived in the more prosperous west. All successful revolutions have begun in the lightly governed eastern provinces and then marched west against Havana.

Spanish efforts to reassert authority over the Americas began under the Bourbon dynasty, which replaced the Habsburgs in 1714. The Bourbons sought greater political and economic control because they needed colonial wealth to develop Spain's economy. Cuba and other relatively prosperous regions now lost the autonomy they had gained during earlier centuries. In 1729, all Cuban *cabildos* thus lost the authority to distribute unoccupied land among local residents. To control smuggling, many municipal governments were brought under the army.

Cuba enjoyed modest economic growth after 1713 because of increased access to French markets. But the Bourbon government obstructed Cuban progress by placing commerce under state-sponsored monopolies. In 1717, it brought all tobacco production under a royal monopoly (the Factoría de Tabacos), and it used the military to crush uprisings by tobacco farmers in 1717, 1729, 1723. Displaced farmers fled to new settlements east and west of Havana, and smuggled their crops out of the island.

In 1740, the Spanish government created a new monopoly with even greater powers. The Royal Company of Commerce (Real Compañía de Commercio) received total control over all trade between Spain and Cuba. The company bought Cuban sugar, tobacco, and hides at low prices, and it sharply marked up Spanish imports. It made enormous profits at the expense of Cuban farmers. The monopoly hampered Cuba's commercial development, and Havana increasingly suffered food shortages.

## THE CUBAN SUGAR BOOM BEGINS

The British conquest of Havana during the Seven Years War (page 146) transformed Cuba. The British controlled Havana for less than eleven months
(1762–63), but their occupation eliminated all the obstacles to Cuban sugar
development. Cuba was thrown open to free trade with Britain's American
colonies. More than 10,000 ships entered Havana harbor—a port that had not
seen more than 15 vessels a year during the previous ten years. The British
occupation freed Cuban planters from the restrictions and high prices of the
Royal Company. Above all, it gave them the labor they needed to expand
production as British merchants brought in some 10,000 slaves—as many as
would normally have entered in two decades. (See Table 22, page 201.)

Cuba had flourished during Spain's absence. Charles III (1759–1788), an
"enlightened despot," was willing to make reforms that would continue commercial growth and increase the king's revenues. From 1765, the Crown
gradually lifted all restrictions on trade between Cuba and the Spanish Empire.
Beginning in 1789, it permitted both Spanish and foreign slavers to bring in
African slaves without restrictions or taxes, and it allowed unlimited cultivation
and unrestricted sale of tobacco from 1817. In February 1818, Spain finally
opened the island to ships of all nations. However, customs tariffs discriminated
against island exports and foreign imports carried aboard non-Spanish ships.

The wars of the American and French revolutions also benefited Cuba's
sugar industry. The Anglo-Spanish war from 1779 to 1783 allowed North
American merchants to visit the island. Trade with the United States—although
still illegal—increased after 1783, and Cuba replaced the British colonies as
America's main source of sugar. Cuban planters similarly profited from the 1791
slave revolution on Saint-Domingue, which removed that producer from the
market.

Sugar prices remained at high levels for sixty years after 1762, reaching their
peak in 1815. Allowed access to the world market, sugar planters rapidly
expanded production. (See Table 8, page 105.) Ten thousand acres were devoted
to sugarcane in 1761, 160 thousand in 1792. The 100 primitive mills of 1763
grew to more than 1,000 in 1827, now larger and technically more advanced.
As cane fields spread, planters cut down and burned the vast forests covering
the island.

## SANTO DOMINGO AND PUERTO RICO

Efforts to develop Puerto Rico's agricultural potential began toward the end of
the 18th century. The Crown sent a trusted representative, Marshal Alejandro
O'Reilly, to tour the island in 1765. Based on O'Reilly's report, Spain bolstered
the defenses of San Juan, reformed governmental practices, and allowed foreigners to sell slaves. A decree of 1778 welcomed skilled artisans and planters who
professed the Roman Catholic faith and took an oath of allegiance to the Crown.
The population tripled by 1800, and the local militia defeated a British army of
10,000 men that attacked San Juan in April 1797.

| TABLE 14. PUERTO RICO POPULATION ESTIMATES, 1765–1802 | | | |
|---|---|---|---|
| | TOTAL | WHITES | SLAVES | FREE NON-WHITES |
| 1765 | 44,883 | — | 5,037 | — |
| 1775 | 71,260 | 29,263 | 7,487 | 34,510 |
| 1802 | 163,192 | 78,281 | 13,333 | 71,578 |
| SOURCE: Watts, *West Indies*, 321. | | | |

Investors tended to favor Cuba, and they paid less attention to Santo Domingo (Hispaniola). Perhaps as few as 6,000 *vecinos* inhabited the entire colony in 1730. The situation improved somewhat after 1740. Ranchers found a ready market for beef in French Saint-Domingue, several ports were opened to foreign commerce, and substantial immigration began from the Canary Islands. By 1785, the total population had risen to about 125,000—one-third of those living under French rule in the western part of the island. Some 40,000 of these are described as "Spanish" or white, and about the same number were slaves.

## TRINIDAD

Until the reforms of the 1770s and 1780s, Trinidad was neglected and undeveloped and had few contacts even with the neighboring mainland province of Venezuela. Cacao became the most important crop until 1725, when the coca trees were blighted, probably by a fungus. Some settlers left, and others were killed by disease, especially by a smallpox epidemic in 1741. A 1733 census reported 162 non-Indian adults, including 28 whites. The Arawak living on Trinidad fared somewhat better than those in the Greater Antilles, who quickly died off; some 2,000 Indians still lived on the island in 1777. From the 1780s, however, the rapid opening up of the island for plantation development brought about the virtual disappearance of Indian villages.[7]

| TABLE 15. TRINIDAD POPULATION ESTIMATES, 1777–1834 | | | |
|---|---|---|---|
| | TOTAL | WHITES | SLAVES | FREE NON-WHITES |
| 1777 | 1,410 | 340 | 200 | 870 |
| 1797 | 17,716* | 2,151 | 10,009 | 4,474 |
| 1802 | 28,477* | 2,261 | 19,709 | 5,275 |
| 1825 | 42,174* | 3,214 | 23,230 | 15,003 |
| 1834 | 44,715 | 3,632 | 22,359 | 18,724 |
| NOTE: "Total" includes native Americans during the following years: 1797 (1,082), 1802 (1,232), 1825 (727). | | | |
| SOURCE: Patterson, *Slavery and Social Death*, 479. | | | |

The lowest point in the colony's life was probably reached following the 1741 smallpox epidemic. In the *Loss of El Dorado*, the Trinidadian author, V. S.

Naipaul quotes contemporary records that describe the *vecinos* of Saint Joseph living "in drunken isolation." A new governor in 1757 commanded its inhabitants to clean up the town, to build a meeting hall for the *cabildo*, and to keep its minutes in "a decent book, properly bound." As Naipaul recounts the incident, the citizens found excuse after excuse to not to comply with his orders.

It would take them more than a year to clear the streets and fill the holes, if they had tools. They didn't have tools and couldn't afford to buy any; and there were no tools on the island anyway. . . . Orders will be given to Pedro Bontur, the only carpenter in the island to make the chest for the records. . . . But his Excellency the Governor must provide the boards, the cabildo knowing no one on the island who can make them; and when opportunity offers, His Excellency must get the locks and hinges for the same from the Main, nothing of the kind being available here. Orders will be given for the papers of the cabildo to be properly arranged; and a book will be made when paper is available, the members of the cabildo not having a single sheet between them at the moment.[8]

## CHAPTER TEN

# THE WORLD OF THE SLAVES

∎

Sugar enriched many planters as well as their European creditors and suppliers—and sugar made slavery necessary. The labor of black slaves was the basis for life on the sugar islands from the 17th century. Economically, socially, and politically, slavery dominated the islands to an extent never matched in human history. By the 1750s, almost nine out of ten men and women were slaves on all the islands where sugar was grown. Never before in human history had so high a proportion of a population been slaves.[1]

Slavery tended to change over time as the island economies developed. At first, most slaves worked as hands on cane estates. By the end of the 18th century, slaves did every conceivable type of task—thus creating an entire range of situations from total bondage to comparative freedom. Blacks condemned to gang labor on sugar estates had the least control over their own lives. White overseers and black drivers controlled every minute of their day. Slaves doing other sorts of work could exercise more initiative and set their own pace. The greatest autonomy was enjoyed by skilled craftsmen and slaves living in towns—for example, in the seaports of the Virgin Islands, Curaçao, or the Bahamas.

In the Caribbean slave societies, sugar and human misery went together. On an individual basis, some slaves may have lived decent lives—as good as or better than those of European laborers during the same centuries. Urban slaves and those on islands without sugar fared the best. Slaves endured the harshest labor and most rigid controls during the early years of development, as planters set up estates. During these years, life on the islands was brutal and rough for both owners and slaves. As their masters prospered, some slaves enjoyed better treatment, and governments strove to improve or "ameliorate" slave conditions from about 1770.

Overall, the sugar islands failed the most basic test of slave well-being—the ability to survive and multiply. Before about 1800, death rates among Caribbean slaves always were much higher than birth rates. Perhaps the most telling indictment of the sugar islands is the happier fate of Africans carried to North America. While island blacks died out, the slave population rapidly multiplied in British North America and the United States. Since Caribbean slaves died without reproducing themselves, the sugar estates could operate only by constantly importing enormous numbers of new slaves. Moreover, the high death rate among slaves in the Caribbean does not tell the entire story. Millions more died while they were being brought across the Atlantic to the sugar islands. The slaughter started during the dread "Middle Passage."

## THE SLAVE TRADE BOOMS DURING THE 18TH CENTURY

Except for the Spanish, all the colonial powers encouraged and were directly involved in the Atlantic slave trade.[2] Until the 1680s, the Dutch West India Company dominated Atlantic commerce, including the slave trade. The British and French then destroyed Dutch commercial power during the Second (1665–1667) and Third (1672–1678) Dutch Wars. Great Britain henceforth flourished as the supreme slaving nation in the Atlantic world. Between 1690 and 1807, British traders exported some 2,500,000 slaves to the Caribbean and Spanish America. Envying British success, the French government tried to foster participation by its own nationals. But French entry into the slave trade was slow and ineffective. During the 18th century, French slavers exported from Africa only half as many slaves as British traders.

Because of the peculiar nature of the slave trade, European governments believed they needed to garrison fortified settlements and warehouses along the coast of West Africa. These forts provided a safe haven where their nationals received and stored slaves provided by African rulers and slave dealers. And the forts also protected them from attack by hostile European powers (especially, at first, the Dutch). These trading posts were enormously expensive, and private capital was not at first ready to enter the business. During the 17th century, the Dutch, French, British, and Danish governments thus set up privileged state companies for Africa. In return for maintaining the African forts, these were granted legal monopolies over the slave trade.

None of these monopoly companies made money or brought over enough slaves to satisfy the Caribbean planters, and all countries turned to free trade. The British government allowed the charter of the Royal Africa Company to expire in 1712. In France, a royal decree in 1716 largely opened the trade to all Frenchmen who fitted out their ships in any of five major ports. Further reforms effectively opened the slave trade to almost all French merchants by 1741. Moreover, the government further encouraged the trade by exempting slaves from certain export and import duties and collecting only a modest tax on slaves imported into its colonies.

## THE MAJOR SLAVE ROUTES TO THE CARIBBEAN

Under the free trade regime, the British and French slave trades dramatically expanded. At their high point in the 1790s, British traders, many headquartered in Liverpool, brought almost 50,000 slaves each year to the Caribbean. At first, they carried most slaves to Barbados. From 1720, Jamaica took the lion's share of British slave exports. The acquisition of the Ceded Islands and especially Grenada opened up new markets after 1763. Although British America also

| TABLE 16. ESTIMATED SLAVE IMPORTS, BY IMPORTING REGION, 1601–1870 (in thousands) | | | | |
|---|---|---|---|---|
| | 1601–1700 | 1701–1760 | 1761–1810 | 1811–1870 | TOTAL |
| **CARIBBEAN REGION** | | | | | 4,059.9 |
| **British Islands** | | | | | 1,664.8 |
| Barbados | 134.5 | 180.4 | 72.0 | — | 386.9 |
| Leeward Islands | 44.1 | 142.4 | 159.5 | — | 346.0 |
| Jamaica | 85.1 | 263.8 | 398.5 | — | 747.4 |
| Windward Islands | — | — | 70.1 | — | 70.1 |
| Trinidad | — | — | 22.4 | — | 22.4 |
| Grenada | — | — | 67.0 | — | 67.0 |
| Other | — | 10.0 | 15.0 | — | 25.0 |
| **French Islands** | | | | | 1,521.0 |
| Martinique | 66.5 | 146.8 | 111.6 | 41.0 | 365.9 |
| Guadeloupe | 12.7 | 160.5 | 76.6 | 41.0 | 290.8 |
| Saint-Domingue | 74.6 | 308.7 | 481.0 | — | 864.3 |
| **Spanish Islands** | | | | | 766.9 |
| Santo Domingo | — | — | 6.0 | — | 6.0 |
| Cuba | — | — | 139.2 | 550.0 | 689.2 |
| Puerto Rico | — | — | 16.6 | 55.1 | 71.7 |
| **Danish Islands** | 4.0 | 20.0 | 33.0 | 0.2 | 57.2 |
| **Dutch Islands** | | | | | 50.0 |
| **SOUTH AMERICA** | | | | | 4,879.1 |
| Brazil | 560.0 | 959.6 | 931.8 | 1,145.4 | 3,596.8 |
| Spanish colonies | 292.5 | 271.2 | 167.6 | — | 731.3 |
| Dutch Guiana | 40.0 | 280.0 | 180.0 | — | 500.0 |
| French Guiana | 2.0 | 21.0 | 14.0 | 14.0 | 51.0 |
| **NORTH AMERICA** | | | | | 455.7 |
| British/U.S.A. | 28.5 | 170.6 | 177.4 | 51.0 | 427.5 |
| French Louisiana | — | 18.0 | 10.2 | — | 28.2 |

NOTES: Prior to 1760, small numbers of slaves illegally were smuggled into the Spanish islands. The British Windward Islands comprise Saint Vincent, Saint Lucia, Tobago, and Dominica. "South America" includes Mexico and Central America. "Dutch Guiana" consists of Surinam, Demerara, Berbice, and Essequibo.

SOURCES: Philip Curtin, *The Atlantic Slave Trade: A Census* (Madison: University of Wisconsin Press, 1969), 35, 40, 44, 85, 216, 234, 268–69; James Rawley, *The Trans-Atlantic Slave Trade* (New York, 1981), 100, 167.

imported slaves, the Caribbean plantations were the main consumer of slaves. The thirteen mainland colonies purchased only half as many slaves as the one small island of Jamaica.

After the Portuguese and the British, the French were the most important slave dealers. French slavers brought in about 150,000 slaves during the 17th century and more than one million during the 18th. However, the sugar plantations on Saint-Domingue consumed slaves so rapidly—especially after 1763—that French traders never met their needs. Between 1701 and 1810, French merchants supplied only two-thirds of the French West Indian market, with British, Dutch, and North American merchants making up the deficit.

French ships invariably stopped first at Martinique, their first landfall out of Africa. A few ships occasionally went to Guadeloupe, but most either sold their cargo on Martinique or continued on to Saint-Domingue. After 1730, Saint-Domingue became the preferred destination, receiving more than three-quarters of all French slaves in the 1780s. Before going on to Saint-Domingue, traders rested the slaves on Martinique or on one of the tiny islands nearby. After the deadly Middle Passage, most needed a few days of rest to regain the appearance of good health.

The Dutch, whose small and arid islands were only minor sugar producers, primarily brought in slaves for sale on the British and French islands and on the Spanish mainland. Although Dutch merchants lost their dominance of the trade during the 1680s, they remained highly competitive carriers. Dutch slave imports actually grew during the 18th century, but their cargoes now formed only a dwindling proportion of an immensely larger trade. Altogether the two West India companies carried about 225,000 slaves to the Caribbean and Spanish America, while Dutch free traders imported another 50,000 into the West Indies between 1734 and 1803.[3] Curaçao flourished as a slave depot into the 1720s. In later years, most Dutch slavers headed for Sint Eustatius to supply the French market.

The Danish West India Company also built forts and factories on the African coast. The company colonized Saint Thomas for use as a slave depot, and the Danish slave trade expanded after it purchased Saint Croix in 1733. Following the Dutch example, the Danish government abolished the company's monopoly in 1734, opening the trade to all Danish merchants. Saint Croix received substantial numbers of Africans for use on its own plantations. As a free port, it also developed into a major center for the inter-island or secondary market in slaves. Generally, larger ships from Africa docked at Christiansted, while smaller vessels from the West Indies used the lesser port at Frederiksted.

## THE SLAVE TRADE IN AFRICA

The Africans brought to the Caribbean already were slaves in Africa, and they were sold to European traders by their African owners. Almost all came from western Africa, usually from tribes living within 200 miles of the coast. Over the centuries, the slave trade tended to move slowly down the coast of West Africa, from the Senegambian region down to the Congo and Angola. During the 1800s, Biafra and the west-central regions contributed most slaves, with perhaps 10 percent coming from Mozambique on the eastern coast.

Slavery always was widespread in West Africa, often taking in one-third or more of the population. However, some scholars believe that African slavery during earlier eras usually involved smaller groups in face-to-face relationships.

Thus, traditional African forms of slavery presumably were less harsh than slavery on Caribbean sugar estates.

In precolonial Africa, no one really was a free individual, and the family, kinship grouping, or lineage was the dominant political and economic institution. African kinship groups sought to assimilate newly bought slaves into their circle—although in a subordinate position or status. Over several generations, the descendants of these slaves might come to belong to the tribe. Many slave villages might then work under their own management, paying a tribute something like that owed by serfs in medieval Europe.

But only settled and assimilated slaves belonged to the tribe. Most new slaves were taken in war, kidnapped on raids disguised as wars, or convicted as criminals. Immediately after capture or trial, a new slave's life was forfeit, and his master could treat him as he liked. Usually the master tried to sell new slaves as far away as possible from the region where they were taken. This prevented them running away to their own kinship group.

Since African societies contained many slaves, an extensive internal slave trade had developed. When the Portuguese landed on the West African coast in 1450, they found that a complex system of trade routes already crossed the continent. Since the 600s, organized intercontinental slave trades had transported millions of Africans north and east to the slave-holding Islamic states. A northern route carried perhaps seven to ten million slaves across the Sahara to North Africa and Egypt. An eastern network took some five million slaves north to Egypt and the Middle East, or across the Red Sea to Arabia.

After the Europeans arrived, Africans continued to control the supply of slaves to the transatlantic trade. Because they had no immunity to malaria and yellow fever, Europeans (and North Africans) literally could not live in West Africa.[4] Moreover, African warriors were equal or superior to Europeans, and their weapons were as effective until the end of the 19th century. European traders visited the slave coast at the sufferance of its African rulers. They did not create trade networks. They simply set up forts along the coast that tapped into the routes of Africa's already existing slave trade.

African slave dealers charged high prices in trade goods. As more and more slave ships came to the West African coast, prices rose sharply during the 18th century. Obviously, selling prices could vary between widely separated African ports. Overall, the average price of a male slave probably doubled from about £10 in the 1700s to £20 in 1740. It then dipped before rising again in the 1780s, to an average of £25 on the Gold Coast.

European purchasers, who competed for supplies with both the internal and Middle East trades, had to take what African sellers offered them. Thus we cannot identify the precise origins of Caribbean blacks. European traders named slaves after the port where they purchased them, even though many had been captured hundreds of miles away. With rare exceptions, Europeans knew little about the political or cultural origins of the slaves they bought.

Because of the strong African demand, sellers tended to offer Europeans only the "least indispensable" slaves.[5] African owners valued female slaves more highly than males. Thus fewer women than men showed up at slave markets, and the European slave traders mainly shipped adult males. Overall, European slavers carried twice as many men as women to the Americas, and children under ten years of age made up less than 10 percent of their cargoes.

## THE MIDDLE PASSAGE

Slave traders often spent several months purchasing slaves at various ports. As soon as they accumulated their cargo, they sailed for the Americas with their captives on the notorious Middle Passage. Most followed a direct route due west to near the Ascension Islands and then turned north toward the West Indies and Martinique or Barbados. Tropical storms or the doldrums near the equator could delay the voyage, which might take as little as one month or as long as half a year.

As the trade boomed during the 18th century, slavers of all nations carried, fed, and treated slaves in similar ways. Slave ships tended to be small and narrow. Into their limited cargo space, their captains packed an average of three hundred captives and a relatively large crew of thirty-five to control the slaves. On average they allotted each captive only half the amount of room afforded convicts, emigrants, or soldiers transported during the same years.

All traders used temporary platforms between decks to provide sleeping space. Male slaves, but not women or children, were shackled together in pairs—left leg to right leg, left wrist to right wrist. Some captains removed the shackles once the ship was at sea, others took them off during the day, and some left their captives chained throughout the voyage. Most fed the slaves on dried beans, rice, corn, yams, and palm oil—with meat a rare treat.

The Middle Passage took a heavy toll of Europeans as well as Africans. All told, 13 percent of the slaves carried aboard French ships during the 18th century died before reaching the West Indies. And almost one out of five seamen sailing out of Nantes did not return to France. During the early years, outbreaks of smallpox, measles, or other highly communicable diseases caused astronomical death rates on some voyages. At all times, anemic dysentery and scurvy were the biggest killers. Contrary to legend, overcrowding or "tight packing" was not the major cause of death on board. Since the risk of dysentery increases with time at sea, the death rate instead rose with the length of the voyage, the quality of food and water during the passage, and epidemics and health conditions at the time of departure in Africa.

Slaves were expensive. Since they could not resell dead or diseased slaves, all captains had a strong economic motive to minimize losses. Most ships carried surgeons, but their medical efforts did the sick little good. Death rates dropped after 1750 because Europeans used faster ships, learned more about hygiene and diet, and introduced crude forms of vaccination against smallpox. On average, about 20 percent of the slaves died during the Middle Passage before 1700, compared to some 5 percent around 1800.

Although it killed fewer victims as slavers improved their techniques, the Middle Passage deserves the universal condemnation it has received. Whether it was caused by cruelty or by ignorance, even a 5 percent death rate (in 1800) is extraordinary among young adults during a two to three month voyage. Moreover, many additional slaves died on the way to the ships before leaving Africa. No precise accounting is possible. But as many as eight million Africans may have died to bring four million slaves to the Caribbean islands.

## THE UNIQUE NATURE OF CARIBBEAN SLAVERY

Slavery is difficult to define precisely. Individual freedom, the logical opposite of slavery, is a modern concept. Before the 19th century, hardly anyone was free in our sense of the word. Ties and obligations, which they could not unilaterally dissolve, constrained most persons and limited their freedom of action. Every individual belonged to one or more communities and was bound by family traditions, village customs, obligations to lords, or craft regulations. Even today, it is questionable whether we can accurately describe as "free" the many men and women laboring at jobs they dislike in order to purchase food, clothing, and housing.

What made slavery on tropical plantations unusual was the master's total freedom of control over his or her slaves. In most agricultural societies, serfs were members of a village governed by communal traditions. Their lord usually could not interfere with the customary ways of doing things. By contrast, Caribbean sugar plantations resembled factories in a modern capitalist society. To meet the demands of the world market, the owner and his agents had to manage rigorously all steps of production. Until the end of the 18th century, most sugar estates used the "gang" system. The owner treated dozens or hundreds of slaves literally as units of production. He organized their labor from day to day and even hour to hour. And he used physical force to ensure that, like cogs in a well-oiled machine, the slaves performed their assigned tasks on time.

Slaves working on cane estates always suffered the harshest conditions and labored under the most rigorous controls. The very nature of the sugarcane industry partially explains the master's need for total control. The weight and bulk of harvested cane are enormous compared to other grasses. (As a rule of thumb in the 18th century, planters needed 20 pounds of cane to make 1 pound of sugar.) Thus growers can not export cane unless they first concentrate the sugar by milling it. In this process, machines squeeze out the cane juice, which then is boiled to evaporate excess water, producing crystalline sugar and a by-product called molasses.

Milling is crucial and must be done quickly. Laborers must cut sugar as soon as it is ripe and then take it to the mill within 24 hours or it will ferment. For this reason, immediate access to a sugar mill is essential. From the 1860s, most notably in Cuba, several dependent farmers (*colonos*) brought their cane to a large mill (*central*) owned by a dominant planter or corporation. During the 18th century, however, every planter thought it necessary to have his own mill under his total control.

A sugar plantation—a "factory set in a field"[6]—thus combined agriculture and manufacturing. It was a novel social, economic, and political organization, which brought together large amounts of capital and human labor and combined them on tropical soils. To make a profit, a planter had to manage and coordinate a complex series of tasks. For the slaves, most of these tasks involved intense and monotonous labor.

## ISLAND LAWS GIVE PLANTERS UNLIMITED POWER OVER THEIR SLAVES

Planters, especially on cane estates, had to exercise close control over their slaves. At least through the 18th century, island laws granted them the unlimited powers they needed, and the courts seldom bothered with the relationships between slaves and masters. Since slavery now was rare in western Europe, the colonies had to develop new laws regulating slavery. The legislature of each British island made its own laws—with the consent of the governor and Crown—for and peculiar to that colony. Laws were harshest where slaves greatly outnumbered their owners (Jamaica) and less severe in islands without sugar plantations (the Bahamas).

French, Dutch, Danish, and Spanish islands in theory enjoyed less local initiative, since they were governed by royal laws. In 1685 the Crown proclaimed one single Code Noir (Black Code) governing the treatment of slaves in all French colonies. However, although it was drawn up in the mother country, French jurists based the Code Noir on practices and precedents in the Antilles. Thus, it was at least as oppressive in many areas as the laws passed by legislatures on the British islands.

All islands sought to protect the planter and not the slave. Whether British, French, Spanish, Dutch, or Danish, all courts savagely punished slaves who rebelled or struck their masters. In these cases, the penalties included slow death by torture and the loss of an ear, hand, or leg. Early slave codes also authorized mutilation for persistent runaways and theft.

Except for the Spanish, slave codes treated the slaves as property and thus allowed planters to do as they pleased with their slaves. British slave laws often did not mention slave marriages, families, education, or religious conversion. The French Code Noir did recognize marriage and required slaves to be baptized. But slaves could not marry without their master's consent, and owners did not have to provide time off for religious education or worship.

The differences between these slave laws mattered little in practice. The sugar planters and their agents dominated colonial society and controlled local affairs. London, Paris, Copenhagen, and The Hague sent governors to the islands under their flags. But these governors could act effectively only with the support of the colonial planters. On all islands, slavery was regulated by local courts and customary law.

The French Code Noir and Spanish colonial laws were more generous than British laws in their treatment of manumission (the gaining of free status). By prohibiting manumission without the owner's consent, the British colonies made it almost impossible to gain freedom. More slaves became free in the Spanish colonies, such as Cuba. Courts in these colonies frequently allowed slaves to own personal property, make contracts, and buy their freedom with their own savings. To a more limited extent, self-purchase also became part of the customary law in the French islands. French (and Spanish) courts also permitted marriage between white males and freed female slaves, whose children thus became free as well.

French law gave freed slaves full legal rights of citizenship. But British colonies usually denied freed slaves all legal privileges except that of a jury trial. Even if free, blacks and persons of color in British colonies could not vote or hold political office, and laws forbade them to enter certain trades. Thus freedmen were both more numerous and more powerful in the French colonies. They were especially influential in the South and West provinces of Saint-Domingue, where they took a major part in the revolution of 1791.

## THE HARSH LIFE OF A FIELD SLAVE

By the 18th century, sugarcane estates could not function without the labor of African slaves, who were bound to the soil by strict laws. The slave in turn became bound up in a rhythm of unceasing labor determined by the needs of the sugar plant itself. Work routines fell into a fixed and unvarying pattern. In a set sequence of steps, the slaves prepared and manured the soil, then planted, weeded, harvested, crushed, cured, boiled, and sometimes distilled the cane. As soon as they had completed one task, another demanded the attention of the planter and slaves.

Before land could be used for sugarcane, slaves with axes removed and burned the existing trees and brush. Once they cleared the land, owners laid out sugar plantations in patterns that made crop rotation easier, saved on transportation costs, and simplified slave management. Most planters divided their property into three to five large cane fields. Each year they harvested canes from one part of the land, with the other fields divided among growing canes and fallow. On the larger islands of Jamaica and Saint-Domingue, a sugar plantation usually took up about four times the amount of land given to cane. The cane mill and the boiling and refining houses occupied a central location in the middle of the fields. The remaining acres were taken up by food plots ("provision grounds"), grazing land, the planter's house, slave quarters, workshops, and animal pens.

## THE PLANTATION AS FARM: PLANTING AND HARVESTING SUGARCANE

Planters generally harvested cane about eighteen months after it was planted. They timed planting and harvesting to coincide with the island's rainy and dry seasons. During the rainy season—May/June to December/January—the slaves dug holes and dunged, planted, fertilized, and weeded the growing plants.

African slaves harvesting sugar in Cuba, 19th century. ("Raza Negra-Negros de Guinea en Cuba.") Tools similar to those shown also were used during previous centuries. Field gangs often contained more women than men.

During the dry season, from January to May/June, they harvested and processed the mature crop, cutting the canes and carrying them to the mill to be ground.

Sugarcane is propagated through cuttings from the tops of mature plants. Originally these were planted in long trenches. From the 1720s, most planters adopted holing to prevent soil erosion and conserve moisture. Using hand-held hoes, the slaves dug holes 5 to 6 inches deep and about 5 foot square. They then laid one or two cane tops in the center of each hole and covered them with about two inches of soil. As the plant sprouted and grew taller, the slaves filled the hole with mold and dung until the field was level. During the following weeks, they weeded and thinned the growing plants and inserted new cuttings to replace any failing to grow. After five or six months, the canes were large enough to keep down the weeds.

This method of planting involved extremely heavy labor. Particularly on clay soils baked hard by the sun, holing is arduous work, and only the fittest of the slaves could endure it. Because the land was cut up by the cane holes, slaves had to spread dung by hand. Long files of slaves, usually women, carried the heavy dung baskets to the fields.

To spread out the harvest, planting was staggered over several months early in the rainy season. Cane planted in July was ready to be harvested 18 months later in January. Thus, the slaves performed one difficult task after another during the entire period from July through March. The heavy labor of holing, dunging, and weeding had barely ended, when it was time to begin cutting, hauling, and milling the mature cane.

Harvesting the cane was as difficult as holing. Using machetes, cutlasses, or long heavy "bills," the slaves chopped off the canes close to the ground. They then stripped the canes of leaves and cut them into shorter pieces 3 or 4 feet in length. These heavy bundles were then carried to the mills by the slaves, on pack animals, or in carts drawn by cattle or mules.

## THE PLANTATION AS FACTORY: SUGAR MILLING AND REFINING

At the mill the slaves crushed the cane to remove the liquid or juice, which boiled and clarified until it crystallized into sugar. As a final step, they might distil molasses (the residue remaining after the cane is clarified) into rum at the still house. The first step, crushing or milling the cane, used a vertical three-roller mill.[7] Wind, water, slaves, or cattle turned the middle roller. Through interconnecting cogs and teeth, it turned the two rollers on either side.

Two slaves fed the newly cut canes into this mill. One in front of the rollers inserted the canes. The other behind the rollers received the crushed stalks and passed them back to extract the rest of the liquid. The cane juice from the rollers ran off into a series of as many as seven copper vats of decreasing size. Slaves added lime water to the boiling cane syrup, and they removed the gross matter with a long-handled skimmer. From the last boiler, the liquid sugar was emptied into wooden troughs or coolers. If the boiling was successful, the liquid cooled into a mixture of crystals and molasses. After thirteen or fourteen hours, a plug at the bottom of each trough was removed, permitting the molasses to drain off.

This first stage of grinding and boiling produced a coarse brownish product known as *muscovado*, from a Portuguese word meaning "less finished." Many planters shipped the sugar in this state, but some went on to make a semi-refined grade known as clayed sugar. Slaves placed the muscovado into cone-shaped clay molds, and covered the top of each mold with a whitish clay. This helped to purge the sugar of molasses as the water drained down through the sugar toward a small hole in the bottom of the cone. Work in the sugar mill, where the constant heat of the fires raised the temperature above 120 degrees, was as

demanding as field labor. It also demanded considerable skill. The slave supervising the boiling operations had an especially demanding job. More than any
one else his judgment could mean the difference between a profit or loss.

On most islands, cattle, horses, mules, or even the slaves themselves turned
the sugar mill's rollers. On low-lying islands open to the trade winds—especially
Barbados but also on Antigua, Saint Kitts, and lowland Guadeloupe—planters
introduced windmills during the 18th century. Water mills primarily were found
in the French islands. Many plantations on Saint-Domingue introduced water
mills in the 1740s and 1750s. To a lesser extent, planters also built water mills
on Guadeloupe, Martinique, and Jamaica.

Refining represents the third and last stage in sugar making. The raw
product was reheated, and egg whites, white vinegar, or bullock's blood was

Stone windmill, Saint Croix. One of dozens of windmills that provided power to grind
sugarcane. Wind-powered mills were especially popular on low-lying islands (such
as Barbados and Antigua) and along the windward coasts of Saint Croix, Saint Kitts,
Nevis, and Guadeloupe.

added. This solution was clarified by the removal of scum, reboiled, and cooled in molds with a layer of wet clay to separate the crystals. Almost all sugar was refined in Europe or in North America. Some Martinique and Guadeloupe planters built their own refineries at the end of the 17th century, but the government forced them to close to protect the French refining industry.

Besides muscovado and clayed sugar, many plantations sold several liquid by-products of the milling process. They produced the coarsest—known as *garapa* by the Portuguese and *grappe* by the French—by collecting cane juice skimmed from the boiling syrup and allowing it to ferment. This produced an inexpensive but very strong liquor popular among slaves and poor whites. From the molasses left by the boiling and claying processes, the planters distilled a milder and smoother liquor known in French as *tafia* and in English as rum. All of the colonists enjoyed rum, but the British colonies in North America and the Caribbean formed the largest market. Thus the French sold most of their rum to foreigners, contrary to both British and French law.

## SLAVE GANGS, SLAVE TASKS

During all periods, slavery was harshest on sugar estates under the "gang system." Sugar gangs enjoyed the least personal freedom, suffered the worse conditions, and endured frequent physical punishments. These slaves worked under close control at repetitive tasks, with each member of the gang doing the same work. Throughout the 1700s, planters rigorously standardized the gang system to increase production. Under the supervision of drivers, large gangs dug cane holes, weeded the growing plants, and cut mature cane. A long line of slaves moved down the field in order, urged on by the whips of the drivers. At other times—when the slaves carried dung baskets, cane, or grass on their heads—the gang marched in a file, with the drivers in the rear.

Many planters divided their field slaves into three or more gangs. They assigned slaves by age and strength, trying to match the strongest slaves to the hardest tasks. The drivers put mature men and women into the first or "great" gang, which they trained to do the hard work of holing and harvesting. The second gang—youths from twelve to eighteen and elderly men and women—was given lighter field work. Children six to twelve went into the third gang, and the drivers put them to work weeding or gathering grass. Women as well as men formed part of the first gang. Indeed, more women than men worked in the fields. Since men held almost all the skilled jobs as drivers and craftsmen, women filled up the field gangs, even though men usually outnumbered women overall.

These gangs worked from dawn to dark, six days a week and more than 300 days a year. Although they usually did not work on Sundays, owners expected field slaves to spend their spare time growing food on their provision grounds. The slaves marched to the fields about 5 A.M. in the summer and a little later during the winter months. They continued to labor until dusk, with two breaks to cook their meals. The normal workday thus lasted ten to twelve hours. But it was much longer during the sugar harvest, when milling and boiling continued around the clock and slaves worked sixteen or eighteen hours a day.

The harsh gang system was most prevalent on the sugar estates. Slaves in towns or on smaller farms worked under the "task system." This meant that their owner or a driver assigned them a set amount of work to accomplish within a certain time limit. Skilled craftsmen—carpenters, barrel makers, masons, brick-layers, women spinners and weavers—always worked by the task. Moreover, tasking was employed in growing products other than sugar—including arrow-root, cocoa, coffee, long-staple cotton, pimento, rice, and lumber. Some sugar estates also switched from gang to tasking from the late 18th century. On the British islands, tasking replaced ganging as part of a policy of "amelioration" that sought to keep slaves alive as prices for new slaves increased.

## FIELD SLAVES MUST FEND FOR THEMSELVES

On large plantations, owners and managers cared about the slaves only as laborers and only during working hours. After the days' gang labor was done, whites left the slaves to do as they pleased. In most cases, they expected the slaves to feed, clothe, and house themselves. As a result, estate slaves lived under miserable conditions, and they also had little contact with whites. These two facts are related. On a large cane plantation, eight to ten whites managed hundreds of slaves. To these white managers, the slaves literally were faceless "hands" working in anonymous "gangs."

Field hands and most skilled slaves lived away from their owners in what often were miniature African villages. Estate slaves usually constructed their own houses out of straw and mud, thatching them with guinea grass, cane tops, or palmetto fronds. Rarely larger than 12 feet square, slave huts typically contained only two rooms, without floors or windows. Other than a few wooden bowls, a water-jug, and an iron pot for boiling their meals, most slaves had no furniture and slept on the floor.

These flimsy slave huts have disappeared without a trace. Old maps show that they often were set close to the sugar mill and within sight of the overseer's house. In the French West Indies, slave huts usually were constructed in a circle around a common open area. On some estates they were laid out in rows, with the huts of the headmen and drivers closer to the more solid houses of the managers.

Estate owners also took little responsibility for slave clothing and food. In most colonies, laws required owners to give every slave clothes each year. On the British islands, these laws became more generous during the period of amelioration after 1770. But most owners simply gave out rolls of coarse cloth and expected the slave women to make it into clothes. As late as 1800, travelers described slaves—both male and female—as working naked or nearly so in both the fields and sugar factory. For Sunday and holidays, slaves might dress up in better clothes that they had bought or made for themselves. House servants and town slaves were more decently dressed, though often barefoot.

The wholly inadequate housing and clothing of the field slaves contributed to their high death rate. Caribbean evenings and mornings can be quite cool, particularly in the winter months. West Africans have relatively little tolerance for cold. Already weakened by overwork and malnourishment, slaves easily fell victim to the "fevers" that killed so many.

More than anything else, however, plantation slaves suffered from a lack of adequate food. Planters used two methods to feed their estate slaves. Those on Barbados and the Leewards (and later Cuba) devoted all their land to sugar. To feed the slaves, they imported corn from North America and beans from England. On Jamaica, Saint-Domingue, Puerto Rico, and some of the Windward Islands, land remained more abundant. Here owners assigned the slaves "provision grounds" and expected them to grow their own food when they could.

Slaves often went hungry between June and September, the very months in which heavy work digging cane holes exhausted their energies. Many starved following hurricanes or during war-time naval blockades. At the best of times, a slave's diet was limited and monotonous. Most slaves lived on gruels or stews of cornmeal, rice, millet, and kidney beans ("pigeon peas"). To these they added the root plants—yams, potatoes, cassava, sweet potatoes—that formed the main diet of many West Africans. Some slaves also raised greens and fruit as well as hogs and chickens. However, they often sold both produce and animals, using their earnings to buy a few innocent pleasures, such as clothing, liquor, and tobacco.

Field slaves were seriously malnourished because they consumed little protein or fat. Planters rarely supplied fresh meat and fed their slaves from imported supplies of dried and salted fish, pork, and beef. Few slaves got as much as a pound a week, and the imported meat and fish often turned putrid before they received it.[8] A diet low in meat and fat condemned field slaves to poor health and low fertility. The lack of these essential elements led to high death rates—among newly born children and infants as well as adults.[9] Planters did not deliberately set out to starve their slaves. However, most planters—especially during the 18th century—did not provide a diet that could maintain health or even an efficient work force.

Overwork and underfeeding rather than deliberate cruelty were the main causes of high slave mortality. There is little reliable information about whipping and other punishments during the course of everyday life on rural estates. Occasional anecdotes describe cases of exceptional brutality, especially during the earlier years. In the British colonies at least, punishments apparently became less frequent and brutal toward the end of the 18th century. Most owners were sane enough not to deliberately destroy the expensive species of human machinery that provided their income. However, many planters—out of greed, carelessness, or mere stupidity—did allow their slaves to die of hunger and disease.

## SLAVES TAKE ON EVERY SORT OF WORK

As the sugar islands prospered, their economies became more complex, and some planters became more polished. By 1800, slaves performed a wide variety of tasks. On some long-settled islands, probably fewer than half the slave population now lived on the sugar estates. Moreover, plantation records show that only about half of the slaves on rural estates actually worked as part of the field gangs.

Throughout the islands, slaves did virtually any job that provided an income to their owners and that the free population could or would not do. Since advanced schooling was not available, whites monopolized (at least for other whites) the "lettered" professions of accounting, law, medicine, and the clergy. Slaves performed virtually all other tasks. Many worked as domestic servants. Visitors frequently commented on the enormous staffs of servants maintained by Caribbean whites. In 1795, for example, the overseer on the Worthy Park estate in Jamaica assigned 36 slaves to serve six white persons.

In the towns as well as on the estates, slaves were responsible for every type of unskilled and skilled labor. In the ports, slaves worked as sailors and fishermen as well as dock hands. Slaves provided most of the internal marketing system. Slaves worked in many shops. Traveling saleswomen—called "higglers" or *revendeuses* (*révadèz* in Creole)—carried provisions from the country to towns and also brought imported goods from the ports back to the rural estates. Town slaves commanded and often excelled at every kind of artisan skill—including carpentry, masonry, barrel making, cooking, baking, tailoring, hairdressing, performing, weaving, silversmithing, and cigar making.

## THE AMBIGUOUS LIFE OF URBAN SLAVES AND FREEDMEN

It always is dangerous to generalize about the mysterious relationship between master or mistress and servants. Nevertheless, town slaves did enjoy more freedom and better treatment than field hands. A skilled artisan is a valuable property precisely because he or she can work without direction. Slave craftsmen and higglers often controlled their own time. Some were rented out and had a say as to who they worked for—or even who might buy them. Free persons of color supported themselves in many of the same ways as slaves. Thus the distinction between slavery and freedom eventually blurred in many towns.

Urban slaves also enjoyed better living conditions and thus lived longer than field hands. Since many were owned by poor whites and black freedmen, they were not luxuriously housed. But at least they slept under a solid roof, and they had access to a variety of fresh food and cotton clothing. Moreover, they could mingle at town taverns and dances with other slaves and sometimes with poor whites.

Freedmen and urban slaves could amass large sums of cash money. Rented slaves might keep tips above the contract price (legally under Spanish law). Higglers often controlled their receipts. In competition with other vendors, they charged that day's market price, kept the receipts, and settled up with their owner days or weeks later. On some islands, slaves controlled far more liquid cash than many sugar planters, who often were heavily in debt. After emancipation on most islands, former slaves, as well as freedmen, drew upon their cash hoards to buy thousands of acres from failed planters.

## THE SUGAR PLANTATION AS A KILLING MACHINE

On all the sugar islands, death rates for black slaves were always higher than birth rates. Africans sold to Caribbean cane estates suffered a much harsher fate than those carried farther north to America. In contrast to the remarkable natural decrease (excess of deaths over births) in the Caribbean, the American slave population rapidly increased. Since the slaves in both cases came from the same regions of West Africa, this difference provides perhaps the harshest indictment of Caribbean slavery. In 1825, both the United States and the islands had an African population of about two million. But slave traders had carried (through 1810) about 3,500,000 slaves to the islands and only some 375,000 to British North America.

It sometimes is said that Latin or Roman Catholic countries enjoyed a milder or more humane form of slavery compared to the Dutch or English. The survival rates do not support this belief. African slaves fared as badly in the French colonies as in the British. In the Greater Antilles, it is possible to compare British Jamaica to French Saint-Domingue (today Haiti). From 1655 through 1807, Jamaica imported about 750,000 slaves. In 1834, only 310,000 slaves were freed. Saint-Domingue took in about 800,000 slaves prior to the slave rebellion in 1791. A census in 1789 counted only 435,000. The death rate was even higher on the smaller Leeward Islands. Although Barbados received 387,000 slaves, the planters only freed 81,000 in 1834. From 1635, Martinique imported 366,000 slaves; only 100,000 Africans remained in 1848, when the French abolished slavery.

The record is slightly better for Spanish Cuba and Puerto Rico. On these islands, the African population did not increase over time; but at least the slaves did not die off as rapidly as on the French and British islands. Cuba, for example, imported about 700,000 slaves from 1761 through 1870. The census of 1877 counted 480,000 Africans.[10]

Because the slaves died without reproducing themselves, the sugar estates could operate only by constantly importing new workers from Africa. A vicious cycle existed. The slave traders brought in new slaves, many of whom soon died—making it necessary to bring in yet more slaves to die. We could continue this catalog of human misery for every island (except the Bahamas and Curaçao). As with the extermination of the Arawak in the 1500s, the word *genocide* precisely describes the fate of Africans carried to the sugar islands as field slaves.

This "natural decrease" continued for some two centuries. Contemporary critics blamed cruel masters, poor food and housing, intense work schedules, disease, and the rigors of the Middle Passage. All of these worked together to make the tropical sugar plantation a true killing machine. Caribbean slaves suffered from both high death rates and low birth rates, and both factors hindered population growth. Very high infant mortality provided the most important check on the slave population. A low-protein and low-fat diet reduced births and also made adults more susceptible to disease.

There is an obvious connection between sugar plantations and high death rates. Slave deaths increased as agriculture intensified after 1700. At least in the

British colonies, death rates fell toward the end of the century. Slavery thus was most deadly during the early years when planters rapidly developed sugar estates and introduced the factory-type discipline of gang slavery.[11] The population decline slowed in the older colonies as the economy matured and more slaves worked away from the fields.[12]

Overall, the natural decrease averaged about 3 percent per year in Jamaica and 4 percent a year in the Leeward and Windward islands. By the 19th century, the African population fell only 1 percent a year or less in the older colonies. The French colonies may have had a worse record. Some planters on Saint-Domingue had to replace 10 percent of their hands every year.

African slaves (and white immigrants) died most rapidly during their first three years in the islands, when they were said to be undergoing "seasoning." During these first years, at least 15 to 20 percent died and sometimes as many as one in three. Already weakened by confinement and malnutrition during the Middle Passage from Africa, many perished from the sudden exposure to a new disease environment. Dysentery (the "bloody flux") killed many new arrivals. Others succumbed to tuberculosis, typhoid, and varieties of malaria and yellow fever to which they had not been exposed in Africa.

Slaves also died rapidly during their first years of life. Three out of every four babies died before the age of five. Thus, the effective birth rate was very low. Abolitionists and other critics accused planters of believing that it was "better to buy than to breed." Since both pregnant women and young children ate without working, these critics charged, planters did not encourage slave births. However, most planters probably favored births—at least in principle. Yet, as one planter said, despite all he did, "the children do not come."[13]

Recurrent epidemics continued to kill off both creole slaves living past childhood and Africans that outlasted the seasoning process. A few lived into their sixties or seventies. But the average life expectancy, among those surviving infancy, probably was less than forty years. A field hand's chance of survival to middle age finally began to increase after 1800. Second and third-generation creoles adapted to the West Indian disease environment. When the slave trade ended in 1807, it brought a halt to epidemics introduced by the constant influx of new Africans. The number of creole slaves actually began to increase in Barbados by about 1810, in Jamaica from the 1840s. The development of natural immunities and better food probably helped the most—18th-century medical care the least.

## CHAPTER ELEVEN:

# ENGLAND AND FRANCE
# STRUGGLE TO CONTROL THE
# ISLANDS

■

The great wealth of the sugar islands made them immensely valuable prizes during the world wars that pitted France against Great Britain from 1744 to 1783. The sugar estates now were much too valuable to destroy. Although England and France were at war during sixteen of these thirty-nine years, neither nation pillaged the other's Caribbean colonies. Both sides wanted to take the enemy's colonies intact. In sharp contrast to its policy during the 17th century, the British government thus ordered its invading armies to protect French plantations, and it gave generous terms to the islands it conquered. During all wars, French, British, and sometimes Spanish privateers destroyed thousands of merchant vessels, seriously disrupting trade with Europe and North America. Since many islands depended on imported food, the African slaves suffered greatly, and thousands died. But the cane estates themselves suffered little lasting damage.

During the War of the Austrian Succession (1740–1748), the Seven Years War (1756–1763), and (in its international aspects) the War for American Independence (1776–1783), Great Britain and France fought to gain commercial and colonial supremacy throughout the world. Although the Caribbean certainly was a major theater of battle, these were true world wars, also fought in Europe, North America, Africa, and India. In Europe, the Franco-British contest over foreign colonies became entwined with continental wars of plunder that did not directly affect the Caribbean. The fortunes of war in Europe did influence decisions at the peace conferences. British statesmen in 1763, for example, gave up overseas gains in return for restoration of territories lost by their European allies.

During earlier wars between England and France, only one territory was permanently transferred.[1] In contrast, several islands changed hands many times during the 18th century. Saint Lucia probably holds the record for frequent changes of ownership. Although the island is mountainous with comparatively poor soil, Saint Lucia has in Castries one of the finest small harbors in the West

Indies. Unlike those based in more distant Barbados and Antigua, British ships at Saint Lucia could watch the principal French base at Fort Royal, Martinique—less than 25 miles away. The island thus had strategic importance to the security of the French Islands. It was from Saint Lucia, for example, that Admiral Rodney sailed to win the decisive battle of the Saints in 1782. British forces conquered Saint Lucia in 1762 and 1778, but returned it to France in 1763 and 1783 (Treaties of Paris and Versailles). The British took the island again in 1794 and 1796 and again returned it to France in 1802 (Treaty of Amiens). Retaken yet again in 1803, Saint Lucia finally was ceded to Britain in 1814 (Treaty of Paris).

However, even changes of flag did not deeply affect the society or economy of an island. Sugar dominated the economies of all the islands, and the planters in turn influenced local governments under both the French and the British. Some have argued that rule by one empire—either French or British—might have led to greater unity between the islands. This seems unlikely. An islander's loyalty is to his own homeland. The Leeward Islands—close neighbors under one flag—always resisted British pressures to form a federation. We may safely assume that Antigua and Martinique would not today form one country if the British had retained the latter in 1763.

## THE MILITARY WEAKNESS OF SLAVE SOCIETIES

The wars between 1740 and 1783 did little damage in the colonies. However, the planters could not know this in advance. The British in particular were thrown into terror by any rumors that a French fleet had arrived. French attacks during earlier wars proved that even a small armed force could cause very great loses.[2]

To defend their ports and provide places of refuge during an invasion, island leaders hurriedly erected forts, some still extant. But the regular navies of England and France provided the main defense of the colonies. The islands were extremely vulnerable to attack because they had no local forces. Both Britain and France were reluctant to station large numbers of regular troops on the islands, since the planters refused to contribute toward their pay during years of peace. The island militias were very small, wretchedly trained, and almost wholly unwarlike.

With the growth of large estates worked by slaves, the number of white men able to join the militias had fallen. Guadeloupe was supposed to contain between 3,000 and 4,000 armed men, but not more than 1,600 appeared with weapons when the British invaded in 1762. To make up the gap, the militias included free blacks and mulattos, especially in the French islands. However, the planters generally did not trust their slaves with weapons and primarily used them as laborers. It was not until 1795 that the British government formed twelve West India regiments of black troops.

## BRITISH AND FRENCH NAVAL STRATEGIES

Fleets sailing from Europe decided these wars, and the British and French developed different naval strategies. The West India Interest enjoyed substantial political influence in England. It insisted on squadrons of warships permanently stationed in the West Indies. Following the earthquake of 1692, the Crown rebuilt Port Royal's dockyard, and a second naval station was set up in 1743 at English Harbour in Antigua. In May 1757, the Admiralty decided to keep eight line warships at both stations, though it could not always fulfill this resolution.

Unlike the British, the French did not have permanent naval bases until 1784 and sent fleets from Europe for specific purposes. The British system probably was superior over the long run. Certainly British fleets dominated the Caribbean during the Seven Years War. Britain's permanent fleets could not defeat major French expeditions, but they did command the seas during several months each year and interrupted French trade.

Caribbean bases contributed to British victory by allowing British fleets to stay in the region longer than fleets from France. To avoid the hurricane season, French ships intended to leave by October or November and return to Europe by the end of June. But large expeditions often were delayed in port and did not get off until the middle of January. In 1759 and 1762, French fleets thus arrived too late to prevent the British conquests of Guadeloupe and Martinique.

The French and British strategies both had advantages and disadvantages. French fleets arrived in the West Indies fresh from the dockyard and in good repair, whereas British ships quickly rotted under tropical conditions. Once they arrived in the region, however, the French fleets quickly ran out of food, while British ships could obtain provisions from the permanent naval stations. Because they had to carry their own supplies and provisions, French ships could stay in the Caribbean for no more than six months—or even less in the case of small frigates. Stores rarely lasted long in the tropics, and some French fleets left early because their supplies had rotted.

French naval forces could purchase little food once they arrived. The French islands could not feed themselves in peacetime, and the British blockade hindered shipments from North America. Crews arriving from France immediately fell ill of yellow fever or malaria, often so severely that several squadrons could not sail. As soon as these epidemics began to subside, the food had run out, and it was time to go home. Thus, French squadrons sent to the West Indies took hardly one offensive measure between 1744 and 1763, even against British merchant ships.

Illness was the main killer during all the wars of the 18th century. Over and over, disease killed dozens of sailors and soldiers for every casualty in battle. After only a few days in port, men fresh from England or France began to sicken of yellow fever, malaria, and other tropical diseases. Any victory had to be won almost immediately, for a long siege led to staggering death rates. William Beckford was precise in September 1758, when he warned Prime Minister Pitt that—

> Whatever is attempted in that climate must be done *uno impetu*; a general must fight his men off directly, and not give them time to die by drink and disease; which has been the case in all our southern expeditions.[3]

## THE "WAR OF JENKINS'S EAR," 1739–1748

In October 1739, Britain began to war with the Spanish empire, in what became known as the War of Jenkins's Ear. France joined the Spanish side by declaring war on England in March 1744. The War of Jenkins's Ear continued a centuries-old struggle between Britain and Spain. In this conflict, the British again sought both to force their commerce on the Spanish and to annex parts of their empire. In an ironic reversal of their traditional roles, however, the British now accused the Spanish of piracy.

The Spanish Crown had closed its empire to foreign merchants in 1502, opening colonial ports only to Spanish vessels licensed by the Casa de Contratación. Since these legal shipments were expensive, Spanish colonists in Cuba, Puerto Rico, and Santo Domingo eagerly bought cheaper slaves and goods smuggled from Jamaica. The Spanish responded by allowing Cuban and Puerto Rican privateers to seize British ships throughout the Caribbean.

The Queen Regent of Spain had issued the first Spanish privateering commissions in 1674, copying a British device previously abused by pirates such as Henry Morgan. Under these commissions, Spanish ships (called *guarda costas*) roamed the Caribbean, searching British ships for cargoes illegally acquired in Spanish ports. Like Henry Morgan, their captains were private men who paid themselves by seizing merchant ships as prizes and selling them in Spanish ports. Between 1714 and 1737, the *guarda costas* seized over 200 ships, and most were condemned by courts on the Spanish islands. A mini-war raged in Caribbean waters, with right and wrong on both sides. Jamaican smugglers made thousands of pounds each year through illegal trade with the Spanish islands. But the *guarda costas* seized both smugglers and innocent merchant ships legally passing a Spanish coast.

From 1713, Spanish and British diplomats continuously quarreled over the seizures by the *guarda costas*. For domestic political reasons, the British government drifted toward war in the spring of 1738. Captain Jenkins's ear provided the excuse it needed—as well as a name for the war. Jenkins was a master mariner of dubious reputation. In 1731, a *guarda costa* stopped his ship in open Caribbean waters and searched his cargo for contraband. The Spanish captain allegedly cut off one of Jenkins's ears. As Jenkins told the story, the dastardly Spaniard told him to take the ear to England as a token of the punishment awaiting British seamen who broke Spain's trade laws.

With war fever raging in 1738, Captain Jenkins appeared before a committee of the House of Commons. There he produced a piece of shriveled flesh said to be his severed ear. Although his enemies alleged that both Jenkins's ears were safely hidden under his wig, the opposition party took up his case. British merchants, eager to take new markets, joined in the call for war, and the government felt obliged to act.

Britain (and later France) fought the resulting war in traditional ways. Privateers based in the islands again proved their most effective weapon. The British also sent larger naval expeditions to conquer the Spanish colonies, but these failed as miserably as the British attack on Santo Domingo in 1655. A small squadron under Admiral Edward Vernon (1684–1757) harassed the Spanish Main early in the war, seizing Portobelo (November 1739) and Chagres (March 1740) and bombarding Cartagena. Vernon succeeded in these attacks by acting quickly before his men could fall sick of the fever.

A larger British fleet came to disaster in 1741. Its commanders—Vernon and General Wentworth—mistakenly tried long sieges during which most of their European and North American troops (some 15,600 men) died of tropical diseases. From March to May 1741, the Spanish repulsed a six week siege of Cartagena. They had greatly strengthened the city's defenses after the French attack in 1697, and disease ravished the British soldiers. Fewer than a third of the force lived to return to Jamaica.

After taking on fresh troops, the British fleet seized Guantánamo Bay in Cuba (July 1741), intending to march on Santiago. Sickness again killed most of the expedition (at least 208 officers died), and the fleet returned to Jamaica in November. Disease thwarted an even more ambitious plan to capture Panama City in March 1742, and a second attempt to take Santiago in 1748 also failed. The deputy governor of Anguilla led the only British land expedition that entirely succeeded. With some 300 soldiers, he captured the French part of Sint Maarten (Saint-Martin) and Saint-Barthélemy in 1744. The Anguillan militia also successfully repelled a small French force that attacked the island in July 1745.

The Treaty of Aix-la-Chapelle (1748) ended hostilities, and all parties returned their conquests. The treaty did not mention a principal cause of the war—the Spanish practice of searching British ships for contraband. The British and French confirmed the neutrality of Dominica, Saint Lucia, Saint Vincent, and Tobago. Both sides promised to reserve these islands for the resident Carib, and they agreed to remove their nationals from the small camps of squatters. The latter paid no attention, and French colonists continued to settle these islands. They were especially attracted to Dominica, located only a few miles between Martinique and Guadeloupe.

## THE SEVEN YEARS WAR, 1756–1763

After a brief and troubled truce, Britain and France in 1756 resumed their struggle for naval and commercial supremacy. The Seven Years War was actually two wars—a European land war in which Prussia fought Austria and Russia, and a worldwide sea war between Britain and France. Friction between Britain and Spain continued, with Britain declaring war in December 1761. But Britain and France were the main rivals and the chief combatants both in the Caribbean and around the world.

The previous war began in the Caribbean. In this case, the major colonial rivalries between France and Britain centered on North America and the Indian subcontinent in Asia. As it went on, however, the sugar islands became valuable and vulnerable prizes in this worldwide war. Britain and France both sent larger forces to the West Indies than in any of their previous wars.

William Pitt (1708–1778), who directed the war for Britain from 1756 to 1761, sought nothing less than to destroy France as a colonial and extra-European power. His policies found wide support among both agricultural and commercial interests. Both India and North America formed extremely valuable parts of the British commercial empire. Merchants engaged in the American and Indian trades had great political influence in Britain.

The West India Interest also was wealthy and well-represented in Parliament. Unlike the East Indian and American interests, however, the West Indians initially did not want to annex French territory. British planters did not want to increase the number of sugar islands because this would reduce the price of sugar in the protected British market. As it turned out, the British subdued all of the Lesser Antilles in this war and annexed the neutral Windward Islands also. Both sides changed their attitude toward West Indian conquests during the course of the Seven Years War. Britain launched major expeditions, and their commanders now had orders to annex the enemy's sugar colonies, not merely to pillage them. The French government also sent out large fleets, although these arrived to late to save their colonies.

Both sides thought of the sugar islands as valuable bargaining chips at the next peace conference. Early in 1756, the French navy conquered the important British naval base at Minora in the western Mediterranean. In July 1758, British forces seized Cape Breton Island, whose great fortress, Louisbourg, was the key to French naval power in North America. Both governments wanted to recover these crucial bases, and the British looked for other conquests—such as the French islands—to trade during peace talks.

*The British Occupy Guadeloupe, Martinique, and Havana*   In contrast to the previous war, all British expeditions took their objectives. No major battles occurred in the West Indies until 1759, although British and French privateers again destroyed the other side's merchant fleet. At the end of 1758, now possessing Louisbourg, Pitt launched two attacks against the French islands. A British force captured France's slave factories in Africa, thus crippling the French slave trade. In January 1759, a naval force with some 5,000 soldiers unsuccessfully attacked Fort Royal (now Fort-de-France) in Martinique. Its commanders then turned against Guadeloupe, seizing Basse-Terre and besieging the French positions in the interior of the island.

During the siege of Guadeloupe, more than half the soldiers were sick within a month, and the British commander died late in February. His successor, Brigadier-General John Barrington, decided to adopt a divide-and-conquer strategy. Instead of attacking the main French positions, the British invaders plundered and destroyed outlying plantations. Members of the French militia deserted and came over to the invaders to protect their property, and the island surrendered on May 1. The French had sent a fleet, but when it finally arrived a few days later, Guadeloupe already had fallen.

To encourage surrender, Barrington offered the French planters very generous terms. The articles of capitulation granted the French access to British markets and imposed no new taxes. They guaranteed complete religious freedom, protecting church as well as secular property. The islanders retained the existing French laws, courts, and judges. Planters fighting for France could control their estates through attorneys. The articles even promised that the government would prevent British subjects from buying island properties before a peace treaty was signed.

Under these terms, the British conquest helped the Guadeloupe planters. They sold their sugar for high prices to British and North American merchants, who rushed in supplies and thousands of cheap slaves. The conquest also wiped out their enormous debts to French creditors, allowing them to borrow even more money from Antiguan factors.

During the second half of 1759 and through 1760, the conquest of Canada fully occupied the British forces. Troops from Canada easily took Dominica in June 1761. In November, Admiral George Rodney (1719–1792) arrived at Barbados with more than 13,000 British soldiers. They turned against Martinique, taking Fort Royal in February 1762 after only three weeks of siege. Many of the Martinique militia deserted to save their estates, when the British commander, General Robert Monckton (1726–1782), offered them terms similar to those granted at Guadeloupe. The articles of surrender again maintained existing laws and taxes and confirmed the rights and properties of the religious orders.

The French rushed a strong squadron under Admiral Blénac to the Caribbean. Again, it reached the Caribbean too late to save Martinique. With Martinique gone, small squadrons quickly took Saint Lucia and Grenada. Although small French camps still existed on Saint Vincent and Tobago, the British now occupied all of the major French islands except for Saint-Domingue.

Throughout the war, British privateers had molested Spanish merchant shipping. Moreover, the Spanish government feared total British control of the Caribbean islands. Thus in 1761 it promised France to declare war before May 1762. The British government anticipated events by declaring war on Spain in January 1761 and fitting out a large expedition to take Havana.

Admiral George Pocock (1706–1792) commanded the Havana fleet, which carried 15,000 soldiers under the command of George Keppel, the earl of Albermarle (1724–1772). Instead of taking the traditional route along Cuba's southern coast, Pocock surprised the Spanish by taking his armada through the dangerous Old Bahama Channel, north of the island. Moro Castle fell in August 1762, after a two-month siege. Some 5,000 troops died from fever or dysentery, while only 560 died in battle. The British force took enormous booty, including twelve ships of the line and nearly a hundred merchant vessels. The total prize money reached the staggering sum of £750,000.

## THE TREATY OF PARIS

The conquest of Havana was the last major engagement in the Seven Years War. With Britain victorious in the Americas and the European land war at a stalemate, it was time to negotiate a peace. The British had won more than enough prizes to set trade against their loses and those of their Prussian ally. Which should they keep? Pamphlets thrashed out this question in the celebrated controversy of Canada against Guadeloupe. The West India Interest was divided, but many sugar planters now were converted to keeping at least some of the French islands.

In the end, this noisy debate probably did not influence the British ministers. By the Treaty of Paris in February 1763, France gave up most of her conquests in the Germanies. In return, Britain returned the French slave stations as well as Martinique, Guadeloupe, and Saint Lucia. The British kept Canada[4] as well as Grenada and the Grenadines and the formerly "neutral islands" of Dominica, Saint Vincent, and Tobago. They returned Havana to Spain, taking Florida in exchange. Spain also received Louisiana, which France ceded as some compensation for Spanish loses during the war. Even though it was still unsettled, the French negotiators had insisted on keeping Saint Lucia in order to defend Martinique and Guadeloupe. The British agreed to give up Saint Lucia in return for concessions in North America. Thus the British conquered in the islands in order to annex territory on the continent.

## THE WAR FOR AMERICAN INDEPENDENCE, 1776–1783

The Treaty of Paris marks the high point of the old mercantile British Empire. Spain, Holland, France, and England had fought—almost since 1492—a fierce competition for sea power and colonial wealth. The sugar islands had been invaluable prizes of battle. Much of the fighting had taken place in the Caribbean seas, crossroads of the Atlantic trade. Now Britain was supreme in North America, free to expand territorially in India, and ready to absorb the commerce of Spanish America. Within twenty years, the British had lost the largest part of their overseas possessions, and their mercantile empire was gone. France and England now fought one more great war—the fifth since 1688—for colonial dominion. One last time, European navies fought for control of the wealthy sugar islands. This time the French won.

*The French and Spanish Seek Revenge*  The French and Spanish courts, both under Bourbon rulers, looked upon the peace of 1763 as a mere truce. Their chief ministers sought revenge and altered governmental policies to obtain it. Under the influence of the intellectual movement known as the Enlightenment, they reduced governmental regulations, restored state finances, and enlarged and improved their armies and navies. These enlightened ministers succeeded only partially in reforming French society and politics. However, even these partial reforms enabled the French to defeat Britain in the West Indies.

In France, the duc de Choiseul (1719–1785), as foreign minister and minister of marine, rallied the nation in a campaign to rebuild the navy. When royal funds proved inadequate, Choiseul turned to public fund drives. Private subscribers financed fifteen ships of the line (the largest type), the most impressive being the 104-gun *Ville de Paris*. Choiseul also built a new naval station at Fort Royal on Martinique as a base for future military operations.

Choiseul's successors continued to build up a strong navy. By 1778, when France declared war on Britain, its navy had 78 ships of the line and 186 frigates and smaller craft. Compared to the British, many were better built, their gunners better trained. Although less efficiently manned, the Spanish fleet added 60 ships of the line to the combined force against England. The Royal Navy had as many ships. But some were not fit for sea, and many were tied down blockading the North American coasts. French and Spanish forces thus dominated the Caribbean for the first time in a century. Peace in Europe enabled the French government to concentrate all of its energies on the naval struggle with Britain.

In 1774, Louis XVI succeeded to the throne, and the comte de Vergennes (1717–1787) became foreign minister. Vergennes sought war as eagerly as Choiseul, and the American Revolution gave him his opportunity. Although war would bankrupt the country, France began secret aid to the rebels in 1776. When the campaign ending at Saratoga (June to October 1777) proved that the Americans could win, the French government signed an offensive and defensive alliance in February 1778, declaring war on Britain in June. Spain entered the war in June 1779 when England refused to return Gibraltar.

France and Spain fought England to take the Caribbean islands.[5] The French ministers were indifferent to American independence, and the French navy mainly kept to the West Indies until the siege of Yorktown in 1781. The Spanish monarchy—openly hostile to all rebels—also sought territory in the West Indies. Spanish policy looked to the expulsion of Britain from both the Mediterranean and the Caribbean, long a base for British commercial infiltration into Spanish America. Spanish goals thus included the reconquest of Florida and even of Jamaica.

**The British West Indies Fall to French Attack**  Many West Indians favored the American cause and flagrantly traded with American ships. Nevertheless, their location tied the British islanders to the British navy—which now failed to protect them. The French blockade cut Jamaica and Barbados off from food and supplies, and thousands of slaves died of hunger and disease. Most of the other British islands suffered actual capture.

European troops rather than colonial militia again did most of the fighting. The weather strongly influenced British and French naval strategies. To avoid hurricanes, their fleets usually visited the Caribbean only from November through June or July. This shortened fighting season proved to be a wise precaution. The great hurricane of October 1780 (page 10) destroyed those men-of-war that the French and British had left in the West Indies for guard duty.

The governor of Martinique gained the first French conquest by taking Dominica in September 1778. A strong French force under Admiral d'Estaing (1729–1784) captured Saint Vincent and Grenada early in the summer of 1779. Only a brilliant British victory in Saint Lucia in December 1778 thwarted French domination of the Lesser Antilles. Acting quickly—before West Indian fevers destroyed his forces—the British commander landed soldiers from New York near Castries and successfully beat off a French counterattack.

The following season (winter 1779 to spring 1780) proved indecisive—although both sides dispatched large fleets commanded by their best officers. From March 1780, Admiral George Rodney commanded the British fleet, supported by a squadron under Admiral Samuel Hood (1724–1816). Rodney fought several inconclusive battles near Martinique in April and May. He also failed to intercept a Spanish armada that reached Martinique in June, carrying some 10,000 troops. The French and Spanish planned a joint attack on Jamaica or another major island. But their commanders waited too long. Disease—the islander's best defense against European invasion—ravaged the Spanish crews and troops, and the fleet retreated to Havana.

Admiral Rodney spent most of the next season (winter 1780–summer 1781) plundering the Dutch colony of Sint Eustatius. When Rodney took Statia in February 1781, the "Golden Rock" was at the height of its prosperity. Statia became a free port in 1756, when the Dutch abolished customs duties to compete with Danish Saint Thomas. At all times, its harbor provided a convenient haven where merchants and smugglers could trade during both war and peace. Its warehouses now became a vast depot for the guns and powder (largely French) used by the American rebels.

Great Britain declared war on Holland in December 1780, and Rodney seized defenseless Statia in February, along with Saba, Sint Maarten, and Saint-Barthélemy. With Statia, he took 150 merchant ships and an immense booty valued at two to three million pounds—more even than the plunder seized at Havana in 1762. An ardent gambler, Admiral Rodney had fled to Paris in 1774 to avoid debtor's prison. He plundered Sint Eustatius so thoroughly that the island never regained its importance.

Rodney spent the next months supervising the sale of prizes at Sint Eustatius. While he delayed, a powerful fleet under the comte de Grasse, France's ablest commander, safely made its way to Martinique, took Tobago in May 1781, and then sailed north for the siege of Yorktown. In November 1781, after the British and French fleets had left the Caribbean, the governor of Martinique surprised the British during a storm, retaking Sint Eustatius and the other Dutch colonies.

*The Battle of The Saints and the Treaty of Versailles*   Cornwallis's surrender at Yorktown (October 1781) released the French fleet under Admiral de Grasse for a final season of naval war in the Caribbean. The following year began with continued victories for the French. It ended with the battle of The Saints, one of the few decisive sea battles in world history. Only Admiral Rodney's memorable victory saved her sugar colonies for Britain.

In January 1782, de Grasse's fleet captured Saint Kitts, Montserrat, and Nevis. The Saint Kitts planters surrendered when the French offered lenient terms, similar to those the British gave Guadeloupe during the previous war. However, a small British garrison boldly defended the fortress of Brimstone Hill against overwhelming odds for almost a month. The French held all the Leeward Islands, except Antigua, and most of the Windwards. The French and Spanish sea forces now planned an invasion of Jamaica. The outlook for the British planters was dark indeed when, on April 12, 1782, Rodney's victory over de Grasse suddenly turned the tables.

Brimstone Hill fortress, Saint Kitts. The sugar islands were tempting targets during wars between Britain and France. To protect themselves, planters constructed large fortresses. In 1782, a British garrison on Brimstone Hill held out for a month against a much larger French force.

Rodney returned from England in February, with a fleet that was—when joined with Hood's squadron—slightly stronger than that of the French. He took up his station at Saint Lucia and waited for de Grasse to act. At Martinique, de Grasse had collected a great convoy of transports with some 10,000 troops intended for the attack on Jamaica. Now he had to get them safely to the rendezvous at Cap Français on the northeast coast of Saint-Domingue.

With Rodney in pursuit, de Grasse turned north from Fort Royal and found himself trapped in the narrow channel between Dominica and Guadeloupe. A group of small islands called Les Saintes (after which the battle is named) blocked progress to the north. With the wind blowing from the east, de Grasse's only open route lay to the south. The French fleet doubled back on its pursuers. Suddenly the wind fell off. Rodney's flagship, the *Formidable*, broke through the French line of battle, as did another of his fleet. Several British ships now could concentrate their fire on one of the scattered French vessels.

By nightfall, de Grasse had surrendered his flagship, the great *Ville de Paris*, and four other ships. The rest of the French fleet retreated. The French put off and finally abandoned the attack on Jamaica, whose inhabitants erected a statue to Rodney in Spanish Town. The Spanish force moved to Havana, taking New Providence in the Bahamas in May 1782. The British public reacted with pent-up hysteria to the Royal Navy's most decisive victory since the Seven Years War.

With the combatants financially exhausted, peace negotiations now began. Britain, despite military defeat, was in a relatively strong bargaining position because of disagreements between her four opponents. Thus the Treaty of Versailles (February 1783) that recognized American independence also restored to England the French conquests in the Caribbean. France kept Tobago and regained Saint Lucia and its African slave forts, while Spain retained Florida (taken by troops from New Orleans in 1781). Tobago was a trivial prize after so much cost and loss of life. But the French ministers hoped that defeat in America meant the end of Britain as a great power. Without North America's resources to exploit, they believed that Britain soon would relapse into the position of a second-class power on the periphery of Europe.

# RUNAWAYS AND REBELS

■

Two different societies—European and African—occupied the islands throughout the slave era. Both existed to make sugar. But each led its own life, with owners generally leaving slaves to their own devices after working hours. Every planter or white employee knew he was vastly outnumbered by his slaves. Blacks exceeded whites at least ten to one on most islands. The disparity was even greater in the countryside, where black slaves might outnumber white masters fifty to one. The slaves' working tools—machetes, axes, and even hoes—easily could become effective weapons. The very harshness of the slave codes shows that the planters distrusted and feared their slaves. Particularly on Jamaica, fears of slave rebellion were well founded.

There are few diaries or other firsthand accounts about the internal life of those—white or black—living on plantations. Some slaves doubtless accepted their condition and tried to make the best of the circumstances in which they found themselves. There were also many who refused to become the passive instruments of their owners' needs and whims. Although most rural slaves were grossly overworked and underfed, they resisted their owners' demands in many ways. Individual slaves frequently ran away, avoided work, or did it poorly. And groups of slaves—sometimes hundreds of slaves—met together to plot their escape or even an uprising against the whites. Especially on Jamaica and Saint-Domingue, some slaves, called Maroons, created separate African communities that survived for many years. Others went even further and sought to kill the whites and destroy the entire plantation system. Hundreds of rebellions marked the entire slave era. But only the 1791 revolt on Saint-Domingue eventually succeeded in permanently freeing an entire island, renamed Haiti in 1804 to celebrate its liberation.

## THE PLANTATION WORLD AND SLAVE RESISTANCE

Owners often complained that slaves refused to work consistently, regularly, and efficiently. Slaves dragged their feet, working at their own pace or pretending to be sick. Some ran away to the woods or, in later periods, to the towns. Despite almost inevitable recapture and savage flogging, most plantations always had one or more slaves absent without permission. Many went for personal reasons, to visit lovers or kin. Others ran away repeatedly, removing their labor as a kind of—in modern language—spontaneous strike.

Theft by slaves also was a fact of life for planters. Many slaves stole food because they were hungry, but others stole as a form of aggression against their owners. Slaves might deliberately sabotage their owner's property by damaging machinery, seting fire to cane fields, or wounding and poisoning animals. A few slaves even attacked whites, although slave codes punished such assaults with painful forms of death. More careful slaves sought to kill a particularly hated owner or overseer by using poison. Planters on all the islands lived in fear of poison, and the French in particular believed that slaves often poisoned whites and other slaves.

Theft and their slaves' refusal to work harder reduced their profits, but plantation owners could survive defiance by individuals. As the slave codes recognized, coordinated resistance by groups of slaves was far more serious. The planters could blame individual acts of protest on the stupid or uniquely brutal management of one planter. Organized rebellion by slaves from several plantations represented a political statement against the entire system of slavery. If the rebellious group grew too large or powerful, the slaves could threaten the very lives of the planters. Planned permanent escape and revolution thus represented the most serious and feared forms of slave protest. The two were closely related, since many rebels sought to separate themselves from—rather than take over—white society.

## THE MAROONS CREATE INDEPENDENT BLACK STATES

Wherever slavery existed, there were runaways. When runways banded together and sustained themselves in the wilds, they are called *Maroons*. The islands initially offered a natural refuge for runaways. Areas of dense brush and broken terrain marked every island, and high mountains dominate the Greater and many of the Lesser Antilles. Thus most islands sheltered Maroon bands during the early years of settlement. Runaway slaves formed bands on Cuba and Puerto Rico almost as soon as the Spanish imported Africans to replace the exterminated Arawak. During the 16th century, these Maroons joined in pirate and buccaneer attacks on Cuban cities. Rebel slaves also escaped and set up armed camps on Saint Kitts, Barbados, and Antigua during the first years of settlement.

These early Maroon communities usually disappeared as planters cut down the forests to create cane estates. Survival was never easy. To last for more than a few years, Maroons had to fight off white attacks, plant fields or *conucos*, and attract women. After about 1700, sugar plantations occupied all of the available land on the smaller islands, and the Maroons vanished. Organized Maroon communities survived only on the unsettled Carib islands of Saint Vincent and Dominica and in the mountains of Jamaica, Hispaniola, Guadeloupe, and Cuba. *The Jamaican Maroons* On the British islands, Maroon communities prospered only on Jamaica, which is heavily wooded, mountainous, and covered with broken limestone caves and "cockpits." A smaller Windward group (Nanny Town) formed soon after the British conquest in 1655. When the British took

"Pacification with the Maroon Negroes, Saint Vincent." The Black Carib (descendants of the Carib and escaped slaves) defeated British efforts to drive them off the island. A 1773 agreement—modeled on earlier treaties with the Jamaican Maroons—granted the Black Carib autonomy.

Jamaica, the Spanish colonists freed their slaves, some of whom fled to the mountains (page 86). These "maroons" ultimately settled on the northern slopes of the Blue Mountains, which rise to 7,000 feet. There they built their main camp, Nanny Town, on the brink of a 900-foot drop above the junction of two branches of the Rio Grande.

A larger Leeward group (Trelawny Town) also existed in the western part of the island. In 1690, slaves in Clarendon Parish rebelled under the leadership of Cudjoe, a Coromantee warrior. Cudjoe's band ultimately found refuge in the terrible Cockpit Country—some 200 square miles of harsh sinkholes, jagged rocks, and dense vegetation. Both Maroon settlements survived by growing crops and hunting wild hogs. Their numbers grew to more than 1,000 by 1730, as more slaves escaped from the plantations.

As planters settled Jamaica's interior provinces, Maroon bands raided isolated frontier plantations, setting fire to the cane fields and carrying off food, cattle, and female slaves. Hostilities increased as the planters feared that Maroon successes would encourage a mass slave revolt. The British government sent two regiments of regular troops from Gibraltar in 1730, and the Jamaican Legislature formed companies of freedmen and also recruited Mosquito Indians from Nicaragua. A fierce guerrilla war raged for eight years. The British finally succeeded in destroying Nanny Town in 1734. But its survivors temporarily joined forces with Cudjoe's band. The black troops and Mosquito Indians systematically destroyed the Maroon's provision grounds, but they could not take Cudjoe's main settlements.

In March 1738, Governor Edward Trelawney (1699–1754) finally signed a treaty that guaranteed the Maroons two homelands with more than 2,500 acres. Cudjoe enjoyed complete jurisdiction except for the death penalty, and this semi-independent status lasted until Jamaica became independent in 1962. The Jamaican legislature in 1739 signed a similar treaty with the Windward or Nanny Town Maroons. However, the Jamaican Maroons preserved their own freedom only by agreeing to capture and return runaway slaves and to assist in the suppression of slave rebellions. The Maroons kept their part of the bargain, and the whites paid them £2 for each returned slave. In 1760, the Maroons captured Tacky, the leader of a major slave rebellion. As late as 1861, they also helped to suppress the Gordon riots. (See page 194.)

A Second Maroon War broke out in the summer of 1795 that involved only the Trelawney Town Maroons, as Cudjoe's settlement was now called. As governor, the earl of Balcarres (1752–1825) feared that French agents had spread revolutionary doctrines from Saint-Domingue to Jamaica. He led a large force of regular troops to destroy the Maroons' crops and threatened them with trained dogs imported from Cuba. Over 590 Trelawney Maroons surrendered and were exiled to the bitter cold of Nova Scotia. The British government finally transported the survivors to Africa in 1800.

*Maroon communities on the French Islands*   Stable Maroon communities also flourished on the French islands of Guadeloupe and Saint-Domingue. On Guadeloupe, Maroon bands with hundreds of members existed by the 1730s, and some communities survived until French slaves were freed in 1848. Saint-Domingue's rugged terrain favored runaways. By 1750 more than 3,000 escaped slaves lived in the mountainous no-mans-land between French Saint-Domingue and Spanish Santo Domingo. From their hidden villages, they harassed plantations in frontier districts throughout the 18th century. In 1752, a charismatic leader named Mackandal united the Maroon bands of Saint-Domingue and created a network of secret organizations among slaves on the estates. The planters believed that Mackandal planned to drive all the whites from the colony through the use of poison. Although he was betrayed, captured, and burned alive in 1758, other large bands continued to raid isolated plantations. The most famous band, that of Le Maniel, numbered 137 in 1784. As in Jamaica, the governor could not defeat Maniel's Maroons and had to negotiate a treaty protecting the estates from attack.

On the smaller islands, marronage became impossible after planters felled the forest. Slaves now fled by boat, often to the Spanish colonies or to the Carib

"A Family of Charaibes, drawn from the life, in the island of Saint Vincent." Another group of Carib—known as the Yellow Carib—maintained their separate racial identity and culture. A few dozen of their descendants survive on Saint Vincent.

islands of Saint Vincent and Dominica. The Spanish Crown frequently was at war with England during the 17th and 18th centuries. Thus it instructed colonial officials to receive escaped slaves as free men—if they accepted baptism as Catholics and took an oath to the king. Puerto Rico became a haven for slaves fleeing plantations on the British Leeward Islands, Dutch Sint Eustatius, and the Danish and British Virgins. Over the years, thousands of slaves also fled from Saint-Domingue to the thinly populated Spanish colony of Santo Domingo, which welcomed them as ranch hands and dock workers. A smaller number of slaves fled from Jamaica to Cuba, and fugitives escaping from British Tobago to Spanish Trinidad also became free. In 1798, a general decree to all Spanish officials reaffirmed the freedom of fugitives reaching their colonies.

The Windward Islands, Saint Vincent and Dominica—which international treaties reserved for the Carib—provided another haven for escaped slaves. Until the British occupation in 1763, a steady steam of runaways fled from Saint Lucia and Barbados to Saint Vincent, where they gradually absorbed the more pacific Carib. By 1763 more than five thousand Black Carib formed an unusual community on Saint Vincent. The Black Carib were African and spoke a French dialect, but they had adopted the Carib's political system, culture, and religion. On Dominica, north of Saint Vincent, a mountainous land with very high rainfall supported a dense virgin jungle. Here the Carib managed to maintain their ethnic identity, and the runaways formed separate black villages similar to those of the Jamaican Maroons.

## AFRICAN SLAVE REBELLIONS

The Maroons sought to separate themselves as much as possible from white society, although they had to trade with the plantations, especially for guns. Rebellious slaves sometimes went farther and sought to totally destroy the plantation system and kill the whites. Table 17 summarizes the available evidence about slave rebellions and lists both actual revolts as well as the conspiracies that the planters uncovered and crushed.[1]

Slaves rebelled much more frequently in the Caribbean than in the United States. The largest slave rebellion in the United States involved fewer than 500 slaves, and no rebellion seriously threatened white society. In the Caribbean, however, hundreds or even thousands of slaves joined in widespread violence on dozens of occasions, destroying plantations and killing their owners.

Caribbean slave rebellions followed a general pattern, with later colonies failing to learn from earlier experiences. The introduction of sugar plantations inevitably called up slave revolts. Whenever planters set up new cane estates, they imported thousands of slaves, most taken directly from Africa. Some of the newly arrived Africans refused to accept slavery. They either fled and set up Maroon communities or, when this was impractical, sought to exterminate their masters.

### TABLE 17. CARIBBEAN SLAVE REBELLIONS, 1522–1844

| ISLAND | CONSPIRACY | UPRISING | NUMBER INVOLVED | COMMENT |
|---|---|---|---|---|
| Antigua | 1687 | | Dozens | Maroons seek to incite slave rebellions |
| | | 1701 | Dozens | Coromantees, Christmas |
| | 1729 | | Hundreds | Christmas, Crump Estate |
| | 1735–1736 | | Thousands | Island-wide, Africans and some creoles |
| | | 1831 | Thousands | Widespread unrest, arson |
| Bahamas | 1734 | | Hundreds | General slave plot |
| | | 1830 | Dozens | Exuma Island |
| | | 1832–1834 | Hundreds | Exuma, Eleuthera, Cat Island |
| Barbados | 1649 | | Dozens | Simultaneous revolts by white servants |
| | 1675 | | Hundreds | Coromantees |
| | 1683 | | Dozens | Africans |
| | 1686 | | Hundreds | Africans |
| | 1692 | | Thousands | Creole elite as well as Africans |
| | 1701 | | Hundreds | Africans and some creoles |
| | | 1816 | Thousands | Bussa's rebellion |
| Cuba | | 1713 | | Santiago copper miners |
| | | 1729 | | |
| | | 1805 | | |
| | | 1809 | Hundreds | Several provinces and Havana |
| | | 1825 | Hundreds | Matanzas |
| | | 1826 | Dozens | Guira |
| | | 1830–1831 | Dozens | Coffee estates |
| | | 1833 | Several | Sugar estates |
| | | 1837 | Dozens | Manzanillo |
| | | 1840 | Dozens | Cienfuegos and Trinidada |
| | | 1841 | Dozens | Havana |
| | | 1843 | Hundreds | Several provinces |
| | 1843–1844(?) | | Hundreds | Conspiracy of La Escalera |
| Curaçao | | 1795 | Hundreds | Led by Tula and Carpata |
| Dominica | | 1785–1790 | Thousands | First Maroon War |
| | | 1791 | Hundreds | New Years, Windward slaves |
| | | 1795 | Hundreds | Colihaut uprising |
| | | 1802 | Hundreds | 8th West Indian Regiment mutinies |
| | | 1809–1814 | Thousands | Second Maroon War |
| Grenada | | 1765 | Hundreds | Revolt and maroon actions |
| | | 1795 | Thousands | Fédon's Rebellion; freedmen, slaves |

| ISLAND | CONSPIRACY | UPRISING | NUMBER INVOLVED | COMMENT |
|---|---|---|---|---|
| Guadeloupe | | 1656 | Hundreds | Almost all slaves on island |
| | | 1737 | Hundreds | Revolt of Latulipe |
| | | 1789 | Thousands | Tied to French Revolution |
| Jamaica | | 1673 | Hundreds | Coromantees, Saint Ann's Parish |
| | | 1678 | Hundreds | Saint Catherine's Parish |
| | | 1685 | Hundreds | July, Guanaboa Vale |
| | | 1690 | Hundreds | Clarendon, elder Cudjoe among leaders |
| | | 1730–1740 | Thousands | First Maroon War |
| | 1742 | | Dozens | Coromantees, Saint James |
| | 1745 | | Hundreds | Africans, Saint David's |
| | | 1760 | Thousands | Tacky's Revolt, Coromantees |
| | | 1765 | Dozens | Coromantees, Saint Mary's |
| | | 1766 | Thousands | Westmorland |
| | 1776 | | Thousands | Africans and creoles, Hanover Parish |
| | | 1791–1792 | Hundreds | Unrest after Haitian revolt |
| | | 1795–1796 | Hundreds | Second Maroon War |
| | 1806 | | Dozens | Saint George's Parish |
| | | 1808 | Hundreds | 2nd W. Indian Regiment mutiny |
| | 1815 | | Hundreds | Led by Ibos |
| | | 1822–1824 | Thousands | Widespread unrest, Hanover |
| | | 1831–1832 | Thousands | Christmas, "Baptist War" |
| Marie-Galante | | 1789 | Dozens | French Revolution |
| Martinique | | 1752 | | |
| | | 1789–1792 | Thousands | French Revolution |
| | | 1822 | | |
| | | 1833 | | |
| Montserrat | 1768 | | Dozens | |
| | | 1776 | | |
| Nevis | 1725 | | Dozens | Two executions |
| | 1776 | | | Williams |
| Puerto Rico | | 1527 | Dozens | Africans |
| Saint Croix | 1759? | | Dozens | Plot may not have existed |
| Saint-Domingue | 1752–1758 | | Hundreds | Mackandal unites Maroon bands |
| | | 1791 | Thousands | French Revolution |
| Saint John | | 1733–1734 | Hundreds | Africans, slaves take island |
| Saint Kitts | | 1639 | Dozens | French section of island |
| | 1770? | | Dozens | Plot probably did not exist |
| | 1778 | | Dozens | Plan to liberate island |
| Saint Lucia | | 1795–1796 | Thousands | Brigand's War |

| ISLAND | CONSPIRACY | UPRISING | NUMBER INVOLVED | COMMENT |
|---|---|---|---|---|
| Saint Vincent | | 1769–1773 | Thousands | Black Carib, First Carib War |
| | | 1795–1796 | Thousands | Second Carib War |
| Santo Domingo | | 1522 | Dozens | 40 African slaves |
| Tobago | | 1770 | Dozens | Courland Bay |
| | | 1771 | Dozens | Bloody Bay |
| | | 1774 | Dozens | Queens Bay |
| | 1801 | | Hundreds | Christmas, creoles |
| | | 1807 | Hundreds | March on Government House |
| Tortola | | 1790 | Hundreds | Pickering's estates |
| | | 1823 | Hundreds | Pickering's estates |
| | | 1830 | Hundreds | Lettsome slaves |
| | 1831 | | Hundreds | Island-wide slave plot |
| Trinidad | 1805 | | Hundreds | Plot among French slaves |
| | | 1837 | Hundreds | 1st West India Regiment mutinies |

SOURCE: The references to rebellions on the British islands are based in part on Michael Craton, *Testing the Chains* (Ithaca: Cornell University Press, 1982), 335–339.

As the older colonies became settled after 1700, slave revolts became less frequent, except on Jamaica. Rebellions were rare on the smaller islands, such as Barbados, Antigua, and Saint Kitts. Cane estates entirely occupied their soil, and slaves did not have an interior into which to flee and create Maroon colonies. Many slaves were creoles born on the islands, and they understood the enormous power the white settlers could bring to bear to crush any rebellion. Among the larger islands, Jamaica holds the record for slave unrest prior to the Haitian Revolution of 1791–1804. Jamaica had more rebellions than all the other British colonies put together. More slaves participated in Jamaican revolts, which also did more damage, than in other colonies.

Slave revolts also were common in the Windward Islands after the British occupied them in 1763. Planters set up new plantations and imported thousands of slaves directly from Africa. Dominica, Grenada, and Saint Vincent all saw major rebellions as these newly arrived Africans resisted their captors. Slave rebellions reached their peak in 1795 because the revolutionary government in France encouraged them during its war with Great Britain.

In the same way, few slave revolts scarred the Spanish islands until the growth of the sugar industry after 1800. Slavery existed, but it took a mild form on the cattle ranches dominating Cuba, Puerto Rico, and Santo Domingo. From the end of the 19th century, the number of cane estates rapidly increased in Cuba, bringing in immense numbers of African slaves. With sugar, slave revolts also became commonplace.

Until the 1770s, most rebellions involved newly imported Africans, who planned, prepared and fought in African ways. Most were led by a powerful charismatic leader, who drew support from the large number of alienated and vengeful slaves. Members of Akan-speaking groups from the Gold Coast (modern day Ghana) were especially likely to rebel. Planters highly valued the strength and hardiness of these slaves, whom they called Coromantees. Several of the Akan peoples, including the Asante or Ashanti, had created warrior kingdoms that supplied slaves to the European forts along the coast. Coromantee warriors (themselves slave owners) retained their pride and military skills even after they were defeated in battle and sold to slave traders.

The goals of these African rebels were "restorist" rather than revolutionary. They did not seek universal freedom for all men. They wanted to recreate contemporary West Africa, as they remembered it. When marronage became impracticable, the rebels sought to destroy white society and replace it with an Akan-style autocracy. In the great Jamaican revolt of 1760, Tacky and his followers wanted to kill the whites and partition the island into small principalities. Their own slaves would grow crops (the Maroons also owned black slaves) for sale to white traders along the coast.

Savage punishment invariably followed all slave rebellions, whether large or small. The planters slaughtered many slaves during the initial stages of fighting. Colonial courts killed rebel leaders through slow tortures—by progressive mutilation, slow burnings, breaking on the wheel, or starvation in cages. They then dismembered the bodies of the dead slaves, leaving their severed heads to rot in public places.

At least twice, these African slave revolts almost gained their ends. In 1733, slaves on the Danish island of Saint John captured the only fort, burned almost half of the plantations, and killed most of the whites. The rebels controlled the island for six months, defeating reinforcements from Saint Thomas as well as British Saint Kitts and Tortola. They were suppressed only when the French governor of Martinique sent two ships with 228 soldiers under an experienced commander.

An even more ambitious rebellion scourged Jamaica in 1760. Tacky, its main leader, was a Coromantee from the Gold Coast. He had as many as 30,000 followers who sought to kill all of the whites and bring the entire island under their rule. Their revolt began in April 1760 and spread to many of Jamaica's parishes. The Maroons honored their treaty and joined the Jamaican militia and British army in fighting the rebellion. But the forces of control only slightly outnumbered the rebel warriors. The latter held out until October 1761, and they were almost as bloodily effective as the more famous Haitian rebels of 1791–1804. Some sixty white persons and at least as many freedmen died. Five hundred slaves were killed or committed suicide, and as many were transported to the bay of Honduras. A contemporary historian estimated property damage at more than £100,000—perhaps as many millions in modern dollars.

## THE FRENCH REVOLUTION AND THE NAPOLEONIC WARS

Events in Europe during the French Revolution and Napoleon's First Empire (1789–1815) directly affected all of the Caribbean islands. The French Revolution began because the government was bankrupt—largely due to its wars with

Great Britain. In May 1789, an advisory body called the Estates-General met in Paris. Calling themselves the National Assembly, its members made radical changes in the laws and institutions governing France and its colonies. On August 4, 1789, they abolished the rights of the nobles and clergy, declaring that "all citizens, without distinction of birth, can be admitted to all ecclesiastical, civil, and military posts." Three weeks later, on August 26, the Assembly published the Declaration of the Rights of Man, which began "Men are born and remain free and equal in rights." Few members of the National Assembly thought of France's Caribbean colonies as they legislated for the homeland. But clearly, their decrees were inconsistent with a regime based on human slavery.

A Legislative Assembly took power in October 1791 and seized control of the king. France began to combat much of Europe—declaring war on Austria and Prussia (April 1792), on Great Britain and Holland (February 1793), and also on Spain (March 1793). A world war, involving all of Europe's colonies in the Americas, had begun. Hostilities lasted for twenty-three years until the final overthrow of Napoleon in 1815.

The most radical stage of the French Revolution began during the summer of 1792. King Louis XVI was overthrown in August 1792, and a National Convention, dominated by extreme revolutionaries or *Jacobins*, took power in September. Under the leadership of Maximilien Robespierre, the Jacobins murdered the king and his family (January 1793). They then created the first totalitarian government and began a "reign of terror and virtue." Their rule was terrible but brief. On July 27, 1794, more moderate Jacobins turned on Robespierre. Assuming power as the Directory, they ruled until October 1799, when they in turn were overthrown by Napoleon Bonaparte.

## SAINT-DOMINGUE IN 1789

Saint-Domingue was the most valuable colony in the world in 1789. Cane estates along the coastal plains produced 40 percent of the world's sugar, more than all the British colonies combined. Other tropical products also flourished, with the mountainous interior (rapidly developed since 1750) growing half the world's coffee. This one small colony provided 40 percent of France's foreign trade, and its 7,000 plantations also had substantial commercial links with the United States and the British and Spanish colonies. The planters complained that little of this wealth remained on the island. Although rich in land and pretensions, most colonists were heavily in debt to French merchants.

French law divided Saint-Domingue's inhabitants into three racial castes. In 1789, the island held about 31,000 whites, 25,000 freedmen (most of mixed race), and 435,000 slaves. All three groups were growing in number, with planters importing some 40,000 African slaves each year during the 1780s. Contrary to the British and Hispanic islands, however, racial caste and economic class did not neatly coincide. Both the whites and the *gens de coleur* (persons of color) comprised many competing groups, ranging from the very rich to very poor.

The highest ranks of white society included the top royal officials and the *grands blancs* (literally, "big whites"), who owned the largest and most prosperous sugar plantations in the Caribbean. Next in status and wealth came the *petits blancs* ("little whites"), a widely diverse group that included self-made coffee planters, merchants, and artisans as well as soldiers, sailors, waterfront drifters, and criminals. More than on any other island, the *petits blancs* directly competed with the members of the large free colored community. Thus many—but not all—were strongly racist.

| TABLE 18.   POPULATION ESTIMATES FOR THE FRENCH ISLANDS, 1750–1805 | | | |
|---|---|---|---|
| | TOTAL | WHITES | SLAVES | FREE NON-WHITES |
| Martinique | | | | |
| 1751 | 79,386 | 12,068 | 65,909 | 1,413 |
| 1789 | 96,158 | 10,636 | 83,414 | 5,235 |
| Guadeloupe | | | | |
| 1750 | 50,160 | 9,134 | 41,026 | |
| 1790 | 109,639 | 13,969 | 92,545 | 3,125 |
| Saint-Domingue | | | | |
| 1754 | 191,352 | 11,540 | 117,411 | 4,911 |
| 1775 | 288,803 | 32,650 | 249,098 | 7,055 |
| 1789 | 490,108 | 30,831 | 434,429 | 24,848 |
| 1805 | 380,000 | — | — | — |

NOTE:   The French colony of Saint-Domingue became the independent state of Haiti in 1804.

SOURCES:   Patterson, *Slavery and Social Death*, 480–81 (1751–1789); Leo Elizabeth, "The French Antilles," *Neither Slave nor Free*, 148–151; Lasserre, *Guadeloupe*, 284, 297; James Leyburn, *The Haitian People*, revised edition (New Haven: Yale University Press, 1966), 321 (1805).

The free coloreds of Saint-Domingue were both more numerous and also more prosperous than those living on the Spanish, British, or even the other French islands. Most resided in the country, where they made up the rural police force and militia. Many worked as overseers on the estates of absentee white owners. Others became coffee and cotton planters, and they probably outnumbered white planters in the mountainous South and West provinces. While not all freedmen were wealthy, those with money could buy slaves and land without any restrictions. In 1790 their spokesmen claimed that the coloreds owned a quarter of the colony's slaves and between a quarter and one-half of its productive land.

Despite the wealth of some freedmen, they had many grievances. French law had become increasingly racist since the 1730s as the colored population increased. The law now prevented freedmen from becoming priests, physicians, or lawyers. It also restricted them in many petty but irritating ways. Freedmen of mixed birth resented these restrictions because they tended to identify with their white ancestors. They typically despised the newly arrived slaves because of their African origins and customs. They copied white habits, and they looked for whiteness in their marriage partners.

The slaves, outnumbering whites and coloreds eight to one, formed the bottom of society. Nevertheless, as in other colonies, some slaves enjoyed a higher status than others. The great number of Africans arriving during the 1780s endured the hard work and poor food of the plantations. The creole élite of urban slaves and domestics—men like Toussaint L'Ouverture—might enjoy a comparatively mild slavery under considerate or even indulgent owners.

## THE FRENCH REVOLUTION BRINGS CIVIL WAR TO SAINT-DOMINGUE

The revolution on Saint-Domingue began in 1788, when the king announced the forthcoming meeting of the Estates-General. It ended sixteen years later with the creation in 1804 of the black republic of Haiti. During the first stage (1788–1791), whites fought whites, and whites also battled the colored freedmen. The black slaves looked on. Together with the legislative assemblies of Martinique and Guadeloupe, wealthy landowners from the North Province sent representatives to the Estates-General in 1788. In June 1789, the National Assembly admitted six West Indian deputies—the first colonial representatives accepted by any European legislature. There they opposed the members of the Société des Amis des Noirs (Society of the Friends of Blacks), a newly formed club seeking the abolition of slavery.

The same landowners that had sent representatives to Paris also established assemblies on the island, one for each of the three provinces as well as a General Assembly meeting at Saint Marc. As in France, however, the Haitian revolution became more radical during the summer of 1789, and these *grands blancs* lost control to other white factions. A virtual civil war existed by the spring of 1790, as these factions raised troops and fought for control of the assemblies and town governments. Except for the royal officials, all parties wanted to gain autonomy from France while maintaining slavery and a hierarchy of race on the island. Thus many whites refused to make any concessions to the colored freedmen. Only whites would share in the "liberty, fraternity, and equality" promised by the French Revolution.

Rebuffed by most white factions, some free coloreds also began to organize. In Paris, the coloreds, joined by the Amis des Noirs, demanded full legal equality. In May 1791, the National Assembly grudgingly granted full voting rights to colored men born of two free parents and otherwise qualified. Although it would have empowered perhaps 400 people, this decree infuriated the *petits blancs* factions. Toward the end of July 1791, the people of color in the West Province began to gather in armed bands, their patience exhausted. As disorder spread, some freedmen fortified their plantations and even armed their slaves. Wealthy coloreds returning from France initially provided leadership. Vincent Ogé (c.1750–1791), one such figure, already had led an abortive colored revolt in 1790 near Cap Français.

Governmental power had collapsed, and the whites and colored slave owners were divided into many warring factions. Yet no one expected the slaves to join the revolution. Suddenly, on the night of August 22, 1791, thousands of slaves near the city of Cap Français rose up and took a terrible vengeance on their masters. Within ten days, slaves had revolted throughout the entire North Province, leaving the whites in control only of Cap Français and a few fortified camps in the western mountains. Within two months, rebel slaves killed 2,000 whites and destroyed 280 sugar plantations. Ash from the blazing cane fields rained down on the city of Cap Français.

The Haitian revolution now became a many-sided struggle, with white, colored, and slave factions forming temporary alliances. The slave uprising was at first confined to the North Province. Sporadic slave uprisings in the other two provinces gradually died down by January 1793. In The West Province, André Rigaud (1761–1811) led the colored planters, who armed their slaves and gained control of the countryside, while a petits blancs mob controlled Port-au-Prince. In the South Province, the white planters generally maintained control.

## FRENCH SLAVES GAIN THEIR FREEDOM

While these local factions fought for power, the revolution in France had become more radical. On April 4, 1792, the Legislative Assembly decreed full political and legal equality between all free men, both white and colored. To enforce its decrees, it sent a Revolutionary Commission with autocratic powers and 7,000 troops, who arrived at Saint-Domingue in September 1792.

Léger Sonthonax, who dominated the Revolutionary Commission, was a Jacobin closely associated with the Amis de Noirs. Sonthonax was convinced that Saint-Domingue's whites—whether grands blancs or poor townsmen—were royalists or separatists. He now allied himself with the colored militias as his French troops died of malaria and yellow fever. Establishing a Jacobin reign of terror, Sonthonax purged and deported his enemies, dissolved the colonial assemblies and municipal governments, and levied heavy fines and taxes on the towns and merchants. Sonthonax's despotism destroyed any remaining white military power in the North Province, and alienated white colonials throughout the island. Some of the coloreds, now in positions of power, persecuted their former persecutors.

Sonthonax initially did not intend to free the slaves. Indeed, he used the people of color to crush both rebel slaves and the island's whites, whom he believed to be counterrevolutionaries. To retain power, however, he was forced to end slavery in June 1793—the first abolition of African slavery anywhere in the world. On June 20, 2,000 sailors from the French fleet landed in Cap Français to help its white citizens oust Sonthonax. While a fierce battle raged, Sonthonax promised freedom to all black warriors joining the republican cause. Taking up his offer, a large insurgent band attacked and burned the town during the night of June 20/21. More than 10,000 persons were killed, many of them whites. The surviving whites in the North Province fled to the United States, Cuba, Jamaica, and Puerto Rico.

While the French warred with each other, a Spanish army bore down on Sonthonax from the east. When war broke out in March 1793, a Spanish army of 14,000 men launched a two-pronged offensive towards Cap Français and Port-au-Prince. As it advanced, many rebel bands joined its ranks. With the Spanish and their black allies closing in on his remaining bases, Sonthonax on August 29 decreed the abolition of slavery throughout the island. On February 4, 1794, the National Convention in Paris approved his act by unanimously abolishing slavery throughout the French dominions.

## THE REVOLUTION ON GUADELOUPE AND MARTINIQUE

The French Revolution also exported political and social disorder to Guadeloupe and Martinique. Here, however, the white planters managed to maintain political control. In January 1793—frightened both by the Jacobin reign of terror and the massacre of whites in Saint-Domingue—their representatives placed both islands under British rule. On Guadeloupe and Martinique, the white planters succeeded in gaining the measure of autonomy Haiti's *grand blancs* had sought in 1789. Both islands enjoyed relative peace because they had fewer extremes of wealth and poverty. Thus the whites remained more united, while the free coloreds were fewer and less wealthy than on Saint-Domingue. (See Table 18, page 163.)

On Guadeloupe the royal governor and the colonial assembly welcomed the constitution of 1789, which strongly guaranteed property rights. The *petits blancs* in the towns called for more radical changes. However, the assembly easily crushed their demonstrations, and they fled to France, Dominica, or Saint Lucia. Curiously, Marie-Galante, perhaps seeking independence from its larger neighbor, chased out the royalist governor and adhered to the republican cause.

On Martinique the French Revolution primarily pitted the planters against their *petit blancs* creditors in Saint-Pierre. Troops commanded by the governor and assembly blockaded the capital by land and sea throughout the autumn of 1790, finally taking it with the help of a volunteer militia from Guadeloupe. Most people of color sat out the revolution—some because the planters were their kin, others because the *petits blancs* were their commercial rivals. All factions supported slavery, and they united to crush small-scale slave revolts in 1790 and 1791.

The white planters thus retained power on Guadeloupe and Martinique. When the Jacobins dismissed the king in August 1792, the assemblies of both islands declared their loyalty to the Crown, thus effectively seceding from France. In October 1792, the Jacobins sent a revolutionary commissioner to regain control of the islands. Raising an army among the exiled republicans on Saint Lucia, the commissioner invaded Guadeloupe (January 1793) and introduced a Jacobin reign of terror. Some planters sent representatives to Britain, which had treated the islands well during an earlier occupation (1758–1763). On January 17, 1793, planter envoys in London transferred their allegiance to the British Crown. The latter agreed to restore the islands to France, if the Bourbons regained the throne.

## THE FIFTH CARIBBEAN WAR BETWEEN FRANCE AND GREAT BRITAIN

A British army invaded Saint-Domingue in September 1793, thus beginning the fifth great war with France for control of the Caribbean islands. British forces easily seized the French islands in the Lesser Antilles. But the invasion of Saint-Domingue became a costly disaster that dragged on until 1798. Altogether, the British government poured over ten million pounds and more than 20,000 soldiers into Saint-Domingue. Almost 13,000 men died—perhaps 1,000 in battle, the rest of malaria and yellow fever.[2] Tropical diseases played a major role in the British loss. But they were also defeated by the determined resistance of the insurgent generals, black and colored, who fought to preserve the freedom granted by France in February 1794.

British forces entered Saint-Domingue at the invitation of its remaining white planters. During the summer of 1792, 420 planters in London joined those from Guadeloupe and Martinique in transferring their allegiance to George II. The murder of King Louis XVI horrified the colonists, and many despaired of regaining their estates while the revolution raged in France. If the islands must be ruled from Europe, then the planters preferred British government to Spanish.

Prime Minister William Pitt's decision to intervene defies any simple explanation. The prime minister was no friend of slavery.[3] His motives probably were both defensive and aggressive. Some Jamaican planters feared that the rebellion in Saint-Domingue might encourage an uprising among their slaves— the most rebellious in the Caribbean. Conquest of the French West Indies also would serve traditional British goals. Even if Pitt did not intend to keep the French Caribbean, its occupation would be useful at the peace conferences. As it had during previous wars, Great Britain would use its navy to capture France's colonial empire, while leaving land battles on the continent to its European allies.

British troops invaded Saint-Domingue from Jamaica in September 1793. The white planters turned over the port cities and naval bases without a struggle, and many fought on the British side. By June 1794, the British forces had taken all the major ports and much of the South and West provinces, and the Spanish and their black allies dominated the North Province. The French army controlled only Cap Français and Port-de-Paix. Early in 1794, a British expeditionary force with 6,000 solders under Admiral Sir John Jervis (1735–1823) and General Sir Charles Grey (1729–1807) took Martinique (February 20), Saint Lucia (April 4), and Guadeloupe (April 21). Since they already occupied Tobago, the British appeared on the verge of total victory in the French West Indies by mid-May 1794.

Suddenly the tide of battle turned against the British. In June, a French squadron landed troops on Guadeloupe under the command of Victor Hugues (1770–1826). As fanatical and bloodthirsty as Sonthonax but more effective, Hugues recaptured Guadeloupe in November. More than 1,200 white planters went to the guillotine at his order. Using Guadeloupe as a base, Hugues and the other commissioners sent from France encouraged rebellions in the French islands. They also sent agents to stir up the French-speaking free coloreds and slaves of Dominica and Grenada and the Black Carib of Saint Vincent, which Britain had occupied only since 1763.

French planters on Martinique managed to suppress Hugues's agents and remained under British rule. But serious slave revolts broke out concurrently on Saint Vincent, Saint Lucia, and Grenada. Pressed by the rebels—primarily black slaves joined by some free coloreds and Jacobin whites—the British had to flee Saint Lucia in July 1795. Joined by some African slaves, the Black Carib controlled almost the entire island of Saint Vincent for six months. On Grenada, the British army held only the fort at Saint George in February 1796. Under the leadership of Julien Fédon, a colored planter, the slaves established a virtual black republic. Even Jamaica itself was not immune, and July 1795 also saw the uprising of the Trelawny Town Maroons.

Simultaneous slave rebellions on so many different islands seriously challenged British rule in the West Indies. The British sent 17,000 troops to the Windward Islands in March 1796. This expedition ultimately did retake the French islands, but the black and colored rebels proved to be tough opponents. Those on Saint Vincent and Grenada surrendered only after offering sharp resistance, and some slaves on Saint Lucia held out for almost two years.[4] In contrast, British troops seized Trinidad (February 1797) and the Dutch islands without fighting, when Spain and the Netherlands came under French dominance.

## TOUSSAINT L'OUVERTURE LEADS THE HAITIAN SLAVE REVOLT

Because of the slave revolts in the Windwards and Jamaica, Britain could not send reinforcements to Saint-Domingue, where yellow fever and malaria were annihilating its army. Quarrels between the British and the French planters also slowed their advance. In June 1794 the French National Convention finally recalled Sonthonax and gave command of the French forces to General Étienne Laveaux, a less divisive leader. Although disease, dissension, and the Windward rebellions weakened the British army, Toussaint L'Ouverture (1743–1803) still deserves much of the credit for its defeat. Haitian independence became possible in May 1795 when Toussaint betrayed his Spanish allies and offered his services to the French under General Laveaux.

A creole slave from the North Province, Toussaint had organized a small band of loyal black followers.[5] With the outbreak of war, he entered the Spanish service and built up a force of some four thousand black troops skilled in guerrilla warfare. When news arrived that the French Assembly had freed the slaves, he decided to cast his lot with the remnants of the French army. On May 6, 1794, Toussaint suddenly turned on the Spanish in Saint Raphael and slaughtered many as they came out of church after Mass.

An untrained but brilliant general, Toussaint effectively used both guerrilla tactics and frontal attacks against the British. By early 1795, he controlled much of the North and West provinces. Two of Toussaint's lieutenants—Jean-Jacques Dessalines (1758–1806) and Henri Christophe (1767–1820)—especially distinguished themselves during these campaigns and later succeeded him as rulers of Haiti. Moreover, Toussaint's victories inspired renewed attacks by André Rigaud, who commanded a force of several thousand colored and black troops in the South.

English forces had been driven back to four ports along the coast by June 1795, and the Spanish had retired to Santo Domingo. In July, the Spanish government officially withdrew from the war and ceded Santo Domingo to France (Treaty of Bâle). The British sent another army under a new general, but Toussaint retained control of the North and West, while Rigaud kept the initiative in the South. In March 1798, General Thomas Maitland made one last attempt to hold the South Province, closest to Jamaica. When it failed, he sued for peace, signing a secret military and commercial treaty that treated Toussaint as an independent ruler. By October 1798, the last British troops had left Saint-Domingue.

As European power in Saint-Domingue collapsed, Toussaint and other black and colored generals fought for control. One by one Toussaint skillfully eliminated his rivals. In 1796, he defeated a plot by Rigaud and Villatte, the colored commander of Cap Français. Although professing loyalty to the French government, he expelled its commissioners when they attempted to check his autonomy. By 1799, only Rigaud retained an independent power base.

With an army of 55,000 blacks, Christophe and Dessalines invaded the south in November. Because Rigaud had retained ties to France, an American fleet assisted their advance. Although his army contained black solders as well as whites, Rigaud's power rested on the colored planters, who distrusted the former slaves. The colored troops now fought as valiantly against Toussaint as they had against the British. At Jacmel, the defenders and their able commander, Alexandre Pétion (1770–1818), held out against savage attacks for six months.

When Jacmel fell, Pétion—and later Rigaud—escaped to France. To break the power of the colored forces, Toussaint appointed the brutal Dessalines to govern South Province. Despite Toussaint's earlier promises of no reprisals, Dessalines slaughtered thousands. Resistance was crushed, but Dessalines's brutality left a great bitterness among the people of color. Toussaint now controlled all of Saint-Domingue, but his experiences made him fear invasion from the Spanish part of the island. In January 1801, his forces invaded Santo Domingo, taking the capital after a triumphant three-week campaign.

## TOUSSAINT L'OUVERTURE'S NEW ORDER

Toussaint had won the war. Now he had to govern a devastated and impoverished country. Eleven years of civil war and invasion had destroyed Saint-Domingue's fabled prosperity. The cities were charred ruins, and war and neglect had devastated the elaborate irrigation systems. The island lacked both skilled technicians and laborers. Perhaps two-thirds of the whites and one-third of the colored freedmen had died or emigrated. More than a third the 435,000 slaves had perished, and many of the rest had fled for safety to the mountains. Moreover, the civil war also had destroyed the traditions and the institutions of self-government. As C. L. R. James noted in his classic history of the revolution,

> For nearly ten years the population, corrupt enough before, had been trained in bloodshed and soaked in violence. Bands of marauders roamed the countryside. The only disciplined force was the army, and Toussaint instituted a military dictatorship.[6]

Toussaint's victory and the unification of Hispaniola posed in stark terms fundamental questions that have troubled Haiti ever since. The most important immediate problem was money. France, now ruled by Napoleon Bonaparte, was likely to invade its wealthiest colony. The export of tropical products grown on large plantations provided the obvious source of revenues to support an army. But any system of wages would make Haiti's sugar and coffee more expensive than crops produced on islands still under slavery. Moreover, few former slaves wanted to work on cane estates under any system. Prior to the revolution, the slaves had grown most of the island's food on their provision grounds. Now that they were free, they wanted to live as independent peasant farmers cultivating their own bit of family land. Freedom meant the right to control their own labor and keep the crops they grew with their own hands.

Toussaint sought to restore Saint-Domingue's prosperity by creating a centralized and authoritarian state based on forced labor. The constitution of July 1801 gave all power to Toussaint and granted him the right to name his successor. He controlled major appointments to the army, administration, and church. Each of the six provincial governors reported directly and only to him. Perhaps, given Napoleon's obvious ambitions, Toussaint had no choice. But his system gave Haiti a centralized and authoritarian government that has endured to the present.

Toussaint's constitution and subsequent decrees restored the plantation system under state control. Toussaint's government took over abandoned estates and rented them to revolutionary generals. Altogether, perhaps two-thirds of the land was state-controlled, and Toussaint also encouraged absentee white and colored planters to return to their estates. Half the profits went to the government, one-fourth to the owner, and one-fourth to the workers.

While whites and coloreds received key governmental and military posts, the former slaves were forcibly returned to the plantations. The blacks became subject to military discipline. A system of internal passports was introduced, and the army prevented workers from leaving the plantations. Dessalines, as inspector general, authorized physical punishment to keep them at work. Some plantations even purchased Africans slaves from slave traders. This system of "militarized agriculture" resembles modern socialism, and it borrowed from earlier decrees by Sonthonax, the Jacobin commissioner in Saint-Domingue.

Toussaint's policies stimulated a modest economic revival, but they also alienated his black followers. Some of Toussaint's own generals resented the return of white proprietors. In September 1801, Moïse, his adopted nephew and rumored successor, led a major revolt against the whites of the North. Toussaint

"Revenge taken by the Black Army for the Cruelties practised on them by the French." Napoleon Bonaparte sent more than 45,000 soldiers to reconquer Saint-Domingue (now Haiti). French troops acted brutally, and the former slaves tried to kill all whites remaining on the island.

quickly crushed the revolt, executed Moïse, and purged 2,000 of his followers. But he could not regain the trust of the population. To the newly liberated slaves, the work regimen imposed by the revolutionary state closely resembled the slavery they thought they had left behind. Some escaped to the mountains. Most were indifferent when French armies invaded the following year.

## NAPOLEON INVADES SAINT-DOMINGUE

Napoleon became determined in 1801 to reestablish the French Empire in the Caribbean. The Peace of Amiens (October 1801) freed his hand by halting hostilities with Great Britain. In return for other concessions, Britain returned all French territories except Trinidad. Napoleon dreamed of a great western empire that would include Louisiana (returned by Spain in March 1801), Florida, and French Guiana as well as the West Indies. A prosperous Saint-Domingue was crucial to his plans, and he decided to restore slavery in the French Caribbean.

Commanded by General Charles Leclerc (1772–1802), Napoleon's brother-in-law, 20,000 soldiers—including many Swiss and Polish conscripts—reached Saint-Domingue by February 1802. Napoleon would lose 40,000 of his best soldiers before the French withdrew twenty-two months later. The French invasion thus repeated Britain's earlier defeat. But it also turned into a vicious war to the death between the races.

After destroying Cap Français on February 4, Henri Christophe withdrew to the interior. The troops holding Santo Domingo and the South Province surrendered without resistance. By February 12, Leclerc held all the important coastal positions and launched an attack on the interior. His victories proved costly as Toussaint's generals fiercely resisted. Dessalines was especially effective in the South and West provinces, where he killed the whites and burned towns and plantations. By the middle of April, half of Leclerc's soldiers were dead or sick of yellow fever. Suddenly, and somewhat mysteriously, first Christophe, then Toussaint, and finally Dessalines surrendered at the end of April. A month later Leclerc invited Toussaint to dinner. During the course of the meal, Toussaint was seized, bound, and hurried on board a ship for France—where he died in a freezing dungeon on April 7, 1803.

Leclerc's victory lasted barely five months. By mid-July, the yellow fever epidemic reached a peak. With fewer than 8,000 soldiers, Leclerc had to depend on Dessalines and Christophe to carry out his policies. At this crucial point, slavery and the slave trade were restored in Guadeloupe and Martinique (May 20, 1802), and Leclerc began to reimpose slavery in Saint-Domingue itself. Spontaneous revolts broke out across the island. The colored, who no longer trusted the French, increasingly joined forces with the black rebels. Leclerc replied with ruthless brutality, shooting entire brigades of black soldiers.

The black generals who had deserted Toussaint for Leclerc now swung back again to the opposition. Pétion (who had returned with the French army of invasion) and Christophe rebelled in the north, while Dessalines took the west. While he had served the French, Dessalines had eliminated many of his rivals.

In late November 1802, the black and colored generals recognized him as leader of the resistance.

On the French side, General Rochambeau (1725–1807) replaced Leclerc, who died of yellow fever on November 2. Reinforced by another 25,000 French troops, Rochambeau fought on for a year, acting with extraordinary brutality verging on genocide. Dessalines and Christophe responded with equal ferocity, determined to exterminate every white they could reach. In May 1803, England again declared war on France, shattering the Treaty of Amiens. British forces quickly retook Saint Lucia and Martinique, and they also captured Guadeloupe. Early in July, a British fleet blockaded Saint-Domingue and bombarded French positions on the coast. On November 30, the remaining French soldiers left Cap Français accompanied by 18,000 refugees.

Saint-Domingue finally belonged to the black majority after 15 years of devastation. On January 1, 1804, Dessalines and his generals proclaimed Haiti's independence, choosing an aboriginal word (meaning "the land of the mountains") to replace the French name, Saint-Domingue. Dessalines became governor general for life. In 1805 he had himself crowned emperor in imitation of Napoleon.

# PART FOUR:

## THE ABOLITION OF SLAVERY AND THE CHALLENGES OF FREEDOM

■

# THE BRITISH COLONIES

∎

Slavery dominated every aspect of life in the Caribbean islands. It made sugar plantations possible, shaped social and familial relations, and dominated the laws and politics of the islands. Thus the abolition of slavery represented a radical and dramatic change in island life. Great Britain was the first European state to permanently end slavery in its Caribbean colonies. Many Britons now felt that slavery was both cruel and economically inefficient. They believed that the slaves only needed freedom to become happy and productive. Unfortunately, freedom was all the Abolitionists wanted to give the slaves. In 1846, Parliament adopted free trade and began to tax imports of West Indian sugar at the same rate as foreign sugars—which were cheaper precisely because they still were produced by slaves. Thus the British islands were forced to create an entirely new society while their incomes were rapidly falling. Many island governments failed this difficult test. From the 1860s, Britain thus abolished the island legislatures and ruled its colonies directly from London.

## THE LONG ROAD TO FREEDOM

Until the 1780s, European statesmen and governments accepted slavery as inevitable and necessary. Through the labor of thousands of slaves, the island colonies produced extremely valuable exports of sugar and other tropical goods for European empires. Enormous amounts of capital invested in the sugar industry provided income to many Europeans and tax revenues for their governments. Since all European rulers agreed on the need for slavery, they let the planters rule their slaves and stood ready to help suppress slave rebellions. Events in Europe affected the islands, as we have seen, primarily when they led to international wars.

First in Great Britain and later on the continent, many Europeans came to believe that slavery was wrong and even evil. In most cases, they then forced abolition on island planters, who generally wanted to keep slavery. Even had they wanted to, the Caribbean whites could not abolish slavery until European governments turned against it. Except for Haiti and Santo Domingo, all of the islands were colonies, and their laws had to be approved by the European nation ruling over them. Beginning in 1792, European rulers began to force emancipa-

| TABLE 19. THE ABOLITION OF AFRICAN SLAVERY IN THE CARIBBEAN, 1792–1886 | | |
|---|---|---|
| COLONIAL POWER | SLAVE TRADE OUTLAWED | SLAVERY ABOLISHED |
| Denmark | March 1792 (partial ban effective ten years later); 1807 (total ban) | 1848 |
| France | February 4, 1794 (reimposed 1802 for Guadeloupe and Martinique); April 15, 1818 | February 4, 1794 (reimposed 1802 for Guadeloupe and Martinique); 1848 |
| Great Britain | 1806 (bans sale to foreign colonies); March 25, 1807 (import of slaves into British colonies outlawed from March 1, 1808) | August 1834 (unpaid labor as "apprentices" required to 1838) |
| Holland | 1814 | 1848 (Sint Maarten) 1863 (other colonies) |
| Spain | Formally banned in 1820. But illegal trade tolerated to Puerto Rico (until the 1850s) and Cuba (to 1865) | 1873 (Puerto Rico) 1879 (Cuba; unpaid labor required to 1886) |
| Sweden | 1824 | 1846 |

tion on their colonies. But the road to freedom was long. Almost a century passed before Caribbean slavery finally ended with its abolition on Cuba in 1886.

## THE ANTI-SLAVERY CRUSADE IN GREAT BRITAIN

The British Empire was the first to put a permanent end to slavery, and emancipation was a momentous event in the history of the British colonies. In 1833, the British islands were inhabited by many black slaves and a few slave owners, and there were only a relatively small number of black and colored freedmen. Crops grown by slaves formed the only export. No one knew whether crops grown by free-wage labor could compete with those from regions where slavery still existed—the French islands, Cuba, and Brazil. Haiti provided the only earlier example of black freedom, and abolition in Haiti had ruined a once buoyant economy and caused the massacre of many thousand whites. In abolishing slavery, the British government thus took a decisive step with unpredictable consequences.

Most historians now agree that this extraordinary act resulted from a profound change in the moral values of ordinary men and women. During the last quarter of the 18th century, anti-slavery sentiment suddenly spread throughout Great Britain. Intellectuals had long attacked slavery as uncivilized, unjust, and unproductive, but the abstract arguments of philosophers have little influence in themselves. Abolitionism prospered in Britain because it became part of a great religious revival associated with John Wesley's Methodist movement and the Evangelical reformers in the Anglican church.[1] Eighteenth-century revivalism stressed both sin and spiritual rebirth expressed in good works. The converted believed that God rewards the good and punishes sin and evil. Thus they became convinced that abolition would ensure God's blessings. But continuing the sin of slavery would call down God's wrath upon Britain.

The religious revival provided not only ideas but institutions that could bring pressure on the government. Methodists in Britain and North America— perhaps 300,000 strong by 1830—formed a vocal and highly organized pressure group. Moreover, compelled by their beliefs, Methodist and Baptist missionaries flocked to the British West Indies, where they began to convert growing numbers of black slaves. The black now was not only a brother—a fellow human—but also a born-again member of the same church.

## THE STRUGGLE TO END THE BRITISH SLAVE TRADE

Anti-slavery forces formed the Society for the Abolition of the Slave Trade in 1787. Given contemporary politics, they felt it would be easier to abolish the trade than to attack slavery head on. In abolishing slavery, the government would confiscate existing property rights, and laws passed by the colonial assemblies protected these rights. In contrast, Parliament alone had the power to regulate maritime commerce, and one law would thus end the slave trade.

The anti-slavery leaders thus began by asking supporters to send petitions against the slave trade. To their surprise, thousands responded, and Parliament received more than 100 petitions by the end of May 1788. William Wilberforce (1759–1833), a wealthy politician and close friend of the prime minister, William Pitt, became the chief parliamentary spokesman for the abolitionists. Because the number of petitions impressed the government, Wilberforce was able to accomplish a great deal, although later legends probably overstate his effectiveness.

Working behind the scenes with the king's ministers, Wilberforce initiated a series of parliamentary inquiries that brought out the horrors of the Middle Passage. To document its iniquities, Thomas Clarkson (1760–1846) provided expert witnesses and accumulated massive data on all aspects of the trade—as well as collecting shackles, thumb screws, teeth chisels, and branding irons that vividly demonstrated its horrors. Between 1787 and 1794, Clarkson collected information showing that the slave trade was one vast graveyard both for the slaves and also for British sailors, who died even faster than the Africans.

Despite Clarkson's evidence, many in Parliament opposed the sudden interruption of a business long sanctioned by law. In April 1791, the Commons overwhelmingly defeated Wilberforce's first motion to introduce an abolition bill. The abolitionists only redoubled their campaign in the country. Pamphlets publicized the most telling evidence presented to the parliamentary commissions. Josiah Wedgwood sold 200,000 copies of a china medallion that showed a kneeling slave in chains with the inscription "Am I Not a Man and a Brother?"

Over 500 petitions from regional abolition committees reached Parliament. A second crushing defeat of abolition would be politically dangerous. Prime Minister Pitt, in what many consider his most eloquent speech, carried both houses for gradual, not immediate, abolition.

After much debate, the Commons decided to end the British slave trade on January 1, 1796. But the Jacobin reign of terror and the war with France in 1793 discredited radical ideas. Pitt and other parliamentary leaders now gave only tepid support, and 1796 passed without an abolition bill. Some abolitionists charged that Pitt had lost interest because the British had conquered Dutch Guiana and Trinidad and were seeking to take Saint-Domingue from Toussaint L'Ouverture's black rebels. Thousands of new slaves would be needed to restore Saint-Domingue's prosperity as well as to grow sugar on the rich lands of Britain's new colonies.

The majority of politically influential Britons had accepted the goal of abolition, but fourteen more years of parliamentary maneuvering was needed to end the trade. The government first gained passage of the Foreign Slave Bill (May 1806), which prohibited the shipping of slaves to foreign colonies (like Cuba) or to Britain's new conquests, such as Trinidad. In 1807, Parliament finally abolished import of slaves into British colonies as of March 1, 1808, and imposed large fines on transgressors.[2]

## THE ILLEGAL SLAVE TRADE TO THE FRENCH AND SPANISH ISLANDS

Abolition was much less popular on the continent than in Great Britain. In European countries the anti-slavery movement never became a religious crusade as it did in England. Only intellectuals and government officials joined groups such as the French Société des Amis des Noirs. Most were Protestants in Roman Catholic countries, and the pope did not condemn the slave trade until 1839. Without pressure from Great Britain, therefore, most European countries would have continued to permit the slave trade.

Britain's abolition of the trade affected all the islands, since British ships had carried most slaves imported by the Spanish and French colonies. Following its victory in the Napoleonic wars, the British government tried, with varying success, to persuade other states to end the slave trade. The 1806 law ending the slave trade in newly conquered colonies applied to the Dutch West Indies as well as to the Danish Virgin Islands, captured in 1807.[3] Treaties with Sweden (1813) and the Netherlands (1814) confirmed the abolition of the slave trade to their Caribbean colonies.

It proved more difficult to suppress the slave trade in the French and Spanish islands. The British forced the defeated French to sign an 1814 treaty (confirmed in 1818), ending the trade. However, an illegal trade continued until 1831, delivering some 80,000 slaves to Guadeloupe and Martinique. The Spanish adamantly refused to conform to British demands, and continued to tolerate illegal traders. By a treaty in 1817, Spain agreed to end the slave trade in 1820. But Spanish officials refused to enforce laws passed under British pressure. The

George Cruikshank del.

Re-published from the Westminster Review, No. XXII, on the 1st Jan. 1830; by Robert Heward, at the Office of the Westminster Review, 2, Wellington Street, Strand, London. Sold there, and by Cowie and Strange, 55, Paternoster Row; and by all Agents of the Westminster Review.

STEREOTYPE.—Printed by T. C. HANSARD, 32, Paternoster Row, London.—PRICE ONE PENNY.

ART. I.—1. *Trial and Condemnation of Esther Hibner.* From the Morning Chronicle of April 11, 1829.

2. *Despatch of Mr. Secretary Huskisson to the Governor of the Bahamas, on the Subject of the Cruelties perpetrated by Henry and Helen Moss on a Female Negro Slave who died under the infliction, and the Application for Remission of their Punishment. Dated Downing Street, Sept. 28, 1827.* From the Anti-Slavery Monthly Reporter for April, 1829.

HISTORY tells of an individual, who believed he had travelled for seven years in foreign countries and there done many notable acts, when the truth was that he had dipped his head into a pail of water and taken it out again. Very much like this is the history of that metaphorical personage, the type of all that is foolish and deceivable in nations, in whom under one bestial appellation is concentrated the description of the ignorance and *gullibility* of the British community. Believing himself to be wise, it is impossible to tell the time when he became a fool. He said, 'I am rich, and increased with goods, and have need of nothing ; and knew not that he was wretched, and miserable, and poor, and blind, and naked.' Puffed up with the idea that he was something and somebody, he winked and ran his head quietly into the endurance of such frauds, as could never have befallen any body that was in the habit of walking with his eyes open, or was humble enough to conceive that he might possibly be made a dupe.

Not that the man positively would not take his fingers out of the fire when they were burning. On the contrary, nobody made more turmoil when he knew that he was hurt. But his coat might be taken off his back, by any body that would tell him a long story. He

"Slavery in the West Indies." An engraving by George Cruikshank on the cover of an abolitionist "penny pamphlet." To arouse public opinion against the slave trade and slavery, British abolitionists published millions of these inexpensive paper booklets from the 1770s.

British navy ended the minor trade to Puerto Rico during the 1850s, after some 55,000 slaves entered that island. In Cuba, slave prices soared since illegal traders had to bribe governmental officials at all levels. But Cuba's growing sugar industry demanded slaves at any price. Until it was ended in 1865, the illegal trade brought in more than 500,000 slaves.

## SLAVE EMANCIPATION IN THE BRITISH ISLANDS

The British Empire was the first to end slavery. The slaves gained their freedom sooner than those in the United States and without the enduring bitterness caused by the Civil War. Nevertheless, emancipation was not achieved without great difficulty, and twenty-five years passed between the end of the slave trade in 1808 and the abolition of slavery in 1833.

The British government was now committed to improving the conditions of the slaves. Sir James Stephen (1789–1859), the son of a leading abolitionist, managed Caribbean matters at the Colonial Office and relentlessly exposed abuses by the planters. After the American Revolution, the government did not want to force emancipation on its West Indian colonies. Instead it sought to persuade the planters to accept abolition through a series of major initiatives—slave registration (1815), amelioration (1823), and emancipation (1831).

The abolitionists sought slave registration both to prevent illegal imports and also to provide statistics proving that slaves were badly treated. Pushed by the British government, all the colonial legislatures by 1820 required masters to register their slaves. The five-year struggle to impose slave registration convinced the abolitionists that Britain must bring stronger pressures to bear on island legislators. In January 1823, they formed the Society for the Mitigation and Gradual Abolition of Slavery, whose name stated its goals.

The campaign to free the slaves repeated the tactics of the earlier crusade against the slave trade. The abolitionists set up local committees and solicited petitions from members of all parties, and especially from clergy. To whip up support, the Abolition Society published millions of pamphlets, won the support of newspapers, and sponsored public lectures across the nation.

Pressure from the Abolition Society forced Parliament to commit itself in May 1823 to eventual freedom. As an immediate goal, the government issued a series of Amelioration Proposals and began to press for their adoption by the colonial assemblies. These measures limited a master's control in many ways. New laws encouraged religious instruction and church marriages, restricted physical punishment, safeguarded a slave's private property, prohibited work (or markets) on Sundays, outlawed the breakup of families, and allowed slaves to testify in court under certain conditions. Despite their initial indignation, all island legislatures adopted at least some of the government's amelioration proposals. The legislatures of Barbados and Jamaica were the least willing to introduce these reforms, and the Jamaicans passed a Slave Act acceptable to the government only in 1831. During the 1820s, island assemblies also lifted the remaining restrictions on free coloreds, who could now vote and be elected to office.[4]

## VIOLENT REBELLIONS END SLAVERY IN THE BRITISH ISLANDS

Abolitionists in Britain campaigned to end slavery, just as they earlier had pressed for an end to the slave trade. This time, however, the slaves themselves took an active role in the campaign. For the first time, slave revolts strongly influenced public opinion in Britain. Although they received freedom from the Crown in 1833, black slaves themselves played a major role in making abolition inevitable.

Slave rebellions significantly increased after 1815 on all the British islands.[5] Slaves rebelled both in the major sugar colonies and on the smaller islands. Unrest grew even in the Bahamas, which had no cane estates. Significantly, blacks no longer informed on conspiracies among their fellow slaves. During the 18th century, the planters usually heard about plots in time to arrest their leaders. From 1815 on, they stopped only one out of fourteen major revolts. The masters' position was becoming untenable.

In 1816, a revolt ravaged Barbados, which had not known a slave conspiracy since 1701. Slaves on seventy of the largest estates suddenly rose up on Easter Sunday. Within a few hours, a third of the island was in flames. Many believed rumors that the British governor was bringing a "free paper" and that imperial troops would not march against them. Although only one white civilian was killed, the Barbados courts reacted with the usual ferocity. Fifty slaves died during the rebellion and 214 were executed after it was crushed.

On some—but not all—of the estates, slave unrest grew out of worsening conditions following the abolition of the slave trade. Slaves did not reproduce themselves, and the slave population thus fell temporarily when the trade ended. Since they had fewer hands, some masters forced their slaves to work harder. For example, cane estates shifted women, children, and colored slaves from domestic service to the field gangs. However, we can attribute only part of the unrest after 1815 to harsher treatment. The Jamaican rebellion in 1831 occurred when conditions were improving, and revolts also took place on islands without cane estates.

The extremely rapid spread of Christianity among the slaves also contributed to unrest—or so the planters complained. The established Anglican church, which enjoyed a monopoly until 1754, had made little effort to convert blacks. On the islands taken from France in 1814, Roman Catholic clergy, who did baptize slaves, generally accepted slavery as licit. From the 1780s, dozens of Moravian, Methodist, and Baptist missionaries flocked to the West Indies. Most found it impossible totally to ignore slavery's manifest inhumanity. Moreover, their teachings emphasized spiritual rebirth in ways that increased a convert's self-esteem. Chapels with all-black congregations also provided black and colored deacons and preachers with a means of leadership. Several black deacons were at the head of the Jamaican revolt of 1831–32, often called the Baptist War.

These leaders gained the support of a large number of more ordinary slaves who could no longer endure slavery. Slavery remained intolerable even after amelioration laws limited a master's powers during the 1820s. Indeed, amelioration probably made revolution more likely. Thus the right to assemble at black churches on Sundays made it possible for slaves from many estates to coordinate an uprising.[6] The slaves now had more to lose, and they wanted to keep their gains. Many rebel slaves believed that the king soon would grant freedom or already had given it. They feared that the planters would use force to take it away.

The African slaves who rebelled during the 1700s had wanted to kill their masters and restore the African community they had left behind. The goals of the creole slaves in these rebellions were less extreme. They wanted to live in their own family groups on their own land. For most slaves, freedom now meant the right to live as self-reliant small peasants. They sometimes might work for a planter, but only for wages and only on their own terms.

Beginning in 1830, both British abolitionists and Caribbean slaves became increasingly impatient with the slow progress of the government's amelioration policies. But it was a Jamaican slave rebellion—and not the British anti-slavery movement—that finally brought slavery to an end. None of Jamaica's earlier slave rebellions matched the scale of this revolt. Led by the Baptist lay preacher Sam Sharpe, the uprising began on December 27, 1831. Before it was suppressed at the end of January, more than 60,000 slaves took part throughout an area of 750 square miles. Over 200 sugar estates in the northwestern parishes were burned and pillaged, the whites fleeing to Montego Bay and other coastal ports. Regular troops and militia put down the insurrection with the customary savagery, and 540 slaves and 14 whites died. The convicted leaders were members of the slave élite, and most were Baptists, including many black deacons. Blaming them for the revolt, incensed whites tore down the chapels of Baptist and Methodist ministers throughout Jamaica.

## THE EMANCIPATION ACT OF 1834

News of the revolt and of its repression provoked outrage in Britain, and it especially energized groups, such as the evangelical churches, already recruited to emancipation. Missionaries who had fled Jamaica aroused audiences with graphic stories of the revolt. The new Parliament meeting early in 1833—the first after the Reform Act of 1832—received petitions signed by more than 1.5 million persons. Emancipation was ensured. Remembering the fate of Haiti, the government decided to compel the freed slaves to remain at work for a period of years. Justice also required that owners be compensated when the government seized property lawfully acquired.

The Abolition Act passed in August 1833 ordered the ending of slavery as of August 1834. Agriculture workers were compelled to work for their former masters as apprentices until 1840, domestics until August 1838—but they also could buy their immediate freedom. In return for food, clothing, lodging, and medical attendance, apprentices owed forty-five hours of unpaid labor per week. Special magistrates from England (rather than local justices of the peace) would judge all disputes between masters and servants. Parliament voted an outright grant of £20 million—some £25 per slave on average—to compensate owners. Since these terms appeared to be the best they could get, the colonial assemblies quickly passed the Emancipation Bill. Bermuda and Antigua freed their slaves immediately. The other colonies enacted apprenticeship.

The Anti-Slavery Society continued to fight for complete emancipation, using its customary tactics. Thousands of pamphlets described such abuses as the employment of treadmills in the workhouses and the flogging of women. In April 1838, Parliament ended apprenticeship two years early, and the colonial assemblies approved the necessary laws. At midnight on August 1, 1838, the 750,000 slaves in the British colonies became free men and women. Thousands of blacks peacefully celebrated at churches, chapels, thanksgiving parades, and public meetings throughout the islands. Their high hopes quickly evaporated, but few would have been willing to return to the hated system that had dominated the British islands since the 1640s.

## THE PAINFUL TRANSITION TO FREEDOM IN THE BRITISH COLONIES

The British West Indies were totally unprepared for slave emancipation. The slave society had tailored governments, taxes, and laws to its particular needs. Island governments furnished few public services, since masters provided their slaves with what passed for justice, education, and medical care. Schools, hospitals, police forces, and jails simply did not exist in 1838. Island governments had to build them for the first time, just as legislators had to rewrite the law codes. Moreover, they had to pay for services to an ever larger number of citizens. Despite several severe epidemics, the population soared after emancipation. Overall, the British colonies had almost twice as many inhabitants in 1891 (1,607,218) as in 1841 (863,971).

Unfortunately, the British colonies found themselves forced to create a new, free society while their incomes were falling rapidly. Emancipation sharply increased a planter's costs precisely as his income from the harvest was dropping. When prices fell by half—as they did between 1840 and 1848—planters had to double their output merely to stay even. But cane production fell after emancipation—by 50 percent on Jamaica—as the former slaves fled from the harsh routines of field labor. Many plantations operated at a loss, and government revenues plummeted.

Labor on a cane estate is arduous and boring. But a comparison between Jamaica and Trinidad—the two largest islands—shows that there was no substitute for a prosperous sugar industry during the 19th century. The industry collapsed on Jamaica, while indentured laborers from India sustained it on Trinidad. As a result, individuals enjoyed a higher standard of living on Trinidad. The steady growth of tax revenues allowed Trinidad—but not Jamaica—to improve its economic infrastructure and public institutions.

| TABLE 20. POPULATION ESTIMATES, SELECTED BRITISH COLONIES, 1773–1911 | | | | |
|---|---|---|---|---|
| | TOTAL | WHITES | SLAVES | FREE NON-WHITES |
| **Jamaica** | | | | |
| 1834 | 376,200 | 20,000 | 310,000 | 46,200 |
| 1861 | 441,300 | 13,800 | — | 427,500 |
| 1881 | 580,800 | 14,400 | — | 566,400 |
| 1891 | 639,500 | 14,700 | — | 624,800 |
| 1911 | 831,400 | 15,600 | — | 815,800 |
| **Trinidad** | | | | |
| 1834 | 44,715 | 3,632 | 22,359 | 18,724 |
| 1851 | 69,609 | — | — | — |
| 1861 | 84,438 | — | — | — |
| 1871 | 109,638 | — | — | — |
| 1901 | 258,000 | — | — | — |
| **Barbados** | | | | |
| 1833–1834 | 100,242 | 12,797 | 80,861 | 6,584 |
| 1851 | 135,939 | — | — | — |
| 1881 | 171,860 | — | — | — |
| 1911 | 172,337 | — | — | — |
| **Saint Kitts** | | | | |
| 1861 | 24,440 | — | — | — |
| 1881 | 29,137 | — | — | — |
| 1891 | 30,876 | 2,343 | — | 28,533 |
| 1911 | 26,283 | — | — | — |
| **Nevis** | | | | |
| 1861 | 9,822 | 260 | — | 9,562 |
| 1881 | 11,684 | — | — | — |
| 1891 | 13,087 | 182 | — | 12,905 |
| 1911 | 12,945 | — | — | — |
| **The Bahamas** | | | | |
| 1773 | 4,394 | 2,053 | 2,341 | |
| 1838 | 21,794 | — | — | — |
| 1851 | 27,519 | — | — | — |
| 1881 | 43,521 | — | — | — |
| 1911 | 55,944 | — | — | — |

SOURCES: Patterson, *Slavery and Social Death*, 477–79 (1834); Gisela Eisner, *Jamaica 1830–1930 A Study in Economic Growth* (Manchester, England: University of Manchester Press), 153 (1861–1911); Watts, *West Indies*, 459 (Trinidad, 1851–1901); Bonham Richardson, *Caribbean Migrants: Environment and Human Survival on St Kitts and Nevis* (Knoxville: University of Tennessee Press, 1983), 93, 132; Burns, *British West Indies*, 514 (Bahamas, 1773); Aaron Segal, "Bahamas," *Population Policies in the Caribbean*, 105 (1838–1911).

## THE IMPACT OF FREE TRADE IN SUGAR

Sugar prices plunged as total world production increased 700 percent from the 1840s to the 1890s. Moreover, the British Caribbean now competed with regions that could produce sugar more cheaply and make a profit even as prices fell. The United States, Cuba, and Brazil increased production using slave labor. From the 1820s, European refiners also imported Asian sugar from the Dutch East Indies, the Spanish Philippines, and British possessions in India, Malaya, Mauritius, and (from the 1880s) Australia. Beet sugar also provided a cheap substitute for Caribbean cane. European governments heavily subsidized exports of beet sugar, and production increased tenfold between 1860 and 1895.

To offset the cost advantages of competitors producing with slave or near-slave labor, British planters had one remaining defense. Their products were protected in the British market by the Navigation Acts, which taxed imports of West Indian sugar at a lower rate than foreign sugar (page 108). By the 1840s, however, the Industrial Revolution had made Britain temporarily the world's leading producer of industrial and consumer goods. Manufacturers, workers, and consumers united in demanding an end to all import duties so that they could obtain raw materials and food at the lowest cost. From 1846, Parliament equalized the duties on West Indian and foreign sugar—whether grown by slaves or by free workers. The planters denounced the hypocrisy of this law, which came only eight years after emancipation.

## THE FORMATION OF AN INDEPENDENT PEASANTRY[7]

With emancipation, the freedmen sought to escape the drudgery of the sugar fields. For former slaves, "full free" meant ownership of at least a small plot of land. On this they might grow their own food and sell the surplus to the plantations or towns. Many also planned to work on the estates from time to time, thereby earning cash to buy land or imported products. But they were not willing to remain submissive field hands, and they left the estates when they had met their immediate goals. The freedman's natural desire for freedom only increased as plantations failed and the need for full-time employment fell on most islands.

At first most freedmen expected to remain in their cottages, which they had built with their own labor. They became outraged when owners began to demand that they pay rent in cash or in labor services for their homes. During the 1840s, freedmen moved to free villages everywhere except Barbados. But the rush from the plantations was especially striking on Trinidad and Jamaica. By 1847—only nine years after emancipation—almost half of Trinidad's laborers and fully two-thirds of Jamaica's had abandoned the plantations for free villages.

Individuals purchased land belonging to plantations or owned by the government ("Crown land"). Often entire villages moved together as missionaries bought up large estates and sold them to their congregations. Built with money borrowed from missionary societies or from sympathetic individuals, these planned villages mushroomed during the first decade after emancipation.

On Jamaica, 150 to 200 free villages on 100,000 acres sprang up between 1838 and 1842. Most set aside land for a church and clergyman, and some required good behavior and forbade gambling and liquor.

The creation of planned villages slowed during the 1840s as economic conditions worsened and the British government decided to sell Crown lands only in large parcels. Individuals now squatted on Crown land or on abandoned estates—especially in the interior regions of Trinidad and Jamaica, where the government was incapable of evicting them. Their legal situation became more secure at the end of the 1860s when the governors on Trinidad and Jamaica made it easier to buy or rent Crown lands at fair prices.

## THE VARYING FORTUNES OF THE SUGAR ISLANDS

Except in a few marginal areas, such as the Virgin Islands, planters tried to maintain production. Their success depended on the availability of laborers willing to work regularly for wages that permitted a profit. Overall, the ratio of population to arable land—land that can be used to grow either food or export crops—largely explains why sugar estates survived on some islands and not on others. When an island had many people and little land, planters could find laborers. Where the ratio was low—in the Windwards and especially on Jamaica—most men became independent peasants. Laborers demanded high wages or refused to work during harvest time. Unable to produce at a competitive cost, planters abandoned their estates, and production plummeted.

| TABLE 21. SUGAR PRODUCTION OF SELECTED CARIBBEAN ISLANDS, 1820–1929 (Annual Averages in 1,000 U.S. tons) | | | | |
|---|---|---|---|---|
| | 1820–1824 | 1850–1854 | 1890–1894 | 1925–1929 |
| Haiti | .7 | — | — | 9.3 |
| Jamaica | 77.3 | 26.6 | 22.0 | 58.3 |
| Antigua | 8.1 | 9.6 | 14.1 | 16.8 |
| Saint Kitts | 5.4 | 5.3 | 16.5* | 16.6 |
| Martinique | 21.3 | 22.4 | 31.0 | 40.7 |
| Saint Croix | 23.0 | 7.3 | 13.9* | 7.8 |
| Guadeloupe | 22.3 | 18.1 | 41.7 | 34.8 |
| Barbados | 11.0 | 31.0 | 57.5 | 72.7 |
| Grenada | 11.0 | 5.3 | — | — |
| Cuba | 50.4 | 287.0 | 859.1 | 4,714.1 |
| Trinidad | 8.2 | 23.1 | 47.6 | 73.2 |
| Puerto Rico | — | 91.1 | 49.2 | 614.8 |

NOTES: Saint Kitts's production figures include Nevis after 1883. Average for two years only: Saint Croix (1890–1894), Puerto Rico (1850–1854). Average for three years only: Puerto Rico (1890–1894).

SOURCE: Averages for 1820–1929 compiled from annual data reported in Deerr, *History of Sugar*, volume I.

Antigua, Saint Kitts, and Barbados—with the highest population density in the Caribbean—continued to grow sugar into the 20th century. Indeed, Barbadian planters actually doubled their harvests between 1845 and 1865. Planters already owned most of Barbados's land in 1838. After emancipation, they converted their estates entirely to cane, and the island now imported two-thirds of its food. In order to eat, landless black laborers had to earn wages on the estates. With an abundant labor supply, Barbadian planters could ignore the worldwide trend toward large, company-owned estates. Most estates continued to use old-fashioned machinery powered by windmills. But they led all others in the use of fertilizers and manicured their fields until they resembled closely cropped gardens.

The Barbadian system of intensive cultivation could not succeed on Nevis or on most of Britain's Windward colonies. These islands had a good deal of empty land, both on abandoned estates and in the mountainous interiors. Many laborers took over small plots of land in the hills and grew food crops, cocoa, nutmeg, arrowroot, and bananas for export. To attract workers and preserve their estates, planters resorted to sharecropping or métayage. Under this system, the sharecropper (métayer) grew the cane and worked in the mill in return for half his crop. Sharecropping was cumbersome, and disputes were common. It also encouraged soil erosion and prevented investment in new equipment. Thus most owners could not compete when prices fell even further at the end of the century. Production for export ceased on Grenada, Saint Vincent, Dominica, and Tobago as well as on the Leeward island of Montserrat.

## HARD TIMES ON JAMAICA

Jamaican planters could not attract laborers on an island with an abundance of vacant land. Sugar production fell off sharply, with devastating effects on Jamaica's people. Exports dropped by half immediately after emancipation, and one-third of the estates were abandoned. Most planters had to use their slave compensation payments to repay estate debts. Since profits were low (or nonexistent), they could not obtain loans for new technology, and large modern mills were introduced only after 1900. When sugar prices fell even further during the 1870s, many of the remaining planters also abandoned their estates. The island had exported almost 80,000 tons of sugar in the 1820s. By the 1900s, it shipped barely 13,000 tons a year. The pre-emancipation level of production was regained only in 1934.

Jamaicans found no alternative source of income as sugar exports fell. The coffee industry also collapsed as labor became scarce and foreign competition increased. Increased exports of new crops by black farmers—including logwood, pimento, ginger, and bananas—could not compensate for the loss of sugar and coffee revenues. Total exports were lower in 1890 than in 1832, while the population had doubled.

Sugar's decline brought hard times to Jamaica's black population. As the estates failed, the free peasantry could no longer earn wages or find a market for its food crops. Without income, Jamaicans could not buy imported goods, and revenues from import and property taxes also fell. Neither individuals or the colonial government had the money to pay missionaries, teachers, or medical doctors. Schools and churches closed, and entire districts had no qualified physicians.

From the 1860s, there really were two Jamaicas. Along the coasts, the remaining white and colored planters elected the legislative assembly and maintained limited public services. In the interior, free villages originally built next to active estates now were totally isolated. The villagers struggled to survive on the produce of their tiny and often eroded plots. Hunger, disease, and theft became common. Prejudice on both sides intensified the division between the races. Black villagers had no say or interest in government and less faith in Jamaican justices of the peace, generally white and colored men of property. Racial relationships had been unusually hostile on Jamaica, where slaves rebelled more frequently than on any other island. Economic decline only increased the conflict between two incompatible cultures.

## NEW IMMIGRANTS AFTER EMANCIPATION

The flight of creole laborers threatened to destroy plantations on several islands. Migrations from one island to another met only part of the need. Most migrants sought jobs in construction, while the better-educated looked for work as policemen, teachers, and nurses. Few wanted full-time work on the cane estates. Thus Caribbean planters and British officials resorted to various schemes of large-scale immigration to supply additional workers. The most successful of these brought 144,000 Indian laborers to Trinidad under five-year contracts or indentures.

While the 19th century saw vast numbers of European laborers immigrate to the United States and Canada, very few were attracted to the Caribbean. The islands were deadly for whites, who also shunned the forms of estate labor that freed blacks so obviously despised. Jamaican planters recruited some 2,500 northern Europeans, and 6,000 workers also immigrated to several islands from Portuguese Madeira. Many died of disease during their first year, and immigration from Europe practically ceased by 1860.

A small number of immigrants also arrived from Africa and China. The British government encouraged settlement by African slaves it liberated from captured Cuban and Brazilian ships. By 1865, some 23,000 Africans were placed as free wage-laborers in Jamaica, Trinidad, and the Windwards. Entitled to a free return passage after five years' work, about a third went back to Africa. The others often settled in separate villages and cultivated small farms. About 8,000 Chinese also came as indentured laborers to Jamaica and Trinidad before 1893. Most bought out the final years of their indentures, left the plantations, and set up small shops or farms. Like the Indians on Trinidad, many succeeded in retaining their ethnic identity into the 20th century.

## INDENTURED INDIAN LABOR HELPS TRINIDAD PROSPER

Europe, Africa and China had added new elements to the already diverse peoples of the islands. But these small influxes did not satisfy the needs of disciplined field workers, and other sources were sought. After 1850, most immigrants were indentured laborers from India, Britain's most populous colony. Indians made ideal farm laborers, and the British government also preferred Indians since its officials could closely supervise recruitment and prevent abuses. Despite these advantages, indentured labor was costly, and island governments had to subsidize transportation to and from India. Trinidadian planters supported the scheme, but the Jamaican legislature was less enthusiastic. Altogether, between 1838 and 1917, almost 144,000 East Indian laborers came to Trinidad. Jamaica brought in 39,000, while smaller numbers reached Saint Lucia, Grenada, Saint Vincent, and Saint Kitts.

Like Jamaica, Trinidad had been hit hard by labor shortages. To attract workers, planters had to offer high pay for each task they performed, and most laborers could complete two or three tasks a day.[8] Some also forced laborers to work in return for their cottages and grounds. But neither high wages nor coercion could keep workers on the cane estates, and most estates ran at a loss in the 1840s. In 1851, the British government offered to guarantee loans made to transport immigrants, and Trinidad's planters turned to Indian labor as their only salvation.

The British and Trinidad governments subsidized the indenture system, and they also closely regulated it. An Indian laborer had to work for five years, and signed an initial three-year contract on arrival. After ten years of residence, he received a subsidized return ticket to India. The indenture system contained a great deal of deception and injustice. Some planters skimped on housing and medical care, and planters also ignored laws guaranteeing Indians the same wages paid to creole workers. In practice, the regulations tended to favor the master. The courts fined or jailed workers found to be negligent, absent, or frequently tardy. Yet planters breaking the ordinances only paid a small fine.

Bad as some masters might be, the indenture system—unlike African slavery—ended after five years. Perhaps one-third of the workers returned to India. Many saved significant sums of money and established shops and businesses. Others bought land and sold cane to the large central mills that began to dominate Trinidad's sugar industry during the 1880s. East Indians made up almost one-third of Trinidad's population when the Indian government ended the indenture system in 1917. They formed a permanent and settled community that voluntarily segregated itself from other groups. Almost all married other Indians and continued to practice the Hindu (accepted by 85 percent) or Muslim religions. Their language, food, and culture also remained distinctly Indian, although obedience to caste rules inevitably weakened over time.

The Indians staying in Trinidad presumably felt they had profited by immigrating as indentured laborers. Their labor fostered a long period of economic growth. Many took part as small farmers or contractors during the cocoa boom that lasted from the 1870s to the First World War. However, it was the sugar industry that gained most from Indian immigration, and its prosperity after 1854 largely was due to Indian laborers. When prices fell again in the 1880s, British capitalists—confident that the industry would survive on Trinidad—financed larger and more efficient mills. By 1897, eleven central factory units produced most of Trinidad's sugar. They purchased cane from independently owned farms, thus creating something like the Cuban *central-colono* system (page 204).

A flourishing sugar industry promoted the island's economic well-being. The influx of Indian workers allowed planters to expand cultivation, thereby increasing the demand for creole workers. Moreover, the plantations also afforded creole farmers and traders a profitable market for food and provided work to skilled artisans. With their wages, Trinidad's peoples could import needed goods. As tax revenues steadily increased, the legislature could create a rudimentary medical service and build hospitals, public baths, roads, sewer systems, and railroads.

## CROWN COLONY GOVERNMENT REPLACES THE OLD REPRESENTATIVE SYSTEM

When emancipation came in 1838, British colonies were governed in two different ways. Most operated under a system of representative government that had evolved since the 1640s. Each island had a governor who appointed a council with limited powers. An elected legislature or assembly made local laws and raised taxes to pay officials. An assembly's statutes could not contradict British laws and could be vetoed by the Crown. But it had almost total control over its own taxes. On most islands, the legislative assembly levied taxes, supervised their collection, approved expenditures, supervised many legislative boards, and audited its own accounts.

The island assemblies often proved incompetent during the wars of the 18th century. Nevertheless, after some hesitation, Britain also extended representative government to the Windward islands—Grenada, Dominica, Saint Vincent, and Tobago—it occupied in 1763. However, after Britain seized Spanish Trinidad (1797) and again took Saint Lucia from France, it did not create elected assemblies for these new conquests. For a time, the British government retained the laws and courts already in force. In 1810 it decided that direct rule by the British Crown was needed to end the slave trade and to protect the free people of color.

Trinidad and Saint Lucia thus became the first Crown colonies. An appointed governor, a number of top officials, and a few local advisors formed an executive council responsible for the day-to-day running of the colony's affairs. A slightly larger body, known as the Legislative Council, advised the governor and passed local laws. In addition to the governor himself, the Legislative Council was made up of British officials and a number of "unofficial members" chosen by the governor. By 1898, Crown colony government had replaced elected legislatures everywhere except in Barbados, the Bahamas, and the

Cayman Islands.[9] With some exceptions, elected representatives did not again participate in island governments until the 1920s.

The extinction of representative government in the West Indies ran counter to the general trend in Britain and in its colonies with a white majority. Throughout the 19th century, the British Parliament steadily lowered voting requirements. All men over twenty-one received the vote in 1918, all women in 1928. Parliament also extended representative government to Canada, Australia, New Zealand, and the Cape Colony in South Africa. By contrast, authoritarian government replaced legislatures throughout the West Indies. Here the British government suspended democracy both to rescue the white planters from their own ineptitude and to protect them against black majority rule.

Emancipation in 1838 made 750,000 former slaves free British citizens, able to vote if they passed the same tests as whites and colored freedmen. On most islands, voters had to own only a small amount of property. Over time, the rules would have allowed many blacks to vote in elections to island assemblies. To prevent this, assemblymen throughout the Caribbean revised the laws after 1838. They raised property qualifications for new voters, while allowing existing voters (usually whites) to qualify under the old rules. In practice only white or colored landowners, merchants, lawyers, and other professional men could vote in elections to the island assemblies.

As plantations were abandoned on many islands, the number of voters meeting these property tests sometimes fell to ludicrous levels. By the 1850s, Barbados registered 1,350 voters. Grenada had 191 voters, Saint Vincent had 273, and Tobago registered 135. In the 1863 election for the Jamaica assembly only 1,457 persons voted out of a population above 440,000. Not all were white. In Dominica, Montserrat, and Nevis, middle-class men of color dominated public affairs. On Jamaica, one-third of the representatives were men of color from the 1850s.

The Colonial Office did not protest the undemocratic nature of island legislatures. But it strongly objected to their financial carelessness and failure to provide needed governmental services. Many islands labored under huge debts because their assemblies did not operate under a budget, and any member could introduce bills to spend money. In 1849 and again in 1853, all government stopped on Jamaica because the assembly refused to approve taxes.

In 1853 the British government offered Jamaica a low-interest loan if the assembly would vote permanent taxes, place its finances in the hands of responsible salaried officials, and allow its accounts to be audited. The assembly gave in, setting up a three-member Executive Committee with responsibility for financial matters. Six islands in the Lesser Antilles also set up executive committees by 1859. However, this reform did not solve the main problem—the ease with which a small faction could prevent an assembly taking desperately needed actions. By the 1860s, the Colonial Office had lost patience with Caribbean legislatures and looked for an excuse to destroy the old representative system. Its chance came in 1865 with a tragic rebellion at Morant Bay in Jamaica.

## MORANT BAY: THE END OF AN ERA

Economic and racial tensions in the British colonies were aggravated by the American Civil War, which sharply increased food prices. Riots broke out on several islands, including Saint Vincent and Barbados. Because Jamaica was the largest and best-known colony, British public opinion was most strongly affected by a rebellion in 1865 at Morant Bay, east of Kingston in Saint Thomas parish. Disturbances began at the Saturday market on October 7. The local justices found a young black man guilty of assaulting a black woman. When the court ordered the arrest of a disruptive spectator, the crowd rescued him and beat the police.

The following Tuesday, eight black policemen set off to arrest Paul Bogle (1822–1865), the alleged leader of the riot. Bogle was a local property owner and a deacon and preacher in the Native Baptist church. He also was a close associate of George Gordon (1820–1865), a colored member of the Jamaica assembly who enjoyed considerable influence in the neighborhood. Several hundred armed men quickly overpowered the police. Bogle then sent them back to Morant Bay with his threat to bring his forces to the vestry meeting scheduled for the following day. The Custos,[10] the chief official in the parish, notified Governor Edward Eyre, who sent one hundred men to Morant Bay on a small British warship.

On Wednesday, October 11, Bogle arrived in the town with a group of about four hundred men, armed with guns, cutlasses, pikes, and bayonets. They attacked the local police station, seized the weapons kept there, and marched toward the courthouse where the vestry was meeting. The parish Custos appeared on the stairway calling for peace, but the mob began to throw stones at perhaps two dozen volunteer militiamen stationed before the courthouse. The volunteers fired, but the crowd quickly drove everyone back inside the court-house. The mob set the building on fire and brutally beat to death many of its occupants as they fled into the open.

In all, several dozen were murdered at Morant Bay, including the Custos, several other magistrates, the entire volunteer force, and two sons of the Anglican priest. The mob then looted the village and released the prisoners in the jail. Parties of rebels fanned out in several directions, killing four white plantation owners and several colored magistrates who attempted to reason with them. Whites and coloreds fled their homes, many escaping to Kingston on ships. There they told Governor Eyre stories of horrible atrocities at the battle of the courthouse.

Panic swept the island, as many planters feared that the Morant Bay massacre was part of a conspiracy to turn Jamaica into a second Haiti. Governor Eyre declared martial law, dispatched troops to the area, and appealed for reinforcements. He also enlisted the aid of the Maroons, whose trackers captured and executed Bogle. The government forces quickly crushed the rebels, who apparently enjoyed limited popular support. Without suffering a single casualty, soldiers marched through the parish killing any blacks they came across.[11]

White and colored planters and the Jamaican newspapers applauded Governor Eyre. However, his handling of the rebellion provoked intense controversy in England. There, influential clergymen, professors, authors, and scientists formed rival committees attacking Eyre as a murderer and defending him as a hero. For three years, the media and Parliament debated the issue, which provoked riots in the streets.

Eyre's arrest and execution on October 23 of George William Gordon aroused the greatest controversy. Gordon, the son of a Scotch planter and a slave, had made money as a produce broker in Kingston. Driven by religious fervor, he was a leader of the Native Baptists and had many followers among the black laborers. Hating both the Custos of Saint Thomas and Governor Eyre, he used his immunity as a member of the assembly to attack them in long, unrestrained tirades. In one speech, Gordon called on the people of Jamaica to throw out Eyre, the oppressor.

> When a Governor becomes a dictator; when he becomes despotic, it is time for the people to dethrone him. . . . I have never seen an animal more voracious for cruelty and power than the present Governor of Jamaica. . . . If we are to be governed by such a Governor much longer, the people will have to fly to arms and become self governing.[12]

Gordon had his largest following in Saint Thomas, where he worked closely with Paul Bogle, leader of the rebels. During the months before the riot, he had called on the parish's black poor to speak and act out against its vestry. Eyre and other Jamaican officials believed he had been involved in the uprising, even though he had not been in Morant Bay when it occurred. Gordon was arrested in Kingston, where marital law was not in effect. Eyre then had him taken to Morant Bay, where he was hanged after a grossly unfair court martial.

The British government suspended Eyre in 1866 and then dismissed him from office. Before he left Jamaica, he presided over the assembly's suicide. Under pressure from the Colonial Office, the assembly abdicated. On December 12, 1865, it asked the queen to set up whatever form of government she thought best. The following June, Britain imposed the Crown colony form of government with a nominated legislative council. The British government soon forced most other island legislatures to follow Jamaica's lead. By the end of 1875, only Barbados and the Bahamas retained their old constitutions. After a period of transition, a legislature named by the governor existed on all other British islands by 1898.

The Morant Bay rebellion uprising was confined to one small section of Jamaica, and it did not involve a large segment of the population. Indeed, few would remember Morant Bay if Governor Eyre had not so vigorously suppressed the uprising. Strictly speaking, it was not a war between the races. The rebels beat and killed black men, while black troops, Maroons, militiamen, and judges joined in suppressing the uprising. But both the Jamaican assembly and the British government viewed the riots as racially motivated. Thus the public outcry over Eyre's actions gave the Colonial Office an excuse to abolish representative government.

By 1865, the government was convinced that only direct rule from Britain could protect the black laborers, who could not yet govern themselves. The planters and merchants in the island assemblies were financially incompetent and did not represent the interests of the black majority. But the latter were equally unready for democracy. Thus only authoritarian government by British officials could protect the interests of the entire community. An official dispatch in 1868 clearly expressed the British view.

> The population at large, consisting of uneducated negroes, neither had, nor could have, any political powers; they were incapable of contributing to the formation of any intelligent public opinion; and the consequence was that the Assemblies performed their office of legislation under no real or effective responsibility. They became aware apparently that irresponsible legislation by small local bodies was not for the interest even of the members of those bodies themselves, or of the class which they represented, and still less of the inhabitants at large.[13]

## THE RECORD OF CROWN COLONY GOVERNMENT

The unrepresentative governments that ruled Britain's Crown colonies until the Second World War generally met the relatively limited goals they set themselves. They maintained public order, provided courts, and made useful improvements in the economic infrastructure and public services. They placed less emphasis on economic growth, and many islands stagnated. No substitute product was found to replace sugar, and American companies generally preferred to invest in cane estates on Cuba and the Dominican Republic.

Crown colony government put an end to the bickering that had stalemated the former assemblies. The governor, who ruled the nominated legislatures, had both clear responsibilities and the power to achieve them. Whether or not the system worked thus depended on the energy and character of individual governors. The most successful—such as Sir John Peter Grant in Jamaica (1866–1874) and Sir Arthur Gordon in Trinidad (1866–1870)—came immediately after the Morant Bay riots, when the British government expected improvements. Over time, colonial government became less active, and it fell into the lazy habit of routinely following precedents.

Basic public services were provided throughout the colonies. Public works departments were created, which built roads, bridges, and railroads. By the First World War, every British colony—including the smaller Leeward and Windward islands—had a police force and fire department, a government medical service, and at least one hospital. Nearly all had public libraries. Noticeable improvements were made in the towns, and especially in the capital cities. Sewage systems and public water supplies did much to cut the death rate. As one consequence, European and North American tourists began to visit some of the islands, especially the Bahamas and Jamaica.

Crown colony governments also carried out legal and social reforms, especially during the early years. They simplified the court system and modernized law codes. Because of streamlined procedures and lower costs, more peasant farmers could obtain clear titles to their lands. The Anglican church was disestablished on Jamaica, where it primarily served the tiny white population. In Trinidad, the government began to allot funds to the Roman Catholic as well as to the Anglican church, in proportion to the number of members each served.

One of the first aims of the Crown colony governments was to increase the number of elementary schools. The government gave grants to private and denominational schools according to the results they achieved. However, since most schools charged fees, fewer than half the black children attended, and only 52 percent of Jamaicans could read and write according to the 1921 census. A small number of secondary schools also were established. A few of the brightest students—including several future West Indian leaders—won a scholarship to a British university, where most studied law or medicine. Perhaps the greatest weakness of public education was its lack of attention to technical and scientific subjects, such as tropical agriculture.

Any argument in favor of democracy can be used with justice against the Crown colony system of government. Under the former system, with all its faults, at least some non-whites had achieved influence as judges or members of the assemblies. Now officials thousands of miles away made major decisions. Educated blacks could be teachers or lower-level civil servants, but posts as senior administrators usually went to whites, frequently sent from Great Britain. The lack of representative institutions contributed to low self-esteem among many islanders. The Crown colony system strengthened the belief that the black "natives" could not rule themselves and needed the help of white men from Great Britain.

## THE LEEWARD AND WINDWARD FEDERATIONS

The British government had tried to bring the Leeward islands under one federal government at the end of the 17th century. From 1671, one governor supervised Saint Kitts (with Anguilla), Nevis, Antigua (with Barbuda), Montserrat, and the Virgin Islands—with Dominica added from 1770 to 1940. However, each island retained its own deputy governor, council, and assembly, and thus had its own laws and treasury. Six legal systems and six civil governments served fewer than 100,000 residents.

In 1869, the Colonial Office again tried to impose federation, primarily to cut costs. However, the relatively more prosperous islands (especially Saint Kitts and Nevis) did not want to share their funds with Antigua and Montserrat, which both were bankrupt. After eighteen months of negotiations, a quasi-federal system was set up in 1871. A federal legislative council and appellate courts unified many laws. But each island maintained a separate treasury and taxes. Britain did unite Saint Kitts and Nevis in 1882, over the bitter opposition of many on the smaller island.

The British government had wanted the Leewards federation to be part of a larger union that would include Barbados and the Windward colonies. But all efforts to establish a federation of the Windwards failed. Governor John Pope-Hennessy (1834–1891) arrived in Barbados in 1876 with orders to arrange a federation between that colony and the smaller Windwards. The Barbados assembly, which did not want to support its poorer neighbors, strongly opposed a federation. Planters, both white and colored, united to form the Barbados Defense League. Pope Hennessy turned to the cane workers for support. In March 1876, political agitation culminated in a riot that killed eight persons and destroyed much property. The Colonial Office transferred the governor to another colony and dropped the scheme. Ten years later, it united Grenada, Saint Vincent, Saint Lucia, and Tobago under one governor. But each had its own legislative council, police force, judicial system, public services, and treasury. Other than the governor, the only common institution was a lunatic asylum in Grenada. In 1889, Britain removed Tobago from the Windward group and joined it with Trinidad.

# CHAPTER FOURTEEN:

# THE SPANISH ISLANDS FIGHT FOR FREEDOM

■

England, victorious in 1815, gained colonies in the West Indies. Spain—and not France—was the great loser during the Napoleonic wars. The French occupation of Spain (1808–1812) allowed the creole aristocracy to seize control throughout the Americas, and the last Spanish garrison (in Peru) surrendered early in 1826. The Spanish empire once again was confined to the Caribbean islands—almost exactly three hundred years after Cortés sailed from Cuba to begin the conquest of the mainland.

For many years, Spanish officials refused to recognize they had lost the Americas. Power in Madrid alternated between supporters of absolutist monarchy and various varieties of reformers. But all Spanish governments were determined to preserve the remnants of their empire. Moreover, all sought to keep the Puerto Rican and Cuban markets as privileged preserves, reserved to Spanish merchants by discriminatory tariffs. This policy subordinated West Indian needs to Spanish commercial lobbies, reflecting the Spanish government's pressing concerns at home. Spain had remained a very poor country, while Cuban sugar planters became wealthy. Indeed, it is probable that all Cuban whites and free coloreds—perhaps even Cuban slaves—lived better than the peasants in the poorer regions of the mother country.

## CUBA, THE RICHEST ISLAND

Cuba, equal in size to Pennsylvania, is by far the largest of the Caribbean islands. Ten times bigger than Jamaica and 250 times larger than Barbados, it is almost as large as all the other Caribbean islands put together. Cuba's natural riches make it an ideal producer of tropical products, such as sugar and tobacco. Cuba is the only major island not dominated by mountains. Almost three-quarters of the land forms a rolling plain at sea level, endowed with rich soil and generally adequate rainfall. In contrast to other islands, roads and railroads could be built from one end of the country to the other.

Cuba's location at the western edge of the Caribbean and an abundance of natural harbors facilitates the movement of goods and people by water. Havana

Black workers operating a sugar mill in Cuba. Semi-mechanized mills were introduced by the middle of the 19th century. Earlier mills used smaller rollers—often vertical rather than horizontal—to crush the sugarcane.

is one of the finest ports in the world, while Guantánamo and Santiago de Cuba provide excellent harbors at the eastern end of the island. Its location also gives Cuba major strategic importance. The island dominates the Windward Passage separating it from Hispaniola, as well as the Yucatan and Florida Channels into the Gulf of Mexico. Cuba was, therefore, essential to the defense of the Spanish empire, and it continues to control the sea lanes to the Panama Canal.

Only Spanish trade regulations kept Cuba from prospering before the 1760s. Under British or French rule, it would have become a major sugar producer long before. As soon as Spain opened Cuban ports to foreign ships, a great sugar boom began that lasted—almost without interruption—until the 1880s. Cuba surpassed all other Caribbean islands because of its great size and natural resources. Cuban planters also benefited from improved technologies and better types of sugarcane. They enjoyed higher yields both because their fields were virgin and not depleted and because they used better methods than Jamaican planters.

Using Spanish and later American loans, Cuban planters introduced modern milling techniques that increased production of higher quality sugar. French refugees from Haiti introduced water mills and enclosed furnaces, and steam engines were successfully used in mills from 1817. By 1860, mills that were at least semi-mechanized produced 92 percent of Cuba's sugar. Vacuum pans— which increase the amount of sugar derived from each cane—were installed from 1841, centrifuges during the 1850s.

The expansion of the cane estates into virgin lands also spurred the expansion of transportation networks. Old roads were improved, and new ones were constructed. The first railroad opened in 1838, reducing transportation costs by 70 percent. By 1860, railroads linked the major sugar regions to seaports, and planters built private feeder tracks connecting their fields and mills to the main lines.

Cane estates continued to expand throughout the island during the 19th century. Sugar plantations replaced cattle ranches, tobacco farms, and coffee estates. For a time coffee rivaled sugar as a major export. However, a series of devastating hurricanes between 1844 and 1846 destroyed many estates, and prices fell as Brazilian coffee entered world markets. Many coffee growers failed, and their plantations were replanted in cane.

The history of the older sugar islands repeated itself on a larger scale in 19th-century Cuba. Since only the mills were mechanized, sugar continued to demand vast amounts of labor. Cuban planters thus brought a truly astonishing number of slaves from Africa.[1] The island had absorbed only 60,000 slaves between 1512 to 1763. As the cane estates flourished, more than half a million slaves were imported between 1808 and the end of the trade in 1865.[2] The number of slaves increased tenfold between 1774 and 1841—almost twice as fast as the white population.

| TABLE 22.  CUBA POPULATION ESTIMATES, 1759–1899 | | | | |
|---|---|---|---|---|
| | TOTAL | WHITES | SLAVES | FREE NON-WHITES |
| 1759 | 140,000 | — | — | — |
| 1774 | 171,620 | 96,440 | 38,879 | 36,301 |
| 1792 | 272,300 | 153,559 | 64,590 | 54,151 |
| 1827 | 704,486 | 311,051 | 286,942 | 106,492 |
| 1841 | 1,007,624 | 418,291 | 436,495 | 152,838 |
| 1861 | 1,396,530 | 793,484 | 370,553 | 232,493 |
| 1877* | 1,509,291 | 1,032,435 | 211,247 | 265,609 |
| 1899* | 1,572,797 | 1,067,254 | — | 505,543 |

NOTE:  The category "Whites" includes persons of Chinese origin in 1877 (43,811) and 1899 (14,857).

SOURCES:  Franklin Knight, *Slave Society in Cuba during the Nineteenth Century* (Madison: University of Wisconsin Press, 1970), 22 (1774, 1841); Susan Schroeder, *Cuba: A Handbook of Historical Statistics* (Boston: G. K. Hall, 1982), 40.

In contrast to the English and French islands, black labor did not totally replace white labor. The Spanish government encouraged immigration from the impoverished homeland, and Cuba also served as a place of refuge. French and Spanish planters fled Hispaniola during the 1790s. After the collapse of the Spanish empire on the mainland, Spanish soldiers and colonists flooded the island, and many settled in Cuba permanently. But slaves arrived in greater numbers than white settlers. As a result, whites formed less than half the population according to the censuses of 1827 and 1841.

Slave unrest became more common with the influx of Africans. Remembering the Haitian revolt and the Jamaican uprising in 1831–1832, whites lived in fear of their slaves. In 1843, Spanish authorities claimed they had discovered a far flung plot, known as the conspiracy of *La Escalera* after the ladders to which jailers tied their prisoners for flogging. They pursued suspects with the same ferocity seen during slave revolts on the English and French islands. Perhaps as many as one thousand slaves and free coloreds were executed or tortured to death.

As Cuba devoted itself almost totally to sugarcane, it came to depend on outside suppliers for food, clothing, furniture, manufactured goods, even wood for the sugar mills. Economic logic made the United States Cuba's single most important trading partner, taking the bulk of its sugar exports. By 1877, The United States took 82 percent of Cuba's total exports, Spain only 6 percent. For their livelihood, Cubans thus relied on the production of one crop for one market.

## CUBAN PLANTERS SEEK FREEDOM FROM SPAIN

By the 1860s, Cuba was devoted—like 18th-century Jamaica or Saint-Domingue—to growing sugar. At the same time, Cuba had a much larger white population, and its social order was more complex than that of the older sugar islands. The creole élite of planters and property owners was urban and involved in the world market. But they had no say in the island's government and disliked the rapacity and petty tyrannies of Spanish officials and merchants. Spain had curtailed Cuban autonomy during the 1700s, and it further increased military control as it lost the mainland colonies. A decree of 1825 gave the captain-general virtually unlimited powers, including the authority to deport, without trial, anyone he thought undesirable. Only their own inefficiency limited the oppressive power of Spanish officials.

Cubans especially resented an economic policy that enriched Spain at the expense of Cuba. By the mid-19th century, Spain's effect on the Cuban economy was wholly negative. Its taxes on imports and exports and freight charges on foreign carriers cut into the profits of producers, while sharply raising prices for all Cuban consumers.[3] Moreover, Spain's abolition of the slave trade in 1820 forced planters to use illegal slavers, greatly raising the price of new slaves.

Unlike other islands, conflict and revolution in Cuba thus pitted white creoles against white *peninsulares* (the name given to recent Spanish immigrants). At first, few creoles supported independence, partly because they feared that a white revolution against Spain might trigger a black uprising against the planters. Indeed, Spanish officials threatened to liberate the slaves if Cubans sought independence. Thus the independence struggles on the mainland inspired several conspiracies during the 1820s, but none enjoyed widespread support.

Until the 1850s, Cubans dissatisfied with colonial rule rejected independence in favor of annexation as a slave state by the United States. Many creoles sincerely admired the United States, where African slavery comfortably coexisted with democracy, economic growth, and intellectual progress among whites. Some Cubans, losing patience with diplomatic maneuvers, tried to incite annexationist rebellions. With the financial support of exiles in New York, General Narcisco López led three expeditions to Cuba between 1849 and 1852. During the same years, three annexationist uprisings on the island also failed. Many in the United States, especially in the southern slave states, also favored Cuba's annexation. President James Polk—who fought the Mexican War to acquire California and New Mexico—unsuccessfully offered Spain $100 million for Cuba. Six years later, in 1854, President Franklin Pierce raised the offer to $130 million, but the Spanish refused to sell.

Both in Cuba and in the United States, support for annexation peaked in the 1850s. The growth of abolitionist sentiment and the American Civil War ended the principal reason for seeking union. Planters—hit hard by the financial panic of 1857—now wanted the government to buy and free their slaves (the policy adopted by Britain in 1834). In 1865, many of the same planters that had earlier advocated annexation organized the Reformist party to seek changes in Spanish rule.

The Reformists published a lengthy petition to the Spanish parliament in May 1865. They had four basic demands: reform of the tariff system, Cuban representation in the Spanish parliament, legal equality with peninsulars, and the suppression of the slave trade. A reform government, temporarily ruling in Spain, responded favorably. Madrid authorized the election of Cuban representatives to a commission (the Junta de Información) studying changes in colonial administration. However, any hope of reform was short-lived. In 1867, a new government in Spain imposed harsh laws that almost called out for rebellion. It increased the authority of military tribunals, closed opposition newspapers, banned political meetings, and imposed higher export fees and new taxes on landowners, businessmen, and professionals.

## THE TEN YEARS WAR AND SLAVE EMANCIPATION

Discontent rose everywhere, but it was especially high among ranchers and planters in the economically depressed eastern provinces. On October 10, 1868, the Revolt of Yara (Grito de Yara) proclaimed Cuban independence and the establishment of a provisional republic led by Carlos Manuel de Céspedes (1818–1874). The war dragged on for ten years, with neither the rebels nor the Spanish army able to win a decisive victory. The rebel leadership was divided over the issue of slavery. The military leaders, many men of color, called for immediate abolition. The creole leadership temporized, hoping to gain support from wealthy landowners in the west.

The Ten Years War turned into a series of guerrilla campaigns that devastated the eastern provinces without seriously affecting Havana and the west. A civil war in Spain hindered efforts to crush the rebels. When it ended in 1874, the government poured more soldiers into Cuba and constructed a fortified ditch the entire width of the island. In 1877, General Arsenio Campos arrived in Cuba with even more troops and promises of compromise. Negotiations culminated in the Pact of Zanjón (February 1878), which promised a variety of constitutional and financial reforms.

During the Ten Years War, both the insurgents and Spanish loyalists had promised to abolish slavery. In February 1880, the Spanish government issued an abolition law without compensation to owners. The freed slaves were subject to the tutelage (*patronato*) of their former masters for eight years. Like the apprenticeship system imposed by England in 1834, this system required the former slaves to work for their masters in return for monthly wages, food, and clothing. The *patronato* proved unpopular both with landowners and freedmen, and the Crown abolished it on October 7, 1886, two years before it was due to expire.

The seventeen years of uneasy truce that followed the Ten Years War began with a severe economic depression. The war had permanently ruined the coffee industry, and higher American tariffs hurt cigar exports. In Europe the production of beet sugar dramatically increased, leaving the United States as the only market with the capacity to absorb Cuban production. The Madrid government did nothing to help the Cuban economy. In fact, it worsened conditions by confiscating the estates of insurgent landowners as well as by raising tariffs and taxes, making Cuba pay the entire cost of suppressing the rebellion. Hundreds of estates went into bankruptcy and thousands of workers were unemployed.

As world prices fell, Cuban sugar plantations had to reduce their costs to remain competitive. Milling was concentrated in gigantic factories (*centrales*) equipped with advanced machinery and connected by private railways to the cane fields. The number of mills fell by 40 percent from 1877 to 1895, while output steadily rose. Production reached one million tons for the first time in 1895. One gigantic mill, Central Constancia, produced as much sugar as the entire island of Jamaica, burdened with 140 outmoded mills.

The vast sums of money needed to erect these immense factories generally came from the United States, usually from companies that marketed tropical products. Some Cuban planters survived as sugar farmers (*colonos*) supplying the *centrales*, others became salaried administrators for the companies owning the mills. By 1895, fewer than 20 percent of mill owners came from the old planter class. American capital and influence increasingly dominated Cuba's most important industry.

A reciprocal trade agreement between Cuba and the United States brought two years of prosperity in 1892 and 1893. However, the United States rescinded its tariff concessions in 1894, and Madrid swiftly restored a wall of protectionist duties around Cuba. An outcry of indignation and protest against Spain arose across the island. Madrid also had failed to deliver the political reforms promised in the 1870s. Creoles still had no say in government, as peninsular officials rigged elections to retain power. By 1895 the economy was in crisis, and political discontent was increasing.

After the Ten Years War, the most dedicated separatists chose exile rather than submitting to continued Spanish rule. Most of the thousands of workers forced to seek work in other countries also were devoted to independence. A commitment to armed struggle held together the ranks of exiled separatists in the United States, Latin America, and Europe. José Martí (1853–1895) led New York's intransigent patriotic society, the Cuban Junta. Martí was an extraordinary leader, simultaneously a skillful politician, a poet and journalist, and a philosopher with a compelling vision of *Cuba Libre*. His propaganda promised a Cuban republic free of racial and social inequalities, although he never drew up specific plans to obtain these goals. It rallied both American support and the unemployed of eastern Cuba, where Martí raised the standard of revolt in 1895.

The horrors of this civil war (1895–1898) far surpassed those of earlier rebellions. Martí soon died in one of the first skirmishes. Leadership of the rebel forces passed to Máximo Gómez (1835–1905) and the colored general Antonio Maceo (1845–1896), who had distinguished themselves as daring guerrilla leaders during the Ten Years War. Poor blacks and whites swelled their forces, while boats brought arms from America. Tens of thousands of peasants provided food and supplies and spied on the Spanish army everywhere in Cuba. The war became a savage guerrilla conflict, pitting rural against urban Cuba. The insurgents sought to drive the peasants into their ranks and make Cuba valueless for Spain by burning crops and estates. General Gómez banned all sugar production, and rebel forces raided across the island with the simple torch as their most devastating weapon.

A new captain-general, Valeriano Weyler arrived in January 1896. Weyler, a non-smoker and military technician, saw that he could not win by defending isolated plantations. To deny the insurgents recruits and supplies, Spanish and loyalist forces rounded up as many as 300,000 peasants. They forced them into hastily erected concentration camps, where thousands died of hunger, abuse, and epidemics. This policy of "reconcentration" and reinforcements from Spain allowed Weyler to regain the initiative after Maceo's death in December 1896. But the rebels denied him victory by refusing to fight major battles. Gómez retreated to the eastern provinces and continued guerrilla operations against towns and forts. When a new government in Madrid dismissed Weyler and gave Cuba autonomous government in January 1898, Gómez rejected any compromise short of total independence.

Many Cuban property owners called for U.S. intervention, and the war devastated American investments. In New York, the Cuban Junta waged a propaganda war to sway American public opinion. Mass newspapers (called "yellow journals" from their shoddy paper) took up the Cuban cause. Their articles graphically depicted and sometimes exaggerated Spanish cruelty and mistreatment of Cuban civilians. In 1898, the United States finally intervened in the conflict. President McKinley disliked war, as did his business friends, and he did not believe in Cuban freedom. But he could not resist public opinion.

In January 1898, Spanish army officers led riots in Havana against Madrid's new policy of autonomy. McKinley ordered the battleship *Maine* to Havana to protect American lives and property. On February 15, an explosion—which American experts attributed to a Spanish mine—tore through the hull of the *Maine*. It sank quickly, and 266 lives were lost. When Spain rejected McKinley's

"Starvation by Proclamation in Cuba." In 1896 and 1897, Spanish forces drove many thousands of peasant families into concentration camps. An example of illustrations and articles in American newspapers and magazines, which fostered support for war with Spain.

demands for an armistice and an end to the concentration camps, war became inevitable. Congress proclaimed Cuba independent on April 11, pledging in the Teller Amendment not to annex the island. Spain severed diplomatic relations, and Congress declared war on April 25.

The war was over in ten weeks with little fighting in Cuba. At Manilla Bay in May, Admiral Dewey blew Spain's Pacific fleet out of the war in one hour, without a single American casualty. In July, the Atlantic squadron was as swiftly destroyed off Santiago Bay in eastern Cuba. After the two most complete naval disasters of modern times, Madrid had to surrender. By the Treaty of Paris (December 1898), Spain granted independence to Cuba, and ceded Puerto Rico and the Pacific island of Guam to the United States.

The American Congress established a military government, which at first concentrated on relieving the starving population, disarming both the insurgents and loyalists, and controlling yellow fever. Elections (under a restricted suffrage) were conducted in 1900 for town governments and an assembly to write a constitution. Most representatives supported immediate independence, and some came from radical factions.

The McKinley administration was determined to set out terms that would protect American property and the rights of minorities. Congress enacted eight provisions, which together are known as the Platt Amendment. These stipulated that Cuba would lease naval bases to the United States, make no treaties with a foreign power that might impair its independence, and acquire no debts it could not pay. On June 12, 1901, the Havana constitutional convention (by a majority of one) added the Platt proposals. The constitution, modeled on that of the United States, also provided for universal suffrage, separation of church and state, a powerful president who could serve two terms, and a relatively weak senate and chamber of deputies.

## PUERTO RICO DEVELOPS A PLANTATION ECONOMY

Puerto Rico's economy and society developed in different ways, and its peoples avoided the bitter civil wars that ravaged Cuba from 1868 to 1898. Nevertheless, their common obedience to Spain linked the two islands throughout the 19th century. Spanish governments—whether constitutional or authoritarian—tended to consider the two islands together. Spanish ministers hesitated to grant reforms to Puerto Rico because they feared the Cubans would demand similar concessions.

Puerto Rico is less than one-tenth as large as Cuba. It is less generously endowed with natural assets and more closely resembles Jamaica or Haiti. Mountains and hills dominate the center of the island with plains along the coasts—about 5 miles wide in the northeast and rather less than that elsewhere. Only about one-third of the island is relatively level, and the soil often is poor. Since the rain-bearing winds come from east, the southern coasts are dry, and some areas must be irrigated.

Spain saw both Cuba and Puerto Rico primarily as military bastions and did little to foster economic growth until the 1760s. During the 19th century, a sugar boom based on African slavery transformed Cuba, and it became the largest producer in the Caribbean. On Puerto Rico, however, the sugar industry flourished only after the American occupation in 1898.

Without cane estates, Puerto Rico's population remained smaller and more rural, without sharp divisions of class. Planters on Puerto Rico were not as rich as their Cuban counterparts, and they imported many fewer slaves. Whites formed a much higher portion of the population than on other major islands, and most persons of color were free. Thus a steady blending of the races, beginning early in the colonial period, continued uninterrupted through the 19th century.

| TABLE 23. PUERTO RICO POPULATION ESTIMATES, 1820–1900 | | | | |
|---|---|---|---|---|
| | TOTAL | WHITES | SLAVES | FREE NON-WHITES |
| 1820 | 230,261 | 102,432 | 21,730 | 106,459 |
| 1836 | 357,086 | 188,869 | 41,818 | 126,399 |
| 1860 | 583,181 | 300,406 | 41,738 | 241,037 |
| 1872 | 618,150 | — | 31,635 | — |
| 1900 | 953,243 | 589,104 | — | 364,139 |

SOURCES: Arturo Morales Carrión, *Puerto Rico: A Political and Cultural History* (New York: Norton, 1983), 114, 137; Deerr, *History of Sugar*, II:281 (1836); Knight, *The Caribbean*, 238 (1860); Watts, *West Indies*, 321, 459.

Economic development became essential when the Mexican subsidies (*situado*) supporting the island's government and military ceased in 1811. By a decree of August 1815 (the Real Cédula de Gracias), the Spanish Crown, increasingly unable to keep out foreign shipping, finally opened Puerto Rico to world trade—although non-Spanish goods paid higher tariffs. It also confirmed the 1778 decree opening the island to immigration and offered free land to settlers. (Black and colored freedmen received half the grant to whites.) Settlers arrived from Haiti, Santo Domingo, Venezuela, and Spain itself.

Coffee, primarily sold in Europe, became Puerto Rico's principal commercial crop during the 19th century. Coffee plantations, initially introduced in 1736, now opened up the interior. They spread rapidly in the western mountains with their high rainfall, helping to develop the ports of Mayagüez and Ponce, which were nearest to the coffee regions. Production reached 6,000 tons in 1897 and peaked at 27,000 tons in 1920. The number of sugar estates along the coastal plains also increased, but Puerto Rican sugar production always lagged far behind that of Cuba.[4] Since coffee plantations tended to be small to medium-size family holdings, a comparatively large portion of Puerto Ricans owned at least some land.

## SLAVERY IS ABOLISHED IN PUERTO RICO

A lack of slaves held back the expansion of sugar estates. In 1845, Great Britain and Spain agreed on stronger provisions to end the slave trade, nominally banned in 1820. Puerto Rican owners could not afford the higher prices of illegal imports, and the trade effectively ended after about 1850. Puerto Rico was developing into a nation—something like Haiti—of independent farmers growing food for their own needs on lands to which they had no legal title. Fully 80 percent of the population still lived in rural areas in 1899.

Seeking to make use of this large pool of peasant labor, the Spanish governor established a system of forced labor in 1849. The law set minimum landholding requirements and forbade the common practice of squatting. It required day laborers to congregate on the fringes of towns and compelled them to carry a booklet listing their employers. The law (Reglamento de Jornaleros) was difficult to enforce and was abolished in 1873.

Puerto Rico's creole élite strongly supported slave emancipation and helped to organize the Spanish Abolitionist Society in 1864. The island's mixed population encouraged egalitarian sentiment, and reformers also believed that they could not win other gains until the slaves were freed. Puerto Rican representatives to the Spanish National Assembly (Cortes)—several of them persons of color—pressed the government to end slavery.[5] After a bitter debate, a law of March 22, 1873, freed the remaining slaves with compensation to their owners.

## PUERTO RICANS SEEK AUTONOMY

After its mainland colonies gained independence, Spain imposed authoritarian government on Puerto Rico, as well as on Cuba. From 1825, the governor—always a military officer—exercised unlimited powers. Municipal governments remained responsible for local administration, and judicial officials retained some autonomy. But the governor could intervene in local matters and arrest or deport individuals at will. Some members of the small educated élite sought limits on the governor and more say in local government. Only a few initially wanted complete independence, and several conspiracies in the 1820s and 1830s met with little success.

The Revolt of Lares (Grito de Lares) on September 23, 1868, was the most serious challenge to Spanish domination in Puerto Rico. Ramón Betances, a physician trained in France, led the independence movement from Saint Thomas. It enjoyed greatest strength in the west among laborers protesting the passbook system and planters heavily indebted to Spanish merchants. On September 23, several hundred men occupied the town of Lares, near Mayagüez. The next morning they declared the independence of Puerto Rico and set up a provisional government. When the rebels tried to take San Sebastian, the next town, they met organized resistance and fled. During the following month, small guerrilla battles took place in the mountains of the region, as troops hunted down the rebels. This revolt has become a symbol to many Puerto Ricans, and September 24 is celebrated as a holiday.

Autonomist sentiment increased among the creole élite from the 1870s. After the overthrow of the Spanish republic in 1875, the governors manipulated the electoral laws in favor of *peninsulares* residing on the island. In 1887, the Liberal party—later reorganized as the Autonomist party—called for self-government within a federal union with Spain. Convinced that the Liberals were plotting subversion, a new governor instituted a year-long campaign of repression and torture, which ended only when he was replaced by the Spanish government.

The autonomists hoped to gain influence by an alliance with one of the Spanish political parties, but they disagreed in their choice of an ally. Luis Muñoz Rivera (1859–1916), an influential newspaper editor, strongly favored affiliation with Spain's Liberal Fusionist party headed by Mateo Práxedes Sagasta (1827–1903). An alliance finally was ratified early in 1897. When a terrorist killed the Spanish prime minister in August 1897, Sagasta returned to power and kept his promises. Royal decrees in November 1898 granted autonomy to Cuba and Puerto Rico.

Puerto Rico now enjoyed political freedom—at least on paper. The decree weakened the powers of the governor appointed by the Spanish Crown. Puerto Rico's legislature had authority over local laws as well as the island's budget, tariffs, taxes, and public works. All males over twenty-five could vote for delegates to both houses of the Spanish Cortes. They also elected the island's legislative assembly as well as eight of the fifteen members of the Administrative Council, a kind of senate.

Puerto's Rico's experiment in autonomy was brief. General elections were held in March, and the legislature took office on July 17. Eight days later, the first U.S. troops landed on the southern coast. Some Puerto Ricans mourned the loss of their brief independence. However, nothing in Spain's history during the 19th century suggests that later governments would have honored its commitments to its former colony.

## CHAPTER FIFTEEN

# HISPANIOLA AND THE LEEWARD ISLANDS

■

After the Revolutionary and Napoleonic Wars (1791–1815), England and Spain controlled the largest and richest of the Caribbean islands. Two independent republics shared the island of Hispaniola after 1844, when Santo Domingo expelled the Haitian army of occupation. With the loss of Haiti, France now possessed only the Leeward islands of Guadeloupe and Martinique, with some 75,000 free men and 175,000 slaves. The Danes continued to occupy the Virgin Islands, and the Netherlands retained Curaçao and its three Leeward colonies.[1]

The same worldwide trends—and especially the oversupply of sugar—affected all the islands. The 19th century was an era of centralization. France, Denmark, and the Netherlands now ruled their colonies directly from Europe, and all abolished slavery—France and Denmark in 1848, the Netherlands in 1863. Like the British colonies, these islands had to look for alternative sources of income as slave emancipation hastened the decline of sugar estates. Although certainly not wealthy, the French islands were comparatively prosperous and among the least torn by social strife. Unlike Britain and Spain, France viewed these colonies as integral parts of the homeland. It allowed island delegates to sit in the French legislature, protected Caribbean sugar from foreign competition, and promoted economic development.

Haiti and Santo Domingo—the only islands without ties to a European power—virtually ceased to grow sugarcane. Both developed into nations of free peasants owning small plots of land. Political authority was unstable, as venal and opportunistic rulers took power through military coups. Particularly in Haiti, these ambitious adventurers took advantage of enduring hostility between the light-skinned élite and the darker-skinned peasants.

## THE FRENCH ISLANDS ABOLISH SLAVERY

Napoleon's empire had restored slavery and the slave trade in 1802. Britain forced the French government to outlaw it by 1818, although illegal imports continued until 1831. Inspired by the success of British abolitionists, Parisian intellectuals formed an Abolition Society in 1834. Their main spokesman was Victor Schoelcher, who poured out a torrent of books, pamphlets, and speeches during the next fifteen years. Continuing slave unrest on Guadeloupe also weakened support for slavery, since French officials never forgot that Haiti had been lost through a slave revolt. A series of laws attempted to improve the treatment of slaves. In 1833, branding and mutilation of slaves was forbidden. Free coloreds—rapidly growing in numbers—became equal in law to whites.

| TABLE 24. MARTINIQUE AND GUADELOUPE POPULATION ESTIMATES, 1827–1848 | | | | |
|---|---|---|---|---|
| | TOTAL | WHITES | SLAVES | FREE NON-WHITES |
| Martinique | | | | |
| 1831 | 109,916 | 9,362 | 86,499 | 14,055 |
| 1848 | 113,357 | 9,490 | 67,447 | 36,420 |
| Guadeloupe | | | | |
| 1827 | 127,574 | 14,958 | 98,368 | 14,978 |
| 1848 | 129,050 | 9,926 | 87,719 | 31,405 |

SOURCES: Patterson, *Slavery and Social Death*, 480; Leo Elisabeth, "The French Antilles," *Neither Slave nor Free*, 148–151; Lassère, *Guadeloupe*, 297.

French abolitionists gained power with a revolution in 1848. The provisional government abolished slavery and appointed Schoelcher head of a committee to enforce emancipation. He compensated the owners but did not require freedmen to serve a period of apprenticeship. The slaves, while celebrating news of their freedom, feared that the planters would refuse to accept the new law. Thousands fled the estates, and rebellious slaves on Martinique killed dozens of whites. To end the disorder, the governors of the islands declared all slaves free even before they received Schoelcher's orders. The 1848 uprising in Martinique ensured that subsequent governments could not retract the emancipation decree.

## INDENTURED LABORERS FROM INDIA

As in the British colonies, many freedmen showed their contempt for field labor by moving out and squatting on vacant land. With emancipation, sugar production was halved on Guadeloupe and fell by almost one-third on Martinique. French planters, noting the apparent success of British estates using indentured labor, sought governmental help. Some imported free blacks from French colonies along Africa's western coast as well as small numbers of Chinese and Indochinese workers. Most used indentured laborers recruited in India by agreement with the British government. Between 1852 and 1887, Guadeloupe planters took in 45,000 Indians and 5,800 Africans, while Martinique received 29,400 Indians and 10,500 Africans. About three-quarters of the Indians stayed on after their indentures expired. As in Trinidad, most settled in separate communities and tried to maintain their own traditions.

Successive French governments continued to protect and support the sugar and rum industries. High tariffs kept foreign sugar out of France, and the main competition came from French beet sugar. After intense debate, a French law of 1843 taxed both products equally and gave the colonial sugar growers almost a legal right to priority in the home market. Henceforth, France effectively treated Caribbean sugar as a domestic product, and the government increased protective measures during depressions in the 1890s and 1930s. Indeed, since 1967, sugar from the French overseas departments is regulated as a European product by the European Common Market.

In addition to subsidizing immigration and offering a protected market, the government also encouraged investment by French banks. Modern central mills were built on both islands, and sugar production substantially exceeded pre-emancipation levels by the 1870s. Production again dropped at the end of the century with the end of Indian immigration and lower prices for French beet sugar. Only the most efficient creole planters survived, and French companies owning the central factories became large landowners.

## A CREOLE SOCIETY WITH FRENCH LAWS AND SCHOOLS

Black and colored peasants also bought up abandoned plantations as well as public lands, growing food for local consumption on their small farms. Two separate societies evolved here as on several other islands. As large companies consolidated the plantations, the number of whites fell—especially relative to the soaring black and colored population. High French officials, white landowners, and merchants enjoyed the greatest prestige. White and colored businessmen and professionals came next, with black smallholders and farm laborers at the bottom. The various races lived in segregated communities, and racial antagonisms sometimes broke out into violent riots.

Social peace normally was maintained because French laws offered opportunities to ambitious blacks and coloreds that were lacking in Spanish Cuba or the British Crown colonies. Especially under the Third Republic after 1870, the islands were increasingly integrated with France, and French colonial officers enforced French laws. Each island sent three representatives to the National Assembly, and each also elected a General Council, created in 1854 to discuss its budget. In addition, each town had an elected mayor and a municipal council with limited powers. While elections were not always totally honest, all adult males could vote from 1849 to 1854 and again after 1871. Blacks were elected to the local councils, while men of color tended to hold the more important positions and to represent the island in the National Assembly. Although blacks and coloreds keenly appreciated their differences, they did not, as in Haiti, form opposing factions.

Elementary education was generally available after the government took over the schools in 1886. The government also opened secondary schools (*lycées*), set up a law school on Martinique in 1882, and provided a small number of scholarships to French universities. Island schools taught French courses in

French under the supervision of officials from Bordeaux. Black and colored islanders who spoke French and had a French education could take posts with the government or work for the colonial administration, especially in French Africa.

## THE DUTCH COLONIES SURVIVE

The Dutch West India Company had occupied several islands from the 1630s, during its failed attempt to conquer Brazil. Despite French and British efforts to destroy Dutch commerce, the company held on and kept two groups of islands as trading posts. In the Leewards it governed Sint Eustatius, Saba, and Sint Maarten, which it shared with France. Just off the coast of the mainland, it held Curaçao—with a superb harbor at Willemstad—and its two small dependencies of Aruba and Bonaire. When Napoleon occupied Holland in 1795, the British occupied all the Dutch colonies until 1815. It then restored the islands and Holland's mainland colony of Surinam.

The last remnants of its empire in the Antilles brought few profits to the Netherlands during the century after 1815. Dutch traders had prospered during the 18th century by smuggling goods and slaves into Spain's mainland colonies and the French and British islands. Britain forced the Dutch to end the slave trade in 1814, and the Spanish mainland colonies won their independence and opened their ports to European shipping. Since smuggling and the slave trade had been their most lucrative business, many Dutch traders moved to Latin America or the United States. With their small populations and arid climates, the islands had few sources of income. Thus, the Netherlands, which had to subsidize their budgets, paid little attention to its Caribbean possessions, which it treated as extensions of Surinam.

Like the Spanish, British, and French colonies, the Dutch islands now came under direct rule from Europe. The Netherlands had abolished the West India Company in 1791. It now brought its Caribbean possessions under Dutch law enforced by governors-general sent from Europe. After unsuccessfully combining all of its Caribbean possessions under one administration (1828–1845), the Dutch established two governors-general. One governor enforced Dutch policies in Surinam. The other had authority over the three Leeward islands and the Curaçao group to the south. These officials were assisted by a variety of advisory councils, whose members were appointed by the governor and had no independent authority.

The Netherlands ended slavery in its Caribbean colonies on July 1, 1863, considerably later than Britain or France. Abolition enjoyed little support in Holland. Only a few academics called for emancipation, and the Reformed church—the official state church before 1795—did not petition the government on the issue until 1858.

In spite of sporadic efforts to promote agriculture or salt mining, the islands produced few cash crops, and only 6,500 slaves remained by 1863. But the sugar planters on Surinam refused to accept emancipation without compensation. When France ended slavery on Saint-Martin in 1848, slaves in the Dutch section simply took their freedom. Thrifty planters kept records of births among the blacks they still theoretically owned, while the Dutch government leisurely debated how much compensation to pay owners.

Curaçao was by far the most prosperous of the Dutch Antilles during the 19th century. Trade with Venezuela now became the mainstay of Curaçao's economy. The Dutch government negotiated a commercial treaty that lifted import taxes on all merchandise imported from the Netherlands and some products from other countries. Despite tensions during Venezuela's many revolutions, Dutch merchants profited by exchanging Venezuelan products for European manufactured goods.

Curaçao's economy was wholly based on trade. Although the Dutch government heavily subsidized agriculture during the 1830s, few cash crops can live on the island's dry soils. Aruba and Bonaire grow the aloe plant, whose leaves produce a liquid used in medicines and insect repellents. Farmers on Curaçao also introduced Seville oranges. They shipped the dried bitter peels to Holland, where they are distilled into a liqueur also called Curaçao. The end of slavery had little effect on this commercial economy. Emancipation did end production at Bonaire's salt ponds, which had attracted the Dutch to the islands in the 1630s.

Holland's three tiny islands in the Leewards suffered a severe economic decline during the 19th century. Sint Eustatius's traders had prospered by smuggling goods and slaves into the neighboring French and English islands as well as to the Spanish colonies on the mainland. In February 1781, a British fleet under Admiral Rodney occupied Sint Eustatius, destroying its warehouses and plundering the ships in its harbor. Most merchants and trading companies moved to the nearby Danish island of Saint Thomas, safely neutral during European wars.

Sint Maarten was less arid and had more fertile soils. Small plantations grew sugarcane and raised cattle, and hundreds of slaves also worked at the island's huge salt ponds. When emancipation came in 1863, planters could not pay wages and make a profit. They deserted these marginal estates, which soon were overgrown by tropical brush. The freed slaves and small white populations of the three Leeward islands survived by growing their own food, making shoes, and building ships. The men migrated each year as seasonal laborers—cutting sugarcane in Cuba and Puerto Rico, mining salt on Saint Kitts, or working in the phosphate mines in French Guiana.

## THE VIRGIN ISLANDS UNDER THE DANISH CROWN

The Danish Virgin Islands were under the direct rule of the King of Denmark from 1754. As in the British and Dutch islands, the royal governor had virtually unlimited powers. In 1863, two colonial councils with legislative powers were granted. Because of strict property requirements and other qualifications, only wealthy whites could vote in elections to these councils.

Prosperous conditions generally prevailed until the 1830s, when both foreign trade and the sugar industry began to decline. Unlike sailing ships, steam-driven merchant ships did not need to stop at Saint Thomas on the way to the British and French islands. Moreover, the adoption of free trade by the British empire took away many of Saint Thomas's advantages as a free port. As the harbor at Saint Thomas declined, planters and merchants found it difficult to ship their goods.

The Danish Virgin Islands had many ties to the British colonies, and Denmark could not maintain slavery after Britain ended it in 1833. The British abolition law prompted the Danish governor-general to decree various reforms, limiting the powers of owners and preparing the slaves for freedom. An 1839 decree called for free elementary education for both free and slave residents. Schools soon opened on Saint Croix, but Saint Thomas had to wait until 1878, Saint John even longer. English was the dominant language, used in the public schools after 1850.

A slave rebellion speeded up emancipation on Saint Croix, as on other islands. In 1847, a royal decree promised slaves their freedom in 1859. The slaves on Saint Croix decided not to wait for twelve years. Led by a young man named Buddhoe, blacks near Frederiksted secretly organized a revolution. In July 1848, they sacked several houses, and most whites fled to ships in the harbor. The slaves besieged the fort, demanding immediate emancipation and threatening to burn the town. When the governor finally came across the island from Christiansted, he quickly wrote out an emancipation decree that the Crown confirmed on September 22, 1848.

| TABLE 25. DANISH VIRGIN ISLANDS POPULATION ESTIMATES, 1835–1911 | | | | |
|---|---|---|---|---|
| | TOTAL | WHITES | SLAVES | FREE NON-WHITES |
| Saint Thomas | | | | |
| 1835 | 14,022 | 3,520 | 5,298 | 5,204 |
| 1848 | 14,000 | — | 3,500 | — |
| 1880 | 14,389 | — | — | — |
| 1911 | 10,678 | — | — | — |
| Saint Croix | | | | |
| 1835 | 26,681 | 1,892 | 19,876 | 4,913 |
| 1848 | — | — | 26,000 | — |
| 1880 | 18,430 | — | — | — |
| 1911 | 15,467 | — | — | — |
| Saint John | | | | |
| 1835 | 2,475 | 344 | 1,929 | 202 |
| 1850 | 2,228 | — | — | — |
| 1880 | 944 | — | — | — |
| 1911 | 941 | — | — | — |

SOURCE: Boyers, *America's Virgin Islands*, 40, 48, 53; Patterson, *Slavery and Social Death*, 482.

Sugar estates on Saint Croix became less profitable after emancipation increased expenses. Like freedmen on other islands, the former slaves refused field labor, and the cane estates faced bankruptcy. In 1849, the Danish government imposed a system of compulsory labor and internal passports that tied black laborers to the soil through yearly contracts. To cut milling expenses, it also opened a central factory in 1878, but it operated at a loss.

Full legal freedom came only after a second revolt destroyed much of Frederiksted in 1878. When they were free to leave, many black laborers emigrated to other Caribbean islands. The population of the islands continued to decline, falling by about a third between 1835 and 1911. (See Table 25.) The races remained separate, and the white minority retained economic as well as political power. Most whites sent their children to private schools rather than to the public schools established in 1839, and churches also were segregated by race.

The Danish government now found the colony an economic liability as revenues failed to cover its costs. Negotiations to sell the islands to the United States began in 1865, although they were not concluded until 1917. Indeed, the Danish government approved the sale of Saint Thomas and Saint John in 1867. However, the American U.S. Senate, caught up in the impeachment of President Andrew Johnson, failed to ratify the treaty.

## THE FORMATION OF MODERN HAITI

Victorious over Napoleon's armies, Jean-Jacques Dessalines made himself emperor of Haiti in 1805. Dessalines and later Henri Christophe (ruling in the north until 1820) tried to keep the plantations going with forced labor. But both blacks and colored persons resisted their system, which effectively reimposed slavery under a different name. Under their successors, Haiti became a nation of two castes. In the country, black peasants produced their own food on small plots, while the colored élite in coastal towns dominated commerce and politics. Although the hated and despised white masters were gone, racial divisions continued to trouble the new nation. With some exceptions, skin color has corresponded with wealth, with lighter Haitians being richer and darker ones poorer.

## EMPEROR JEAN-JACQUES DESSALINES

African by birth, the new emperor had begun life as a field hand on a cane estate owned by a black freedman. Scarred for life by his master's whip, Dessalines hated both whites and people of color. Following the defeat of the French, he ordered his soldiers to kill every remaining white, and some light-colored Haitians also perished. Haiti was to be a totally black nation in which no white would ever again own any property.[2]

Dessalines wanted Haiti to be black, but he did not want a nation of free black peasants. The emperor continued Toussaint's system of state socialism and made it even more rigid. The government would become the only landlord, with his generals and high officials leasing the estates at his whim. Dessalines thus seized all estates that had been owned by white Frenchmen—as well as all lands that blacks and coloreds had acquired since October 1802. Using forgery and murder, Dessalines also took other estates that he considered valuable. By 1806, his government owned more than two-thirds of all productive plantations, and Dessalines reimposed slavery on Haiti's blacks. He decreed that all persons must labor either as soldiers or as laborers bound for life to a specific estate. The army drove the majority of men and women back to the plantations, where the overseers used physical punishments to increase production.

A system of state socialism requires an army of literate officials and managers. Although he hated them, Dessalines had to fill these important posts with people of color. Many blacks continued to flee with their families into the hills. But the most effective opposition came from the colored landowners who had held estates during the colonial period. In October 1806, an insurrection began that had the secret approval of Henri Christophe, the most senior army officer. When Dessalines moved south to crush the rebels, he was killed in a roadside ambush near Port-au-Prince on October 17, 1806.

Christophe considered himself Dessalines's successor and did not bother to attend the assembly called to name the new head of state. Alexandre Pétion's supporters packed the meeting and drew up a new constitution providing for a powerless president and a powerful head of the national assembly. They then elected Christophe president, while Pétion became leader of the assembly. When Christophe brought his army south, Pétion's troops forced him to retreat. From 1807 to 1820, Haiti was divided into two states. In the north, Christophe crowned himself king in 1811, while Pétion ruled a republic in the South and West provinces.[3]

## THE KINGDOM AND THE REPUBLIC

King Henry I was Haiti's most relentlessly effective and dramatic ruler.[4] He retained Dessalines's system of disguised slavery and used it to enrich his realm. The peasants remained a separate caste, bound to the soil and forbidden to marry non-workers. Christophe's largely dark-skinned followers—who now became dukes, counts, and barons—received long leases and paid one-fourth of the annual crop in taxes. As hostile as Dessalines toward the coloreds, Christophe preferred foreign whites and used them in his administration. But he entrusted his own security to the Royal Dahoments, a personal bodyguard of 4,000 warriors recruited directly from Africa and thus loyal only to the king.

Under Christophe's stern rule, sugar, indigo, and coffee once more flowed profitably from the plantations to foreign markets. Cap Henri (the new name for Cap Français) flourished as a commercial center, and the king issued gold and silver currency. Using the unpaid labor of his people, he built a colossal fortress (La Citadelle La Ferrière) on a high mountain as well as his own exquisite palace, called Sans Souci. His harsh measures finally provoked a popular uprising in 1820. Stricken by paralysis and faced with defections in his army, King Henry I shot himself at Sans Souci—according to tradition, with a silver bullet.

Pétion's republic adopted very different policies. The republic did not preserve the plantations as undivided units worked by unfree labor. From 1809, Pétion broke up many estates and divided them among the populace, while

Sans Souci Palace, near Cap Haitien, Haiti. With his subjects' unpaid labor, King Henri Christophe (1807 to 1820) erected Sans Souci and a colossal fortress (*La Citadelle La Ferrière*) on a nearby mountain peak. Modeled after European palaces, Sans Souci was richly ornamented and furnished.

squatters settled on others. Pétion did keep some large estates and gave them to his colored generals, but their owners often could not find laborers. Thus they divided their plantations into several farms, which they leased to tenants against a share of the crop.

Most farmers in the south and west stopped growing export crops and instead planted garden crops for their own consumption. Sugar, cotton, and indigo virtually disappeared from the south. "Wild" coffee, cacao, and logwood collected in the mountains henceforth became the main export crops.[5] Both agriculture and governmental revenues steadily dwindled. But the former slaves, now secure on their own small parcels of land, loved Pétion as their *Papa bon kè* ("kind-hearted father"). Pétion's republic endured to become a reunited Haiti. The kingdom had perished with Christophe.

## PRESIDENT BOYER

Pétion's light-skinned secretary and friend, Jean-Pierre Boyer (1776–1850) succeeded him as president for life in 1818. When Christophe died in 1820, Boyer reunited the two states under the laws of the republic. In 1822 the Haitian army easily occupied the Spanish part of the island, where Haitian officials abolished slavery. Boyer, an amiable and refined man, ruled the whole of Hispaniola until a revolution removed him from office in 1843. During these two decades, Haiti enjoyed relative peace and stability. In 1825, France accepted Haiti's independence after Boyer agreed to pay a large indemnity to compensate the planters expelled in 1804.

Boyer at first continued Pétion's policy of land distribution, but his government ran out of funds even before the imposition of the French indemnity. Boyer thus made one final attempt to conserve what was left of the plantation system. His Rural Code of May 1826 restored the disguised slavery imposed by Toussaint L'Ouverture, Dessalines, and Christophe. The code attached workers for life to specific estates, forbade them to leave the plantations, and ordered them to work under military supervision. This time the effort failed totally, since Boyer's government lacked the officials or the military force to reimpose slavery.

Haiti now became a nation of small farmers, who grew only enough to feed their own families plus a small surplus sold at the local market. Some owned their own plots and others became sharecroppers. As the population soared many simply squatted on land in the mountains. There they cleared the forests and opened the land to massive soil erosion.

| TABLE 26.   HAITI POPULATION ESTIMATES, 1824–1919 | |
|---|---|
| 1824 | 590,000 |
| 1843 | 830,136 |
| 1863 | 1,100,000 |
| 1888 | 960,000 |
| 1900 | 1,270,000 |
| 1919 | 1,631,250 |
| NOTE:   All totals are estimates, since Haiti never has had an accurate census. | |
| SOURCES:   Watts, *West Indies*, 459 (1824–1900); Aaron Segal, "Haiti," *Population Policies in the Caribbean*, 182 (1919). | |

Few Haitians wanted to work on cane estates under any system. Prior to the revolution, the slaves had grown most of the island's food on their provision grounds. Now that they were free, they wanted to live as independent peasant farmers cultivating their own bit of family land. Freedom meant the right to control their own labor and keep the crops they had grown with their own hands.

Boyer's perennially bankrupt government invested nothing in the nation's infrastructure or in education. The state did not offer public education, and Roman Catholic schools did not exist until the Vatican recognized Haiti through the Concordat of 1860. In the absence of formal institutions, government was highly personalized and based on family ties and face-to-face friendships.

Haiti increasingly developed into a society of two castes. An élite group composed almost entirely of people of color controlled political power and patronage. A small number of coloreds were poor, and a small black élite group existed, especially in the north. But racial caste and economic class generally coincided. Blacks controlled the army, which was unusually large for so small a country. The colored élite dominated commerce and governmental offices and lived in the coastal cities, especially Port-au-Prince. Some collected rents from estates of varying size, but they otherwise turned their backs on and despised the black peasants.

## SEVENTY YEARS OF POLITICAL INSTABILITY

By 1843, Boyer had lost the confidence of the ruling élite. His ouster launched a long era of political instability. During the next seventy-two years, Haiti had twenty-two heads of state, only one of whom served out his term of office. Three died in office, one was blown up with his palace, another was hacked apart by a mob. The other fourteen were overthrown by revolutions after a tenure lasting from three months to twelve years. Color and the north-south split contributed to political turmoil. Politics became the game of the army and a small ruling élite. Factions within these groups made short-term alliances—sometimes crossing color lines—as they struggled to obtain and keep the spoils of office.

A series of short-lived governments ended in 1847 when the Senate elected Faustin Soulouque (1788–1873), the elderly head of the presidential guard. If the colored politicians planned to control Soulouque as a figurehead, he soon surprised them. Like Duvalier 110 years later, Soulouque purged the army, and installed black-skinned administrators loyal to himself. He created a personal army and secret police. He also used priests of the *voudon* religion to influence their followers among the rural population. In August 1849, Soulouque—now Emperor Faustin I—imitated Dessalines and Christophe by turning Haiti into an empire and creating a black nobility. Soulouque's costly and unsuccessful attempts to reconquer the Dominican Republic (which became independent in 1844) weakened his government. His magic ran out in 1859, and a conspiracy led by General Fabre Nicolas Geffrard (1806–1878), an élite *griffe* (born of mulatto and black parents), brought an end to the empire.

During Geffrard's eight years in power (1859 to 1867), the colored élite now reasserted the political and social supremacy it had lost under Soulouque. Since he wanted to keep the peasants quiet, Geffrard renewed the sale of state-owned lands on easy terms and was lenient toward squatters. Exports and government revenues based on customs dues both fell to new lows. Nevertheless, Geffrard's regime did make some progress in education and religion. To weaken the *voudon* religion, he signed a concordat with the Vatican in 1860, ending the schism dating from 1804. The Roman Catholic church assumed an important role in education. Members of religious orders, usually Frenchmen, ran most of the principal schools, which were reserved for the French-speaking élite.

Public office now provided one of the few remaining ways for an ambitious man to become rich. Members of the colored élite and ambitious black generals competed to seize power. In addition to the army, bands of irregular soldiers, known as Cacos, also began to install presidents. Primarily owners of small farms and usually from the north, the Cacos frequently took up arms against the government until the U.S. occupation suppressed them in 1920. President Geffrard put down several rebellions, but he was overthrown in 1867 by Major Sylvain Salnave (died 1869). Salnave's term in office saw almost continuous civil war between various factions. His successor, Nissage-Saget was among the most successful of Haiti's military dictators. He became the first Haitian president to serve out his prescribed term (1870–74) and retire to private life.

Nissage-Saget's retirement led to renewed turmoil. The black and colored élites became increasingly antagonistic and formed two political groups—the Liberal party (mainly colored) and the National party (mainly black). During the 1870s and into the 1880s, these two parties battled to control the army and government. Louis Salomon (1815–1888), leader of the Nationalists, served one seven-year term and began another (1879–1888). One of the most qualified presidents during this period, he founded a National Bank, with financial assistance from France, distributed some state land to the peasants, and allowed foreign companies to own property in Haiti.

Political disorder, rebellion, and financial corruption now were accepted as normal. Solomon's antagonism toward the colored élite worsened racial tensions. The eleven generals gaining the presidency between 1888 and 1915 often appealed to color prejudice in attacking their opponents. However, color and political allegiance did not entirely coincide, and personal and regional loyalties also complicated the political situation.

Europeans dominated what remained of Haiti's once flourishing economy and they also openly intervened in the nation's political struggles. France bought most of Haiti's coffee and about half of her total exports, while German companies controlled wholesale and retail trade. During their brief period in office, the various presidents borrowed heavily from foreigners but spent little on useful projects. They then pawned the customs revenues to pay off the loans and granted generous concessions to unscrupulous foreign promoters. Despite their patriotic talk, many politicians depended on foreign whites to keep their opponents out of power. Foreign gunboats intervened in Haitian rebellions, and some German merchants routinely sponsored uprisings as business propositions.

## SANTO DOMINGO UNDER HAITIAN OCCUPATION

The western third of Hispaniola, which became Haiti in 1804, was at the height of its prosperity under French rule in 1789. Santo Domingo, its larger neighbor to the east, was lightly inhabited, primarily by cattle ranchers. The first capital of the Spanish empire in the Americas, Santo Domingo soon lost its economic and political importance. By 1789, 125,000 Dominicans faced more than 500,000 Haitians. Santo Domingo provided an obvious target to the despots ruling Haiti during the first half of the 19th century. Toussaint L'Ouverture and Dessalines seized the neighboring Spanish colony from 1801 to 1805. And it was occupied again from 1822 to 1844 by the armies of Jean-Pierre Boyer.

Many Spaniards fled in 1801, and most of the remaining whites followed them during the second Haitian conquest in 1822. The population fell to only 63,000 in 1819, and it again reached 150,000 only in the 1860s. The Spanish estates were broken up into small farms, and Santo Domingo became a rural nation of independent peasants, most of mixed race. The nation had little commerce and no industry. A few thousand persons occupied the capital city, whose old monuments recalled its former greatness.

| TABLE 27.  DOMINICAN REPUBLIC POPULATION ESTIMATES, 1789–1897 | |
|---|---|
| 1789 | 125,000 |
| 1819 | 63,000 |
| 1871 | 150,000 |
| 1887 | 382,312 |
| 1897 | 486,000 |

SOURCE:  H. Hoetink, *The Dominican People 1850–1950: Notes for a Historical Sociology* (Baltimore, Maryland: Johns Hopkins University Press, 19.

The two periods of Haitian domination and subsequent invasions in 1849 and 1853 created an enduring hatred between the two neighboring peoples. President Boyer deliberately tried to destroy Santo Domingo's Spanish culture. He closed the universities and forbade communications between the Roman Catholic church and Europe. The Haitians created no lasting governmental institutions, and illiterate soldiers ruled by brutal extortion.

## MILITARY STRONGMEN RULE SANTO DOMINGO

In 1844, on Boyer's death, Spanish-speaking reformers proclaimed an independent republic. As in Haiti, power fell into the hands of armed bands led by rival chieftains (called *caudillos* in Spanish). The strongest of these, Pedro Santana (1801–1864) and Buenaventura Báez (1810–1882), generally alternated in power until 1874. Anxious to keep out the Haitians, Santana in 1861 persuaded the Spanish government to reoccupy Santo Domingo with himself as captain-general. But Spanish military rule proved unpopular here as elsewhere. In 1865, when the end of the Civil War allowed the U.S. to express disapproval of European intervention, Spanish armies withdrew for the last time.

After several years of chaos, Ulíses Heureaux (1845–1899) seized power in 1882. Heureaux—a dark-skinned Haitian—ruled as a severe, often sadistic, and corrupt dictator until 1899. The comparative tranquility of his regime encouraged foreign investment, and American, European, and Cuban planters began to establish sugar estates. Nevertheless, the nation was bankrupt by the end of Heureaux's reign. His government borrowed heavily from Dutch and American investors to build railroads, roads, and a telegraph system. And Heureaux also spent lavishly on himself, his family, and his mistresses.

In 1895, the Santo Domingo Improvement Company, an American firm, purchased the country's foreign debts in return for the right to collect its customs revenue. Heureaux's assassination in 1899 thus left the republic without an effective government and burdened with an enormous foreign debt that could not be paid. President Theodore Roosevelt, fearing that a European power might take advantage of this vacuum to establish bases near the Panama Canal, took over the collection of customs in 1905. American supervision of Santo Domingo's finances continued to 1940, with American marines directly occupying the nation from 1916 to 1924.

# PART FIVE:

# POVERTY AND PROGRESS IN THE CARIBBEAN SINCE 1914

■

# CHAPTER SIXTEEN:

# THE UNITED STATES AND THE INDEPENDENT NATIONS

■

From the end of the 19th century, the United States succeeded the European powers as the main economic and political force in the Caribbean. Under the centralized political systems in place until the 1950s, laws governing the Caribbean continued to be made in London, Paris, and The Hague. However, in setting policies for this area, governments in Europe now had to take American economic and political power into account.

After almost a century of economic decline, American capital provided the means to rebuild the sugar, banana, and coffee industries. American companies became the dominant growers in Puerto Rico, in Cuba (until the 1940s), and in the Dominican Republic. These companies created enormous plantations sometimes covering millions of acres and using the most modern equipment. The older and smaller plantations on Jamaica and in the eastern Caribbean could not compete with the new giants. By the 1920s, American-owned companies produced most of the world's cane sugar.

American power affected the British and French islands indirectly by setting the world market in which they competed. Between 1904 and 1934, the United States intervened more directly in several of the independent states in the western Caribbean. During these years, the United States especially sought to protect the Panama Canal. Both Republican and Democratic administrations were highly sensitive to the canal's commercial and strategic importance. They acted to forestall two possible dangers. The first threat was direct foreign invasion. To prevent this, American military bases were constructed both in the Canal Zone and in Cuba, Puerto Rico was brought under direct American control, and the Danish Virgin Islands were purchased in 1917.

A second threat was continuing chaos that might tempt a European power to take over the government. To preserve order and also to protect American commercial interests, the United States intervened in Cuba, Haiti, and the Dominican Republic. Between 1906 and 1917, American troops were sent to Cuba three times, and the United States again forced governmental reforms in 1922. On the island of Hispaniola, American intervention lasted longer and took the form of direct occupation. For many years, American officials administered the customs, the government's only source of revenues. And U.S. Marines occupied both the Dominican Republic (1916–1924) and Haiti (1915–1934) to end chaotic violence.

In both countries, American administrators reorganized the national finances, created schools and public health systems, and made many physical improvements—building roads and sewage systems and securing safe water supplies. In both cases, the United States also established a trained, disciplined, and well-armed local police force.

In the Dominican Republic, General Rafael Trujillo (1891–1961) soon used the American-trained army to seize control (1930–1961), installing an autocratic but efficient regime. In 1965, American troops again occupied the country until free elections could be held. Since 1966, a series of moderate regimes have been elected, giving the Dominican Republic its first twenty-five years of democracy in five centuries. Foreign investment has been encouraged, and land reforms have increased peasant ownership.

In Haiti events have taken an different course. After the U.S. withdrew in 1933, several dishonest and opportunistic presidents looted the treasury until they were overthrown by palace revolutions. François "Papa Doc" Duvalier (1907–1971), who seized power in 1957, made himself "President-for-Life" in 1964. Duvalier established a strong dictatorship and retained power until his death in 1971. Duvalier was succeeded by his son, the nineteen-year-old Jean-Claude (1951–   ), called "Baby Doc." Under both Duvaliers, Haiti became economically isolated and politically bankrupt. After Jean-Claude was ousted in 1986, a series of short-lived governments, usually military, has ruled Haiti.

## THE CREATION OF THE CUBAN REPUBLIC

José Martí's vision of a politically mature nation failed to materialize during the years after independence. Cuba had many advantages. The largest and most populous Caribbean nation, its people occupied an entire island and had no immediate enemies. Cubans enjoyed the highest standard of living in the region, and the U. S. government agreed to purchase their exports and protect them against foreign powers.

| TABLE 28.   CUBA POPULATION ESTIMATES, 1919–1970 | |
|---|---|
| 1919 | 2,889,004 |
| 1943 | 4,778,583 |
| 1970 | 8,495,404 |
| SOURCE:   Schroeder, *Cuba: A Handbook of Historical Statistics*, 40. | |

Yet the Cuban republic never lived up to its promise. After four centuries under Spain, its citizens regarded any government as something to exploit or fight, while their leaders treated public funds as a source of personal wealth. Power remained both too concentrated and too personal after independence. While the American-style constitution of 1902 called for separation of powers and a federal system, effective rule remained with the president. Two parties emerged after independence—the Republicans or Conservatives and the Liberals. But neither stood for strong principles, and politicians easily switched allegiance. Both parties operated simply as groups of friends and relatives who banded together to win the spoils of political office. In their maneuvers, both combined the worst aspects of the Spanish and American systems.[1]

The first president, Tomás Estrada Palma (1835–1907), accomplished a great deal. Despite the opposition of American sugar growers, he pressed the United States to sign a reciprocity treaty cutting tariffs on imports from Cuba. In another treaty, the U.S. gave up its claim to the Isle of Pines. Unlike his successors, President Estrada did not personally loot the treasury, and it contained a surplus. Estrada believed he deserved another term, and won reelection in 1905 after fraud on both sides.

In August 1906, Estrada's Liberal opponent, José Miguel Gómez (1858–1912) led an insurrection that quickly spread over the island. Estrada, who had only a tiny army, appealed for help to President Theodore Roosevelt. Roosevelt, refusing to intervene, instead sent William Howard Taft, the secretary of war, to negotiate a compromise. Standing on principle, Estrada and his vice-president resigned in September 1906, leaving the country without a government.

Roosevelt now had no alternative and named Charles E. Magoon, the former head of the Panama Canal Zone, to supervise governmental operations. Magoon stayed until the Cuban political parties were ready to hold elections in December 1908. Assisted by Enoch Crowder, Magoon imposed a number of needed laws, including one giving the vote to all males. Some Cubans later accused Magoon of condoning graft and theft of government funds. But the evidence shows that Magoon was personally honest.

## ECONOMIC BOOM AND GAUDY POLITICS

Gómez again ran as the Liberal candidate, and his inauguration in January 1909 ended the second U.S. occupation. President Gómez, ruling during a period of general prosperity, became a millionaire and also allowed his subordinates to plunder state funds. Although Gómez—a major general during the independence struggle—was generally popular, Alfredo Zayas (1861–1934) disputed his control of the Liberal party. Their personal feud allowed the Conservative candidate, Mario García Menocal (1866–1941), to win the presidency in 1913. Another hero of the wars of independence, Menocal began his rule with major initiatives in education, public health, and government finance. However, as sugar profits soared during the First World War, Menocal's administration became even more corrupt and ineffective than that of Gómez, and Menocal increased his own fortune to $40 million.

Despite his promise not to stand for reelection, Menocal ran again in November 1916, opposed by the Liberal party's Alfredo Zayas. Both sides padded the vote in the localities they controlled. Altogether, 800,000 votes were cast by fewer than 500,000 eligible voters. When it seemed likely that Zayas had won, the minister of the interior lost the ballots from the eastern provinces and declared Menocal elected.

The Liberals put off their plans for a revolution when the U.S. announced that it would support only governments that took power constitutionally. President Wilson, who was about to enter the First World War, wanted a quiet Cuba. After some disorder, Menocal took office on May 1917, while the United States sent 2,600 troops—who remained until 1923—to the eastern provinces. Until 1921, Menocal reigned more or less as a dictator, governing largely by decree. He made huge profits from the sugar boom, while all Cuba embarked on a drive for unprecedented wealth.

The November 1920 presidential election was held during a period of acute economic depression following the collapse of the wartime sugar boom. Alfredo Zayas now left the Liberals and enjoyed President Menocal's support against ex-president Gómez. As in 1916, the election was marked by fraud and violence, and Menocal's government declared Zayas the winner. The 1920 election triggered another American intervention in Cuba. The collapse of sugar prices in June 1920 threatened to bring down the banks, and Cuba desperately needed an American loan. In January 1921, President Wilson sent General Crowder to Havana on the battleship *Minnesota*. The Republicans under Warren G. Harding kept Crowder in Cuba, where he briefly became the real power.

When Zayas finally took office in May 1921, the Cuban economy was prostrate. Large stocks of unsold sugar filled the warehouses, and all Cuban-owned banks had failed. Crowder used the urgent Cuban need for a North American loan to force reform on Zayas. Pressed by Crowder, Zayas appointed the so-called "Honest Cabinet." The government cut the budget in half, dismissed unneeded employees, levied a sales tax, and renegotiated corrupt contracts. In return, the U.S. government sponsored a long-term loan of $50 million in January 1923.

Almost as soon as the loan was final, President Zayas declared that Crowder's reforms offended Cuban sovereignty. He dismissed the Honest Cabinet, and his government soon degenerated into a carnival of nepotism and graft. Large sugar harvests and higher prices from 1922 to 1925 restored a surface prosperity. But many Cubans, and especially many intellectuals, lost all respect for the republic and abandoned hope of achieving progress through it.

Zayas's last years as president saw the beginning of large demonstrations by students and veterans protesting Cuba's dishonest and incapable political system. Rejected as a candidate by the Conservatives, President Zayas returned to the Liberal party and endorsed General Machado y Morales (1871–1939). Although Zayas used force on his behalf, Machado probably would have won a majority in any case.

## THE MACHADO DICTATORSHIP

Despite episodes of American intervention, Cuba remained Spanish in population and culture. The Treaty of Paris had guaranteed the private property of Spaniards, and more than 400,000 new immigrants arrived between 1902 and

1916. Many came as penniless workers. But Cuba's prosperity (when sugar prices were high) also attracted businessmen and professionals, who were influenced by political and intellectual trends in Europe. Thus Machado's dictatorship was inspired by and may be compared to the authoritarian governments that took power everywhere in Europe during the 1920s.

Like Mussolini in Italy, Machado tried to create a strong one-party state under his personal control. He controlled the army (some 12,000 strong), the congress, and the courts through threats and bribery. In 1926, as sugar prices again began to fall, he imposed production quotas to cut output, thus beginning the state intervention that culminated in Castro's government takeover. Like Mussolini, Machado sought to promote prosperity by a vast program of public works. His pride was the great central highway that ran for 750 miles from the western to the eastern tip of the island.

Machado did not tolerate opposition. He took over the Conservative party and combined it with his own Liberals and other smaller parties, thus running as the only candidate in November 1928. He attacked the Cuban Communist party—founded in 1925—and crushed strikes by labor unions associated with the European Anarchist movement. American officials remained silent about Machado's crimes and illegal changes in the 1901 constitution. After the failure of the 1923 intervention, the U.S. government had decided to refrain from political meddling.

Machado's dreams of imitating Mussolini or Salazar in Portugal ended with the Wall Street crash of October 1929. The worldwide depression crushed the already weak Cuban economy, and new U.S. tariffs made matters worse. In mid-1930, the Hawley-Smoot Tariff Act increased the import tax on Cuban sugar to protect producers in the United States, the Philippines, Hawaii, and Puerto Rico. Cuba's share of the U.S. market was cut in half between 1930 and 1933. As both sugar prices and output collapsed, foreign trade dropped to one-tenth of the 1929 level. Government revenues also fell and American banks—many themselves failing—had no money to lend Cuba. Unemployment, wage cuts, and bankruptcies brought widespread misery.

Since Machado had absorbed both the Liberal and Conservative machines, his opponents formed extra-legal organizations. Moderate politicians led an armed uprising in August 1931 that failed ingloriously, and more radical groups took over. By far his loudest and most dangerous enemies were the university students, often led by professors and men who had already graduated. In September 1930, Machado closed the university and many high schools. Students, intellectuals, and young professionals formed the ABC, a terrorist group organized in secret cells. Machado's gunmen retaliated, paying murder for murder. The countryside became as lawless as it had been during the final days of Spanish rule.

The new administration of Franklin Roosevelt wanted to find a peaceful solution before civil war made armed intervention necessary. The president named Sumner Welles (1892–1961), a State Department expert on the Caribbean, as ambassador extraordinary to Cuba. Welles arrived in Havana on May 8 and began to press for Machado's resignation. President Machado at first defied the United States to intervene. But he lost the support of many officers, and a general strike paralyzed Havana. Machado fled to the Bahamas on August 12, 1933, narrowly escaping fire from ABC terrorists as his plane left the runway.

## BATISTA'S FIRST DICTATORSHIP

Ambassador Welles installed Carlos Manuel de Céspedes (1871–1939) as provisional president. A son of the man leading the 1868 rebellion, Céspedes had a famous name but little support from any faction. His government could not control growing violence as the economy continued to collapse. Looting and riots ravaged Havana, while armed gangs took over sugar mills in the country.

After only a few days, student radicals temporarily allied with soldiers led by Fulgencio Batista y Zaldívar (1901–1973), a thirty-two year old sergeant. On September 4, 1933, Batista walked into the office of the chief of staff and arrested him at gunpoint. Declaring himself a colonel and the new military head, he fired 500 officers and replaced them with common soldiers loyal to himself. With the support of the Directorio Estudiantil Universitario, the main student group, Batista took possession of Havana. Despite several pleas by Welles, President Roosevelt refused to intervene under the Platt Amendment.

The revolution in September 1933 gave power to two armed political forces, the army and university students. It at first became more radical under Dr. Ramón Grau San Martín (1887–1969), a fashionable physician and professor who became provisional president on September 10. Grau abrogated the 1901 constitution and proclaimed a socialist revolution that both alienated many groups in Cuba and that also aroused American hostility. U.S. refusal to recognize Grau encouraged opposition by the Communists, displaced army officers, and ABC terrorists. While Grau's power melted away, Batista solidified his hold on the army. On January 14, 1934, Batista forced President Grau to resign, naming Carlos Mendieta (1873–1960) as provisional president two days later. The United States, which saw Batista as the one leader capable of maintaining order, soon recognized Mendieta's government.

After crushing student unrest and a general strike in March 1935, Batista maintained tight political control through a series of puppet presidents. President Roosevelt's "good neighbor" policy strengthened his regime. In May 1934, the United States signed a treaty that annulled the hated Platt Amendment, while retaining the naval base at Guantánamo. In August, the two nations agreed to a new reciprocity treaty that repealed the Hawley-Smooth tariffs. The American import tax on sugar was reduced, while Cuba allowed most American goods to enter with little or no duty. For the next twenty-five years, Cuba received a fixed quota of the American market that rose to 49 percent by 1949.

Batista was in no sense a conservative. In the Latin-American context, he can be compared to other left-wing soldier-presidents, including Juan Perón of Argentina and Lázaro Cárdenas of Mexico. His policies during the 1930s installed a form of state socialism popular with the Cuban masses. Laws providing pensions, insurance, and limiting working hours largely satisfied the demands of the urban workers. At this time, Cuban Communists under Russian direction worked closely with Batista. Communists directed a labor confederation created in 1939, which bargained directly with the government rather than employers.

The government extended these social security benefits to farm workers in 1941, gave out state lands to small growers, and built many rural schools. A more radical step was a law of September 1937 that brought the sugar and tobacco industries under close state direction. The law organized small farmers in cooperatives and agricultural workers in unions. Above all, it guaranteed the jobs of the *colonos*, the small farmers that supplied sugarcane to the mills. Mills could not lay off a cane farmer, and they could never cancel a farmer's lease, as long as he worked the land.

## DEMOCRACY IS RESTORED

His control of the army and alliance with the Communists gave Batista a strong political position by 1939. In November, he held honest elections that gave the opposition a majority in an assembly to write a new constitution. Although it was ignored in later years, the 1940 constitution created a democratic and mildly socialist state—at least on paper. Under its provisions, the president served only one four-year term, women received the vote, and many social welfare benefits were guaranteed. With the constitution accepted, Batista resigned as chief of the army to run against Dr. Grau in the July 1940 presidential election—the first reasonably honest presidential election since 1912. Although the Communists proved his strongest allies, Batista enjoyed wide support and won almost 60 percent of the vote.

Batista was fortunate to hold office as elected president during the Second World War. As it had during the First World War, Cuba concentrated on producing sugar. From 1942 through 1947, production surged as the United States bought Cuba's entire crop at a guaranteed price, and the war also benefited steel and manganese mines in eastern Cuba. Given this economic boom, Batista was confident that Cubans with property backed him. Thus he continued to court the labor unions, established diplomatic relations with the Soviet Union, and gave the Communists two seats in his cabinet.

Batista assumed his prime minister would win the 1944 presidential election, and he thus permitted an honest count. Despite vigorous Communist support for Batista's candidate, his old opponent Dr. Ramón Grau won. Batista had not stopped the theft of government funds, but Grau used the continuing sugar boom to set a new record in corruption. Although he was already a rich man, Grau turned his presidency into an orgy of theft behind a mask of emotional nationalist speeches. He also tolerated the growth of private armies, in many cases placing their leaders on government payrolls. Armed gangs took over the University of Havana, which now became totally corrupt. As the cold war between Russia and the United States worsened, Grau broke with the Communists and created a rival labor confederation. Overall, Ambassador Sumner Welles apparently was correct in refusing to accept a Grau presidency in 1933.

The election of 1948—the last free election to date—brought in Dr. Carlos Prío Socarrás (1903–1977). Prío promised to restore an effective administration, end violence, and remove Communists from powerful positions. He failed in all of these goals, while personally stealing millions. Labor racketeering discouraged honest businessmen, and violence by armed gangs increased. In 1951, Prío's government finally indicted ex-president Grau for stealing $40 million. But the courts never convicted Grau, whose trial was constantly delayed by frivolous appeals and open violence.

## BATISTA'S SECOND DICTATORSHIP

In March 1951, Batista returned to Cuba from Florida and announced his candidacy for president in the 1952 elections.[2] Fearing that he might not win, Batista overthrew Prío's regime on March 10 in a bloodless coup. Within two hours, his men were in charge of the army and police, and President Prío sought asylum in the Mexican embassy.

The Cuban economy prospered during Batista's second regime. A sugar stabilization fund helped hold up prices when overproduction weakened the world market. Partly because of the rigid labor laws imposed during the 1930s, few foreigners now wanted to invest in sugar mills, which were mainly Cuban-owned. However, Batista's return to power did encourage foreign investment in mining, cattle raising, and tourism. The government financed low-cost housing as well as completing a new water system for Havana and other public works Grau and Prío had neglected, albeit with the usual graft. As in the 1930s, Batista won over the major labor leaders as well as most of union members. However, the Communists now refused to cooperate with the president because of his close ties to the United States.

On July 26, 1953, a delayed revolt against Batista finally broke out. Probably sponsored by deposed President Prío Socarrás, some 130 young men attacked the Mocada army barracks near Santiago. Their leader was Fidel Castro Ruz (1927– ), a 26-year-old lawyer from a wealthy family and long involved in university intrigue and terrorism. The effort failed miserably. Some of the attackers were massacred, and another 68 died in prison. Castro himself escaped to the mountains but was captured and sentenced to fifteen years in prison.

Pardoned by Batista, Castro opened his second attack in December 1956. Castro promised that he would replace Batista's dictatorship with free elections, end the stealing of governmental funds, and develop the domestic economy. Believing these promises, Roman Catholic bishops, businessmen, and landowners persuaded the United States government to halt the sale of arms to Batista. On January 1, 1959, Batista and his family flew from Cuba to Florida, taking with them a substantial part of the national treasury.

## CASTRO'S TOTALITARIAN RULE

At first Castro's government had the support of most of the population. However, it soon alienated many of its supporters. Within a few months, Castro showed that he intended to create a Communist society. The government almost immediately seized the agricultural estates, factories, and utilities—whether owned by Cubans or by foreigners. Through its control of raw materials and money for investment, it sought to end any form of private property, which was outlawed in 1968. Instead, all economic activities were to be run by governmental officials and their Russian advisors.

Increasing numbers of Cubans went into exile to the United States, especially to south Florida. Like earlier groups of exiles during the 19th century, they sought American support in overthrowing a dictatorship in Cuba. But these attempts were discredited in 1961 by the total failure of the Bay of Pigs invasion. The following year, American spy planes verified the presence throughout western Cuba of launching pads for surface-to-air nuclear missiles. When President Kennedy threatened a blockade and invasion, Premier Khrushchev of Russia agreed to remove the missiles. The United States in turn promised not to invade Cuba.

Despite the general failure of his economic programs, Castro has remained in power with the help of efficient police terror, large Russian subsidies, and the continuing emigration to Florida of hundreds of thousands of Cuban dissidents. During the 1960s, Castro sought to export his revolution to the Latin American mainland. While some Caribbean politicians (for example, President Manley in Jamaica) praised Castro's policies during the 1970s, few imitated his close ties to the Soviet Union.

## THE U.S. INTERVENES IN THE DOMINICAN REPUBLIC

Following the murder of President Ulíses Heureaux in 1899, several governments under self-proclaimed generals ruled the Dominican Republic. The nation was bankrupt, and the European states holding its debt threatened to take over to recover their investments. President Theodore Roosevelt thus forced the Dominicans to place their customs—the major source of revenues—under U.S. supervision. As president, Ramón Cáceres (1868–1911) gave the nation five years of firm and quiet government (1906–1911). But Cáceres's assassination plunged the republic once more into chaos. A series of short-lived presidents gutted the national treasury to pay bribes and purchase loyalty.

President Woodrow Wilson believed in America's responsibility to foster democracy around the world. He found the Dominican Republic in turmoil and increased U.S. efforts to avert total financial collapse and political anarchy. In November 1915, he demanded that the Dominican government allow U.S. officials to control government finances and train a new police force, replacing the existing army and militia. The Dominican Chamber of Deputies refused to accept Wilson's proposal, and anti-American feeling became intense. In May 1916, American marines landed in Santo Domingo, beginning an eight-year U.S. occupation.

American commanders, who could not find a compliant Dominican politician to act as president, ruled the country under martial law. The American occupation forces reformed the nation's courts and finances. In order to improve life in the rural areas, they built roads, created public schools, and improved public sanitation. Due to better medical care, the population rose sharply.

| TABLE 29.   DOMINICAN REPUBLIC POPULATION ESTIMATES, 1897–1960 | |
| --- | --- |
| 1897 | 486,000 |
| 1920 | 1,140,000 |
| 1940 | 1,759,000 |
| 1960 | 3,030,000 |

SOURCES:   Hoetink, *Dominican People* 19 (1897); Carmen A. Miró, *La poblacion de America Latina en el Siglo XX* (Santiago de Chile: Centro Latinoamericano de Demografia, 1970), page 2 (1920–1960).

Armed bandit gangs formed the most serious problem in the countryside. The United States therefore replaced the old army with a new National Guard trained by American solders. Criticism by the Republicans during the 1920 presidential campaign hastened the end of U.S. rule. American forces left in 1924, after the U.S. and Dominican politicians negotiated an agreement that retained American supervision of the customs. (U.S. supervision ended in 1940.)

## TRUJILLO'S LONG DICTATORSHIP

The Dominican National Guard was the most lasting legacy of American occupation. The United States wanted it to keep order and to stay out of politics. In 1927, Rafael Leónidas Trujillo Molina, received command of the guard, which turned itself into the Dominican army the following year. By 1930, the army had regained control of Dominican politics, and General Trujillo gained the presidency (1930–1961).

Trujillo took power during a time of crisis. A hurricane in September 1930 killed thousands and almost totally destroyed Santo Domingo City. The worldwide economic depression increased unemployment and made reconstruction more difficult. Trujillo gained extraordinary powers to deal with the emergency, retaining them until his death in 1961. The president soon eliminated his enemies and erected an autocratic but effective regime. He insisted on being treated with something approaching worship and changed the name of the rebuilt capital to Trujillo City (Ciudad Trujillo).

Under Trujillo, exports of sugar, tobacco, and cacao boomed, especially during the Second World War. The government built new roads, railways, public buildings, hotels, and airports, and encouraged tourism. But Trujillo ran the country as a ruthless dictator, freely using torture and murder to suppress possible rivals. He also enriched his family, which built up a fortune of more than $500 million and owned companies controlling 60 percent of the nation's assets and workers.

Trujillo's empire began to crumble in the late 1950s. Sugar provided most foreign revenues, and prices plummeted. In 1960, Trujillo tried to assassinate the president of Venezuela. The Organization of American States banned the sale of weapons, the U.S. Congress cut price supports for Dominican sugar, and rumors of unrest kept away tourists. Despite Trujillo's usual elaborate precautions, a seven-man team killed him on May 30, 1961. The assassins were

Dominican army officers who wanted Trujillo dead for personal reasons. While the U.S. Central Intelligence Agency was not directly involved in Trujillo's murder, it helped to plan it and supplied some of the weapons used.

Ramfis, Trujillo's eldest son, took command of the army, while Joaquín Balaguer (1907– ) became president. However, the U.S. government would not allow the Trujillo family to retain power. Some of the family temporarily seized control, but they fled when the United States sent warships to Trujillo City. In December 1962, Juan Bosch (1909– ) became president after the first democratic election since 1930.

During his six months as president, Bosch tried to impose major economic and social changes with substantial financial aid from the United States. The government confiscated more than 7 million acres of Trujillo-owned land and gave it out to 70,000 landless peasants. A new constitution weakened the Roman Catholic hierarchy, and Bosch threatened to reduce the power of the army. His toleration of the Communist party—not long after Castro seized Cuba—angered the more conservative army officers. On September 25, 1965, the military arrested Bosch and exiled him to Puerto Rico.

## THE SECOND U.S. OCCUPATION

The new military government promised to hold free elections, but various factions plotted to seize power. Bosch's party allied with the Communists, and the former president published a book attacking the ruling groups and calling for sweeping changes. On April 24, 1965, young army officers supporting Bosch seized sections of the capital and seemed on the verge of defeating the loyalist forces. Although he wanted to stay out of this civil war, President Lyndon Johnson felt he could not be reelected if he permitted a "second Cuba" under Communist rule. On April 28, U.S. military forces flew into the capital city to halt the rebel advance. In a repeat of the 1916–1924 occupation, 23,000 American U.S. troops ultimately occupied the country.

American forces—augmented by small numbers of Brazilian, Honduran, and Costa Rican troops—remained in Santo Domingo for a year. A political solution eventually emerged after four months of military stalemate in which some 2,000 Dominicans were killed. In June 1966, Joaquín Balaguer won 57 percent of the vote in a relatively honest election and was reelected President in 1970 and 1974.

## THE DOMINICAN REPUBLIC TODAY

Balaguer's government was authoritarian and paternalistic. The president frequently transferred senior officers to prevent them from gaining a personal power base. But he also let elements of the military use illegal force against left-wing terrorists. With substantial U.S. aid, higher sugar prices, and growing investments, the country generally prospered through the mid-70s. The nation's gross national product increased almost 10 percent each year. However, the income of the rural poor actually fell under Balaguer, and unemployment began to increase during his third term as petroleum prices exploded while sugar prices dropped drastically. Moreover, in 1979, two devastating hurricanes ravaged the repub-lic, killing more than one thousand persons and leaving another 400,000 homeless.

Seeing an opportunity to win power, Bosch's old party, the Dominican Revolutionary Party (PDR), revived its grass-roots organization. Its candidate in 1978, Antonio Guzmán (1911–1982), was a moderate millionaire rancher acceptable to the United States. When the vote count showed Guzmán with a strong early lead, military officers seized the ballot boxes and tried to annul the election. With considerable pressure from U.S. President Jimmy Carter and threats of a massive general strike, Balaguer convinced the military to return the ballots. In August 1978, Balaguer gave up his office to Guzmán, arguably the first democratic and peaceful transfer of power after almost two centuries of political disorder.

The economy remained depressed throughout the 1980s as sugar prices remained low and the population continued to grow rapidly. Encouraged by governmental subsidies, tourism boomed, replacing sugar as the republic's most important source of foreign currency. By 1988, more than 1.2 million tourists visited each year. (See Table 33.) Nevertheless, almost half the population continued to work in agriculture, primarily growing sugar, cacao, and coffee. Incomes remained low, unemployment was high, and the republic continued to depend on the United States and Europe for economic assistance. In 1984, the International Monetary Fund persuaded the government to adopt a policy of austerity and free trade.

Despite these economic problems, the country has continued to follow a democratic course. President Guzmán moved cautiously to implement socialist policies, but the country's large foreign debts forced his successors to reduce governmental spending. After his PRD successor, Salvador Jorge Blanco, was elected president in 1982, Guzmán killed himself following accusations of corruption against members of his government. Jorge Blanco also failed to restore economic growth. Joaquín Balaguer, now leader of the Christian Reform Party, was again elected president in 1986 and reelected to a fifth term in 1990. Economic prospects brightened with rising sugar prices, a smaller trade deficit, and the restructuring of foreign loans.

## THE U.S. MARINES OCCUPY HAITI

The United States failed to create stable, democratic governments in Cuba and the Dominican Republic. But the occupation of Haiti (1915–1934) undoubtedly represents America's least successful interventions in the Caribbean. President Woodrow Wilson occupied Haiti in 1915 to prevent Germany from taking over the country. He also wished to create an honest and effective government that would foster economic development. Instead, after the United States withdrew, a series of dishonest presidents were followed by François Duvalier and his son, Jean-Claude. Under the two Duvaliers—"Papa Doc" and "Baby Doc"—the Haitian people endured thirty years (1957–1986) of cruel and greedy tyranny.

Like the Dominican Republic, Haiti's government was deeply in debt to foreign companies by the early 1900s, and German merchants and companies were dominant. German nationals controlled nearly 80 percent of Haiti's foreign trade, owned major public utilities, and frequently sponsored revolutions to install client governments. Some American companies also had interests in Haiti, but direct American investment in Haiti was tiny. In 1913, U.S. ventures amounted to no more than $4 million, compared to $200 million invested in Cuba by American companies.

President Wilson feared that France or especially Germany—now enemies in the First World War—might occupy Haiti. The government's bankruptcy and continuing political chaos offered foreign powers both an opportunity and an excuse. Between 1908 and 1915, there were seven presidents and about twenty uprisings and attempted insurrections. Although poor, Haiti had great strategic and military importance since it controlled the Windward Passage—the most direct route to the Panama Canal. Wilson's government thus drafted the necessary plans for an occupation as early as July 1914.

A particularly gruesome violation of diplomatic immunity gave Wilson a reason to intervene in 1915. President Vilbrun Guillaume Sam (d. 1915) seized power in February 1915 but was himself suddenly overthrown late in July. As rival forces took Port-au-Prince, Sam ordered the massacre of 167 political prisoners, many members of prominent families. Sam took refuge in the French legation, while the chief executioner, General Oscar Etienne, fled to the Dominican legation. Enraged mobs invaded both sanctuaries, killed Etienne, and literally tore President Sam limb from limb. They paraded portions of his body around the streets of the capital.

American sailors and marines took Port-au-Prince on July 18, 1915. Within six weeks, some 2,000 marines occupied the country's customs houses and other governmental offices. Wilson needed a compliant Haitian government to legitimize American rule. Protected by American soldiers, the Haitian congress elected Sudre Dartiguenave as president on August 12. Dartiguenave, the first colored southerner to hold the office in a generation, believed that cooperating with the United States would benefit Haiti. However, hostility toward American troops increased, and the American commander declared martial law, allowing American military courts to try Haitian political offenders.

On November 11, the United States also forced a reluctant Haitian senate to sign a treaty that legalized the American occupation. This act placed Haitian finances and government under American control, abolished the existing army, and created a single police force (the Gendarmerie d'Haiti) under American officers. A new legislature, elected early in 1917, rejected a constitution written by the Americans. The American authorities quickly dismissed the assembly and submitted the constitution to a popular referendum. It was approved overwhelmingly, but fewer than 5 percent of Haitians voted. The 1917 constitution allowed white foreigners to own property in Haiti for the first time since 1805. It also made the American-led *gendarmerie* the only legal armed force.

## THE PÉRALTE REBELLION, 1918–1919

American troops found it difficult to move between towns because the roads— most built before 1789—had fallen into ruin. Since the Haitian government had no money, the Americans revived an 1864 law requiring peasants to work on local roads for three days a year. Although conscripted Haitians built a large network of roads, some American officers abused this system of forced labor, known as the *corvée*. Gendarmerie guards brutally abused Haitian laborers, forced them to march tied together by ropes, and made them work outside their own districts for weeks or even months. Haitians naturally resented these practices, which recalled French slavery. Aware of increasing hostility, the marine commandant abolished the *corvée* in August 1918. However, the officer in charge of the northern and central regions illegally continued it into 1919.

The American invasion of July 1915 had met little resistance. During the first year of occupation, American forces quickly crushed the Cacos, armed peasant irregulars supporting President Sam's onetime interior minister. Late in 1918, Charlemagne Péralte and Benoit Batraville led a more serious rebellion protesting the *corvée*. The rebels—variously estimated at 2,000 to 40,000—easily defeated the local *gendarmerie*, took over much of the northern mountain country, and twice threatened Port-au-Prince. From March 1919 to November 1920, the marines systematically destroyed the rebels, using, for the first time ever, airplanes to support combat troops. According to official records, the marines lost thirteen of their number while killing 3,071 Haitians.

## THE RECORD OF THE U.S. OCCUPATION

The new constitution went into effect in 1918, and legislative elections were held the following year. President Dartiguenave and an appointed Council of State served as figureheads for American officers and officials. However, Dartiguenave refused to sign an agreement repaying existing debts with a new loan from the National City Bank (now Citibank). In 1922, the American officers simply replaced Dartiguenave with the more compliant Louis Borno (1865–1942), another member of the colored élite. The Wilson administration, fully occupied with the First World War, paid little attention to Haiti after the 1915 invasion. In 1922, the new Republican administration appointed General John H. Russell as high commissioner in 1922. Russell coordinated all American activities in Haiti until 1930 through a joint dictatorship with President Borno, an avowed admirer of Mussolini.

Under the Russell-Borno dictatorship, Haiti was comparatively tranquil and prosperous, thanks to good coffee crops during years of high prices. Long-term economic progress was limited because the American administration used most tax revenues to pay off old debts, and few American companies invested in Haiti. However, Russell's administration did build needed public works. New roads and bridges made it possible for peasants to market their crops in the cities. American engineers also installed telephones, built wharves, lighthouses, schools barracks, schools, a courthouse, and a college. Temporary progress was made in public health, sanitation, and rural education. Until it was abandoned, an agricultural service (the Service Technique) gave a vocational education to several thousand students.

Despite these improvements, racial and cultural tensions remained high. The marines, who were white and mainly from the Deep South, imposed a rigid system of segregation that excluded both black and colored Haitians. Commissioner Russell and his wife—one of the few Americans who spoke good French—were scrupulously polite in their relations with the Haitian élite. However, not even President Borno could enter the American Club, the social center for U.S. residents. While some American officers and officials were personally kind, almost all held the Haitians in contempt. The colored élite responded in kind, pretending a French disdain for American crudeness. For the rural peasants, the Americans were merely oppressors from the dreaded white race.

Instead of seeking to win popular support, Commissioner Russell strengthened American authority. In 1928, the joint dictators imposed constitutional amendments increasing presidential power and extending Borno's term from four to six years. From October 1929, students throughout Haiti went on strike. Riots spread to the towns, and Russell declared martial law. Tensions reached a high point at Les Cayes on December 6. Fifteen hundred angry peasants, armed with stones, machetes, and clubs, surrounded a detachment of twenty inexperienced marines. When they were attacked, the marines fired into the crowd, killing twenty-four and wounding scores.

The 1929 uprisings attracted worldwide attention. President Herbert Hoover, who had introduced a "good neighbor" policy, was especially concerned about adverse reaction in Latin America. Hoover wanted out of Haiti and sent two special commissions to ease tensions. Borno was ousted, and an unusually fair election selected a new legislature in October 1930. As president, the National Assembly elected Sténio Vincent (1874–1959), a member of the colored élite and an articulate nationalist.

Vincent pressed for immediate departure, and the American withdrawal was carried out in haste. Haitians quickly replaced Americans throughout the government, and the Gendarmerie became the Garde d'Haiti under Haitian officers. In August 1933, Vincent and President Franklin D. Roosevelt signed an executive agreement under which all American troops left in August 1934. The National City Bank sold the Banque Nationale to Haiti for $1 million, although Americans continued to supervise government finances until Haiti paid off the 1922 loan in 1947.

The occupations's influence sometimes is exaggerated. The new roads and telephones soon ceased to function. The occupation briefly reduced government corruption and reduced the foreign debt, but it also centralized economic and political power in Port-au-Prince. In contrast to the Dominican Republic, American occupation did not make the army all powerful. Although the Haitian Garde or army quickly grew in size, its commander failed to carry out a revolution in 1938 and was forced into exile.

Perhaps the fairest judgment is that the American occupation worsened unfortunate tendencies in Haitian political and cultural life. For example, the occupation aggravated the hatred between black and colored Haitians, which had existed since the revolution of 1791. American administrators installed three puppet presidents from the colored élite, and they generally appointed only light-skinned officials. At the same time, by constantly showing their contempt for these colored men, the Americans led black intellectuals to reaffirm their African roots. François Duvalier later came to power as a representative of this "black power" movement.

## FROM VINCENT TO DUVALIER

Haiti's internal power structure had changed little since the 1840s. After 1933, a small élite—perhaps 2,000 persons mainly but not exclusively colored—continued to control commerce, the professions, and politics. The rural masses—at least 95 percent of Haiti's people—lived in desperate poverty and did not take part in politics. Given Haiti's mountainous terrain, effective population density approached 1,000 per square mile by the 1930s, and it has continued to soar. The worldwide depression after 1929 further reduced the peasant's modest income from coffee sales.

| TABLE 30.   HAITI POPULATION ESTIMATES, 1919–1970 | |
| --- | --- |
| 1919 | 1,631,250 |
| 1930 | 2,652,290 |
| 1950 | 3,379,813 |
| 1960 | 4,155,597 |
| 1970 | 5,269,392 |
| SOURCES:   Leyburn, *Haitian People*, 128 (1930); Segal, "Haiti," 182. | |

Sténio Vincent was reelected in 1935 for a term extended to 1941 by a fraudulent referendum. Vincent ruled as a dictator, using threats and bribes to gain the loyalty of a small clique of merchants and army officers. Those who objected to his rule were jailed or exiled. Vincent maintained close ties with the United States, which became Haiti's main source of income. However, in October 1937 hostile relations with the Dominican Republic became worse. The Dominican army, acting under orders from President Trujillo, massacred a large number—perhaps as many as 50,000—Haitian laborers. Street riots and pressure from the United States forced Vincent to retire in 1941, and the assembly elected Élie Lescot (1888–1974) to a five-year term (1941–1946). Vincent thus became the first president of Haiti since 1874 to peacefully hand over his office and remain in the country.

During Lescot's reign, coffee sales boomed, and America also imported large amounts of Haitian sisal, a strong fiber made from the leaves of the agave plant. However, Lescot was less politically skilled than Vincent. Corruption and nepotism became even more blatant, and Lescot lost the support of the black élite. Light-skinned men dominated Lescot's administration, his attacks on *voudon* alienated black intellectuals, and his unsophisticated views offended the more radical. In January 1946, using student riots as a pretext, three army officers—including Paul Magloire (1907–　), the head of the palace guard—removed Lescot and dissolved the assembly.

As angry mobs continued to riot, the military staged relatively clean elections for the legislature in May 1946. The National Assembly elected Duamarsais Estimé (1900–1953), the first black president since 1915. Yet another constitution restored the ban on foreign property ownership, gave labor the right to organize, and imposed an income tax. High coffee prices after the Second World War permitted some economic improvements, but Estimé and his followers continued to loot millions in government funds.

Estimé's greatest mistake was to decide, like so many Haitian presidents, that he should rule for life. After a rigged election, he sent a mob to pillage the Senate and threaten his opponents. Two days later, on May 10, 1950, the three army officers who had thrown out Lescot in 1946 also deposed Estimé. Their leader, Paul Magloire, had himself elected president through a popular election. (Under previous constitutions, the National Assembly had elected the president.)

Continuing high prices for Haiti's exports raised tax revenues, and Magloire's government made some improvements in urban areas. However, arbitrary arrests continued, and corruption remained obvious as Magloire and his police chief lived in ostentatious splendor. Once again, Haiti's president seamed unlikely to retire when his term ended. A general strike paralyzed Port-au-Prince in December 1956. On December 10, told that many young army officers opposed him, Magloire left the country with $12 to 18 million in stolen government funds. His fall showed that the military could no longer ensure order. In a larger sense, it indicated a loss of power by the small élite that had controlled Haitian politics for more than a century.

## PAPA DOC TAKES POWER

Eight months of chaos followed Magloire's fall. By September 1956, François Duvalier had captured the allegiance of the army, and he also enjoyed significant popular support. Duvalier at this time had a reputation for relative honesty. He was a writer in the black power (*noiriste*) tradition who had wooed the more important *voudon* priests and peasant leaders. Young members of the black middle-class followed him because he had helped to write major social legislation under President Estimé. With the help of the army, Duvalier won an overwhelming majority in the September 1957 presidential election.

François Duvalier surprised both his supporters and his opponents by creating a totalitarian dictatorship. Duvalier's single purpose was to remain in power. A true master of political techniques, he took over or destroyed all possible sources of power that a rival might use against him. Duvalier perfected terror and bribery, the traditional means of control in Haiti, and brought them under his personal control. Soon after the 1957 election, Duvalier got rid of the chief of staff and seized direct command of the army. He then closed the military academy and created several competing military bodies, headed by his own men. The Tonton Makoutes, a secret police directly under Duvalier, spied on and terrorized the cities. A civil militia (the VSN) recruited major *voudon* priests and prosperous peasants in the countryside.

Duvalier also subverted or closed down civilian institutions that threatened his power. He personally chose the members of the National Assembly, subverted business associations, and gave good-paying government jobs to middle-class intellectuals. He closed down the unions, the press, even the boy scouts. For a time, he weakened the Roman Catholic church by expelling its priests (mostly whites), closing its seminary, and compelling the Vatican to nominate five Haitian bishops of his choice. In 1964, with all national institutions under his control, François Duvalier declared himself "President-for-Life."

Under Duvalier's oppressive rule, many members of the colored élite fled to other countries while the black peasants became even poorer and more desperate. Although he did not threaten other counties, a series of American presidents had to deal with the embarrassment posed by Duvalier and his son. All faced the same problem. Given Duvalier's destruction of civilian and military institutions, American intervention might well install an equally repulsive regime.

## THE OVERTHROW OF BABY DOC

François Duvalier died in April 1971, after naming his nineteen-year-old son, Jean-Claude, his successor as President-for-Life. The uneasy balance of power between the various military forces enabled the dynasty to survive the change

Presidential Palace, Port-au-Prince, Haiti. Begun after rebels blew up the previous palace in 1912, this building was completed during the American occupation. Under "Papa Doc" Duvalier and his successors, it also housed several élite army units and the national armory.

in leadership. At first many Haitians considered the young Duvalier an indolent playboy under the influence of his mother and sister. From 1975 to 1980, the Haitian government, prodded by the Carter administration, proclaimed some superficial freedoms and sought to attract American light industry.

A new wave of repression followed the second Duvalier's marriage to Michèle Bennett in 1980. Jean-Claude now began to replace his father's appointees with his own men. By marrying the light-skinned daughter of an importer, Jean-Claude had made a lie of his father's *noiriste* (black power) rhetoric. Moreover, his wife's arrogance and wanton greed became a symbol of his presidency. In 1985, during a severe food shortage, Madame Duvalier reportedly spent $1.7 million on one shopping spree in Paris. Defiance in the provincial towns received the support of many Roman Catholic priests. Thanks to the first Duvalier's expulsion of foreigners, most priests now were Haitian and from modest backgrounds. Younger army officers also began to lose their enthusiasm for the regime.

As demonstrations grew in size and intensity, so did the U.S. government's disapproval of Jean-Claude's regime. Pressured by allies and foes alike, Duvalier wavered between brutal repression and reform. The army shot at demonstrators, but Duvalier also announced price cuts and dissolved part of the hated Tonton Makoute network. Encouraged by the false news that the government had collapsed on January 30, mass protests spread to Port-au-Prince. On February 7, 1986, Jean-Claude Duvalier and his wife fled to France with their immediate family and a small group of followers.

## HAITI AFTER THE DUVALIERS

Following Jean-Claude's exile, Haiti suffered through an era of political instability resembling the half-century ending in 1914. Brief-lived governments took power in rapid succession, with no president completing his term in office. Industrial production collapsed as fearful foreign investors withdrew their investments. The majority of the population continued to live outside the economy, surviving on the food from their own small plots.

The nation needed patience, strong leadership and some measurable economic progress. But three decades of Duvalier rule had thoroughly discredited its political and military institutions. Most Haitians—including many soldiers— distrusted the light-skinned military, business and professional leaders associated with the former régime. Alternative governments sprang up, as the peasants and urban poor formed local associations and communes, often affiliated with religious factions.

With no effective police force, the country remained prey to violence by rival private armies. The government officially disbanded the Tonton Makoutes, but former Tontons joined together in various gangs, committing crimes for whoever paid them. Some anti-government groups created their own quasi-military forces, which killed thousands suspected of being Tontons or former Duvalierists.

Henri Namphy (1932– ), commander of the army, took power after Jean-Claude's exile. But demonstrations continued, as did also mob executions of lower-ranks Duvalierists. A wave of violence made it impossible to conduct elections in November 1987. More killings and a low turn-out marked the army-run election of Leslie François Manigat (1930– ) as president in January 1988. Manigat, an honest man and a distinguished economist, apparently thought he could outsmart the conniving generals. He lasted barely six months, as General Namphy seized the presidency in June 1988.

Namphy was brought down the following September by a mutiny among non-commissioned officers and enlisted men. Lieutenant General Prosper Avril, a former adviser to both Duvaliers, emerged as president and managed to cling to power for eighteen months. Avril was the commander of the 1,200-men Presidential Guard, an élite battalion housed in the presidential palace. But he never controlled the entire army and had to supress several mutinies.

Although he initially tolerated his critics, Avril declared a state of siege in January 1990 and exiled several opposition leaders. Violent demonstrations against his rule increased, as did robberies and killings blamed on Tontons and members of the Presidential Guard. In March 1990, troops breaking up an anti-government demonstration accidentally killed a young girl, triggering widespread protests and strikes. As rioting spread, mobs burned cars and set up flaming barricades.

Under intense pressure from the American ambassador, Avril resigned and fled to Florida. Supreme court justice Ertha Pascal-Trouillot (1944– ) served as interim president until elections—delayed by a lack of money—could be held. The December 1990 elections were unquestionably the most honest Haiti has known. The provisional government had disbanded the Presidential Guard, and the regular army behaved impeccably. Led by General Raoul Cedras, the soldiers maintained order during the elections. Three weeks later, they crushed an attempted revolution by Roger Lafontant, former head of the Tonton Makoutes.

Jean-Bertrand Aristide (1952– ) won the presidency with more than two-thirds of the vote in a heavy turnout. A Roman Catholic priest—although suspended by his church—Aristide is a fiery orator and proponent of "liberation theology." This philosophy, which merges religious fervor with Marxist theories, holds that the clergy must help the poor improve their lot through radical political action. While liberation theology is most popular in Latin America, it fits well with Haiti's Jacobin tradition of violent revolution. (See pages 164–168.)

Aristide grew up in a poor section of Port-au-Prince. He was educated by and ordained as a member of the Salesian order of missionaries. In 1985, he returned to the slums as a priest, preaching passionately against Jean-Claude Duvalier and his successors. Although the Salesians expelled him in 1988 for "exalting violence and class struggle," Aristide continued to preach. He gained national fame in September 1989 when a band of thugs (possibly sent by the Namphy government) attacked his congregation during services, killing thirteen persons.

Aristide's eloquent speeches and radio broadcasts won him the support of rural communes as well as the poor of Port-au-Prince.[3] Appealing to the nation's pent-up political rage, his electoral slogan, Opération Lavalas (avalanche) referred in Creole to the cleansing flood that follows a tropical rainstorm. Many of his followers sought vengeance through a form of murder popularly called *Pa Lebrun* (after a large Haitian tire store). Encased in a burning rubber tire, its victims suffer horribly before they die. When the Roman Catholic archbishop of Haiti attacked liberation theology in January 1991, Aristide's supporters burned down several buildings owned by the church. At least fifty people suspected of being Tontons died after meeting *Pa Lebrun*.

Inaugurated as president, on February 7, 1991, Aristide retained power for less than eight months. Despite his immense personal popularity, his political party did not win a majority in the National Assembly. Refusing to compromise, Aristide chose a premier and cabinet from among close friends with little government experience, and he refused to send judicial and military appointments to the Assembly for approval. The economy moved perilously close to total collapse. The government imposed high tariffs on imported food (including Dominican sugar and American rice), and it frightened the business sector by proposing to set up collective farms and seize funds that had been banked abroad.

President Aristide's mass support allowed him to circumvent his political critics. In August, his followers surrounded the Legislative Palace, beating several legislators and forcing the Senate to suspend a vote of no confidence. But the president lost the backing of the army. Aristide named General Cedras as acting head of the military. However, he failed to make Cedras's appointment permanent and stopped him from punishing the torture and death of five teenage boys. Raising fears of a new Tonton Makoutes, Aristide also created a special 300-member security force, apart from the armed services and trained by Swiss advisers.

Few Haitian presidents take the risk of leaving the country before they have been deposed. In September, while the president was in New York speaking to the United Nations, the army disarmed Aristide's private security force. On his return, Aristide called for a popular uprising and endorsed the use of *Pa Lebrun*. A mutiny among enlisted men was joined by General Cedras and other officers. On October 31, 1991, Aristide followed so many of his predecessors into exile. The Organization of American States and the United States imposed an economic embargo but decided against military action to restore his rule.

# CHAPTER SEVENTEEN:
# THE ISLANDS REGAIN POLITICAL INDEPENDENCE

∎

The Caribbean islands differ in languages, political systems, and cultural traditions. But all have faced similar economic problems as they look for new sources of income to replace the declining sugar industry. Because they had to compete with more modern plantations in Cuba, Puerto Rico, and the Dominican Republic, conditions were especially harsh for the European colonies between the two world wars. But these years also witnessed the development of island-wide political movements that prepared the way for independence.

Since the Second World War, all the islands except Cuba have regained the self-government they lost during the 19th century. Several islands have become integral parts of larger states in constitutional arrangements that give their peoples management of local affairs. Puerto Rico and the Virgin Islands entered into a unique relationship with the United States, the French Antilles were integrated into France, and the Dutch West Indies became an autonomous part of the Kingdom of the Netherlands. The major British colonies have become totally independent states, and the smaller islands remaining within the British sphere enjoy home rule.

## PUERTO RICO: FROM COLONY TO COMMONWEALTH

Under Spanish rule, Puerto Rico's fate was linked to that of the larger and richer colony of Cuba. The United States went to war in 1898 primarily to expel the Spanish from Cuba and the Philippines. As American forces advanced, the United States decided to end the Spanish empire and sent a small army to take Puerto Rico. After some debate, Congress decided to keep the island, at least for a time. Puerto Rico seemed too small and too poor to be given independence. But American leaders did not want to grant the island statehood because of its Spanish culture and the large number of people of color—40 percent of the population according to an 1899 census.

By the Foraker Act of 1900, Congress imposed a system of government copied from the British Crown colonies. The American president appointed the supreme court and the governor. The governor in turn named an eleven-man

| TABLE 31. POLITICAL STATUS OF THE CARIBBEAN ISLANDS, 1992 (Reading from Northwest to Southeast) | |
|---|---|
| GREATER ANTILLES | |
| Cuba | Independent (1902) |
| Jamaica | Independent (1962) |
| Haiti | Independent (1804) |
| Dominican Republic | Independent (1844) |
| Puerto Rico | Commonwealth associated with the United States (1952) |
| Cayman Islands | British Crown colony (1972) |
| Bahamas | Independent (1973) |
| Turks and Caicos | British Crown colony (1976) |
| LESSER ANTILLES | |
| U.S. Virgin Islands | U.S. territory with local self-government (1968) |
| British Virgin Islands | British Crown colony (1967) |
| Anguilla | Associated state within the British Commonwealth (1982) |
| Saint-Martin | Administrative district of Guadeloupe (1946) |
| Sint Maarten | Member of the Netherlands Antilles (1954) |
| Saint-Barthélemy | Administrative district of Guadeloupe (1946) |
| Sint Eustatius | Member of the Netherlands Antilles (1954) |
| Saba | Member of the Netherlands Antilles (1954) |
| Saint Kitts and Nevis | Independent (1983) |
| Antigua and Barbuda | Independent (1981) |
| Montserrat | British Crown colony (1966) |
| Guadeloupe | Overseas *département* of France (1946) |
| Martinique | Overseas *département* of France (1946) |
| Dominica | Independent (1978) |
| Saint Lucia | Independent (1977) |
| Barbados | Independent (1966) |
| Saint Vincent and the Grenadines | Independent (1979) |
| Grenada | Independent (1974) |
| Trinidad and Tobago | Independent (1962) |
| Aruba | Member of the Kingdom of the Netherlands (1986) |
| Bonaire | Member of the Netherlands Antilles (1954) |
| Curaçao | Member of the Netherlands Antilles (1954) |

NOTE: For independent states, the date in parentheses represents the year in which sovereignty was achieved. For colonies, it represents the year when the political status noted was established. Aruba and the members of the Netherlands Antilles enjoy local self-government within the Kingdom of the Netherlands.

Executive Council, while a thirty-five-member House of Delegates was elected by popular vote. The governor and the nominated Executive Council had to approve island laws, and the U.S. Congress also retained a veto. The Foraker

Act abolished tariffs between the United States and the island from 1902, but the island's peoples became citizens of Puerto Rico and not of the United States.

Influential Americans criticized the Foraker Act as undemocratic. In Puerto Rico, the broadly-based Union party denounced it as granting neither statehood, independence, or even home rule. Reform finally came in 1917 under Woodrow Wilson. President Wilson believed in the military importance of the Caribbean, where Puerto Rico formed a strategic triangle with American bases at Guantánamo and the Canal Zone. To keep Germany out of the region, Wilson intervened in Haiti in 1915 and purchased the Virgin Islands in 1917. From the same defensive motives, he wanted to bring Puerto Rico under the American flag, binding its people to the United States "by ties of justice and interest and affection."[1] On March 2, 1917 Wilson signed the Jones Act, which defined Puerto Rico's legal status until 1948.

Under the Jones Act, Puerto Ricans became American citizens, protected by several of the guarantees in the U.S. Constitution. They were free to travel to the mainland and subject to the draft. However, they did not pay federal taxes or vote in federal elections. The Jones Act also gave Puerto Rico more power over local laws. From now on, the Puerto Rican Senate as well as the House were elected by universal male suffrage, with women receiving the vote in 1929. Both houses enjoyed somewhat greater powers, but Puerto Rico did not enjoy all the powers of an American state. The president continued to appoint its governor and other top officials as well as its Supreme Court judges.

In 1947, Congress amended the Jones law and granted Puerto Ricans the right to elect their own governor. Yet this still made the U.S. Congress the source of Puerto Rican rights. In campaigning to become the first elected governor in 1948, Luis Muñoz Marín (1898–1980) proposed that Puerto Rico become a commonwealth, a free associated state (*estado libre asociado*). When Muñoz won 61 percent of the vote, the U.S. Congress moved with unusual speed. In July 1950, President Truman signed Public Law 600, which invited the Puerto Rican people to draft their own constitution.

As a commonwealth (since July 25, 1952), Puerto Rico enjoys a unique legal status. The island is self-governing in all local matters, and Puerto Ricans do not pay federal taxes. Yet the island is not fully independent. The United States handles defense and foreign relations, and the federal government operates alongside the island government, as it does in mainland states. Thus Puerto Ricans receive federal transfer payments, such as food stamps. Commonwealth status has had distinct economic advantages, but it also denies Puerto Ricans a vote for the American president and other officials whose actions affect their lives. Nevertheless, in a 1967 plebiscite, 61 percent favored retaining commonwealth status, 39 percent voted for statehood, and less than 1 percent called for independence.

## THE SUGAR INDUSTRY DOMINATES THE ISLAND

Before 1898, the sugar industry had been of minor importance. Between the U.S. occupation and the Second World War, it dominated the entire island. Sugar imports from Puerto Rico were free of American tariffs and protected by government quotas. American corporations bought up much of the island's farmlands and constructed large modern sugar mills (*centrales*). The Foraker Act of 1900 had limited a corporation's land holdings to 500 acres. However, it was difficult to enforce and had little effect before the 1940s.

Sugar now became the island's main product. During the generally prosperous years before 1925, sugar exports rose tenfold.[2] During the same years, coffee—produced on smaller farms—became less important. World prices fell, and hurricanes in 1899 and 1928 damaged much of the crop. The United States did not replace Europe as a consumer because Americans preferred South American coffee. Most workers now became landless laborers on large sugar estates, receiving low wages and suffering long periods of unemployment. The Free Federation of Workers (FFW), was founded in 1899 with the support of American labor leader Samuel Gompers. But only a small number of workers belonged to the FFW, which was allied to the Socialist party instead of one of the two major parties.

The island's income did not keep pace as the population rapidly increased. Thanks to American success in checking diseases and a lower infant mortality rate, the number of islanders roughly doubled between 1899 and 1940, and the population density was one of the highest in the world. (See Table 32.) The island's dependence on one crop became especially harmful when sugar prices fell after 1925. In 1929, Puerto Ricans had on average an income of $122 per year, about one-fifth of the level on the mainland. By 1933, during the great depression, the average yearly income fell to $84.

| TABLE 32. PUERTO RICO POPULATION ESTIMATES, 1920–1960 | |
|---|---|
| 1920 | 1,312,000 |
| 1940 | 1,800,000 |
| 1960 | 2,361,000 |
| SOURCE: Miró, *La poblacion de America Latina*, 2 (1920–1960). | |

## THREE DECADES OF RAPID GROWTH

Efforts to improve Puerto Rico's economy began with President Franklin Roosevelt's New Deal. Federal agencies poured hundreds of millions in transfer payments into the island but achieved little. Real progress became possible in 1940 when Luis Muñoz Marin's Popular Democratic party won control of the legislature. The son of independence leader Luis Muñoz Rivera, Muñoz—a charismatic politician—held power for twenty-four years as Senate leader and then as governor (1948–1964). Under his rule, Puerto Rico underwent a profound social and economic transformation. Sugar collapsed and was replaced by manufacturing and tourism. Although the population continued to grow, the economy grew faster. Between 1940 and 1987, the per capital gross national product skyrocketed from only $154 to $4,850.

As a pragmatic reformer, Muñoz was able to work with both Roosevelt's New Dealers and Eisenhower's more conservative Washington. In 1941, President

Roosevelt named Rexford Tugwell, a fervent radical as governor. His administration, ending in 1946, devised the governmental machinery and corps of officials needed to carry out economic planning. In 1942 the government organized a central planning board, a government development bank, and the Puerto Rico Industrial Development company, known as *Fomento*. The return of federal taxes on Puerto Rican rum sold in the United States provided the initial funds for development.

Muñoz's reform program began with the enforcement of the 500 acre limitation on land ownership. The government purchased land from the large sugar companies. Some was held by state farms, with a worker's wages including a share of the profits. Other land was sold in small plots, or given to landless farm workers. The companies continued to run the centrales, but government farms and *colonos* (family-run sugar farms) supplied most of the cane.

Economic growth was relatively slow in the 1940s, as the government attempted to build its own factories, all of which lost money. Real progress began when the legislature passed the Industrial Incentive Act of 1947. This granted new industries direct and indirect subsidies as well as exemption from corporate, personal, and property taxes for periods ranging from ten to thirty years. Investment was especially rapid during the 1960s and early 1970s, when Puerto Rico enjoyed one of the highest sustained growth rates in the world. By the late 1980s, Puerto Rico had become as thoroughly industrialized as many European countries, and manufacturing produced almost half of the island's income.

Tourism has become Puerto Rico's second source of wealth. In 1940, the entire island had only 600 guest rooms. As part of its economic development plan, the government built several large hotels, whose success stimulated private investment. Aided by inexpensive airfares from U.S. cities, Puerto Rico captured much of Cuba's tourist business following Castro's 1959 revolution. By 1988, almost three million tourists and cruise passengers visited Puerto Rico each year.

While industry and tourism have boomed, farm production has sharply declined. As workers found better-paying jobs, sugar production fell more than 80 percent—from a peak of 1.3 million tons in 1952 to only 249,000 tons in 1973. By 1983, only 4,000 cane workers remained, and the government now owns all the remaining mills. Coffee production also has fallen, and almost no tobacco is grown. Indeed, Puerto Rico now has become a net importer of sugar, tobacco and coffee, crops that formerly dominated its list of exports.

## THE END OF CONSENSUS

Until the mid-1970s, the government's industrialization program generally was successful. Since 1975, economic growth has slowed, and output actually has fallen in some years. Since the population has continued to increase, unemployment also has risen. Many have come to rely on federal transfer payments, which were expanded during the 1970s. In the mid-1980s, the government employed about 40 percent of all workers, and about two-thirds of the population received some type of federal aid.

| TABLE 33. TOURIST ARRIVALS IN THE CARIBBEAN DURING 1988 (Thousands of Arrivals) | | |
|---|---|---|
| | TOTAL | OVERNIGHT |
| Bahamas | 3,158 | 1,475 |
| Puerto Rico | 2,801 | 2,077 |
| U.S. Virgin Islands | 2,032 | 599 |
| Dominican Republic | 1,216 | 1,116 |
| Jamaica | 1,020 | 649 |
| Sint Maarten/Saint-Martin | 496 | 480 |
| Barbados | 742 | 451 |
| Bermuda | 585 | 427 |
| Cayman Islands | 535 | 219 |
| Antigua | 416 | 187 |
| Aruba | 359 | 278 |

NOTES: "Total" refers to the number of international visitors arriving for pleasure at each destination and not to the number of individuals; if the same person makes several pleasure trips to the same country, she or he is counted each time as a new arrival. "Overnight" refers to visitors staying in the country one or more nights; it primarily excludes tourists arriving on cruise ships.

SOURCE: World Tourism Organization, March 1990.

As economic growth has stalled, the remarkable political unity of the 1960s ended. No subsequent leader has enjoyed Muñoz's widespread popularity. In elections since 1968, Muñoz's party, the Popular Democratic party, has been locked in close elections with the Progressive National party, which generally favors statehood.

During hard times, many Puerto Ricans find work on the mainland. Mass emigration began in 1946 and reached a peak during the early 1960s. Fewer left the island during the boom years, but emigration increased during the 1980s as the economy stagnated. In 1987, about 2.6 million persons of Puerto Rican descent lived in the United States—nearly as many as lived in Puerto Rico.

## THE U.S. VIRGIN ISLANDS

In 1917, the United States bought the three Danish Virgin Islands for $25 million to prevent their falling under German control. After the war, the threat to the Canal Zone diminished, and the United States almost forgot about the Virgins. At first the Navy administered the islands, and they were placed under the Department of the Interior in 1931. The inhabitants received American citizenship in 1927, but they do not vote in federal elections for president or the Congress.

The United States initially retained the Danish system that gave full powers to an appointed governor, but the political system has become more democratic since the 1930s. The Organic Act of 1936 gave the local government control over all federal taxes collected in the islands, and it guaranteed inhabitants the freedoms included in the U.S. Constitution. The act removed the highly restrictive qualifications for voting enacted in 1863. It gave the vote to all adult residents who were citizens of the United States and able to read English. The islands gained full local autonomy in August 1968, when President Lyndon Johnson signed a bill abolishing the presidential veto of island laws and allowing the islanders to elect their own governor from January 1971. One legislature had replaced the two separate councils at Saint Croix and Saint Thomas in 1957.

Unlike Puerto Rico, the Virgins saw little economic development until the rise of mass tourism after the Second World War. Sugar from Saint Croix remained the main export, and the three islands had a population of less than 17,000 as late as 1950. Tourism began to boom during the 1950s as jet airplanes made the islands an inexpensive destination for increasingly affluent Americans. Many tourists also were attracted by Saint Thomas's status as a free port. The United States has not imposed American tariffs, and many foreign products sold at bargain prices. In 1988, more than two million tourists and cruise ship travelers visited the islands—compared to fewer than 50,000 visitors yearly in the early 1950s. The Virgin Islands, once among the poorest islands, are now among the wealthiest. Thanks to tourism, per capita income has risen dramatically—from about $400 a year in 1950 to almost $8,000 in 1985.

Much of the tourist industry is concentrated on Saint Thomas. The Virgin Islands government has copied Puerto Rico in using tax incentives to encourage manufacturing on the larger island of Saint Croix. A major refinery processes imported oil, and smaller factories make clocks, textiles, rum, and pharmaceutical products. As land values soared, sugar estates were turned into tourist resorts, and the last plantation went out of business in 1966. Saint John, in contrast, is almost entirely a park and has only one small village. The Virgin Islands National Park, originally established in 1956 through gifts from Laurence Rockefeller, now includes almost 80 percent of the island.

## PROBLEMS OF ECONOMIC DEVELOPMENT IN THE EUROPEAN COLONIES

The European colonies generally faced hard times between the two world wars, and the great depression of the 1930s was unusually severe on many islands. Particularly in the British islands, sugar producers found it difficult to compete with modern plantations and factories on Cuba and Puerto Rico. With some exceptions, alternative sources of livelihood were slow to develop. While several islands tried to build up light industries producing consumer products for local consumption, most continued to import even everyday products from Europe and the United States.

Oil provided employment on several islands. In Trinidad, oil production began in 1911, and Trinidad also profits from its remarkable pitch lake, which provides asphalt for roads throughout the world. Oil also benefited other islands that became home to large refineries. In 1916, a subsidiary of the Royal Dutch/Shell Group built an enormous refinery on Curaçao that processed oil

Royal Dutch/Shell Refineries light up the sky, Curaçao. Built from 1916 to process Venezuelan oil, these refineries remained profitable until the late 1970s, giving Curaçao one of the highest standards of living in the Caribbean.

from Venezuela and later from Colombia. Standard Oil of New Jersey built a second large refinery on Aruba in 1929.

The worldwide economic depression of the 1930s was especially hard on the fragile island economies, which depended on one or two major export products. Prices and sales plummeted, government revenues dropped with the fall in income from export duties, and many colonies had to suspend the public works programs that previously had given work to part-time laborers. At the same time, several countries in the region forcibly expelled foreign laborers and closed their doors to further immigration. Unemployment, real hunger, and desperation contributed to strikes, demonstrations, and violent riots on many islands throughout the 1930s.

The British colonies were especially hard hit, and these economic problems were made worse by the absence of political rights. Because of the oil industry, Aruba and Curaçao were spared the worst effects of the depression. In the French colonies, the French government both protected the markets for island products and provided some of the social welfare programs offered in France. Perhaps more important, political participation headed off discontent. Every adult male could vote for representatives to the National Assembly in Paris as well as for the mayors and other officials of towns and cities. There were fewer large disturbances than in the British colonies, and the Caribbean territories remained loyal to France when it was occupied during the Second World War.

## THE FRENCH AND DUTCH ANTILLES

As most Puerto Ricans prefer association with the United States, so too have the French Antilles chosen assimilation with France. In a plebescite in 1945, the peoples of French Guiana, Martinique, and Guadeloupe voted for political union with France.[3] The following year, these former colonies became three additional *départements* (administrative districts) of France. Their political evolution subsequently runs parallel with that of France itself.

Initially, each *département* was under a *préfet* (governor) appointed from Paris. As in France, the *préfet* carries out the directives of the central government and controls local public services. Because of the distance from Paris, he also controls the armed forces and can declare martial law. Local councils continued to be elected, but their powers were purely advisory. In 1960, following a riot in Martinique, the island councils were granted a larger say over local laws and greater powers over public funds.

The six islands in the Dutch Antilles have enjoyed very different economic fortunes. With poor soils, inadequate water, and no commercial importance, Bonaire and the three Leeward islands of Sint Eustatius, Saba, and Sint Maarten underwent little economic development. Many of their inhabitants migrated to other islands, and they now have less than 5 percent of the population of the entire group. In contrast, large oil refineries gave Curaçao and Aruba one of the highest standards of living in the Caribbean and indirectly provided income and social services for the four smaller islands.

This dependence on one industry proved to be dangerous when economic and political changes threatened both refineries. The refinery on Aruba was closed in 1985. Although the government bought the Shell operations on Curaçao and leased them to the Venezuelan state oil company, production and employment both fell sharply. Since the 1970s, tourism has boomed both on the three southern ABC islands and especially on Sint Maarten. The government also has attempted to attract manufacturing on Curaçao and Aruba by establishing duty-free zones and giving tax breaks similar to those offered on Puerto Rico.

Following the Second World War, the Dutch government granted the colonies universal suffrage and internal self-government. On December 15, 1954, the six islands became an autonomous part—with the Netherlands and Surinam—of the Kingdom of the Netherlands.[4] Unemployment caused serious riots in Curaçao in 1969, and some politicians in the smaller islands complain that their interests are not fully represented in the regional assembly. Nevertheless, many islanders feared that separation from the Netherlands would harm their economies, and only Aruba sought full independence. The Dutch government at first would agree to independence only within a federation. In 1986, it finally accepted Aruba's secession. The island became a separate, internally self-governing unit of the Netherlands, with full independence scheduled for 1996.

## THE BRITISH COLONIES GAIN INDEPENDENCE

For the British colonies, the road to self-government was long and arduous. Color prejudice unquestionably played a role in the denial of political rights.

But the British refused to share power even with the white population, who had enjoyed local autonomy prior to the 1860s. From the 1920s, those of both races meeting strict property qualifications could vote for some members of the governor's advisory councils. But these "unofficial" members were expected to support the laws sought by the governor. Not until the late 1940s and early 1950s were universal suffrage and greater autonomy granted to the British islands.

From the 1890s, professional men and planters formed associations to protect their economic interests and lobby the colonial government. But it was the disturbances and riots of the 1930s that gave rise to the first strong labor movements among workers and farm laborers. On some islands, most of the population joined unions that led successful strikes, provided economic help, and developed into political parties. The leaders of these unions—the first important political figures in modern times—frequently dominated their island's politics for several decades.

After the Second World War, as the British were expelled or withdrew from their colonies in Asia and Africa, the Crown colonies in the Caribbean became an anachronism. Although British governments never made their intentions clear, they probably would have preferred an arrangement something like that in the Dutch Antilles—one federated state in some sort of loose association with England. A federation with a relatively weak central government did come into existence in 1959, but it lasted barely three years. Most inhabitants of the former British West Indies feel an intense loyalty to their own island. Only a small group of intellectuals expressed real enthusiasm for federal government.

In 1962, irreconcilable differences between Jamaica and Trinidad broke up the federation, and both of these large islands became independent. Once it began, the process of breakup accelerated, and attempts to create smaller federations also failed. In 1966, Barbados received independence, and the remaining smaller islands worked out their own arrangements with Britain. By the 1980s, virtually all the British colonies had become independent states. Britain retained only a few thinly populated colonies—Montserrat, Anguilla, the British Virgin Islands, the Cayman Islands, and the Turks and Caicos. In these territories, an elected legislative assembly is responsible for local affairs, while an appointed governor handles defense and foreign relations.

## CROWN COLONY GOVERNMENT

Beginning with Jamaica in 1866, the British government had suppressed the island legislatures. Except in Barbados and the Bahamas, it ruled its West Indian possessions directly from London. Under this system of Crown colony government, the British Parliament passed laws regulating their constitutions and overall legal structure. The governor and other chief officials appointed by the Colonial Office formed an Executive Council in charge of governmental operations. A Legislative Council—with from nine to twenty-two members—advised the governor and made local laws and regulations. It generally contained an equal number of officials and "unofficial" members named by the governor from among the colony's most prominent men. Until the 1920s, all the British colonies, except Jamaica and Barbados, had wholly appointed legislatures. Elected town councils or public health boards did survive in most colonies, but these had only those powers granted them by governor and the appointed Legislative Council.

The legislature in a Crown colony government did not represent the island's inhabitants. Officials were named by and responsible to the Crown and not to the island legislature. The governor controlled the vote of official members. Moreover, the British government expected even the appointed members "to give a general and effective support to the Governor's measures in the Legislature" and might force them to resign if they failed to do so. Finally, the governors always retained certain "reserve powers" that gave them the final say over the police, the law courts, and appointment of senior officials.

## THE FIRST STEPS TOWARD SELF-GOVERNMENT

In the absence of elected local officials and political parties, individuals formed associations based on specific economic interests. Between 1880 and 1920, many commercial and professional organizations sprang up. Some represented middle-class professionals such as teachers, lawyers, and retailers. Others helped producers of primary agricultural products—bananas, cocoa, cotton, rice, coconut, arrowroot, and citrus products—negotiate with the large corporations buying their products.

Less affluent black workers also began to form labor unions during the 1890s, some derived from the mutual aid and benevolent societies of the slavery era. But these found it difficult to organize seasonal plantation workers or the many laborers emigrating for a time to other parts of the region. And laws restricting picketing and permitting suits for damages or loses caused by strikes also weakened unions.

While these local self-help organizations often tried to influence the government in their own interest, other groups directly attacked the Crown colony system itself. Popular resentment against Crown colony government increased after 1900, both on Jamaica and Trinidad and on the smaller islands. Its first critics included white and colored professionals—lawyers, merchants, doctors, journalists, and civil servants—in the larger towns. All had attended secondary schools, and some had gone to British universities. They considered themselves more qualified to lead local government than transient British officials.

The self-government movement became more vocal during the 1920s, often led by men who had served in the British West India (BWI) regiment during the First World War. One of its most distinguished early leaders was T. Albert Marryshow (1887–1958) of Grenada. Strongly critical of Crown colony rule and an advocate of federation, he gathered a group of middle-class colored Grenadians who formed the Representative Government Association in 1914. Professional men founded similar associations on most of the smaller islands. All demanded the election of at least some members of the colonial Legislative

Councils and a role in local government for the elected members. Some also supported a political federation of the West Indies colonies.

Labor unions also gained members and won increased recognition during the 1920s and 1930s. New unions emerged throughout the Caribbean in response to collapsing sugar prices and economic depression. In the British colonies, they had the support of the British Labour party, and especially its Fabian or socialist wing. British labor unions helped to create West Indian affiliates, and they encouraged the island unions to adopt relatively moderate policies. In this way, the Fabians hoped to prevent Russian-dominated Communists from taking control, as they had in Cuba and some other parts of the British Empire.

On the British islands, middle-class professionals and rural laborers could work together because Crown colony government provided them with a common foe. As a result of these increasingly vocal protests, a commission headed by the colonial undersecretary, E. F. L. Wood (later Lord Halifax), visited most of the islands as well as British Guiana from December 1921 to February 1922. Following Wood's cautious recommendations, elected members were added to the Legislative Councils. In all cases, voters had to meet high property qualifications. In 1939, the small number of islanders entitled to vote ranged from only 2 percent in Saint Lucia to 7 percent in Trinidad.

On Trinidad, Arthur Cipriani (1875–1945) took advantage of these modest reforms to forge the first successful alliance between a political organization and a mass union. Cipriani, a member of a creole family of Corsican descent, rose to the rank of captain in the BWI Regiment during the First World War. He joined the Trinidad Workingmen's Association in 1919 and became its president in 1923. Cipriani was an outstanding orator with great personal magnetism. Under his leadership, the TWA rapidly increased its membership, and it actively sought to recruit Indian as well as black workers.

Captain Cipriani won a seat on the Legislative Council in the elections of 1925—the first since the British occupied Trinidad in 1797. He was reelected until his death in 1945 and also won election to the Port of Spain city council. Cipriani formed a one-man opposition to the government. One of the first West Indian leaders to consider himself a socialist, Cipriani forged close links to the British Labor party. The avowed "champion of the barefoot man," he campaigned—without immediate success—for a minimum wage, workers' compensation, an eight-hour day, and the prohibition of child labor.

## THE TURBULENT 1930S AND THE MOYNE REPORT

Acute economic distress during the 1930s created bitter resentment, which eventually erupted into strikes and violence throughout the British Caribbean. New leaders emerged who organized effective unions and mass parties, which demanded first self-government and then independence. The political alliances created during these years endured for more than forty years, until the 1970s. Throughout the British Caribbean, labor unions and political parties became fused or merged under one strong leader—usually a persuasive orator with a magnetic and charismatic personality. The leaders of these unions became dominant political figures, often serving as the first heads of government when an island gained independence.

Since most islands depended on one or two major export crops, the great depression was unusually severe. By 1933, prices for the islands' principal exports had been almost halved. Wages fell, taxes rose, and unemployment increased. Funds from laborers employed in other countries also fell drastically. The United States restricted immigration; and Cuba, the Dominican Republic, and the Central American states rounded up and deported laborers from the British colonies. Many workers lacked adequate food, housing, and medical care, and the islands provided only limited welfare programs.

Demonstrations, strikes, and riots were frequent throughout the British Caribbean between 1935 and 1938. In 1933, the oilfield workers in Trinidad organized a hunger march to publicize their difficulties, and there were strikes and riots in the island's sugar belt in 1934. The following year saw violent demonstrations among sugar workers on Saint Kitts and Saint Vincent. The governors of these islands restored order with the help of British warships, and 1935 generally was quiet. But new and more violent outbursts occurred in the larger colonies of Trinidad, Barbados, and Jamaica in 1937 and 1938.

On Trinidad, Cipriani had refused to support strikes and marches because he preferred legal methods. Tubal ("Buzz") Uriah Butler (1897–1977), a Grenadian laborer, emerged as the new leader of the predominantly black oilfield workers. Butler's racially based party won wide support because of his strong personality and his forceful way of speaking at meetings that resembled religious crusades. Butler was firmly convinced that God was on his side. As "God's Appointed" and "Chief Servant of the Lord," he saw himself as a new Moses sent to lead the suffering black workers from the "wilderness of colonialism."

Inter-island launch leaving Nevis. While tourists travel on luxurious cruise ships or crowded jet planes, small motor vessels provide inexpensive if slow transportation between the islands for both freight and passengers.

In June 1937, Butler called a general strike of oil workers that was joined by the cane workers and laborers in Port of Spain. An attempt to arrest Butler triggered widespread riots in which two policemen and twelve civilians were killed. In July, Clement Payne, one of Butler's associates, tried to take his crusade to Barbados. Payne called on black Bridgetown laborers to unite and force employers to raise wages. When the police attempted to deport Payne, a mob looted Bridgetown, and rioting occurred in the countryside. At least thirteen persons were killed, forty-seven wounded, and over five hundred imprisoned. In 1938, violence spread to Jamaica. A series of strikes and riots among sugar workers and Kingston laborers claimed forty-six lives.

Other islands also suffered violence and political oppression during the Great Depression. Rafael Trujillo imposed a police state on the Dominican Republic, while a civil war ended Gerardo Machado's attempt to establish one-man rule in Cuba. Nevertheless, violence in its West Indian colonies alarmed the British government, which sent a series of commissions to inquire into their causes. The most influential, chaired by Lord Moyne, was dominated by Fabian socialists, including the secretary of the British Trades Union Congress. The Moyne *Report* placed much of the blame for the disturbances on the Crown colony form of government. It called for stronger labor unions, more elected members of the Legislative Councils, and the eventual extension of the vote to all islanders.

Great Britain already was at war when the Moyne Commission returned in November 1939. The government temporarily put aside its recommendations for more self-government, but it did take steps to improve economic conditions and to strengthen labor unions. Britain in 1940 created a government office to fund public works and economic development projects. To qualify for grants, colonial governments had to recognize trade unions. They also were required to create labor departments and pass laws regulating working conditions and providing workers' compensation and unemployment insurance.

## GOVERNMENTS, UNIONS, AND PARTIES

Throughout the British colonies, the hardships and disturbances of the 1930s gave rise to strong labor unions headed by emotional and charismatic leaders. Earlier labor organizations often had organized only skilled workers in a specific craft. (Captain Cipriani's broad-based TWA was an exception.) The new movements were island-wide and sought to enroll both skilled and unskilled workers in a wide variety of occupations into one large, comprehensive union. Especially in the larger territories, they attracted support from lawyers, doctors, teachers, and journalists as well as from unskilled farm workers.

The leaders of these unions believed that they could obtain their goals only by taking control of the government. They accordingly formed mass-based political parties that sought autonomy from Britain. Although parties and unions legally may be separate bodies, they are closely integrated in practice. Most political parties depend on trade unions to provide both funds and to get out the vote of their members. One man heads the union and party, and the same individuals hold high offices in both bodies, which thus share a common leadership. While this fusion of unions and parties is not unique, they are more closely integrated in the British West Indies than in most other regions. Many West Indian party leaders in fact come from middle-class backgrounds. But they rise to power through careers in the trade union movement rather than (as in the United States) as lawyers.

Most West Indian parties use the word *labour* in their name and describe themselves as socialist. In fact, their policies have been relatively moderate, and private ownership of industry has survived on most islands. The close union of unions and governments is understandable given the region's history. When the parties were formed, most industries were owned by foreign companies or by a small racial minority. As the majority of people were poor agricultural workers, every party had to claim to represent this group. Most West Indians are socially conservative, embrace their island's traditions, and oppose radical experiments. But any party that called itself "conservative" or that advocated "capitalism" would commit suicide.

No matter what their platforms said, Caribbean political parties united around a forceful leader rather than "issues" or cohesive political principles. And the personalities of leaders continue to be the most important factor deciding elections. There are few sharp differences between Caribbean parties. All initially were concerned with achieving independence, and all subsequently promised better education, more social welfare, and improved economic conditions.

## LABOUR PARTIES IN JAMAICA, BARBADOS, AND TRINIDAD

On the larger islands—Jamaica, Barbados, and Trinidad—the leaders of the unions and parties founded during the 1930s often were light-skinned members of the small élite educated in Britain. Most called themselves socialists or social democrats and tended to borrow the traditions and slogans of the British Labour party. Their party platforms often favored governmental management of the economy, land reform, and the redistribution of incomes through high taxation and welfare payments. These socialist parties include the Peoples National party in Jamaica, the Democratic Labour party and the Barbados Labour party in Barbados, and the People's National movement in Trinidad and Tobago.

*Jamaica*   In Jamaica, two strong parties were founded by distant cousins—Alexander Bustamante (1884–1977) and Norman Manley (1893–1969). Although they initially worked together before becoming political rivals, Bustamante and Manley had very different personalities. Bustamante, the son of an Irish planter and a Jamaican mother, practiced several different trades in North, South, and Central America. He returned 1934, using his sizable fortune to set up a real estate and money-lending business in Kingston. Where Bustamante had an unfailing gift for the common touch, Manley was a cultivated, aloof lawyer who was most at ease with other middle-class professionals. Of Irish and black descent, he won a Rhodes Scholarship to Oxford and became a prominent lawyer, who represented many of the island's largest corporations throughout his life.

Both men became deeply involved in the political unrest that erupted in 1937. A picturesque man of the people with a striking presence, Bustamante helped to organize a series of mass meetings on behalf of the strikers. His following increased when the British imprisoned him in 1938 for sedition and incitement to riot. Norman Manley successfully defended Bustamante in court. On his release, he founded and became president for life of the Bustamante Industrial Trade Union (BITU), a general union of skilled and unskilled workers.

In September 1938, Manley and Bustamante cooperated in forming the People's National party (PNP), which at first served as the political wing of the BITU. Under Manley's guidance, the PNP formally adopted a socialist platform in 1940, and it later joined the Socialist International. The PNP now favored large cooperative farms as well as called for nationalization of major industries and utilities, state management of the economy, and increased welfare payments.

Jamaica gained a second mass party, the Jamaica Labour party (JLP) in 1942. When he threatened a dock workers strike in September 1940, the British had imprisoned Bustamante without trial for seventeen months, further increasing his reputation as a martyr and hero. After he was freed, Bustamante split with Manley and the PNP. Accusing them of betraying his trust, he founded the Jamaica Labour party to contest the elections of 1944, the first under universal adult suffrage. Finding himself without the necessary union support, Norman Manley formed the Trade Union Congress and later turned it into one general union supporting his party.

Jamaica thus found itself with two union-based parties, each under one strong leader. Manley and Bustamante alternated in power for the next thirty years, and the parties they founded continue to dominate Jamaican politics. While both had broad appeal, Manley's PNP enjoyed its greatest strength among middle-class professionals and urban workers. Bustamante's JLP was strongest in rural areas and also had substantial backing from white businessmen.

Bustamante became Jamaica's first elected chief minister (in 1953) when the JLP gained a majority of seats in the lower house in the elections of 1944 and 1949. Bustamante won by attacking PNP leaders as Communists and atheists. Socialism and the creation of cooperative farms did not appeal to small farmers owning their own land. In 1949, Norman Manley thus had to reassure the voters in his own district that the PNP planned to nationalize only the largest manufacturing industries.

Two successive electoral defeats convinced Manley to dilute the PNP's socialist rhetoric. In 1952 a PNP conference expelled as Communists four prominent members, who had controlled its Trade Union Congress. The PNP then formed the more conservative National Workers Union. The economic policies of the PNP and JLP became increasingly similar during the 1950s. Until 1974—when Prime Minister Michael Manley suddenly revived the party's radical tradition—the PNP accepted private property and foreign investment. With these more moderate policies, Norman Manley came to power in 1955 and remained in office until 1962.

*Barbados*   Grantley Adams (1898–1971), who dominated the politics of Barbados from 1937 to 1961, combined Manley's parliamentary skills with some of Bustamante's personal charm. Adams, a colored lawyer who had won an island scholarship to Oxford, was an avowed socialist with close ties to the radical wing of the British Labour party. He founded the Barbados Labour party (1938) and the Barbados Workers Union (1941), building up a wide mass following through his speeches and his powerful charismatic appeal.

In a development reminiscent of the earlier split between Alexander Bustamante and Norman Manley, Barbados acquired a second labor party in 1955, when Errol Barrow (1920–1987) left Grantley Adams's BLP and founded the Democratic Labour party (DLP). Like Adams, Barrow had studied law in London, and he became Adams's protégé in the early 1950s. Barrow now claimed that Adams had become too closely linked to the British governor and had lost contact with union members. His DLP gained popularity by winning benefits for Barbados's sugar workers while Grantley Adams was away from the island, as the first (and only) prime minister of the West Indies Federation. The DLP won the elections of 1961 and 1966, and Barrow became the first leader of an independent Barbados in the latter year.

*Trinidad and Tobago*   Eric Williams (1911–1981), who headed the government of Trinidad and Tobago from 1956 to 1981, was the only West Indian leader to take power without the backing of a major labor union. His People's National movement (PNM) established in 1956, succeeded only because the unions were themselves sharply divided. In contrast to other British islands, where one or two mass parties captured wide support, political loyalties on Trinidad are highly fragmented. When universal suffrage came in 1945, many small parties and organizations appealed to different and competing racial and economic interests.

The fragmentation of political parties reflected the deep divisions in Trinidad's society. Most islands are racially homogeneous, and the colored middle class joined the black majority in the struggle for self-government. Trinidad is a divided or segmented society in which a large number of groups think of themselves as separate and distinct. Before the island gained independence, the small white élite was divided between British officials and Roman Catholic creoles born on the island. The opinions and interests of the colored and black middle class—distinguished by education and white-collar jobs—often differed from those of black oilfield and farm workers. Blacks considered themselves totally distinct from the East Indian population (about 40 percent of the total)—which was in turn divided between Muslims and Hindus. As Bridget Brereton concludes, "Class, colour, caste and race combined to create an immensely complex pattern of human relationships. . . ."[5]

During the 1920s and 1930s, Captain Cipriani's union actively sought to recruit East Indian members. However, Buzz Butler brought race back into Trinidadian politics by presenting himself as a black leader for black workers. The emergence of black nationalism increased race consciousness among all groups, and the nationalist movement in the Indian homeland also encouraged

"An Indian family, Trinidad, B.W.I.," early 20th century. Almost 144,000 Indians came to Trinidad as indentured or contract laborers before 1917. About two-thirds chose to remain, forming separate and distinctive communities of farmers and small businessmen.

a sense of racial identity among East Indians. During the first election under universal suffrage in 1946 and 1950, the labor vote fragmented. Blacks and East Indians clashed, and racial slurs became a common part of campaign rhetoric.

The election of September 1956 set the course of Trinidad and Tobago for the next thirty years. Few expected victory for the People's National movement (PNM), launched the preceding January by Eric Williams (1911–1919). But the PNM took 39 percent of the vote and won fourteen of the twenty-four seats on the Legislative Council. Under Williams's strong-willed leadership, the PNM brought Trinidad to independence in 1962 and retained power until 1986.

Williams was a skilled politician who made the PNM into an effective political machine. He owed his initial success to his own personal magnetism, his speaking ability, and his deep personal identification with the needs of lower-class blacks. A dark-skinned creole, Williams had spent almost ten years in Britain and the United States. Although his family was poor, he was a superb student and won an all-island scholarship to Oxford. There he earned both a first-class degree and a doctorate in history. He taught at Howard University and worked for the Anglo-American Caribbean Commission from 1948 to 1955.

Despite these successes, Williams always believed that he had been discriminated against because of his skin color. He developed a strong sense of West Indian nationalism, which emphasized the contribution of black workers. During 1955, Williams hammered home these views to crowds of thousands in Woodford Square—a public park in front of the colony's legislative building.

His interpretation of Caribbean history aroused tremendous pride among his listeners—as well as adulation of Williams himself. Unlike other parties, the PNM claimed to be a multiracial organization. At this time, the PNM also welcomed investment by foreign companies. With the slogan "nationalism and democracy," it called for "a rally, a convention of all and for all, a mobilisation of all the forces in the community, cutting across race and religion, class and colour."

## THE LESSER ANTILLES

In the smaller and less-developed islands, unions and parties also were fused under one charismatic leader, who took the island to independence and then ruled for several decades. Here, however, political leaders usually came from working-class backgrounds rather than from the British-educated élite. Self-made men who emerged through the labor movement, they had fewer ties to British and European socialism. Their party platforms instead stressed greater opportunities for small businesses as well as farmers and rural laborers. These populist parties, which held power at least until the 1970s, include Saint Lucia's United Workers party, the Grenada United Labour party, and the Labour parties on Saint Kitts, Antigua and Dominica.

On Saint Kitts, Robert Bradshaw (1916–1978), himself a worker in a sugar factory, became vice president of an organization representing black sugar workers in 1932. From 1940, he combined the presidency of an island-wide union with that of the Saint Kitts–Nevis-Anguilla Labour party, which won every election from 1946 until 1980. A former Salvation Army captain, Vere Conwall Bird (1909–  ) won the presidency of the Antigua Trade and Labor Union in 1943. The allied Antigua Labor party has controlled the assembly almost continuously, and Bird became the first (and only) prime minister with the island's independence in 1983. On Dominica, Edward Oliver Leblanc (1923–  ), a small farmer, similarly lead the Dominica Labour party from 1960 to 1974.

Eric Matthew Gairy (1922–  ) of Grenada was the most controversial of the union leaders in the Lesser Antilles. An elementary school teacher and later a union organizer on Aruba, his union and Grenada United Labour party (GULP) were especially popular among rural peasants. In 1951, Gairy forced the British governor to negotiate by calling a strike that turned into a violent insurrection. He lost the 1962 election to the Grenada National party led by Herbert Blaize (1918–  ), who promised to unite with neighboring Trinidad and Tobago. When Prime Minister Williams of Trinidad totally rejected any union, Gairy returned to power in 1967. His corrupt and despotic government became unpopular, preparing the way for a Maurice Bishop's Marxist revolution in 1979.

## THE COMING OF INDEPENDENCE

The Moyne Commission had agreed in its 1940 *Report* that Britain's ultimate goal should be self-government based on universal suffrage. The Second World War increased pressure on the British (and other European empires) throughout the world. Beginning in 1947, Britain began to free its colonies in Asia, Africa, and the Middle East. Influential Britons began to think of their future as linked to Europe, and they increasingly viewed the poor West Indian possessions as a costly anachronism.

After the Second World War, successive British governments reaffirmed Britain's commitment to replacing Crown colony governments with self-government by elected officials. But self-government did not, in the British view, require immediate independence. Most British officials, of all political parties, believed that the island peoples still needed guidance by Europeans. They also were convinced that the smaller colonies were too poor to survive as viable states. Thus British officials wanted to unite the West Indian colonies in some sort of federation and tied independence to union.

The British government never drew up an overall plan for its West Indian colonies. Instead it tended to react to events in each colony, and the speed of progress toward self-government depended on the strength of local political leaders. British officials wanted to turn over political responsibility to men who enjoyed popular support but who also supported relatively moderate policies. For this reason, although the British colonies went through the same constitutional stages in gaining autonomy, the timing of independence varied greatly.

## THE WESTMINSTER MODEL

Most of the former British colonies have had several constitutions since the 1940s. However, all have adopted and continue to use the British system of government. Unlike the United States, all are unitary states in which legislative power is vested in an elected representative assembly. (Most also have a second or upper house—partly or wholly appointed—with only limited powers.) The assembly may delegate certain responsibilities to towns or local commissions, but these have no independent authority.

As in Great Britain, there is no separation between the executive and the legislative branches of government. West Indian constitutions usually provide for a figurehead governor-general representing the queen (or for a president in the case of Trinidad). However the real leader of the government is the prime minister (or premier), who is elected by the party gaining the most seats in the lower house of parliament. The prime minister forms a cabinet that includes the ministers or heads of various government ministries (departments). Each electoral district sends only one representative to the lower house. Victory goes to the man or women receiving the most votes, even if the candidate does not receive a majority. As in Great Britain or the United States, this "winner take all" system makes it very difficult to establish a third party.

The legal and judicial systems also are based on British precedents, and island constitutions separate the courts from the legislature. Judges are appointed for set periods, and their decisions can be appealed to local or regional appellate courts. In some cases, appeals still can be carried to the Judicial Committee of the Privy Council in Great Britain.

Under this system of parliamentary democracy, the British territories evolved from Crown colony government to self-rule in a series of steps or stages.

The first stage involved the granting of universal adult suffrage. This allowed every adult man and woman to vote for members of the governor's Legislative Council—which ultimately became the lower house in the island parliament or assembly. The British introduced adult suffrage first in the larger islands of Jamaica (1944) and Trinidad (1946). New constitutions established adult suffrage in the smaller Leeward and Windward colonies between 1951 and 1953.

Britain took a second step toward self-government when it allowed members of the assembly to take part in the government. Usually they first were chosen to sit on the governor's Executive Council but without any major responsibilities. Then elected members were given charge of a governmental department or ministry. At some stage the Executive Council became a governing cabinet when the majority of ministers were members of the elected assembly. This step—ministerial governments responsible to Parliament—was taken in all the islands by 1956.

Full internal self-government came when the leader of the largest party took over from the governor as chairman of the cabinet and became the territory's chief minister. This stage was reached in Jamaica and in Trinidad in 1959. A territory that achieved internal self-government—thus becoming an "associated state" in the British Commonwealth—was not fully independent. The British Colonial Office remained responsible for the colony's foreign policy and its defense forces.

## THE WEST INDIES FEDERATION, 1958–1962

By the later 1950s, all British territories had taken significant steps toward self-government. But they remained colonies in which British governors retained important powers. Before granting full independence, Britain first tried, between 1958 and 1961, to create a West Indies Federation. The British islands became sovereign states or received full internal self-government only after the federation failed.

For several centuries, the British Colonial Office had tried to unite several islands under one federal government. In this way, it hoped to increase governmental efficiency and thus cut expenditures. But the island assemblies—dominated by a few white planters—strongly resisted federation. Attempts to unite Barbados and the Windwards failed during both the 17th and 19th centuries. The British created looser confederations for the Leewards (1871) and Windwards (1885), but these were generally unpopular and had few powers.

During the economic troubles of the 1930s, many island leaders accepted the British view that the Caribbean territories were too poor to survive without some form of union. Successive British governments favored federation, and it was approved again and again by the West Indian legislatures. Leaders of the parties linked to unions believed that a West Indian federation would speed up the transition from Crown colony government to self-rule. Political union also might help increase economic growth, and it would make it easier for West Indians to bargain with a foreign company operating on several islands.

The British government encouraged federation, but it did not force it upon its colonies. In 1947, it called a conference at Montego Bay, Jamaica, that included representatives of all its territories. The leaders of the labor parties strongly endorsed a federation, and almost all non-governmental organizations also supported it. Several regional bodies, including the University of the West Indies, were added to those already in existence. A permanent committee was set up to plan the new federation, and several more regional meetings were held. On January 3, 1958, a West Indies Federation finally came into existence. It included ten island territories—Jamaica, Trinidad and Tobago, Barbados, Grenada, Saint Kitts–Nevis-Anguilla, Antigua and Barbuda, Saint Lucia, Saint Vincent and the Grenadines, Dominica, and Montserrat. Only the northern territories of the Bahamas and the British Virgin Islands remained outside.

The federation's constitution did not provide full internal self-government. Executive power was vested in a British governor-general, who could veto bills and appointed the Council of State, the federal cabinet. A federal House of Representatives was elected by universal suffrage, and it in turn chose the federal prime minister. Both the national and island legislatures were empowered to make laws, with federal legislation prevailing in case of conflict.

The West Indies Federation began without agreement on three fundamental concerns—inter-island immigration, federal taxation, and common import taxes. To bring the federation into existence, the territories had agreed that it could not make any laws for five years concerning these three issues. Its first prime minister, Sir Grantley Adams of Barbados, sought to keep the new nation alive for those five years while building up a sense of nationhood among the peoples of the ten territories. Unfortunately, the leading politicians in both Jamaica (Prime Minister Norman Manley and Alexander Bustamante) and Trinidad (Eric Williams) did not take part in the 1958 federal elections, which thus aroused little popular interest.

The federation might have succeeded had it been given time to gain popular support. It died after only three years because of major differences between Jamaica and Trinidad, its largest units. During the 1950s, both islands saw substantial economic growth thanks to bauxite mining on Jamaica and increased oil exports from Trinidad. Jamaica became the world's leading exporter of bauxite, the ore from which aluminum is derived. Trinidad and Tobago benefited from higher oil prices and increased exports, with oil production rising by one-third during the 1950s. Jamaica and especially Trinidad also had begun to develop significant manufacturing industries, helped in part by governmental efforts to lure foreign investment.

Because of their relative prosperity, the economic benefits of federation seemed less important. Many political leaders on both islands feared that their economies would be drained by the poorer islands of the eastern Caribbean. Trinidad's representatives vehemently opposed unlimited immigration from the smaller islands. Alexander Bustamante, now leader of the Jamaican opposition, would not accept a binding customs union. He charged that, with free trade,

Trinidadian factories would sell their products below cost to prevent the growth of manufacturing in Jamaica.

The West Indies Federation came to an early end when Jamaica withdrew in 1961. Bustamante's JLP, which originally had supported the federation, denounced it during the 1959 election campaign. Manley's PNP won, but membership remained an issue. Both Bustamante, now seventy-six years old, and Norman Manley, ten years younger, were struggling to maintain control over their parties. In May 1960, Bustamante suddenly demanded a national plebiscite to determine whether the island would remain in the federation. The following day and without consulting his own party, Manley promptly accepted his cousin's challenge. In September 1961, by a small majority, Jamaicans voted to withdraw from the West Indies Federation. The British government accepted the result of the Jamaican plebiscite and introduced legislation granting Jamaica independence. Eric Williams, premier of Trinidad and Tobago, then announced that Jamaica's withdrawal made a strong and unified federation impossible. Britain dissolved the federation, and both Jamaican and Trinidad became fully independent members of the British Commonwealth in August 1962.

Grantley Adams tried hard to hold together a smaller federation of Barbados and the other colonies in the eastern Caribbean. But the smaller islands feared domination by Barbados, while Barbadians did not want to assume financial responsibility for their poorer neighbors. In November 1966, Barbados became independent, and Britain granted new constitutions to its remaining colonies. Most became associated states with internal self-rule and subsequently were granted full independence. The Bahamas broke away in 1973, and they were soon followed by Grenada (1974), Dominica (1978), and Saint Lucia (1979). By the mid-1980s, even the smaller islands of Saint Vincent (1979), Antigua (1982), and Saint Kitts–Nevis (1983) had gained full independence.

Britain retained only a few thinly populated colonies, whose inhabitants feared assimilation with their larger neighbors. In 1966, Montserrat again became a direct dependency of the British Crown—as did several groups of tiny islands that had never joined the original federation, including the British Virgin Islands, the Cayman Islands, and the Turks and Caicos. Each territory made a separate agreement, which usually granted some self-government through an elected assembly and appointments to the governor's council. The appointed governor kept responsibility for defense, foreign affairs, and internal security.

Anguilla's situation was somewhat more complicated. In 1967, Saint Kitts–Nevis-Anguilla  became an associated state with internal self-government, the Anguillans almost immediately evicted the Saint Kitts police force and began to rule themselves through a local council. In 1969, the British government sent army engineers and London policemen to the island, installed a British commissioner, and reluctantly accepted Anguilla's request for a return to colonial status. In 1982, a new constitution granted the island the status of an associated state with internal self-government.

# CHAPTER EIGHTEEN:
## THE COMMONWEALTH CARIBBEAN SINCE INDEPENDENCE

■

The former British territories inherited all the economic problems common to the entire Caribbean region. With few exceptions, they continue to produce raw materials and commodities whose price is set by the world market. A drastic fall in sugar prices created an economic crisis during the 19th century, and the sugar industry disappeared from several of the Lesser Antilles before the First World War. Since 1945, sugar production also has declined in importance on the larger islands. Agriculture now provides less than 10 percent of total national production on Jamaica, Trinidad, and Barbados.

The products and services replacing sugar also are subject to sudden price changes that island governments cannot influence. The sharp rise in world oil prices in 1973 gave Trinidad and Tobago a decade of prosperity. When oil prices fell again during the 1980s, Trinidad's economy again slumped, and unemployment rose. Tourism, now the largest single industry on many islands, is an equally unreliable source of income. Revenues vary with the whims of travelers, and they rise and fall with economic conditions in America and Europe. To diversity their economies, island governments have encouraged manufacturing by subsidizing foreign investment and putting high tariffs on imported goods. These programs rarely have achieved their goals. The domestic products are more expensive than foreign imports, and they provide relatively few jobs for the amount invested.

The British territories became independent nations precisely as the economy faltered throughout the region. Only Trinidad produces significant amounts of oil, and every other island was hit hard when world oil prices sharply increased in 1973. Taking into account the mountainous or arid nature of many islands, the population density is among the highest in the world. With little economic growth, unemployment—especially among young islanders—remained at a high level throughout the 1980s.

Despite their economic difficulties, the islands, with the exception of Grenada, have retained democratic systems of government. Because they have kept British-style parliamentary democracy and share membership in the British Commonwealth, the former British colonies often are referred to as the "Commonwealth Caribbean."

| | TABLE 34. POPULATION ESTIMATES, FORMER BRITISH COLONIES, 1921–1970 | | | | |
|---|---|---|---|---|---|
| | JAMAICA | BARBADOS | SAINT KITTS | NEVIS | BAHAMAS |
| 1921 | 858,100 | 156,774 | 22,415 | 11,569 | 53,031 |
| 1943 | 1,246,200 | — | — | — | 68,846 |
| 1946 | — | 193,680 | 29,818 | 11,388 | — |
| 1960 | 1,605,546 | 232,820 | 38,113 | — | — |
| 1963 | — | — | — | — | 130,220 |
| 1970 | 1,848,512 | 236,891 | 33,737 | 11,147 | 168,812 |

SOURCES: Eisner, *Jamaica 1830–1930*, 153; *Population Policies in the Caribbean*, 26, 50, 105; Richardson, *Caribbean Migrants*, 146.

## NEW LEADERS FOR JAMAICA

Jamaica's two founding fathers, Norman Manley and Alexander Bustamante, dominated the nation's politics until the late 1960s. Under their leadership, Bustamante's Jamaican Labour party (JLP) and Manley's Peoples National party (PNP) adopted similar and generally moderate views, and they alternated in office about every ten years. The JLP won the 1962 elections, but illness forced Bustamante into semi-retirement in 1965. After another but narrow JLP victory in 1967, Hugh Shearer, president of the party's union, served as prime minister until 1972. Despite the world economic boom of the 1960s, unemployment and inflation both increased. Moreover, the Shearer government gained a reputation for weak management, party in-fighting, and corruption.

The two parties began to follow widely different courses when a new generation came to power at the end of the 1960s. Norman Manley died in 1969, and his son, Michael, assumed leadership of the PNP. Under Michael Manley (1924– ), the PNP revived the socialist heritage it had dropped in 1952. Tall, eloquent, and charismatic, Michael Manley took control of the PNP in 1969 because of his own personal dynamism as well as his father's reputation.

Manley, himself almost entirely white, worked hard to gain the support of the black power movement that had grown up during the 1960s. PNP leaders adopted the clothing and manners associated with the black lower classes, and Manley made a special effort to gain support from the Rastafarians.[1] With the slogan, "the politics of participation," the PNP decisively defeated the JLP in the 1972 elections. It gained votes among the Rastafarians and also from Jamaican businessmen and professionals disenchanted with the Shearer government.

## MICHAEL MANLEY AND DEMOCRATIC SOCIALISM

During his first two years in office, Manley increased welfare benefits and cultivated friendships with Fidel Castro and African members of the Non-Aligned movement.[2] In September 1974, the PNP government startled the people of Jamaica by suddenly announcing its conversion to socialism. Prime

Minister Manley declared his intention of seizing or nationalizing Jamaica's largest businesses.

Although many private companies survived, Manley's government took control of large segments of the economy between 1974 and 1978. It set up agricultural cooperatives, and it nationalized (with artificially low compensation) the island's electricity, telephone, and transportation companies as well as many sugar factories and a major bank. It also purchased 51 percent of the bauxite mines owned by foreign-owned aluminum companies. To help pay for these acquisitions, Jamaica in 1974 suddenly broke its existing contracts with the mining companies and sharply increased the levy (tax) on all bauxite production. As a way of emphasizing his socialist goals, Manley traveled to Cuba in 1975. There he and Fidel Castro embraced and expressed enthusiasm for each other's policies. Hundreds of Cubans came to Jamaica, while thousands of Jamaicans went to Cuba for training.

During Manley's first term, Edward Seaga (1930– ) succeeded Shearer as leader of the JLP. Seaga and Manley have continued the personal rivalry that earlier pitted Alexander Bustamante's JLP against Norman Manley's PNP. However, in an ironic reversal of roles, Michael Manley adopted Bustamante's angry and emotional style, while Seaga has preferred the more formal and remote manners associated with Norman Manley. While he lacks Michael Manley's fiery rhetorical style, Seaga is perceived as disciplined, hard-working, and intelligent. Despite being white and wealthy, he won election to parliament from one of the poorest districts in West Kingston. His talents soon brought him high office as minister of development (1962-1967) and minister of finance and planning (1967–1972).

During the December 1976 elections, Manley and Seaga supported totally different policies. The JLP charged that the PNP's socialism inevitably led to godless communism, and it also attacked the PNP's close relations with Cuba. Although the PNP won a sweeping victory in 1976, it no longer represented all Jamaicans. For the first time, different economic groups tended to support each of the two parties—both originally based on nation-wide unions. The PNP won the votes of unskilled workers and the unemployed, while professionals and white-collar workers swung to the JLP.

Manley began his second term by turning to the radical wing of the PNP, which had close ties to Jamaica's Communist party. The government took over more companies, and it created a Ministry of Mobilization to educate the population in socialist beliefs. By the fall of 1977, however, a severe economic crisis forced the government to ask for international help, and the prime minister began to support more moderate elements within the party.

The Jamaican economy had fallen into deep depression partly because of the sharp increase in world oil prices in 1973. But the government's policies clearly made matters worse. The new tax on bauxite agreements frightened off foreign investment, and it encouraged the mining companies to develop new sources of supply in other countries. The government ran up large foreign debts both to pay for higher welfare benefits and also to cover loses by state-owned companies. Manley's friendship with Castro dismayed foreign investors, while bankrupt Cuba had little money for aid to Jamaica.

By 1977, Jamaica had run out of foreign currency to purchase needed imports, and Manley's government was forced to ask the International Monetary Fund for help. In return for its loans, the IMF insisted that the government reduce its huge deficit by cutting spending and raising taxes. Although they were needed, these reforms further reduced wages in the short run. Overall, six years of socialist government led to a severe decline in living standards. By 1980, production had fallen by 16 percent, prices had tripled, and one third of Jamaican workers were unemployed. Ordinary Jamaicans had enough of socialism by the elections of October 1980. Seaga's JLP won a massive victory as one-third of those voting for the PNP in 1976 switched to the JLP in 1980.

## EDWARD SEAGA AND DEMOCRATIC CAPITALISM

The 1980 election was a personal victory for Edward Seaga, who became both prime minister and minister of finance. Seaga imposed the second major shift in economic policy since independence. The Seaga government supported private enterprise, reduced governmental spending, and tried to increase exports. It cut out layers of governmental regulation and returned some nationalized businesses to the private sector.

Prime Minister Seaga had inherited a severely troubled economy, and the JLP did not fully achieve its goals. Jamaica received large amounts of foreign aid throughout the 1980s, which partially insulated it from adverse trends in the price of its exports. But production, employment, and incomes increased very slowly until 1986. Contrary to his plans, moreover, Seaga actually had to increase government ownership in important industries, including oil refining and bauxite mining. Because of the earlier tax increases and nationalization, bauxite production fell drastically during the early '80s. Several foreign companies ceased operations on the island, forcing the government to buy their mines to maintain exports.

The continuing weakness of the economy shattered public faith in Seaga's financial skills, and many PNP supporters came back to the party. The PNP was careful to present a more moderate political image following its defeat in 1980. In a move reminiscent of earlier reforms in 1952, it thus cut all ties to Jamaica's communist party. With the economy the dominant public concern, the PNP led in opinion polls by late 1982. Michael Manley, with his emotional nationalist style, once again became the country's most popular party leader.

The invasion of Grenada in 1983 temporarily reduced support for the PNP by reviving fears of communism and Cuban aggression among Jamaican voters. Manley had supported the revolutionary New Jewel movement, and he now condemned the American invasion. When public opinion polls showed a significant drop in the PNP's popularity, Prime Minister Seaga suddenly called for a new election in December 1983. Under Jamaica's constitution, a prime minister can hold an election at any time during his five year term of office. But the PNP refused to take part because the voting lists had not been revised since 1980. The JLP thus won all sixty seats in the parliament and retained power until 1989.

## MICHAEL MANLEY RETURNS TO POWER

Helped by a fall in oil prices in early 1986, the Jamaican economy improved and grew significantly in 1987 and 1988. Nevertheless, a majority of Jamaicans turned against the JLP, which had reduced government spending on education, health, and housing. Voters also feared increasing violence and drug-related crime, and many Jamaicans simply preferred Michael Manley's more charismatic style. During the election campaign, Manley presented himself as a moderate leader who had learned from his mistakes during the 1970s. Manley pledged to increase spending on education and welfare benefits. But he also stressed the importance of American trade and assistance and promised to cooperate with the Jamaican business community and foreign investors.

Manley's PNP won a landslide victory in February 1989. Following the election, Manley appointed a governing cabinet from the moderate wing of the party, and he has continued Seaga's efforts to encourage investment by private companies. The new Manley also has maintained good relations with the United States and western Europe. While restoring diplomatic recognition of Cuba, he has been careful not to revive his close friendship with Fidel Castro.

## TRINIDAD'S UNIQUE OIL WEALTH

Differences in climate and in the history of settlement and development have given each of the Caribbean islands its own individual character. None is more distinctive than Trinidad—the only Caribbean island to possess oil and natural gas. Although they form only a small fraction of total world production, oil exports provide Trinidad's 1.3 million inhabitants with their main source of income. The highly mechanized oil industry directly employs only about 10 percent of the nation's workers, but it subsidizes the rest of the economy. Trinidad resembles the oil-rich nations in the Middle East more than the other Caribbean states. Indeed, since Trinidad exports oil, which all other islands must import, its economic fortunes are almost the exact reverse of other nations. A rise in oil prices, which harms the economies of the other islands, is good for Trinidad. Falling oil prices benefit the other islands but are disastrous for the Trinidadian economy.

Trinidad also differs from the other islands in its striking ethnic diversity. Blacks and East Indians—each making up about 40% of the entire population—retain their distinctive cultures. Until recently, blacks formed the majority of oil workers and preferred to live in the cities, while East Indians lived in the country and worked on the sugar estates. Because of these ethnic divisions, Trinidad's labor leaders have not succeeded in creating the large, nation-wide unions found throughout the rest of the West Indies.

For thirty years beginning in 1956, Trinidad's politics were controlled by Eric Williams and the party he founded, the People's National movement. Even after his death in 1981, Williams's legend helped win another five-year term for the PNM, and other parties came to power only in 1986. Labor leaders often opposed the Williams government. There were many strikes, and various unions formed parties and alliances against the PNM. But none of these labor parties could win enough votes to gain control of the government.

Despite Williams's compelling personality, the PNM did not retain power without opposition. The Democratic Labour party (DLP), founded in 1958, attracted East Indians and others who felt left out of the PNM. It remained the main opposition party until 1972, although it never won a majority in parliament. Low oil and sugar prices weakened Trinidad's economy between 1962 and 1973. Unemployment rose, and there were many strikes. Nevertheless, the PNM decisively won the 1966 and 1971 elections. Black workers remained loyal to the PNM, while the DLP and other opposition parties were torn by internal struggles for power. The opposition's weakness allowed the PNM to control the parliament, but it won a smaller number of votes in each election. The government became increasingly authoritarian. Williams and a few advisors made most decisions without explaining their actions to the party or to the news media.

## THE BLACK POWER REVOLT

The PNM sought to build up the economy by attracting foreign investment, and multinational corporations dominated the oil, sugar, and banking industries. In 1969 and 1970, Williams's acceptance of foreign (and thus white) ownership came under attack from black power militants and labor leaders, who tried to take over the government by force. However, partly because they failed to gain support from the East Indian community, Williams was able to crush the rebels.

Intellectuals with ties to American black militants created a black power movement in Trinidad during the late 1960s. The most radical group was the National Joint Action Congress (NJAC) at the University of the West Indies. Under the Williams government, the NJAC charged, white and colored businessmen—both Trinidadian and foreign—still owned the nation's industries. NJAC leaders wanted to install a government that would totally control the economy and own all land as well as the entire sugar industry. They rejected parliamentary democracy and were willing to use force to take power. A party publication, Slavery to Slavery, insisted that "We need to destroy . . . the system from its very foundations . . . to get out of our economic mess (and) build a new society."[3]

A major political crisis began at the end of February 1970. Several black power marches attracted thousands of demonstrators, and individuals linked to the NJAC bombed banks, stores, and government offices. Just as these marches and strikes reached their peak in mid-April, the deputy prime minister, A. N. R. Robinson, resigned from the cabinet—suggesting that the PNM was breaking up. Black power leaders and several unions scheduled a general strike and march on the capital, Port of Spain, for April 21. Prime Minister Williams decided to attack first, declared a state of emergency, and arrested the movement's leaders.

Despite riots and arson, the police maintained control of Port of Spain. But the government was further threatened when the junior officers and some men of Trinidad's small (800 men) army mutinied. They apparently sympathized with the black power movement and intended to take power after assassinating members of the government. The coast guard remained loyal and stopped the revolt by shelling the only road to the army base, located on the Chaguaramas peninsula north of the capital.

Following the 1971 rebellion, Prime Minister Williams moved to strengthen governmental powers. One proposed law required police permission to hold public meetings and forbade statements inciting racial hated or violence. Although Williams withdrew this law when it aroused intense opposition, the parliament passed several other laws that introduced licenses for guns and gave the police the power to search for unauthorized weapons. Many Trinidadians were unhappy with the Williams government by the May 1971 elections, but the various factions once more failed to come together. With the opposition parties—and most voters—boycotting the election, the PNM captured all thirty-six seats in the parliament.

## THE PNM CREATES A SOCIALIST ECONOMY

The Arab oil embargo in November 1973 rescued the Williams government by quadrupling the world price of oil. While most Caribbean countries entered a deep recession, Trinidad's enjoyed ten years of economic boom. The Williams government used taxes on oil exports to take control of the economy. It purchased foreign corporations, built ambitious public works, subsidized consumer goods, and created new manufacturing companies.

The government began to buy up key industries before 1973 in response to criticism of foreign ownership by union and black power leaders. Its ownership accelerated as oil revenues grew. The government purchased several oil companies in 1969, and it nationalized the remaining oil firms and all gas stations in 1975. State-owned companies also took control of other major industries—including sugar producers, electricity and water utilities, airlines, banks, and insurance companies.

Throughout the 1970s, oil revenues fueled a continuing boom. As funds poured in, Prime Minister Williams remarked that "Money is no problem."[4] His government used oil revenues to maintain artificially low prices for consumer goods, such as gasoline. And it spent lavishly on education, public works, and welfare programs from food stamps to old-age pensions. It also attempted to create heavy industries that could compete on the world market. (Earlier programs during the 1950s and 1960s had emphasized the manufacture of consumer goods for local use.) State funds were poured into projects such as a multibillion-dollar industrial park at Point Liasas, on the coast about 10 miles north of San Fernando. At enormous cost, factories were built to produce petrochemicals, fertilizers, cement, iron, steel, cement, and automobiles.

By the early 1980s, the government employed two-thirds of all workers, and it had more control over the economy than in any other Caribbean country except Cuba. Although Trinidad had taken socialism much further that the Manley government in Jamaica, Williams escaped criticism. Because of its great oil wealth, Trinidad could afford to pay full market price for foreign companies, which also were invited to participate in joint ventures under government supervision.

As the Williams government increased its control over Trinidad's economy during the 1970s, the prime minister became even more autocratic and aloof.

Commissions under his control supervised the government and state companies. From 1976, one National Advisory Council controlled all economic planning. Since government officials did not have to account for their actions to the parliament, bribery and corruption became common. In 1980, high officials were charged with taking bribes from U.S. companies to influence their choice of air planes for the military and the state airline.

Because of the economic boom and continuing ethnic divisions within the opposition, Williams easily won the 1976 elections. However, Tobago elected representatives from a new party, the Democratic Action Congress (DAC). Founded by A. N. R. Robinson, the PNM minister who had resigned during the 1970 black power riots, the DAC sought greater autonomy for Tobago. Although the British had united the two islands in 1888, they have little in common. In its history and economic development, Tobago resembles the other small islands of the Lesser Antilles rather than oil-rich Trinidad. After the sugar plantations collapsed during the 1870s, the island's primarily black inhabitants (now about 50,000) became independent farmers producing crops such as cocoa and coconuts. Most long have wanted to be independent of their larger neighbor. In 1980, Trinidad's parliament set up a fifteen-member elected assembly on Tobago and gave it responsibility for local finance and economic planning.

## THE ECONOMIC DEPRESSION OF THE 1980S

When Eric Williams died in March 1981, the PNM named George Chambers (1930– ) as party leader and prime minister. Chambers easily won the 1981 election, but his government soon became unpopular. Lower oil prices since

Waterwheel at Speyside, Tobago. Tobago's tranquility provides a distinct contrast to the industrialized activity of neighboring Trinidad. Sugar exports ended about 1900, idling the waterwheels on cane estates.

1982 have plunged Trinidad into a deep economic depression. Unemployment has soared, while per capita income has been cut in half—from $6,800 in 1982 (among the highest in the region) to $3,000 in 1989. The economic down-turn has been especially devastating because Trinidadians became dependent on imported consumer goods during the 1970s boom. Farm production has declined sharply, and Trinidad now must import three-fourths of its food. With falling oil revenues, the island has run up large trade deficits to buy needed imports.

In December 1986, the PNM lost power for the first time since independence. A coalition of four political parties formed the National Alliance for Reconstruction (NAR), headed by A. N. R. Robinson. Campaigning under the slogan "one love," the NAR trounced the PNM by appealing to all ethnic groups and promising to increase employment and end governmental corruption. However, the Robinson coalition began to lose popularity almost as soon as it took office in 1987. The NAR has maintained state control of the economy. Like Chambers, Robinson has balanced the nation's budget by cutting governmental spending and raising taxes and utility rates. These austerity measures have won little applause. Many of the NAR's Indian supporters left to form the United National Congress, while black people began to move back to the PNM.

An attempted revolution in July 1990 failed to overthrow the Robinson government. Led by Yasin Abu Bakra—a former policeman born Lennox Phillip in 1942—several hundred black Muslims occupied the parliament building and state television studios. There they seized fifty-four hostages, including Prime Minister Robinson and seven cabinet ministers, and held them captive for five days. The group—which had received money and weapons from Libya's ruler, Colonel Muammar Gaddafi—issued a statement condemning drugs, corruption, and poverty. The residents of the capital did not join Abu Bakr's rebels, who surrendered when they ran out of food. But many did take to the streets, looting many stores and burning down others. Although order was restored, more than thirty persons died during the worst violence since the black power riots in 1970.

## THE BAHAMAS

Unlike Jamaica and Trinidad, the many small islands and cays forming the Bahamas archipelago have few natural resources. Because of their poor soil and dry climate, sugar estates did not develop, and farming remains of little importance. Bahamians traditionally have made their living from the sea, and they also have profited from their close location to the United States. During the 17th and 18th centuries, the Bahamas provided an ideal base for pirates. They welcomed Confederate blockade runners during the American Civil War and alcohol smugglers during the Prohibition era. They owe their current prosperity primarily to the tourist and banking industries.

Because they lie just off the east coast of the United States and enjoy a moderate climate, tourism flourishes year-round. The Bahamas are the most popular travel destination in the Caribbean, and tourism provides about 70 percent of the nation's income. The Bahamas also lead in "offshore banking"— the provision of services by Bahamian branches of foreign banks. Accounts in

Cruise ships entering Nassau harbor, the Bahamas. As cane estates have disappeared, tourism has become the Caribbean's main industry. Nassau, one of the first major resorts, was visited by steam passenger ships from the end of the 19th century.

these branches escape some of the taxes and regulations imposed on banks in the United States. During the 1970s and 1980s, Bahamians also gained significant—but unmeasurable—income by smuggling cocaine, marijuana, and other illegal drugs to the United States.

The history of Bahamian independence is similar to that of other British territories. Led by Lynden Oscar Pindling (1930–  ), the Progressive Liberal party has won every election since 1968, and Pindling has served as prime minister since independence was gained in 1973. The PLP, founded in 1953, initially faced strong opposition from the United Bahamian party, which represented white business interests on Nassau. When the UBP won several elections during the 1960s, the PLP attributed its loses to unfair electoral boundaries. Pindling, as official leader of the opposition, dramatically protested in 1965 by throwing the speaker's ceremonial mace through a window while the assembly was in session. The PLP came to power in 1968 by appealing to black pride and the interests of workers.

Unlike many other Caribbean parties, the PLP is not closely tied to a labor union. It has carried out major public works, favors free-enterprise, and has held taxation to the lowest level in the Commonwealth Caribbean. The party owes its continued popularity to Pindling's charismatic leadership during twenty-five years of economic prosperity and improved material conditions for most Bahamians. From time to time, members of the PLP have split off and founded new parties, but none has been able to gain a majority in the assembly.

The PLP easily won the 1987 elections despite accusations that Pindling and other government members were involved in the illegal drug trade. Pindling responded to these charges by creating an independent commission of investigation. In its December 1984 report, the commission implicated several ministers and senior governmental officials, who were forced to resign. It found no evidence of direct involvement by Pindling, but did note that the prime minister had spent eight times his income during the past seven years. In wining reelection in 1987, the prime minister skillfully appealed to Bahamian nationalism. In fiery speeches, he accused the United States government of blaming the Bahamas rather than admitting its own inability to control illegal drugs.

## THE CAYMAN ISLANDS AND THE TURKS AND CAICOS

Like the Bahamas, the small and lightly inhabited Cayman Islands and the Turks and Caicos group have thrived by encouraging tourism and offshore banking. The three Cayman Islands are located just south of Cuba in the western Caribbean. The Turks and Caicos, a group of eight inhabited islands and some 40 small islets and cays, form the southeastern end of the Bahamas archipelago. Both groups are low-lying and arid, and their small populations lived, until recently, by fishing and (in the Turks) salt gathering. The British placed them under the governor of Jamaica during the 19th century, and both became separate Crown colonies when Jamaica became independent in 1962.

The 20,000 Caymanians enjoy one of the highest living standards in the Caribbean. Caymanian politics are stable, and islanders strongly favor continued ties to Britain. A British-appointed governor controls external affairs and defense. Local affairs are managed by a legislative council with a majority of elected members. There are no political parties, and candidates run as independents or as members of informal teams.

Tourism and offshore banking provide the main sources of income and employment on the Caymans. The three islands, which rise abruptly from the ocean floor, have a special appeal for scuba divers. Many new hotels and condominiums have been built, especially on Grand Cayman, and more than 500,000 travelers visited the islands in 1988. By the late 1980s, Grand Cayman was second only to the Bahamas as an offshore financial center. Some 500 banks and more than 18,000 other companies have registered as legal residents of the Caymans, where they pay no income, property, or inheritance taxes.

During the 1980s, the Turks and Caicos (current population about 10,000) tried, with some success, to emulate the Caymans as a diving, tourist, and banking center. Major airports were opened and new hotels were built on both Providenciales and Grand Turk. Several thousand companies registered in the islands, attracted by the absence of taxes and exchange controls. Economic development fell temporarily during the mid-'80s due to a major political scandal. In 1985, United States officials arrested the chief minister and two other members of the Legislative Council in Miami, where U.S. courts convicted them of conspiring to protect drug shipments passing through the islands. The British governor on the Turks and Caicos cooperated with the operation, and his strong stand has helped to restore the confidence of foreign investors.

## THE LESSER ANTILLES

In addition to Trinidad and Tobago, Great Britain ruled ten smaller territories in the Lesser Antilles. Some (Barbados, Saint Kitts, Nevis, Montserrat, Anguilla, and the Virgin Islands) were among Britain's first colonies in the Caribbean. Others (Saint Lucia, Saint Vincent, Dominica, and Grenada) were taken from France during the wars of the 18th century. By the 1980s, all except Anguilla and Montserrat had become independent nation states.

These islands share common economic problems. Originally settled as sugar plantations, most have suffered almost continuous economic depression since the mid-19th century. With limited resources and growing populations, all have struggled to find new sources of income as the sugar industry has disappeared since the 1960s. While some governments have encouraged new crops, such as bananas, most now emphasize tourism as the main or only industry. Antigua, Barbados, and Saint Kitts attract the greatest number of visitors. Tourism is least developed on Saint Vincent and on Dominica, which is mountainous and lacks beaches.

With populations ranging from 70,000 (Antigua) to 250,000 (Barbados), these islands are among the smallest of the world's sovereign states. Political parties grew out of and are fused with labor unions, and political loyalties are stable and highly personal as voters respond directly to individuals. The "founding fathers" that brought each island to independence often continue to govern, and many have been succeeded in office by sons or other close relatives. With the striking exception of the New Jewel movement on Grenada, most governments favor free enterprise and seek to foster foreign investment. However, most also have bought up failing companies to maintain employment.

*Barbados*　The Democratic Labour party and the Barbados Labour party have alternated in power since Barbados gained independence in 1966. The two parties have been distinguished mainly by the differing personalities of their leaders, and they have followed similar policies. Both parties have strongly supported private ownership while increasing welfare grants and undertaking large public works to cut unemployment and encourage investment.

The DLP, led by Prime Minister Errol Barrow, ruled Barbados from 1961 to 1976 and was reelected in 1986. In 1976, after fifteen years in opposition, the BLP returned to power under Tom Adams (1931–1985). Like his famous father, Sir Grantley Adams, Tom Adams had won the Barbados Island Scholarship and studied political science and economics in Great Britain. Adams's second term (1981–1986) was marked by a severe economic recession. The DLP won a landslide victory in 1986 by promising to cut taxes, and Barrow again became prime minister until his sudden death in 1987. His successor, Lloyd Sandiford, generally has continued Barrow's policies.

*Antigua and Saint Kitts–Nevis*　Antigua's national life has been dominated by Vere Bird, president of both the Antigua Trade and Labor Union and the Antigua Labour party. With one exception (1971–1976), Bird's ALP has won every parliamentary election since the island achieved internal self-government in 1967. Bird became the first prime minister when Britain granted the colony independence in 1981, and the ALP again won overwhelming victories in 1984 and 1989. During the 1980s, the Bird government bought up companies in a number of industries, and political opponents charge that ALP officials have used these investments for their own personal gain. In 1986 an independent investigation sustained complaints of gross mismanagement against Vere Cornwall Bird, Jr., the prime minister's first son and minister of public works and communications. Nevertheless, the ALP captured fifteen of the sixteen seats in parliament in the March 1989 elections.

Robert Bradshaw's Labour party similarly controlled Saint Kitts from 1946 until Bradshaw's death in 1978. During its long tenure, Labour increasingly intervened to prop up in the failing sugar industry. In 1975, the government took control of all sugarcane fields, and it acquired the island's one central sugar factory in 1976. By the late 1960s, opponents of the Labour government accused it of using illegal means to suppress political opposition, and the inhabitants of Nevis believed that the Labour party ignored their island's needs.

In 1980, the People's Action movement ended Labour's thirty years in power. Led by Kennedy Simmons (1936–  ), a medical doctor, the PAM called for great emphasis on tourism and increased autonomy for Nevis. The 1983 constitution created a federal government for the two islands. A separate Nevis Island Assembly enjoys autonomy in matters of local concern and is subject to the national assembly only with regard to foreign affairs and defense. This constitutional change ended Nevisian threats of secession, and Britain granted the two-nation state independence in September 1983.

*The Virgin Islands, Anguilla, and Montserrat*   These three Leeward islands are among the oldest British colonies.[5] Despite all efforts, however, they did not flourish as plantation islands. With a population of about 12,000, Montserrat is mountainous with little level land. Anguilla (7,000 inhabitants) and the Virgins (12,000) are too arid to support extensive cultivation. Sugar production ended

Workers harvesting sugarcane, Saint Kitts. Cane estates survived into the 1980s thanks to centralized milling. Since 1910, the entire cane harvest has been processed by only one sugar factory, linked to each estate by a road and narrow-gauge railway circling the island.

on the Virgins and Anguilla in the 1830s and it died out on Montserrat by the 1920s. As the economy declined, most of the white planters moved out, and the freed slaves made their living by fishing and growing food crops. During recent years, the three islands increasingly have become dependent on tourism. The British Virgins are especially popular with sailors, while Anguilla emphasizes scuba diving. Montserrat's lush beauty and tranquility attract a growing number of tourists, and the island also has become a retirement haven for several hundred Europeans and Americans.

The three islands lost their local legislatures during the 19th century and were merged into the Leeward Islands Federation until it was dissolved in 1956. All subsequently have become individual Crown colonies. The Virgin Islands chose not to join the 1958 West Indies Federation, and Montserrat reverted to Crown colony status when the Federation collapsed in 1962. Anguilla seceded from Saint Kitts and Nevis in 1969 and received its own constitution in 1982. A British-appointed governor retains control of defense, foreign affairs, internal security and police, the civil service, and the judiciary. Local laws, taxes, and economic development are the responsibility of the Legislative Council, whose elected members choose the chief minister.

Citizens on the three islands favor continued affiliation with Great Britain, which provides substantial financial assistance. Each has a stable political system in which two parties alternate in power. The major parties support similar polices to achieve economic growth, and their leaders' personalities are the main factor deciding elections.

*Saint Vincent*   Agriculture continues to play a major role in Saint Vincent's economy. Since sugar production ended in the early 1970s, the most important exports are bananas and arrowroot—a tuberous root ground into a starch for baby food, biscuits, and computer paper. Many Saint Vincentians earn their living as independent small farmers, and labor unions are less influential than on other islands. The first political party to gain mass support (the People's Political party) had ties to the unions. However, the PPP lost much of its following in the 1960s to the Saint Vincent Labour party, which appealed to the more conservative black middle class.

Led by R. Milton Cato (1915–  ), the SVLP attacked crime and drug abuse, followed a pro-Western foreign policy, and introduced government management of the economy. Cato won the elections of 1967 and 1974, and he became the first prime minister of an independent Saint Vincent in 1979. Concern over Cato's advanced age and ill health contributed to his defeat in 1984 by James Mitchell's New Democratic party, which generally has the same goals as the SVLP.

*Dominica*   Steep volcanic ranges covered by a multilayered rain forest make up Dominica's landscape. One of the last islands to be colonized, Dominica had few sugar plantations and only a small slave population. Its 85,000 inhabitants primarily make their living as independent farmers growing bananas, coconuts, and cotton. For several decades after slave emancipation (1834–1838), Dominica's legislature had a black majority. The island came under direct British rule as a Crown colony in 1898.

With the restoration of elections in the 1950s, a labor party and trade union representing workers and small farmers came to power on Dominica, as on other British Caribbean islands. Edward Oliver Leblanc, a farmer and agriculture instructor, led the majority Dominica Labour party from 1960 until 1974, winning self-government from Britain in 1967. At the end of the 1960s, a radical political organization patterned after the Rastafarians in Jamaica (called "Dreads" on Dominica) emerged among the black lower classes. As unrest grew, the DLP passed a law curbing press criticism of government. Mary Eugenia Charles (1919–  ), a lawyer and member of a prominent family in the capital of Roseau, founded the Dominica Freedom party to protest this legislation.

Leblanc remained popular among rural Dominicans, and the DLP easily defeated the DFP in the 1970 election. In the midst of growing turmoil, Leblanc resigned in 1974 and was replaced by Patrick John (1937–  ). To control the Rastafarians' criminal activities, John's government passed repressive laws, including an act allowing any private citizen to kill members of illegal societies. John won the 1975 election and gained Dominica's independence in 1978. His government increasingly used the army against the opposition and proposed new laws outlawing strikes and limiting freedom of the press. The political crisis reached a peak in May 1979. More than 10,000 demonstrators rallied in front of the assembly to protest the new laws. When the Dominican army fired on the crowd and killed several persons, a general strike shut down the country and forced John to resign.

After a bitter campaign, the Dominica Freedom party gained a landslide victory in 1980. Eugenia Charles became the Caribbean's first female prime minister and won reelection in 1985 and 1990. Under her leadership, the Dominica government has favored private enterprise, sought to increase foreign investment, and strongly supported United States policies in the Caribbean. As chairman of the Organization of Eastern Caribbean States, Prime Minister Charles invited American intervention in October 1983, following the murder of Maurice Bishop in Grenada. Charles opposed a military takeover in Grenada partly because of her own experiences on Dominica. As prime minister, Patrick John had used the Dominica army against opponents, and several army officers plotted with John to overthrow the Charles government in 1981.

*Saint Lucia*   Saint Lucia, another volcanic island, is almost as mountainous as Dominica. Bananas remain the main export, but tourism and light manufacturing are rapidly expanding. Labor unions strongly influence the policies of the major parties. Led by John Compton (1926–  ), the United Workers party—which controlled parliament from 1964 to 1979 and again since 1982—has substantially improved education and public health and fostered foreign and domestic investment. The opposition Saint Lucia Labour party favors increased governmental control of the economy and a foreign policy less tied to the United States. With union support, Allen Louisy led the SLP to victory in 1979, a few months after Saint Lucia became independent. In 1982, internal feuds within the SLP forced Louisy to resign, and the UWP returned to power in 1982.

## REPRESSION AND REVOLUTION ON GRENADA

On Grenada, as on the other English-speaking islands, the personalities of leaders and local concerns influence political choices. Political parties originally grew out of island-wide labor unions led by men with a strong emotional or even charismatic appeal. Some parties have enjoyed greater success than others with agricultural laborers, while still others are popular with urban workers and black and colored merchants and professionals. All, however, seek votes from every segment of society rather than from only one economic class.

The Marxist dictatorship imposed from 1979 to 1983 by the People's Revolutionary Government (PRG) was an aberration. Marxism attracts few islanders in the Commonwealth Caribbean. Most are deeply religious and abhor the militant atheism of Marxist ideology. After centuries of British rule, moreover, most island leaders believe in parliamentary democracy and reject calls for armed revolution. On Jamaica, for example, Michael Manley and Edward Seaga strongly attack the opponent's political philosophy and policies. But neither man has tried to keep power through force when defeated at the polls.

In March 1979, the PRG overthrew Prime Minister Eric Gairy, carrying out the only successful revolution in the history of the British islands. Most Grenadians—who assumed the PRG intended to hold free elections—welcomed the revolution because they held Eric Gairy's government in deep contempt. Gairy, who had dominated Grenadian politics since the early 1950s, became the island's first prime minister when independence was granted in 1974. Gairy now seized complete control, staying in power through fraudulent elections, corruption, and violence.

Gairy's regime resembled that of the Duvaliers in Haiti. He controlled the government and made all decisions. Supporters received import monopolies in return for kickbacks, and Gairy built a personal empire of hotels, restaurants, and nightclubs. Opponents were threatened by laws controlling newspapers, restricting public gatherings, and allowing the police to arrest and hold people without charge. Opposition meetings were broken up by the police, the army (called Green Beasts from the color of their uniforms), and various groups of thugs collectively known as the Mongoose Gang. Almost nothing was spent on education, and hospitals lacked medicine, beds, and linen. The economy was in shambles, and unemployment reached 50 percent.

## THE NEW JEWEL MOVEMENT

Shortly after Gairy won the 1972 elections (partly through fraud), several young Grenadians organized groups opposed to his government. Most belonged to the urban middle class and had earned professional degrees at universities in North America and Europe. During their studies abroad, they became committed believers in a mixture of Marxist and black power doctrines. Maurice Bishop (1944–1983), who had a London law degree, organized a political group in Saint Georges, the island's capital. Unison Whiteman, an economist with a degree from Howard University, attracted rural laborers to his Joint Endeavor for

Welfare, Education, and Liberation (JEWEL). The two groups merged in 1973 to form the New Jewel movement (NJM).

Maurice Bishop and Bernard Coard, who joined the NJM in 1976, became the party's most important leaders. Handsome and tall, with a radiant and optimistic manner, Maurice Bishop was a mesmerizing orator in the tradition of Jamaica's Michael Manley and Cuba's Fidel Castro. Bernard Coard had studied politics and economics at Brandeis University and the University of Sussex. While he totally lacked Bishop's magnetism, Coard was considered an effective manager as well as the party's leading intellectual.

The two leaders shared control of Grenada after 1979, with Bishop taking charge of foreign affairs and Coard running the economy. In 1983, their struggle for power destroyed the NJM and led to Bishop's murder. Both men were committed Marxists who deeply admired Fidel Castro, and Bishop named his son Vladimir in honor of Lenin, the founder of the Soviet Union. Because of his more populist manner, observers outside the NJM sometimes regarded Coard as more radical than Bishop. Judging by the NJM records seized during the 1983 American invasion, however, there was little difference in their basic beliefs or goals.

The middle-class leaders of the NJM tried, at least in their speeches, to reach out to Grenada's poor farm workers. But Bishop and Coard never meant the New Jewel to be a mass party. Copying Cuba and the Soviet Union, Bishop and Coard organized the NJM as a tightly controlled Leninist "party of the vanguard." Only sincere Communists were welcomed, and members were carefully screened during at least two years of probation. At its high point in September 1982, the NJM had only eighty fully qualified members.

Prime Minister Gairy believed in witchcraft and the invasion of the earth by flying saucers, and he often made decisions based on his dreams. On March 12, 1979, he flew to New York, hoping to convince the United Nations to recognize the existence of UFOs ("unidentified flying objects"). At 4 A.M. the next day, forty-six members of the NJM's military wing easily captured the army barracks and state radio station. Gairy's Green Beasts were asleep, and the sentries guarding Radio Grenada fled when they saw the barracks on fire.

## THE PEOPLE'S REVOLUTIONARY GOVERNMENT IN POWER

The jubilant people of Grenada literally danced in the streets at Gairy's overthrow. If the NJM had held elections, Bishop would have obtained a large majority in parliament. However, NJM leaders, firmly dedicated to Leninist principles, intended to keep all power in their own hands. They immediately suspended the 1973 constitution and established a People's Revolutionary Government under NJM control. The PRG assumed all legislative and executive powers, and it also controlled the judiciary. Existing laws were abolished and replaced by "People's Laws" signed by Maurice Bishop.

Bishop, who took the title of prime minister, appointed a cabinet with some twenty ministers—a few of whom were not party members—responsible for specific departments of the government. However, all real decisions were made by the NJM. The party's supreme body was a Central Committee with fifteen to twenty party members, chaired by Bishop. Normally it met about once a month to decide policy matters and give overall direction. Bishop also chaired the Politburo (Political Bureau), whose seven or eight members met weekly and implemented the Central Committee's decisions. Since there were so few party leaders, each usually held several jobs. Bernard Coard sat on both the Central Committee and the Politburo and served as minister of finance and deputy prime minister. Austin Hudson, who led the March 1979 revolution, became commander of the People's Revolutionary Army (PRA), headed two ministries (defense and construction), and belonged to both ruling committees.

As in the Soviet Union, the PRG set up various mass organizations for women, children, and teenagers, as well as "grass roots" groups in each village. These implemented its orders, sought to indoctrinate the people, and might report local concerns. But they had no independent authority, and the PRG immediately moved to head off any opposition to its total control. In March 1979, it authorized Austin's People's Revolutionary Army to imprison anyone, without trial and for as long as it wished. The PRA suppressed opposition newspapers and imprisoned their shareholders. It jailed at least two hundred persons suspected of disagreeing with its policies. Some were held for up to four years, and many were horribly tortured.

The PRG's ultimate goal was Soviet-style communism, with the state owning all industry and farms. It immediately nationalized the electric utility, telephone company, the banks, and some hotels. It also set up state farms and seized the largest private estates. Because it lacked managers, the government temporarily allowed some private ownership of small companies. But it rigidly controlled all exports and imports.

The PRG soon established close ties with Cuba and the Soviet Union. New Jewel leaders virtually worshiped Castro, who now developed a close personal friendship with Bishop. Grenada helped Cuba establish contacts with government and opposition leaders throughout the Caribbean and Latin America. The U.S. government charged that the PRG further assisted Castro in setting up centers of revolutionary subversion. Through its Cuba ally, the PRG became a strident supporter of the Soviet Union. In January 1980, Grenada and Cuba thus were the only nations in North or South America to vote against a United Nations resolution condemning the Russian invasion of Afghanistan.

Cuba and the Soviet Union rewarded Bishop's loyalty with enormous amounts of aid, given both as grants or gifts and as long-term loans. The PRG was so successful in tapping foreign resources that its policies have been called "foreign-aid socialism." The government carefully drew up shopping lists of projects. It then solicited funds from the Soviet Union, other Communist countries, and such oil-rich states as Algeria, Iraq, Syria, and Libya. Altogether, these donors gave the PRG at least $81 million between 1979 and 1983. And it further secured an additional $45 million from Western governments and international agencies. Grenada, with fewer than 100,000 inhabitants, thus ranked among the top five aid receivers in the world.

The centerpiece of Cuban aid was the construction, beginning in December 1979, of a new airport at Point Salines, a few miles from the capital of Saint Georges. Castro gave millions in grants, and hundreds of Cuban workers and engineers worked around the clock at the site. With a runway almost 10,000 feet long, the new airport would be available to the largest aircraft—both civilian and military. The PRG claimed that Grenada needed a modern airport to support an expansion of tourism. The U.S. charged that Port Salines airfield would give Cuba and the Soviet Union a safe base in the East Caribbean. Bishop encouraged U.S. suspicions by refusing to rule out Cuban or Russian military use.[6]

## THE COLLAPSE OF THE PRG AND THE MURDER OF MAURICE BISHOP

The PRG faced serious economic and political problems by the summer of 1983. Despite lavish foreign aid, the government had spent far more than it received. It now ran out of money and could not pay its foreign suppliers, the army, or government workers. Tax receipts were down as the number of tourists fell. Harmed by rigid controls and alienated by the imprisonment of prominent businessmen, private companies stopped investing. The state farms, agricultural factories, and fishing company lost money. Only the construction industry boomed. The PRG had wasted much of the foreign aid. Moreover, since most foreign grants were tied to specific projects, the PRG could not use them to pay day-to-day expenses.

As its economic problems mounted, the PRG became increasingly unpopular. Despite much-publicized Cuban assistance, public services actually decayed, and conditions in the schools and public hospitals remained deplorable. Living standards had fallen under the PRG, and unemployment was rising. The morale of NJM members and the People's Army was low, and most of the party's mass organizations no longer met.

Under the PRG, all decisions were made at the highest level, by the Central Committee and the Politburo. Since he headed both groups, some party members blamed the PRG's problems on Maurice Bishop's ineffective leadership. Bernard Coard escaped blame for party decisions because he had resigned from both governing bodies in October 1982. Moreover, many party members believed that Coard, the party's economic expert, was more likely than Bishop to solve Grenada's debt problems.

A long series of indecisive Central Committee meetings culminated in a three-day gathering between September 14 and September 16. Although they recognized the importance of Bishop's personal popularity, all fifteen members joined in criticizing the prime minister's inept management. The Central Committee then voted to create a joint leadership "marrying the strengths of comrades Maurice and Bernard."[7] Bishop remained prime minister and head of the Central Committee, and he continued to represent the PRG at public and international meetings. Coard became chairman of the Politburo, responsible for day-to-day administration of the party and government.

Bishop accepted the joint leadership proposal at a general meeting of all party members on September 25. During a twelve-day trip to Hungary, Czechoslovakia, and Cuba, he apparently changed his mind and looked for supporters outside the NJM. A combined meeting of the Central Committee and Politburo expelled Bishop from both bodies, and the Central Committee placed him under house arrest on October 13. The following day, Radio Grenada announced Bishop's dismissal as prime minister.

Despite the PRG's failures, Maurice Bishop himself remained popular. On Wednesday, October 19th, more than 10,000 Grenadians (10 percent of the nation's population) gathered at the central market square to protest Bishop's arrest. About 3,000 persons eventually marched uphill from the market to Maurice Bishop's house and liberated the former prime minister. Bishop decided to capture the PRA headquarters at Fort Rupert, which is located atop a high hill south of the market square and approached by only one narrow road. With Bishop and several members of his cabinet in the lead, the crowd stormed the fort. The solders surrendered at Bishop's order, and his supporters armed themselves from the fort's arsenal.

After failing to negotiate a compromise with Bishop, the Central Committee sent three armored personnel carriers to retake the fort. Before Bishop surrendered, the resulting battle killed at least forty of his supporters and three of the attacking soldiers. On the orders of the Central Committee, a firing squad executed Bishop and four of his cabinet ministers. Two hours after this massacre, Hudson Austin, commander of the army, announced the formation of a Revolution Military Council that would rule Grenada for only six days.

## OPERATION URGENT FURY

The murder of Bishop and his closest associates was universally condemned by both the PRG's opponents and its friends, including Fidel Castro and Michael Manley of Jamaica. On October 21, 1983, representatives of the seven other members of the Organization of Eastern Caribbean States met in Barbados.[8] With strong support from the prime ministers of Barbados and Jamaica, they unanimously decided to intervene in Grenada and requested help from the United States and other governments.

Four days later, on October 25, 1,900 U.S. soldiers invaded Grenada in a military action known as Operation Urgent Fury. Three hundred Caribbean soldiers—from Antigua, Dominica, Saint Lucia, Saint Vincent, Barbados, and Jamaica—accompanied the American forces but did not take part in the fighting. The British government did not permit participation by Montserrat, which is still a Crown colony. Prime Minister Chambers of Trinidad strongly opposed military intervention.

U.S. troops occupied the island within three days. Some eight hundred Cuban workers building the Port Salines airport were captured and returned to Cuba. Only a small number among the Cubans and the 1,500-man Grenadian army resisted. The militia was largely pro-Bishop and hardly mobilized. Altogether eighteen Americans, twenty-four Cubans, and sixteen Grenadians died in action.

The OECS states believed that the massacre of a prime minister and his cabinet members justified military intervention. The governments of these small islands, which have minuscule defense forces, also believed that Grenada and its Cuban ally threatened the security of the entire eastern Caribbean. The U.S. government said that it had intervened both in response to the OECS request and also to protect some one thousand Americans living on Grenada— including about six hundred students at Saint George's University Medical School.

Judging by public opinion polls, both Grenadians and the inhabitants of other nations in the Commonwealth Caribbean approved of the invasion. It was condemned by the governments of the Soviet Union, its allies, and many Latin American states. Britain, France, and Germany also initially criticized U.S. intervention. They subsequently supported it when the Reagan administration produced military treaties between Grenada and Cuba and other documents seized during the invasion. Under these agreements, Grenada would have received large amounts of weapons and might well have become a Cuban military base.

## GRENADA REBUILDS

The United States removed its combat troops in December 1983. With the help of some 800 U.S. and OECS troops, an advisory council appointed by the governor-general ruled the island until the December 1984 elections. Herbert Blaize (who had held the office twice during the 1960s) again became prime minister, serving until his death in 1989. Eric Gairy's GULP won one seat, but no candidate of the New Jewel movement—renamed the Maurice Bishop Patriotic movement—was elected. New elections in March 1990 brought in Nicholas Brathwaite, a civil servant in the Fabian socialist tradition. Despite his dismal record in the 1970s, many farm workers remained loyal to Eric Gairy, whose GULP came in second.

A Grenadian jury tried fourteen persons—including Bernard and Phyllis Coard and Bernard Austin—for the murders of Maruice Bishop, his followers, and forty members of the crowd at Port Rupert. Although all received death sentences in 1986, Coard and the New Jewel still had many influential American friends. Repetitive appeals delayed their executions, which were commuted by Prime Minister Brathwaite in August 1991.

Grenada's economy has improved since 1985. Ironically, the island owes much of its new prosperity to increased tourism after the completion of the Point Salines airport. Relaxing the rigid controls imposed by Bishop's PRG, the Blaize and Brathwaite governments have begun returning state companies to private ownership. With substantial foreign aid from the United States and international bodies, they have significantly improved the island's roads, telephones, and health care facilities.

## THE CARIBBEAN TODAY

Despite or because of their small size, each island has individual characteristics, and all are beginning to create new and often unique institutions. The Caribbean nations must be considered a relative success story. The entire region faces grave economic difficulties. It has been affected by the rivalry between the West and Russia. And some islands have seen the growth of powerful and well-armed gangs supplying drugs to the United States. Nevertheless, free elections and individual freedoms still predominate from the Bahamas in the northwest to Curaçao in the southeast. Except in Haiti, Cuba, and (for a time) in Grenada, incumbents routinely are replaced during honest elections. And non-partisan observers give most governments high marks for civil liberties.

In a sense, even Grenada's New Jewel episode shows the region's support for democracy. Most governments in the Commonwealth Caribbean initially accepted Maurice Bishops's 1979 revolution only because they believed he would permit free elections. They refused to tolerate Bishop's murder by an unelected military regime. Both in Grenada itself and throughout the English-speaking Caribbean, the overwhelming majority of islanders backed intervention, and honest elections have been held twice since 1984. Within this framework of political stability, island leaders have begun to address the region's long-standing economic difficulties.

Woman in traditional dress, Guadeloupe.

# A P P E N D I X   A :
## MAPS

■

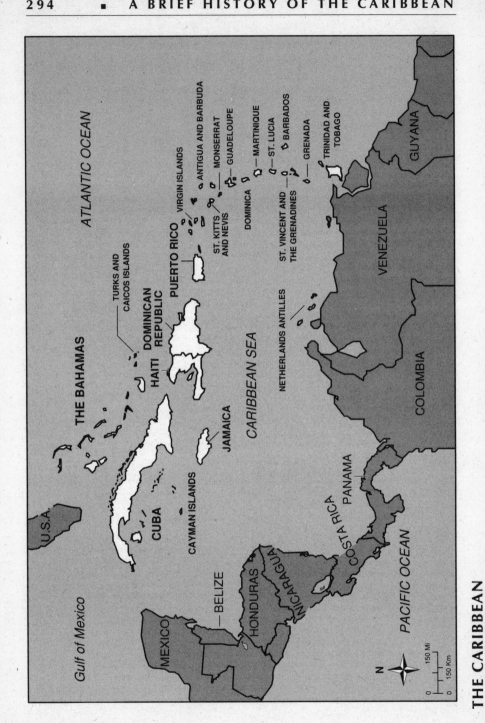

THE CARIBBEAN

## Territorial settlements

1697 (Ryswick). Spain recognizes French colony of Saint-Domingue (today Haiti).

1713 (Utrecht). France cedes its section of Saint Kitts to Britain.

1748 (Aix-la-Chapelle). Dominica, Saint Lucia, Saint Vincent, and Tobago declared "neutral islands."

1763 (Paris). Dominica, Saint Vincent, Grenada, and Tobago to Britain; Saint Lucia to France.

1783 (Versailles). Britain restores Tobago to France.

1795 (Bâle). Spain cedes Santo Domingo to France.

1802 (Amiens). Spain cedes Trinidad to Britain.

1814 (Paris). France cedes Saint Lucia and Tobago to Britain.

ATLANTIC OCEAN

BAHAMAS

CUBA

JAMAICA

SANTO DOMINGO
(Dominican Republic)

SAINT-DOMINGUE
(Haiti)

PUERTO RICO

VIRGIN ISLANDS

ST. KITTS

ANTIGUA AND BARBUDA

MONSERRAT

GUADELOUPE

DOMINICA

MARTINIQUE

ST. LUCIA

BARBADOS

ST. VINCENT

GRENADA

TOBAGO

TRINIDAD

CARIBBEAN SEA

NETHERLANDS ANTILLES

VENEZUELA

COLOMBIA

EARLY TERRITORIAL SETTLEMENTS

CUBA

CAYMAN ISLANDS (GREAT BRITAIN)

JAMAICA

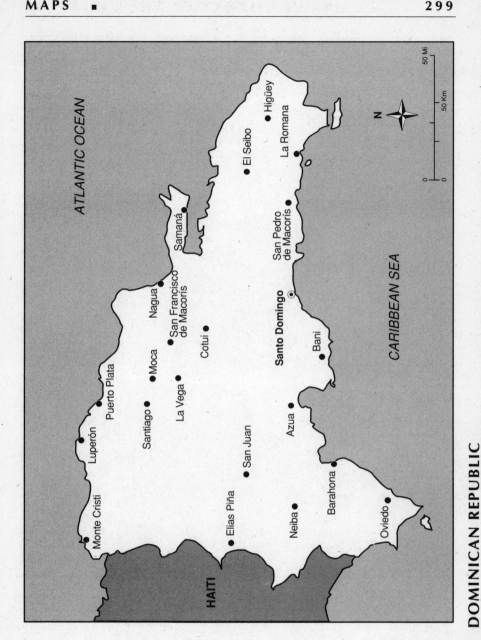

ATLANTIC OCEAN

CARIBBEAN SEA

50 Mi

50 Km

N

Higüey

La Romana

El Seibo

Samaná

San Pedro
de Macorís

Nagua

San Francisco
de Macorís

Moca

Cotui

Santo Domingo

Bani

Puerto Plata

Santiago

La Vega

Luperón

Azua

San Juan

Monte Cristi

Elias Piña

Neiba

Barahona

Oviedo

HAITI

DOMINICAN REPUBLIC

THE BAHAMAS

THE NORTHERN LESSER ANTILLES

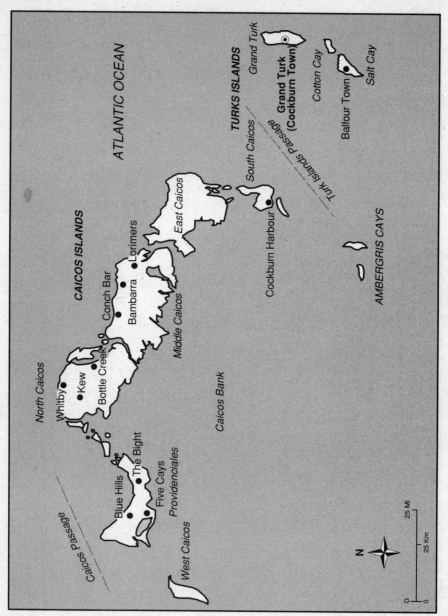

**TURKS AND CAICOS ISLANDS (GREAT BRITAIN)**

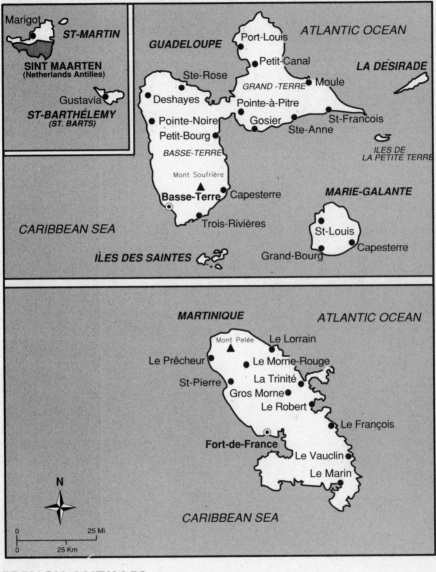

Marigot **ST-MARTIN**

**SINT MAARTEN**
(Netherlands Antilles)

Gustavia
**ST-BARTHÉLEMY**
(ST. BARTS)

**GUADELOUPE**

Port-Louis

*ATLANTIC OCEAN*

Petit-Canal

**LA DÉSIRADE**

Ste-Rose

*GRAND -TERRE*    Moule

Deshayes

Pointe-à-Pitre

Pointe-Noire    Gosier    St-Francois

Petit-Bourg    Ste-Anne

*BASSE-TERRE*    *ÎLES DE*
*LA PETITE TERRE*

Mont Soufrière

**Basse-Terre**    Capesterre

**MARIE-GALANTE**

*CARIBBEAN SEA*    Trois-Rivières

St-Louis

**ÎLES DES SAINTES**    Capesterre

Grand-Bourg

**MARTINIQUE**    *ATLANTIC OCEAN*

Mont Pelée    Le Lorrain

Le Prêcheur    Le Morne-Rouge

St-Pierre    La Trinité

Gros Morne

Le Robert

Le François

**Fort-de-France**

Le Vauclin

Le Marin

N

*CARIBBEAN SEA*

0    25 Mi

0    25 Km

## FRENCH ANTILLES

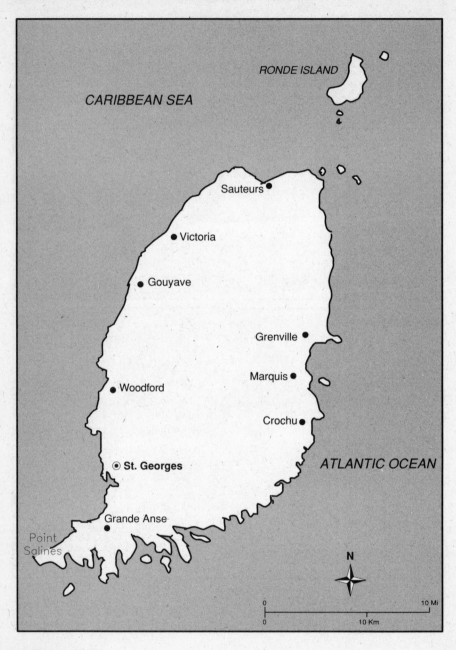

ST-MARTIN
(French Antilles)

Philipsburg **SINT MAARTEN**

CARIBBEAN SEA

SABA

**SINT EUSTATIUS**

Oranjestad

**BONAIRE**

Rincon

Kralendijk

Santa Rosa

**CURAÇAO**

New Port

Soto

Westpunt

St. Willbrordus

St. Michiel

**Willemstad**

CARIBBEAN SEA

20 M

20 Km

N

**ARUBA**

Oranjestad

St. Nicolas

**VENEZUELA**

## NETHERLANDS ANTILLES

# NOTES

■

## PREFACE

1. Some of the significant differences between the Euro-African Caribbean and the Euro-Indian mainland are summarized by Robert West and John Augelli in *Middle America: Its Lands and Peoples*, Third Edition (Englewood Cliffs: Prentice Hall, 1989), pages 12–18.
2. In Latin America, the term *criollo* originally was reserved for native-born whites. In the Caribbean, *creole* denoted all long-established populations and cultural habits, and it was used to contrast them to recent immigrants.

## CHAPTER ONE

1. I use the U.S. system of weights and measures throughout. For example, distances are expressed in miles rather than meters, and temperatures are cited in Fahrenheit and not in Celsius units.
2. This first era of mountain building and volcanic activity began during the Cretaceous period and probably lasted into the Eocene epoch. To emphasize its relative age, the geographical region comprising the Greater Antilles has been called "Old Antillia."
3. Mont Pelée (Martinique) erupted in 1902, Mount Soufrière (Saint Vincent) in 1812, 1902, and 1976. Mont Soufrière (Guadeloupe) erupted in 1956 and showed signs of instability in 1976. In addition, there are volcanic vents (called *soufrières*) or hot sulfur springs on Nevis, Montserrat, and Saint Lucia as well as in the crater of Mont Misery on Saint Kitts.
4. Also referred to as semi-evergreen, semi-deciduous, and semi-evergreen seasonal forests.
5. Carl Sauer, *The Early Spanish Main* (Berkeley and Los Angeles: University of California Press, 1969), page 68.
6. Yellow fever is unusual outside the tropics because the virus dies out at temperatures below 60°, and the mosquito lapses into a coma at 50°. *Aëdes aegypti*, which lives up to four months, can survive long ocean voyages. Thus sailing ships sometimes brought terrible epidemics to Philadelphia, New York, Boston or even northern Europe. But these plagues invariably died out with the first frost.

## CHAPTER TWO

1. Carl Sauer, *The Early Spanish Main*, 194.
2. Slave raids during the early 1500s seem to have totally destroyed the Indian population of the Bahamas. On Hispaniola, a group owned by Diego Colón rebelled in 1522 under the leadership of the cacique Enrique. After a struggle of fifteen years, this group was allowed to establish an independent village at Boya, where some individuals of mixed blood may have lived as late as 1798. In Puerto Rico and Jamaica, a few Indians still survived in 1600, but none are mentioned a century later. Only on Cuba did several villages maintain themselves, and perhaps 400 Indians remained in 1900.
3. Lyle McAlister, *Spain and Portugal in the New World, 1492–1700* (Minneapolis: University of Minnesota Press, 1984), 82.

## CHAPTER FOUR

1. Throughout, this book uses the words *city* and *town* in the usual American sense. That is, a city usually is larger than a town. The royal grants founding municipalities distinguished between a city (*cuida*), a town (*villa*), and a peasant village (*pueblo*). The distinction was a matter of honor and was not based on population or economic importance. Generally, only Indian villages were called *pueblos*.
2. Frank Cundall and Joseph Pietersz, *Jamaica under the Spaniards* (Kingston, Institute of Jamaica, 1919), page 12.

## CHAPTER FIVE

1.  It is inaccurate to group the islands under national labels—as French, British, Dutch, or Danish—for a second reason. Since the settlers came from only a few regions, the islands were developed by provinces rather than by nations. The first French settlers, for example, came almost exclusively from provinces along the Atlantic Coast, such as Normandy, Brittany, and Poitou.

2.  Some confusion arises because the Dutch Windward Islands are located in the midst of the British Leeward Islands. The prevailing trade winds tend to blow more or less from the east to the west—during some months from southeast to northwest. In English and American usage, *windward* denotes the direction or side from which the wind blows. In this meaning of the word, every Caribbean island is thus leeward of those to its east and windward of all those to its west. For its own administrative convenience, the British government arbitrarily divided its colonies in the Lesser Antilles into the Leewards (in the north) and the Windward Islands (in the south). In Spanish, French, and Dutch, the meaning of *windward* is the opposite of English usage. Thus the Dutch, viewing the map from Curaçao, call their northern possessions the Windward Islands (*Bovenwindse Eilanden*, the "islands before the wind").

3.  A different Turtle Island from the famous buccaneer haunt north of Hispaniola.

4.  This is the version given by the French missionary Jean Du Tertre, who came to the region a few years later. According to a less plausible legend, a representative of each group set off from a designated point and walked along the coast until both met again. With the Dutchman drinking gin and the Frenchman wine, this procedure allotted the French the larger share of the island.

## CHAPTER SIX

1.  African slaves did not replace white indentures in British North America until the 1690s.

2.  The restrictions enacted in the 1651 Navigation Act served as the immediate cause of the First Dutch War between England and the Netherlands (1652–1654). However, this war was mainly fought in Europe, and it did not greatly affect the Caribbean colonies.

3.  Including slaves, the king of England had about 73,000 subjects in the West Indies, the king of France about 21,000.

4.  *Basse-Terre* ("low land") seems an inappropriate name for a mountainous island. French sailors used the word to mean "protected," and it is equivalent to the English *leeward*. All towns named Basse-Terre are thus located on the inner or Caribbean coast and often on the southern side of an island. In contrast, the first settlers gave the name Capesterre ("headland"), to towns along the Atlantic or "windward" coast.

5.  The Poinciana tree bears his name, because its scarlet flowers resemble the robes of his order.

## CHAPTER SEVEN

1.  According to legend, the name *buccaneer* is derived from the French or Carib word (*boucan*) for the barbecue on which these hunters smoked beef to preserve it for sale or for later use. The French reserve *boucanier* for these Hispaniola cattle-hunters, and they use *filibustier* ("freebooter") to describe sea bandits. The latter term may derive from the Dutch *vrijbuiter*, describing a type of small "flyboat." The English usage of *buccaneer* to mean pirate must have been common before 1684, when Exquemelin's *De Amerikaensche Zee-Roovers* was translated into English under the title *The Bucaniers of America*.

2.  In 1656, a former governor of Nevis brought over some 1,400 settlers—including families and children—to plant at Morant Bay. Within a few months, one-half to two-thirds had died.

3.  Nellis Crouse shows that Jean Le Vasseur went to Tortuga in 1642—and not in 1640 as most histories indicate. See Nellis Crouse, *French Pioneers in the West Indies, 1624–1664* (New York: Columbia University Press, 1940), page 86.

## CHAPTER EIGHT

1.  British pirates tended to prefer Port Royal, while French pirates operated from Tortuga. However, few among the brethren of the sea were staunch nationalists, and pirates of many nations took part in the larger raids.

2.  *A General History of the Robberies and Murders of the most notorious Pyrates* (London, 1724–28) describes the final great era of piracy, that based in the Bahamas. Defoe's history is based—sometimes loosely—on firsthand materials such as the transcripts of pirates' trials and interviews with pirates, their victims, and their conquerors.

## CHAPTER NINE

1.  See pages 73 and 74 for the 4.5 percent tax on goods exported from Barbados and the Leewards. The government rebated part of the import duties on products reexported from Britain to other countries.

2. Altogether, residents of Great Britain and Ireland received two-thirds or more of Jamaica's annual income and profit in the 1770s. Their European rulers probably took as much from other Caribbean colonies, but precise statistics are lacking.

3. Basil Davidson, *The African Slave Trade: Precolonial History 1450–1850* (Boston: Little, Brown, 1961 [published in hardback as *Black Mother*]), page 51.

4. For example, the profits from slavery represented less than one-half of 1 percent of Britain's annual income. In his influential 1944 study, *Capitalism and Slavery*, Eric Williams (later Prime Minister of Trinidad) argued that Britain's industrial development was directly based on slavery. Williams believed that the profits from the triangular trade "fertilized the entire productive system of the country." He also held that these profits were directly invested in the technological changes we call the Industrial Revolution. The "Williams Thesis" is now seen to be overstated. While the British and North American economies might have developed somewhat more slowly, the Industrial Revolution in Europe would have occurred without the Caribbean slave plantations.

5. Cited Richard Sheridan, *An Economic History of the British West Indies, 1623–1775* (Baltimore: Johns Hopkins University Press), page 60.

6. The Black Carib surrendered to the invading British force in 1796 and were transported to Rattan Island, off the coast of Honduras. More than 40,000 of their descendants—still ethnically and culturally distinct from their neighbors—now live in Honduras, Belize, and Guatemala.

7. Some 200 Indians still lived in the village of Arima before the Second World War. Although referred to as Carib, most probably were of Arawak origin.

8. V. S. Naipaul, *The Loss of El Dorado* (New York: Vintage Books, 1984 [first published 1969]), pages 124–125.

# CHAPTER TEN

1. Slaves thus made up a smaller portion of the population on Bonaire, Curaçao, the Bahamas, and the Caymans, which are too arid for cane estates. Orlando Patterson summarizes information about this and other large-scale slave societies in *Slavery and Social Death: A Comparative Study* (Cambridge, Massachusetts: Harvard University Press, 1982), pages 353–364. For comparison, slaves made up only one-third of the population in the American South during the 1800s (Patterson, page 363).

2. As Table 16 indicates, Portuguese traders brought the largest number of African slaves to the New World, carrying almost four million to their plantations in Brazil.

3. After the bankruptcy of the first Dutch West India Company in 1674, the government chartered another company under the same name. This second West India Company administered its Caribbean possessions (to 1794) and retained a monopoly of the African slave trade until 1734.

4. Six of every ten men sent by the Royal Africa Company between 1695 and 1722 died during their first year in Africa—with this extraordinary death rate contributing to the Company's failure.

5. Herbert Klein, *The Middle Passage: Comparative Studies in the Atlantic Slave Trade* (Princeton, New Jersey: Princeton University Press, 1978), page 241.

6. Richard Pares, "Merchants and Planters," *Economic History Review*, Supplement Number 4 (Cambridge, England, 1959), page 23.

7. According to tradition, this device was invented in Sicily in 1449. It remained standard in Europe and the Americas until long after 1800.

8. Studies of the British islands show that planters imported only about 30 pounds of dried fish annually for each slave. Few Cuban and Puerto Rican planters complied with laws requiring masters to give slaves a half-pound of salted meat or fish daily.

9. In addition to protein and fat, a slave's diet often lacked vitamin C and iron. In the contemporary United States, where some are overfed, meat and fat often are regarded as harmful. In fact, both are absolutely necessary to life. Meat and dairy products are the only natural source of high-quality or perfect proteins that supply all the essential amino acids. These proteins build the muscles, blood, and internal organs as well as form enzymes and antibodies that sustain health and fight infections. For women, a lack of protein also can lower the age of menopause, inhibit ovulation, and increase miscarriages or stillbirths. Among men, a poor diet can lead to a loss of sperm mobility or even of sperm production. Fats also are essential to supply energy, to keep the body warm, to carry the fat-soluble vitamins (A, D, E, and K), and to help the body absorb other vitamins. For an in-depth study of slave diets, see Kenneth Kiple, *The Caribbean Slave: A Biological History* (Cambridge, England: Cambridge University Press, 1984).

10. Table 16 summarizes slave imports into various regions. For the population of the Americas in 1825, see Angel Rosenblat, *La Poblacion indigena y el Mestizaje en America* (Buenos Aires: Editorial Nova, 1954), volume I, chart between pages 36 and 37. For the Cuban population in 1877, see Jack Ericson Eblen, "On the Natural Increase of Slave Populations: The Example of the Cuban Black Population, 1775–1900," *Race and Slavery in the Western Hemisphere*, edited Stanley Engerman and Eugene Genovese (Princeton, New Jersey: Princeton University Press, 1975), page 216.

11.  In the British Leewards, for example, about one-quarter of all slaves perished each year during the 1680s.

12.  In the British islands, the death rate probably also fell from about 1760 because some planters adopted a policy of "amelioration." As prices rose for new hands from Africa, they began trying to reduce deaths among the slaves they already owned. Amelioration later served as the planters' main response to the abolitionist movement described in Chapter 13. To show good faith, island assemblies amended the laws regulating slave treatment. They outlawed cruel punishments—dismembering, for example—and they decreed minimum feeding standards.

13.  Modern historians suggest various reasons why Caribbean slaves had so few live children—the main reason the slave population fell each year. Slaves brought in from Africa literally could not reproduce themselves because African slave dealers offered white traders fewer women than men overall and generally sold them women who already were mature adults. A poor diet and the stress of sugar planting produced many stillbirths and infant deaths as well as reduced fertility among both men and women. West Indians retained the African custom of prolonged breast-feeding—which also may reduce fertility—longer than North American slaves. Lack of opportunity also prevented conception, since slave unions were less regular than in the United States.

None of these modern explanations for low slave birth rates is fully convincing. We can easily understand why slaves died at a high rate. The causes of low fertility remain something of a mystery. Perhaps slave mothers simply did not see much point in raising children solely to provide labor for their masters.

## CHAPTER ELEVEN

1.  After the War of the Spanish Succession, the Treaty of Utrecht (1713) gave the French part of Saint Kitts to Britain.

2.  French expeditions devastated Saint Kitts in 1666 and 1706, Nevis in 1706, and Montserrat in 1712. See Chapter Eight.

3.  Cited Richard Pares, *War and Trade in the West Indies, 1739–1763* (Oxford University Press, 1936), page 286. William Beckford, Lord Mayor of London and Member of Parliament, was a member of the wealthiest family in Jamaica; in 1754, he and his brothers owned plantations totaling 42,075 acres (Sheridan, *Sugar and Slavery*, 228).

4.  France retained fishing rights off the banks of Newfoundland and in the Gulf of Saint Lawrence, with the little islands of Saint-Pierre and Miquelon as fishing stations.

5.  In the treaty of alliance with Spain, the French government renounced all claims to North America east of the Mississippi, but it reserved the right to make conquests in the West Indies.

## CHAPTER TWELVE

1.  Evidence gathered under torture is untrustworthy. Thus historians believe the planters exaggerated the goals and number of participants in several slave conspiracies. The table lists these with a question mark.

2.  Altogether, the British armies fighting in the different West Indies campaigns lost 45,000 men from 1793 to 1798: David Geggus, *Slavery, War, and Revolution* (Oxford: Clarendon Press, 1982), page 463, note 50.

3.  Prime Minister Pitt had personally intervened in Parliament to abolish the slave trade only ten months earlier in April 1792. See page 180.

4.  Because the Haitian Revolution succeeded, Toussaint L'Ouverture has received more attention than equally courageous rebel-slaves on other islands, such as Julien Fédon. History is written by the winners, but failed revolutions also deserve mention, because they too affect subsequent generations.

5.  Toussaint was forty-eight years old in 1791. According to tradition, he had been a slave on the Breda plantation in the North Province. The owner and overseer favored him with unusually good treatment, and he rose from coachman to the important post of steward, responsible for all the livestock on the estate. A devout Roman Catholic, Toussaint was semi-literate and expert in the use of medicinal herbs. Following the slave uprising, he maintained calm on his master's plantation for a month before conveying the whites to safety, and only then joined the rebels. Toussaint himself helped to create this legend. Recent investigations suggest that he was not a slave in 1791, but was instead a freedman who owned both land and slaves.

6.  C. L. R. James, *The Black Jacobins: Toussaint L'Ouverture and the San Domingo Revolution*, Second edition (New York: Vintage, 1989 [originally 1963]), 242.

## CHAPTER THIRTEEN

1.  Both William Wilberforce and Thomas Clarkson belonged to the Clapham Saints, an evangelical group within the established Anglican church.

2. A subsequent law (1811) made slave trading a felony both for foreigners trading in British dominions as well as for Britons everywhere. In 1824 Parliament declared slave trading on the high seas to be piracy punishable by death.

3. The Danish crown had already outlawed the import of slaves into its colonies by an act of 1792 effective in 1802. However, the Danish islands continued to serve as a center for the re-export trade, which shipped slaves to neighboring islands. Inter-island sales were the most profitable part of the trade in the Virgin Islands (see page 125). Thus the 1792 Danish law was less rigorous than it might seem. The United States in 1794 already had prohibited American participation in the slave trade to other countries. By an act of March 1807, Congress prohibited the import of slaves into the United States after January 1, 1808.

4. Island legislatures often required colored voters to meet higher property qualifications than white voters.

5. See Table 17, page 158.

6. The network of conspiracies before the Baptist War in Jamaica involved slaves on almost one hundred separate estates.

7. As used in Caribbean studies, *peasant* and *peasantry* refers to cultivators with small amounts of money working limited plots of land. Although foreign to American usage, these terms do not have a pejorative connotation in this context.

8. A "task" is a set job—for example, hoeing a fixed amount of land.

9. Britain allowed Jamaican taxpayers to elect the Legislative Council's nine "unofficial members" after 1884. The Cayman Islands, with their very small population, retained a highly democratic system. At first, every free man could choose to attend and vote at an annual meeting. Later a legislature, meeting from the 1830s, was elected by all males—without even fixed age requirements. In 1863, Parliament ruled that the governor of Jamaica had to approve Cayman laws, and the governor also appointed a commissioner (from 1898) to represent him on the island.

10. The vestry, which administered local government in each of Jamaica's parishes, included certain elected members and the justices of the peace. The Custos Rotulorum (literally "keeper of the books") was the principal magistrate of each parish. Appointed by the governor and confirmed by the crown, he presided over the vestry's meetings.

11. According to an official inquiry, the soldiers and Maroons destroyed 1,000 homes, executed 85 persons without trial, and hanged 354 after a brief court martial. About 600 men and women were flogged, some receiving hundreds of lashes.

12. Bernard Semmel, *Jamaican Blood and Victorian Conscience: The Governor Eyre Controversy* (Westport, Connecticut: Greenwood Press, 1976 [first published in 1963]), page 41. See also Eric Williams, *British Historians and the West Indies* (New York: Africana, 1972 [first published 1966]), pages 115–118.

13. Circular dispatch signed by the Duke of Buckingham on August 17, 1868, quoted by Hume Wrong, *Government of the West Indies* (Oxford: Clarendon Press, 1923), page 79.

## CHAPTER FOURTEEN

1. Giving into British pressure, the Spanish government outlawed the slave trade in 1820, but local officials did not enforce the laws. See page 180.

2. See Table 16. The high point of the trade came just before it was outlawed. More than 96,000 slaves—19,000 per year—were landed between 1815 and 1820.

3. Thus the 1853 tariff law set the tax on a barrel of Spanish flour at $2.90 while taxing a North American barrel at $9.20.

4. See Table 21, page 188.

5. Following a revolution in September 1868, the Spanish republic gave both Cuba and Puerto Rico representation in the Spanish Cortes. The government canceled its grant to Cuba after the Revolt of Yara, but Puerto Rico continued to send representatives to the Cortes from 1869.

## CHAPTER FIFTEEN

1. In return for some concessions in Europe, France transferred the small island of Saint-Barthélemy to Sweden in 1784. Saint-Barthélemy was returned to France in 1870 and once again became (with Saint-Martin) a dependency of Guadeloupe.

2. According to the imperial constitution of 1805, "No white man (*aucun blanc*), whatever his nationality, can set foot on this territory as master or proprietor, and is unable in the future to acquire any property." Subsequent governments generally enforced this rule until the American occupation in 1915.

3. For a short time, the south seceded to form a third state under André Rigaud, and La Grande Anse formed an autonomous region throughout the entire period of division.

4. Christophe, who was born in Grenada, preferred the English name *Henry* to the French *Henri*.

5. Coffee can grow "wild" up to 3,000 feet in the sense that new plants grow from seeds dropped by parent trees. When the French introduced coffee, the slaves carefully pruned, fertilized, and grafted the plants. The Haitians now let nature take its own course, and quality and production both declined.

## CHAPTER SIXTEEN

1. See Hugh Thomas, *Cuba: The Pursuit of Freedom* (New York: Harper & Row, 1971), page 472.
2. The 1940 constitution permitted an ex-president to run again after an eight-year absence from office.
3. Aristide's book *In the Parish of the Poor* (New York: Orbis, 1991) summarizes the main themes of these speeches, including his justification of revolutionary violence.

## CHAPTER SEVENTEEN

1. Cited Arturo Morales-Carrión, *Puerto Rico, a Political and Cultural History* (New York: Norton, 1983), page 189.
2. See Table 21. Although Puerto Rican sugar was protected by U.S. tariffs and quotas, its price was set on the world market.
3. Including the smaller islands, such as Saint-Barthélemy, associated with Martinique and Guadeloupe.
4. Surinam (formerly Dutch Guiana) withdrew in 1975, becoming an independent republic.
5. Bridget Brereton, *Race Relations in Colonial Trinidad 1870–1900* (Cambridge: Cambridge University Press, 1972), page 212.

## CHAPTER EIGHTEEN

1. The Rastafarian movement or religion, founded around 1930, emphasized its members' racial origins in Africa and rejected Jamaica's creole society and culture. Using old Testament language, Rastafarians condemned Jamaica as Babylon, a land that held them in captivity. They sought a new home in Africa and especially in Ethiopia, whose emperor, Haile Selassie, they regarded as divine.
2. During the 1960s and 1970s, the Non-Aligned movement was a loose association of political leaders, mainly from Africa and Asia. Although all espoused some form of socialism, they claimed to be neutral in the rivalry that opposed the United States and western Europe (the "First World") to the Soviet Union and Eastern Europe (the "Second World").
3. Cited in Selwyn D. Ryan, *Race and Nationalism in Trinidad and Tobago* (Toronto: University of Toronto Press), page 427.
4. Scott MacDonald, *Trinidad and Tobago: Democracy and Development in the Caribbean* (New York: Praeger), page 191.
5. Settlers from Saint Kitts colonized Montserrat in 1632, occupied Anguilla in 1650, and moved on to the Virgin Islands at the end of the 18th century. See pages 73–75.
6. In a 1980 interview, Bishop said "Suppose there's a war next door in Trinidad, where the forces of Fascism are about to take control, and the Trinidadians need external assistance. Why should we oppose anybody passing through Grenada to assist them?" Quoted in *Newsweek* March 31, 1980, page 44.
7. "Extraordinary Meeting of the Central Committee NJM," Minutes, September 16, 1983. Printed in *The Grenada Papers: The inside story of the Grenadian Revolution and the making of a totalitarian state—as told in captured documents*, edited Paul Seabury and Walter A. McDougall (San Francisco: Institute for Contemporary Studies Press), page 294.
8. In addition to Grenada, OECS members include Antigua, Dominica, Grenada, Montserrat, Saint Kitts–Nevis, Saint Lucia, and Saint Vincent.

# SUGGESTIONS FOR FURTHER READING

■

This list is by no means a complete record of all the works and sources I have consulted. It indicates books that I believe will be of general interest. Thus I have not included works in languages other than English, books long out-of-print, or articles in journals for specialists.

## OVERVIEWS AND WORKS ABOUT SEVERAL ERAS

Andrews, Kenneth. *Trade, plunder and settlement: Maritime enterprise and the genesis of the British Empire, 1480–1630*. Cambridge: Cambridge University Press, 1984.

Blume, Helmut. *The Caribbean Islands*. Translated by Johannes Maczewski and Ann Norton. London: Longman, 1974.

Brereton, Bridget. *A History of Modern Trinidad, 1783–1962*. Kingston, Jamaica; Exeter, New Hampshire: Heineman, 1981.

Burns, Alan. *History of the British West Indies*. 2nd edition. London: Allen and Unwin, 1965.

Craton, Michael. *A History of the Bahamas*. Revised edition. London: Collins, 1968.

———. *Searching for the Invisible Man: Slaves and Plantation Life in Jamaica*. Cambridge, Massachusetts: Harvard University Press, 1978.

———. *Sinews of Empire: A Short History of British Slavery*. Garden City, New York: Anchor, 1974.

———. *Testing the Chains: Resistance to Slavery in the British West Indies*. Ithaca: Cornell University Press, 1982.

Curtin, Philip. *The Atlantic Slave Trade: A Census*. Madison: University of Wisconsin Press, 1969.

———. *Death by Migration: Europe's Encounter with the Tropical World in the Nineteenth Century*. Cambridge: Cambridge University Press, 1989.

———. *The Rise and Fall of the Plantation Complex: Essays in Atlantic History*. Cambridge: Cambridge University Press, 1990.

Deerr, Noel. *The History of Sugar*. 2 volumes. London: Chapman and Hall, 1949–1950.

Dupuy, Alex. *Haiti in the World Economy: Class, Race, and Underdevelopment since 1700*. Boulder, Colorado: Westview, 1989.

Goslinga, Cornelis. *A Short History of the Netherlands Antilles and Surinam*. The Hague: Martinus Nijhoff, 1979.

Hamshere, Cyril. *The British in the Caribbean*. Cambridge: Harvard University Press, 1972.

Kilson, Martin, and Robert Rotberg, eds. *The African Diaspora*. Cambridge: Harvard University Press, 1976.

Kiple, Kenneth. *The Caribbean Slave: A Biological History*. Cambridge: Cambridge University Press, 1984.

Knight, Franklin. *The Caribbean: The Genesis of a Fragmented Nationalism*. New York: Oxford University Press, 1978.

Knight, Franklin, and Colin Palmer, eds. *The Modern Caribbean*. Chapel Hill: University of North Carolina Press, 1989.

Lewis, Gordon. *Main Currents in Caribbean Thought: The Historical Evolution of Caribbean Society in Its Ideological Aspects, 1492–1900*. Baltimore: Johns Hopkins University Press, 1983.

Morales-Carrión, Arturo. *Puerto-Rico, a political and cultural history*. New York: Norton, 1983.

Nicholls, David. *From Dessalines to Duvalier: race, color, and national independence in Haiti*. New York: Cambridge University Press, 1979.

———. *Haiti in Caribbean Context: Ethnicity, Economy, and Revolt*. London: MacMillan, 1985.

Ortiz-Fernandez, Fernando. *Cuban Counter Point: Tobacco and Sugar*, translated by H. de Onís. New York: Knopf, 1947.

Perez, Louis. *Cuba: Between Reform and Revolution*. New York: Oxford University Press, 1985.

Rotberg, Robert I. *Haiti, The Politics of Squalor*. New York: Houghton Mifflin, 1971.

Sheridan, Richard. *Sugar and Slavery: An Economic History of the British West Indies, 1623–1775*. Baltimore: Johns Hopkins University Press, 1974.

Suchlicki, Jaime. *Cuba: From Columbus to Castro*. 2nd Edition. Washington, D.C.: Pergamon-Brassey's, 1986.

Thomas, Hugh. *Cuba: The Pursuit of Freedom*. New York: Harper and Row, 1971.

Trouillot, Michel-Rolph. *Haiti, State against Nation: The Origins and Legacy of Duvalierism*. New York: Monthly Review Press, 1990.

Ward, J. R. *Poverty and Progress in the Caribbean, 1800–1960*. Economic History Society, Studies in Economic and Social History. London: Macmillan, 1985.

Watts, David. *The West Indies: Patterns of Development, Culture and Environmental Change since 1492*. Cambridge: Cambridge University Press, 1987.

West, Robert, and John P. Augelli, and others. *Middle America: Its Lands and Peoples*. 3rd ed. Englewood Cliffs, New Jersey: Prentice Hall, 1989.

Williams, Eric. *From Columbus to Castro: The History of the Caribbean*. London: Andre Deutsch, 1970. Reprint, New York: Vintage Books, 1984.

## PART I: THE CARIBBEAN UNDER SPANISH RULE

Andrews, Kenneth R. *The Spanish Caribbean: Trade and Plunder, 1530–1630*. New Haven: Yale University Press, 1978.

Ashburn, P. M. *The Ranks of Death: A Medical History of the Conquest of America*. Edited by Frank Ashburn. New York: Coward-McCann, 1947.

Haring, C. H. *The Spanish Empire in America*. New York: Oxford University Press, 1947. Reprint, San Diego: Harvest/Harcourt Brace Jovanovich, 1975.

Lynch, John. *Spain under the Habsburgs*. Vol. 2, *Spain and America, 1598–1700*. New York: Oxford University Press, 1964–1969.

McAlister, Lyle N. *Spain and Portugal in the New World, 1492–1700*. Minneapolis: University of Minnesota Press, 1984.

Means, Philip. *The Spanish Main, Focus of Envy, 1492–1700*. New York: Scribner's, 1935.

Phillips, William. *Slavery from Roman Times to the Early Transatlantic Trade*. Minneapolis: University of Minnesota Press, 1985.

Sauer, Carl. *The Early Spanish Main*. Berkeley and Los Angeles: University of California Press, 1969.

Wood, Peter. *The Spanish Main*. Alexandria, Virginia: Time-Life Books, 1979.

## PART 2: NORTHERN EUROPEANS COME TO STAY

Beckles, Hilary. *White Servitude and Black Slavery in Barbados, 1627–1715*. Knoxville: University of Tennessee Press, 1989.

Botting, Douglas. *The Pirates*. Alexandria, Virginia: Time-Life Books, 1978.

Bridenbaugh, Carl, and Roberta Bridenbaugh. *No Peace beyond the Line: The English in the Caribbean, 1624–1690*. New York: Oxford University Press, 1977.

Crouse, Nellis. *French Pioneers in the West Indies, 1624–1664*. New York: Columbia University Press, 1940. Reprint, New York: Octagon Books, 1977.

———. *The French Struggle for the West Indies, 1665–1713*. New York: Columbia University Press, 1943. Reprint, Octagon Books, 1966.

Davies, K. G. *The North Atlantic World in the Seventeenth Century*. Minneapolis: University of Minnesota Press, 1974.

Dunn, Richard. *Sugar and Slaves: The Rise of the Planter Class in the English West Indies, 1624–1713*. New York: W. W. Norton, 1973.

Earle, Peter. *The Sack of Panama: Sir Henry Morgan's Adventures on the Spanish Main*. New York: Viking, 1982.

Goslinga, Cornelis. *The Dutch in the Caribbean and on the Wild Coast, 1580–1680*. Gainesville: University of Florida Press, 1971.

Israel, Jonathan. *Dutch Primacy in World Trade, 1585–1740*. Oxford: Clarendon Press, 1989.

———. *The Dutch Republic and the Hispanic World, 1606–1661*. Oxford: Clarendon Press, 1982.

Pope, Dudley. *The Buccaneer King: The Biography of Sir Henry Morgan, 1635–1688*. New York: Dodd Mead, 1977.

Smith, Abbot. *Colonists in Bondage*. Chapel Hill: University of North Carolina Press, 1947.

## PART 3: THE SUGAR EMPIRE

Brathwaite, Edward. *The Development of Creole Society in Jamaica, 1770–1820*. Oxford: Clarendon Press, 1971.

Cohen, David, and Jack Greene, eds. *Neither Slave Nor Free: The Freedmen of African Descent in the Slave Societies of the New World*. Baltimore: Johns Hopkins University Press, 1972.

Gemery, Henry, and Jan Hogendorn, eds. *The Uncommon Market: Essays in the Economic History of the Atlantic Slave Trade*. New York: Academic Press, 1979.

Goveia, Elsa. *Slave Society in the British Leeward Islands at the End of the Eighteenth Century*. New Haven: Yale University Press, 1965. Reprint, Westport, Connecticut: Greenwood, 1980.

Heumans, Gad, ed. *Out of the House of Bondage: Runaways, Resistance and Marronage in Africa and the New World*. London: Frank Cass, 1986.

James, C. L. R. *The Black Jacobins: Toussaint L'Ouverture and the San Domingo Revolution*. 2nd ed. New York: Vintage Books, 1963.

Klein, Herbert S. *African Slavery in Latin American and the Caribbean*. New York: Oxford University Press, 1986.

———. *The Middle Passage: Comparative Studies in the Atlantic Slave Trade*. Princeton: Princeton University Press, 1978.

Kuethe, Allan. *Cuba, 1753–1815: Crown, Military, and Society*. Knoxville: University of Tennessee Press, 1986.

Lovejoy, Paul. *Transformations in Slavery: A History of Slavery in Africa*. Cambridge: Cambridge University Press, 1983.

McNeill, John. *Atlantic Empires of France and Spain: Louisbourg and Havana, 1700–1765*. Chapel Hill: University of North Carolina Press, 1985.

Morales-Carrión, Arturo. *Puerto Rico and the Non-Hispanic Caribbean: A Study in the Decline of Spanish Exclusivism*. Third Edition. Barcelona: Medinaceli, 1974.

Ott, Thomas. *The Haitian Revolution, 1789–1804*. Knoxville: University of Tennessee Press, 1983.

Pares, Richard. *War and Trade in the West Indies, 1739–1763*. Oxford: Oxford University Press, 1936. Reprint, New York: Frank Cass, 1963.

Patterson, Orlando. *Slavery and Social Death: A Comparative Study*. Cambridge, Massachusetts: Harvard University Press, 1982.

Price, Richard, ed. *Maroon Societies: Rebel Slave Communities in the Americas*. Baltimore: Johns Hopkins University Press, 1979.

Rawley, James A. *The Transatlantic Slave Trade: A History*. New York: Norton, 1981

Solow, Barbara and Stanley Engerman, eds. *British Capitalism and Caribbean Slavery: The Legacy of Eric Williams*. Cambridge: Cambridge University Press, 1987.

Stein, Robert. *The French Slave Trade in the Eighteenth Century: An Old Regime Business*. Madison: University of Wisconsin Press, 1980.

———. *The French Sugar Business in the Eighteenth Century*. Baton Rouge: Louisiana University Press, 1988.

Ward, J. R. *British West Indian Slavery, 1750–1834: The Process of Amelioration*. Oxford: Clarendon Press, 1988.

## PART 4: THE ABOLITION OF SLAVERY AND THE CHALLENGES OF FREEDOM

Bolt, Christine, and Seymour Drescher, eds. *Anti-slavery, Religion, and Reform: Essays in Memory of Roger Anstey*. Hamden, Connecticut: Archon Books, 1980.

Davis, David. *The Problem of Slavery in the Age of Revolution*. Ithaca, New York: Cornell University Press, 1975.

Drescher, Seymour. *Capitalism and Antislavery: British Mobilization in Comparative Perspective*. New York: Oxford University Press, 1987.

———. *Econocide: British Slavery in the Era of Abolition*. Pittsburgh, University of Pittsburgh Press, 1977.

Eiser, Gisela. *Jamaica, 1830–1930: A Study in Economic Growth*. Manchester, England: Manchester University Press, 1961. Reprint, Westport, Connecticut: Greenwood, 1974.

Eltis, David. *The Abolition of the Atlantic Slave Trade: Origins and effects in Europe, Africa, and the Americas*. Madison: University of Wisconsin Press, 1981.

Green, William. *British Slave Emancipation: The Sugar Colonies and the Great Experiment, 1830–1965*. Oxford: Clarendon Press, 1976.

Hall, Douglas. *Free Jamaica, 1838–1865*. New Haven: Yale University Press, 1959.

Knight, Franklin. *Slave Society in Cuba during the Nineteenth Century.* Madison: University of Wisconsin Press, 1970.

Moreno-Fraginals, Manuel. *The Sugarmill: The Socioeconomic Complex of Sugar in Cuba, 1760–1860.* Translated by Cedric Belfrage. New York: Monthly Review Press, 1976.

Paquette, Robert. *Sugar is Made with Blood: The Conspiracy of La Escalera and the Conflict between Empires and Slavery in Cuba.* Middletown, Connecticut: Wesleyan University Press, 1988.

Walvin, James. *England, Slaves and Freedom, 1776–1838.* Jackson: University Press of Mississippi, 1986.

## PART 5: POVERTY AND PROGRESS IN THE CARIBBEAN SINCE 1914

Aguila, Juan. *Cuba: Dilemmas of a Revolution.* Revised edition. Boulder, Colorado: Westview, 1988.

Boyer, William. *America's Virgin Islands: A History of Human Rights and Wrongs.* Durham, North Carolina: Carolina Academic Press, 1983.

Langley, Lester D. *The United States and the Caribbean in the Twentieth Century.* 4th Edition. Athens: University of Georgia Press, 1989.

Lewis, Gordon. *The Growth of the Modern West Indies.* New York: Monthly Review Press, 1968.

Lowenthal, Abraham. *The Dominican Intervention.* Cambridge, Massachusetts: Harvard University Press, 1972.

MacDonald, Scott. *Trinidad and Tobago: Democracy and Development in the Caribbean.* New York: Praeger, 1986.

Mintz, Sidney, and Sally Price, eds. *Caribbean Contours.* Baltimore: Johns Hopkins University Press, 1985.

Mintz, Sidney. *Caribbean Transformations.* Chicago: Aldine, 1974.

Payne, Anthony, Paul Sutton, and Tony Thorndike. *Grenada: Revolution and Invasion.* New York: St. Martin's, 1984.

Payne, Anthony. *Politics in Jamaica.* New York: St. Martin's, 1988.

Plummer, Brenda. *Haiti and the Great Powers, 1902–1915.* Baton Rouge: Louisiana State University Press, 1988.

Schmidt, Hans. *The United States Occupation of Haiti, 1915–1934.* New Brunswick, New Jersey: Rutgers University Press, 1971.

Steiner, Stan. *The Islands: The Worlds of the Puerto Ricans.* New York: Harper and Row, 1975.

Wallace, Elisabeth. *The British Caribbean: From the Decline of Colonialism to the End of Federation.* Toronto: University of Toronto Press, 1977.

Wiarda, Howard, and Michael Kryzanek. *The Dominican Republic: A Caribbean Crucible.* Boulder, Colorado: Westview, 1982.

Worrell, Delisle. *Small Island Economies: Structure and Performance in the English-Speaking Caribbean since 1970.* New York: Praeger, 1987.

# PHOTO CREDITS

∎

PAGES 6, 11, 16, 41, 63, 133, 150, 219, 244, 260, and 283.   Courtesy Caribbean Tourism Organization.

PAGE 8.   Courtesy American Airlines.

PAGES 12 and 255.   Courtesy Curaçao Tourist Board.

PAGE 24.   From Bryan Edwards, *The History, Civil and Commercial, of the British Colonies in the West Indies* (London: John Stockdale, 1794), Volume 1, frontispiece. Print courtesy Archives and Special Collections, Richter Library, University of Miami.

PAGE 37.   From Theodore Bry, *Collectiones Peregrinationum in Indiam Orientalem et Indiam Occidentalem* . . . (Franfurt-am-Main, 1590–1634). Print courtesy Archives and Special Collections, Richter Library, University of Miami.

PAGE 67.   Courtesy Saint Kitts and Nevis Tourist Board.

PAGE 70.   Courtesy Barbados Board of Tourism.

PAGES 115, 116, and 292.   Courtesy French West Indies Tourist Board.

PAGE 131.   From a color print published by Montaner y Simon, Barcelona, second half of the 19th century. Print courtesy Archives and Special Collections, Richter Library, University of Miami.

PAGE 154.   Engraving from an original painting by Agostino Brunias in Bryan Edwards, *An Historical Survey of the Island of Saint Domingo, together with an Account of the Maroon Negroes in the Island of Jamaica* . . . (London: John Stockdale, 1801, as Volume 3 of Edwards' *History of the British Colonies* [originally published 1796]), between pages 310 and 311. Print courtesy Archives and Special Collections, Richter Library, University of Miami.

PAGE 156.   Engraving from an original painting by Agostino Brunias in Bryan Edwards, *History of the British Colonies*, Volume 1, before page 391. Print courtesy Archives and Special Collections, Richter Library, University of Miami.

PAGE 171.   From Marcus Ransford, *An Historical Account of the Black Empire of Hayti: Comprehending a view of the Principal Transactions in the Revolution of Saint Domingo* . . . (London: James Cundee, 1805), before page 337. Print courtesy Archives and Special Collections, Richter Library, University of Miami.

PAGE 181.   From a pamphlet published in January 1830 with an anti-slavery article originally printed in the *Westminster Review*. Print courtesy Archives and Special Collections, Richter Library, University of Miami.

PAGE 200.   From *Frank Leslie's Illustrirte Zeitung*. Print courtesy Archives and Special Collections, Richter Library, University of Miami.

PAGE 206.   A color print by W. A. Rogers contemporary with the events illustrated. Print courtesy Archives and Special Collections, Richter Library, University of Miami.

PAGE 265.   A sepia gravure from "Souvenir Views of Trinidad, British West Indies, the Jewel of the Caribbean." Ottawa, Canada: The Photogelatine Engraving Company, no date, [*circa* 1920s or 1930s]. Print courtesy of Archives and Special Collections, Richter Library, University of Miami.

PAGE 278.   Courtesy Trinidad and Tobago Tourist Office.

PAGE 280.   Courtesy Bahamas Ministry of Tourism.

# INDEX

∎